BAND MUSIC NOTES

REVISED EDITION

Norman Smith and Albert Stoutamire

west Neil A. Kjos, Jr., Publisher—San Diego, California

Published by Kjos West/Neil A. Kjos, Jr., Publisher
National Order Desk, 4382 Jutland Dr., San Diego, California 92117

Publishers Edition Number: WB42

International Standard Book Number: 0-8497-5401-1

Library of Congress Catalog Card Number: 79-91984

Printed and Bound in the United States of America.

Cover photo by Pamlyn Smith, New York.

BAND MUSIC NOTES

Revised Edition

Norman Smith
and
Albert Stoutamire

FOREWORD

During many years of conducting public school and university bands, the authors found that the search for information on worthwhile band literature and program notes was often time consuming and frustrating. The principal purpose in writing *Band Music Notes* was to provide a comprehensive reference work for all persons interested in band music: conductors, band members, audiences, scholars, and all other ''great lovers'' of band music.

Biographical information on prominent composers of orchestral, choral and keyboard music has long been available in music history and appreciation texts, and at least one publication *(Great Orchestral Music* by Julian Seaman) contains program notes written for specific professional orchestra concerts. In some instances band program notes are provided by publishers with scores, and many school, service, and professional conductors devote considerable time and effort to provide their audiences with interesting and informative program notes. Detailed knowledge of specific band works can sometimes be found in such periodicals as *The Instrumentalist, Journal of Band Research,* and *School Musician.* However, information concerning much of the band literature being performed at the present time is often difficult to locate and organize in a limited period of time. This book is designed to help solve that problem.

Experienced band conductors will realize that the several hundred titles in the Contents comprise the bulk of worthwhile concert band literature. The titles were selected as a result of a nationwide poll conducted by correspondence with over 200 outstanding school, university, service, and professional band conductors (members of American Bandmasters Association, American School Band Directors Association, College Band Directors National Association, and Phi Beta Mu National Bandmasters Fraternity). The conductors were asked to list ten of their favorite band works selected from any time period or classification, and also to send programs from concerts which had been presented during the last five years. Lists, letters, and thousands of program notes were received from cooperative conductors who saw a need for a book of this type. Titles from the programs were given equal weight with titles listed as favorite band works in the vote-counting process. A few composers and titles were added during the writing period following the survey when performance frequency, as indicated in more recent programs, warranted their inclusion. Contributors' names follow all entries except when the information was written by the authors of *Band Music Notes.*

Possible uses for the text are varied. In a course entitled "Literature for the Concert Band," (taught by one of the authors) the text was used in conjunction with records and scores to plan rehearsal and performance programs. Teachers of humanities, arts, or music appreciation courses might well consider *Band Music Notes* as a reference text. Band conductors who wish to complement performance with knowledge of composers and band literature should consider the book for use as a band class text. In summary, the writers hope that *Band Music Notes* will be a valuable aid to all persons—scholars and laymen alike—who wish to learn more about the music being performed by contemporary concert bands.

The authors are deeply grateful to the band conductors who responded to the difficult challenge of naming *only* ten favorites; to the composers, publishers, and conductors who contributed biographical and program material; to our colleagues and graduate students who provided encouragement while the book was being written; and to Aline, Anne, Linda and Pam for their help in proof-reading and typing.

Names of contributing individuals and organizations are listed in APPENDIX I. In addition to the generous assistance provided by these contributors who sent program notes, biographical information, and favorite votes for both editions, the help of the following colleagues who commented on the book's virtues and shortcomings and often shared valuable research material is gratefully acknowledged: Toshio Akiyama, Paul Bierley, Don Caneva, Claude Christnach, Frederick Fennell, Loren Geiger, Jim Houston, Robert Hoe, Jr., Bob Molenaar, Acton Ostling, James Perkins, James T. Rohner, Leonard B. Smith, Richard Strange, and Paul Yoder.

Publishers of the band music companies are identified by abbreviations in the text and are listed in the "Key to Publishers" and the "Key to Record Companies" in APPENDICES II and III.

The Revised Edition of *Band Music Notes* contains approximately 200 new titles over the 425 listed in the first edition. Biographies of some 60 composers have been added to the 195 listed in the first edition. Grading, estimated duration, and record information have been added to the large majority of the entries (see APPENDIX IV).

Many requests have been made to continue publishing new editions of *Band Music Notes*. A book of this type can be successful only with the assistance of the readers. To this end we ask your continued help in the following matters:

1. PROGRAM NOTES. Please send notes from programs presented during the years 1977 through 1982. *Program notes equal votes* for the next edition. (Band programs without notes will also assist in choosing titles.)

2. BIOGRAPHICAL INFORMATION is needed for composers who are already included in the first two editions, as well as for those recommended for future editions.

3. CORRECTIONS, ADDITIONS, DELETIONS. Regardless of the apparent insignificance or obvious gravity of errors in this edition, your corrections will be gratefully received.

Please include a sentence indicating your permission for the use of your material in future editions of *Band Music Notes,* along with information on your present position and address, in order that you may be given credit.

Norman Smith
Albert Stoutamire

McNeese State University
P.O. Box 354
Lake Charles, Louisiana 70609

CONTENTS

APPENDICES

ABBREVIATIONS

(1)   (2)   (3)   (4)   (5)   (6)   (7)

Four Scottish Dances (Arr = Paynter. Pub = CF, 1971-78. Gr = 4. T = 9:00. Rec = CR-GCIN-403, Interlochen, Wilson; CR-CBDNA-71-4, Shenandoah Conservatory, Noble)

(8)   (9)   (10)

Example Abbreviations

(1) Title of the composition, in italics.

(2) Arr = arranged by; Tr = transcribed by; Ed = edited by; Rev = revised by.

(3) Pub = published by. See Appendix II for Key to Publishers.

(4) One or more dates of publication.

(5) Gr = Approximate grade of difficulty beginning with 1 indicating easy (within the performance range of first year instrumentalists) and continuing to 6 (for highly advanced university and professional groups).

(6) T = Approximate time of performance.

(7) Rec = Recorded by. The first two letters (CR in this example) indicate the recording company. See Appendix III for Key to Record Companies. The remaining letters and numbers should be used to order a recording.

(8) The name of the performing group. The word "band" (wind ensemble, wind orchestra, symphonic band, etc.) is implied unless another type of organization (symphony orchestra, etc.) is specified.

(9) The name of the person who conducted the performance, not necessarily the permanent conductor of the group.

(10) One or more additional reference recordings which have been recommended.

Additional Abbreviations

Col. = College

H.S. = High School

Jr. H.S. = Junior High School

Mid. = Middle School

Mun. = Municipal

Un. = University

AL = Alabama. Other states are abbreviated as standardized by the United States Postal Service.

BAND MUSIC NOTES

HAWLEY ADES
(Born in Wichita, Kansas, 1908)

Hawley Ades received his early musical training in the music education program of the public school system, along with additional specialized instruction in piano, organ, and theory from his mother. He attended Rutgers University where he earned a Lit. B. degree. While at the university he served as chapel organist and choir director and also played with dance bands.

Ades later became staff arranger for Irving Berlin while he was studying with T. Tertius Noble at St. Thomas' Church in New York City. He then joined the Fred Waring staff as arranger and performer and at the same time worked toward an M.M.E. degree at Columbia Teachers College. He has toured with the Fred Waring "Pennsylvanians"—seven months each year—for over twenty years, spending most of the remaining time arranging, composing, and teaching. His textbook on choral arranging has been called the "definitive work" on the subject. His band publications include *Sound Parade, Fred Waring Band Book, A Carol Festival,* and *A Hymn Festival.* Ades now lives in Stuart, Florida.

Sholom Aleichem (Pub = SH, 1974. Gr = 3. T = 5:15. Rec = SH-V8-P-544, Ithaca Col., Gobrecht)

Sholom Aleichem—A Festival of Hebraic Melodies begins with a broad, processional introduction and continues with five short and contrasting sections. The first, "Sholom Aleichem," is translated to "May your coming in and your going forth be in peace." "S'Vivon" includes "Little dreidl, spin, spin, spin. Hanukah is a day of joy." "Hatikvah" means "the hope." This anthem of the Sionist movement is the national anthem of Israel. Long thought to be of anonymous origin the melody was actually written in 1882 by Samuel Cohen and is based on a Moldavian-Roumanian folk song. "Mo'oz Tur" denotes "Rock of ages, let our song praise Thy saving power." The final melody is titled "Hava Nagiela." The dance usually associated with this Hebraic folk tune is the "hors." Both the music and the dance begin slowly and quietly and gradually increase in intensity and excitement to a frenetic climax. (Shawnee Press, Inc.)

SAMUEL ADLER
(Born in Mannheim, Germany, 1928)

Samuel Adler has studied with some of the most illustrious figures in music: composition with Walter Piston, Aaron Copland and Paul Hindemith, musicology with Karl Geiringer and conducting with Serge Koussevitsky. Born in Germany, he came to this country with his family in 1939, settling in Massachusetts. He earned his B.M. degree at Boston University and his M.A. degree at Harvard University. Some of the positions he has held are: conductor of the Seventh Army Orchestra in Europe (culminating in his being awarded the Medal of Honor), music professor at North Texas State University, music director at Temple Emanu-El in Dallas, conductor of the Dallas Lyric Theater, and composition professor at the Eastman School of Music.

Adler has written several operas; five symphonies; concertos for violin, flute, viola, and organ; and much music for chamber music groups. Although he has written pieces in a radical vein, many of his works might be considered in the style of

Copland or Harris. Adler's works for band include *Festive Prelude; Concerto for Winds, Brass and Percussion; A Little Night and Day Music;* and an arrangement of *The Union* by Gottschalk for piano and band. (Chester Mais, Cornell University)

Southwestern Sketches (Pub = OX, 1970. Gr = 5. T = 13:00. Rec = CN-CUWE-8, Cornell Un., Stith)

The music of *Southwestern Sketches* does not tell a story; rather, it is an attempt to translate into musical language the composer's impressions of the Southwest of the United States—the excitement, vigor, youth; the passion; the sudden changes in the weather and terrain; the people—their religious devotion as well as their violence, their happy abandon and their tender hopes. In 1961 Adler had written incidental music to the play by Lewis and Sage, *Joshua Beene and God,* which was set in the Southwest and starred Burl Ives. When commissioned by New Mexico State University in 1962 to write a piece for band in honor of the fiftieth anniversary of New Mexico's statehood, Adler decided to use several of the folk-like tunes from *Joshua Beene and God.* They seemed appropriate and were utilized and expanded in the *Southwestern Sketches.* There is one literal musical quotation—the hymn-tune "Fairest Lord Jesus" ("St. Elizabeth")—which occurs in the latter part of the work. (Gene C. Smith, Baylor University)

TOSHIO AKIYAMA

(Born in Ohmiya, Saitama, Japan, 1929)

Toshio Akiyama is active in both Japanese and international concert band activities as a composer, arranger, teacher, and conductor. He is the international secretary of the Japanese Bandmasters Association and also conducts the SONY Concert Band of Tokyo. He has made numerous trips to music conventions in the United States and has guest conducted the University of Michigan Band and the Goldman Band, among others. In the spring of 1979 he was invited to conduct the "grand finale" at the Tri-State Band Festival in Enid, Oklahoma, and in the summer of the same year his SONY Concert Band was invited to perform at the Texas Bandmasters Association in San Antonio. With a music background which includes both eastern and western cultures (including graduate study at the Eastman School of Music in 1963), Akiyama finds the concert band an ideal vehicle for the expression of ethnic music from around the world. Since 1969, he has been teaching at the Musashino Academy of Music in Tokyo.

Japanese Songs for Band (Pub = EM, 1968. Gr = 2. T = 5:45. Rec = CR-MID-68-8, Northshore Concert, Wilmette, IL, Akiyama)

This set of three folk songs was arranged to promote international understanding of the Japanese culture. The first song, "Night Festival," originated in the Chichibu area north of Toyko and was sung at barn dances and autumn festivals in the hope of having a good harvest. The second song, "Tairyo Utaikomi," originated in the Miyagi Prefecture in northern Japan and is concerned with the expression of joy over a good catch of fish. "Sōranbushi," a name derived from the Ainu word "souran," is also a popular fishing song being sung by fishermen seining for herring. Calls and shouts which appear on the parts of the players were added by Akiyama for a more authentic performance.

RUSSELL ALEXANDER
(Born in Nevada City, Missouri, 1877 — Died in Liberty, New York, 1915)

Russell Alexander spent most of his life as a solo euphonium player and composer-arranger on circus bandstands and vaudeville stages. He performed with the Belford Carnival under the baton of D.V. Burr and wrote some marches for the band. He was euphonium soloist and composer-arranger with Barnum and Bailey's Greatest Show on Earth, in the band directed by Carl Clair, during the European tour of 1897 to 1902. Many of his greatest marches were composed during this time.

After his return to America, Alexander joined with his brothers, Newton and Woodruff, and James Brady to form an act called the "Exposition Four." He died in a tuberculosis sanatorium in Liberty, New York at the age of thirty-eight, leaving a legacy of thirty-six outstanding circus marches and galops. (Loren D. Geiger, Lancaster, New York and Sverre O. Braathen, deceased)

Colossus of Columbia March (Pub = BA, 1901-26-69. Gr = 4. T = 2:40. Rec = CA-265, Ringling Bros.)

The rhythmic drive and excitement of this march reveal the circus band experience of the composer for good reason. In 1897, when Alexander was twenty years old, he signed a contract with the Barnum and Bailey Circus Band for its projected five-year tour of Europe and Great Britain. During that time he played with the band, arranged all of the music, and still found time to compose many marches. It was near the end of the tour in 1901 that Alexander wrote the *Colossus of Columbia March*, dedicating it to "the Continental Congress at Washington."

From Tropic to Tropic March (Pub = BA, 1898-1926. Gr = 4. T = 2:40. Rec = CA-6530, Putnam, TX, H.S.)

Alexander wrote this march in 1898 while he was on a European tour with the Barnum and Bailey Circus Band. He dedicated the march to his good friend, H.A. VanderCook who was musical director of J.H. LaPearl's Railroad Show. According to circus expert Robert Mayer, writing for the *Circus Fanfare* Magazine, "Prof. VanderCook" (founder of the VanderCook College of Music) was the director of the LaPearl Show band until 1897. Although he was only twenty-one at the time, Alexander showed a mature understanding of both craftsmanship and spirit of the circus when he wrote *From Tropic to Tropic March*.

Olympia Hippodrome March (Pub = BA, 1898. Gr = 4. T = 3:00. Rec = IL-83, Un. of IL, Begian)

This march was dedicated to Carl Clair, the director of the Barnum and Bailey Circus Band, at the beginning of a five-year tour of Europe. Alexander must have written the music for the parade of the elephants around the hippodrome as it has a more majestic sound than many of the circus marches. Especially effective is the chromatic build-up to the seventh chord preceding the final grandioso strain.

The original Olympic hippodromes, dating back to the seventh century B.C., consisted of an oval course for chariot races surrounded by seats for spectators. The largest and oldest of these, the Circus Maximus, was large enough in Julius Caesar's time to hold 150,000 spectators. Later, during the time of Constantine, the hippodrome was enlarged to hold 385,000 people.

The Southerner March (Pub = BA, 1908-54. Gr = 4. T = 2:40. Rec = CR-ABA-75-1, LA St. Un., Swor; GC-Revelli Years, Un. of MI, Revelli)

This is one of Russell Alexander's most popular marches. A strong introduction, interesting melodies and countermelodies, dynamic changes that lift the listener out of his seat, and challenging parts for everybody in the band—these are the features of *The Southerner March*. The dedication on the original conductor's part was short and sweet: "To my wife."

HAROLD L. ALFORD

(Born in Blissfield, Michigan, 1883 — Died in Chicago, Illinois, 1939)

Harry Alford studied music at Dana's Musical Institute in Warren, Ohio. He then progressed from church organist to trouper to director of musical comedies, and was best known for his professional arranging bureau in the Chicago area. In the days of vaudeville, his pit orchestra music for *Eva Taguay* made him so famous that every act wanted their music scored by him. He also published many of his own works including an edition of the *Hungry Five* books for German band.

When A.A. Harding was director of the University of Illinois Bands, he commissioned Alford to score some of his first big football band extravaganzas, including *My Hero* and *The World Is Waiting for the Sunrise*. He was thus an important pioneer in this still flourishing area of school band development during the three decades preceding World War II. Although the Chatfield, Minnesota Free Lending Library lists nearly 100 of his compositions and arrangements in its holdings, Alford is best remembered for his *Glory of the Gridiron March* and the *Purple Carnival March*. (Robert Hoe, Jr., Poughkeepsie, New York)

Purple Carnival March (Ed = Erickson. Pub = GS, 1933-69. Gr = 4. T = 3:50. Rec = CR-ABA-75-4, Un. of New Orleans, Bush)

Harold Alford wrote this stirring march in 1933, and its popularity is still as great as ever. The brass fanfare and idiomatic use of the woodwinds show Alford's knowledge of instrumental color and technique. The march was originally dedicated to Glenn Cliffe Bainum and the Northwestern University Band. Frank Erickson edited and revised the work for concert band in 1969.

KENNETH J. ALFORD

(Born in London, 1881, — Died in Reigate, England, 1945)

Alford's actual name was Fred J. Ricketts. He studied both piano and organ as a child and by the age of fourteen was playing cornet in the Royal Irish Regiment Band. He completed the bandmaster's course at the Royal Military School of Music at Kneller Hall in 1908 and wrote many of his marches during the next two decades while he was bandmaster of the Second Battalion Argyll and Sutherland Highlanders. In 1928 Alford became director of music for the Royal Marines at Deal, near the English Channel, and in 1930 he was transferred to Plymouth where he remained until his retirement in 1944. Although he wrote several instrumental duets and suites, Alford is best remembered for his restrained and dignified "poetic" marches. He was as famous in England for his marches as Sousa was in the United States.

Army of the Nile March (Pub = BH, 1941, Gr = 4. T = 3:00. Rec = CR-E-9002, Un. of IL)

The English marches of Kenneth Alford all seem to bear a characteristic stamp of the composer which is not to be found elsewhere. This fine march was composed in 1941, during the dark days of World War II, and is dedicated to the memory of Gen. Charles Gordon and his men who were beseiged at Khartoum for ten months in 1885. Gordon had been sent to this strategic city at the junction of the Blue Nile and White Nile Rivers to rescue the Egyptian garrisons endangered by the revolt of the Mohammedan Mahdi followers. The commander and every member of the garrison were killed two days before a British relief expedition reached Khartoum. (Stuart J. Ling, College of Wooster)

Colonel Bogey March (Pub = BH, 1914. Gr = 4. T = 3:17. Rec = SRI-75004, Eastman, Fennell)

The interval of a descending minor third, apparently basic to childhood communication, appears to be one factor in the composition of this march and a reason for its "basic" appeal. Playing golf in Scotland one day, Alford apparently whistled the interval to attract another golfer's attention and the result was a world famous march (popularized later by the film, *The Bridge on the River Kwai)*, with a familiar golf term, "bogey," in its title.

The Mad Major March (Pub = BH, 1921, Gr = 3. T = 2:55. Rec = MG-SRI-75-Philips, Eastman, Fennell)

Several of Alford's marches indicate a deep interest in British military tradition. *The Mad Major* is a refreshing work, employing soft passages as well as tasteful power, to be performed at a "quick march" tempo of approximately 112 to 116 beats per minute. It was the ninth in a series of seventeen quick marches composed by Alford during a thirty-year period beginning just before World War I. (Maurice McAdow, North Texas State University)

The Vanished Army March (Pub = BH, 1918. Gr = 4. T = 2:40. Rec = CR-ABA-77-6, U.S. Marine)

Kenneth Alford is often hailed as the "March King" of Great Britain, and his compositions are known for their original style and melodic content. Written in 1918, this march is dedicated to the first 100,000 men who died in World War I. Not a brilliant march in color, it is rather somber and stirring in a quiet manner, serving as a reminder of those who gave their lives in the fight against tyranny. A portion of "It's a Long Way to Tipperary" may be heard at the end of the second strain. (Harold L. Hillyer, University of Texas at El Paso)

The Voice of the Guns March (Pub = BH, 1918. Gr = 4. T = 2:30. Rec = PO-2-383-153, H.M. Royal Marines, Mason)

In 1917, when this march was written, England and her allies were engaged in a fierce struggle for survival with the axis powers. The composer's hope for victory is reflected in the transition from a minor to a major key. Although not as widely played today as some of Alford's other marches, *The Voice of the Guns March* has an appeal which warrants repeated performances.

LEROY ANDERSON

(Born in Cambridge, Massachusetts, 1909 — Died in Waterbury, Connecticut, 1975)

Anderson first studied music with his mother who was a church organist. He earned a B.A. degree in music at Harvard University in 1929 and an M.A. degree in foreign language there the following year. As a student he conducted the Harvard Band from 1928 to 1930. He became a music instructor at Radcliffe College from 1930 to 1932 and returned to Harvard as band conductor from 1932 to 1935. Later he served as a church choir director, an organist, a conductor, and a composer-arranger whose works in the "encore" category have few equals. Anderson was a captain in the U.S. Army Intelligence Corps during and after World War II, was a member of the Phi Beta Club, and is survived by four children.

Bugler's Holiday—Trumpet Trio (Pub = MM, 1955. Gr = 3. T = 3:20. Rec = RC-LSP-2687, U.S. Marine; CR-MID-78-10, Vandercook Col., Zajec)

This composition has probably motivated more trumpet players to learn (or improve) the art of double-tonguing in the last two decades than any other piece of music. Although the "Holiday" is relatively uncomplicated harmonically, the performers are given the opportunity to show what they can do with the articulations, the bell tones, and the proper balance of each part. Above all, it's fun to play and fun to hear.

A Christmas Festival (Pub = MM, 1950. Gr = 3. T = 5:45. Rec = MG-71238X45/YW-16161, Eastman, Fennell)

Since Anderson wrote *A Christmas Festival* in 1950, many other composers have also arranged Christmas music for band or orchestra. In spite of the availability of more recent arrangements, this work, like many of Anderson's other compositions, seems to be increasing in popularity. Among the familiar songs included in this arrangement are: "Joy to the World," "Deck the Hall," "God Rest You Merry Gentlemen," "Good King Wenceslas," "Hark! the Herald Angels Sing," "Silent Night," "Jingle Bells," and "Adeste Fidelis."

Rakes of Mallow from Irish Suite (Pub = MM, 1952. Gr = 3. Rec = MG-75013, Eastman-Rochester Pops Orch., Fennell)

Leroy Anderson was associated with Arthur Fiedler as one of the leading arrangers for the Boston "Pops" Orchestra. He also frequently served as the orchestra's guest conductor. In his spare time he tried his hand at composing, and in 1947 he was commissioned by the Erin Society of Boston to write an *Irish Suite* for its annual night at the Boston "Pops." The work consists of six beloved Irish airs and one of the jollier tunes, "The Rakes of Mallow," turns into something quite exciting as the tempo and volume increase. (Harold Hillyer, University of Texas at El Paso)

Serenata (Pub = MM, 1949. Gr = 3. T = 3:55. Rec = DL-8954, L. Anderson Orch.; CA-T-10215, Royal Marines, Dunn)

Serenata begins with the theme in minor, to the accompaniment of a Latin American rhythm, then changes to a bright mood in a major key. Just as the listener might be lulled by the soaring melody and repetitive rhythm, Anderson makes use of a strategically-placed pause to recapture one's attention. The composer's skill at arranging his original orchestra work for band is shown in every phrase of *Serenata*.

Sleigh Ride (Pub = MM, 1948. Gr = 3. Rec = DL-78865, L. Anderson Orch.)

Leroy Anderson believed that musical ideas came to his mind because he was constantly on the alert for them. *Fiddle Faddle,* for example, was inspired by listening to Paganini's *Perpetual Motion.* Memories of sleighride sounds from his New England boyhood suggested the musical themes in the present work. As in his *Typewriter* and *Sandpaper Ballet,* Anderson used sounds from the "real world" for *Sleigh Ride.* More important than the nostalgic bell sounds however, are Anderson's melodies and scoring—their excellence keeps *Sleigh Ride* in the concert band's repertoire.

MALCOLM ARNOLD

(Born in Northampton, England, 1921)

Malcolm Arnold has created for himself a significant and somewhat unique position in contemporary British music. At a time when much new music is foreboding or despairing, his optimistic outlook and high spirits are the more welcome. This is however, only one facet of Arnold's art albeit the best-known one. He has an exceptional facility and his list of works is most impressive. It includes six symphonies, ten concertos, much chamber music, two ballets, and music for several films—he received a Hollywood Oscar for his music for the 1958 film, *Bridge on the River Kwai.*

One aspect of Arnold's work that merits special mention is his mastery of orchestration. In this respect his experience of several years as principal trumpet player in the London Philharmonic Orchestra supplemented the teaching of Gordon Jacob at the Royal College of Music. (Malcolm Rayment and Raoul Camus, Queensborough Community College)

English Dances for Band (Arr = Johnstone. Pub = MM, 1965. Gr = 4. T = 8:00. Rec = AT-MENC-66, AR Tech., Witherspoon)

Arnold's mastery of orchestration is evident on every page of the *English Dances,* the first set of which was completed in 1950 and the second in 1951. Listening to them, one might think that the composer had done considerable research in order to resurrect several forgotten folk-tunes, but in fact, every theme used is original. The Dorian, Mixolydian, and Aeolian modes, those most characteristic of folk music, are used for the set of dances.

The first dance is an andantino in the Dorian mode. The lilting theme is first heard on flute and oboe against an ostinato accompaniment by the horns, timpani, and muted trumpets. The second vivace dance is Mixolydian, having a flattened seventh degree of an otherwise normal major scale. The gloomy, Aeolian third dance has a simple pentatonic theme which is heard four times, each time rising a major third. The final allegro dance is in the Mixolydian mode with the theme being handed from one section of the band to another with the brass playing the chief role. (Malcolm Rayment and Raoul Camus, Queensborough Community College)

Four Scottish Dances (Arr = Paynter. Pub = CF, 1971-78. Gr = 4. T = 9:00. Rec = CR-GCIN-403, Interlochen, Wilson; CR-CBDNA-71-4, Shenandoah Conservatory, Noble)

Supplying his own program notes for the *Four Scottish Dances,* Arnold wrote:

> These dances were composed early in 1957, and are dedicated to The BBC Light Music Festival. They are all based on original melodies but one, the melody of which was composed by Robert Burns.
> The first dance is in the style of a slow strathspey—a slow Scottish dance in 4/4 meter—with many dotted notes, frequently in the inverted (reversed) arrangement of the "Scottish snap." The name was derived from the strath valley of Spey.
> The second, a lively reel, begins in the key of E-flat and rises a semitone each time it is played until the bassoon plays it, at a greatly reduced speed, in the key of G. The final statement of the dance is at the original speed in the home key of E-flat.
> The third dance is in the style of a Hebridean Song, and attempts to give an impression of the sea and mountain scenery on a calm summer's day in the Hebrides.
> The last dance is a lively fling, which makes a great deal of use of the open-string pitches of the violin.

This artistic wind ensemble transcription, made by John Paynter, has a transparency faithful to the original work. (Paul Noble, Shenandoah Conservatory)

FREDERIC H. ASHE

(Born in Detroit, Michigan, 1917 — Died, 1968)

Frederic Ashe graduated from Canonsburg (Pennsylvania) High School where he played cornet in the band. He received both Bachelor and Master of Music degrees from the University of Miami. Later he returned to that university to teach composition, orchestration, and harmony. In 1963 he won the highly coveted Ostwald Award for his *Concert Suite* for band. (Harold Hillyer, Eastern Illinois University)

Concert Suite (Pub = VO, 1963. Gr = 4. T = 10:30)

In the opening Fanfare movement, the horns set the harmonic scheme for both the first and second movements, and the woodwinds announce the germinal motives of the third movement. The second movement, Andante Religioso, is in two parts featuring antiphonal play between the brasses and woodwinds. The third movement, Allegro, begins with light percussion motifs, continues with a Dorian theme by the woodwinds, and closes with three chords utilizing the broadest tonal and dynamic spectrum of which the band is capable. (Robert C. Fleming, University of Tennessee at Martin)

JOHANN SEBASTIAN BACH

(Born in Eisenach, Germany, 1685 — Died in Leipzig, 1750)

With a background which boasted approximately 200 musical ancestors, it is not surprising that Johann Sebastian Bach developed a keen interest in music at an early age. Left an orphan at the age of ten, little Johann lived with his brother, who, though he had no sympathy with the child's musical aspirations, could not prevent him from secretly pursuing a course of self-instruction. At fifteen Johann was engaged as a singer at St. Michael's Church, where, free from his brother's supervision, he continued his study of music. Having mastered the violin and the clavier, he devoted himself to the study and mastery of the organ. Offered a position as organist in the town of Arnstadt at the age of eighteen, he accepted, and proceeded to dedicate himself to the art of composition. As court organist and violinist under Duke Wilhelm Ernst of Weimar, and as director of chamber music to young Prince Leopold of Anhalt-Cöthen, he took advantage of every leisure moment to perfect himself in composition. In his last position, which he held for twenty-seven years, Bach was director of music in the churches of St. Thomas and St. Nicholas and choirmaster at St. Thomas School in Leipzig. Many of his greatest works were composed during this period. (Carl Fischer, Inc.)

During his lifetime Bach was more famous as a player than a composer. A century after his death however, Richard Wagner referred to Bach's compositional ability as "the most stupendous miracle in all music." (Ed.)

Come, Sweet Death—Komm, Süsser Tod (Arr. Leidzen; Reed; Hindsley. Pub = CF, 1936; BA, 1976; HI, ms. Gr = 3. T = 3:50. Rec = IL,-53, Un. of IL, Hindsley)

Come, Sweet Death is one of the sixty-nine chorale preludes by Bach in the group of *Sacred Songs and Airs,* published in 1736. Although usually considered a Bach composition, it is in reality a harmonization by Bach of a beloved traditional German folk song. Bach's chorale prelude adaptation consisted of a single melody line with a figured bass, leaving the harmonization of the inner voices to the keyboard player.

Fantasia in G Major (Arr = Leist & Goldman. Pub = ME, 1960. Gr = 4. T = 6:30. Rec = TE-SD-5038, Cleveland Sym. Winds, Fennell)

The great *G Major Fantasia* for organ was composed between 1703 and 1707 during Bach's residence in Arnstadt. It was here, at the beginning of his career, that his music was found by the Consistory to be too full of "wonderful variations and foreign tones," and certainly the *Fantasia* is strikingly dissonant in its constant texture of suspensions. But the breadth of the five-part polyphonic writing and the richness of the harmonic sonority make the work one of the grandest of all Bach's compositions for organ. It is also one that lends itself most perfectly to the sound and sonorities of the modern wind band. (Harold Jackson, Southwest Baptist College)

Fugue à la Gigue (Arr = Holst.   Pub = BH,   1929.   Gr = 5.   T = 4:00.   Rec = CR-MID-72-5, Durant, OK, H.S.)

Bach, along with Handel, was one of the culminating masters of the Baroque era. This composition was originally written for the organ and has the character of a popular French dance, the gigue, which was well known in Bach's time. Gustav Holst, the noted English composer, arranged this work for the concert band. (Roger L. Beck, Sioux Falls College)

If Thou Be Near (Arr = Moehlmann.   Pub = FZ, 1940.   Gr = 3)

As director of the St. Thomas Church Choir in Leipzig, Bach's duty made it necessary for him to compose and have ready a new composition for each church day. A large number of these works were set aside after only one hearing. Through the efforts of the Bach Society, started by Robert Schumann, many of these beautifully harmonized melodies have been restored to the world. *If Thou Be Near* was transcribed for band by R.L. Moehlmann. (Edmund P. Sedivy, Montana State University)

Jesu, Joy of Man's Desiring (Arr = Leidzen; Hindsley.   Pub = CF, 1936; HI, ms. Gr = 3.   T = 3:45.   Rec = IL-53, Un. of IL, Hindsley)

Bach, the great Cantor of Leipzig, composed nearly three hundred cantatas, of which over two hundred have been preserved. They are especially characteristic of Bach's genius, and they constitute by far the larger portion of his total output. Only one of his cantatas was published during his lifetime, but after his death they were widely dispersed; a large bundle of them being sold by his widow for about forty dollars. They were of little use to his sons, who followed the musical trend of their day, and it remained for Mendelssohn and others to rescue the works of the master composer from oblivion.

The cantata of which this chorale is a part is entitled *Herz und Mund und That und Leben*. It was composed for the Feast of the Annunciation, and the beautiful accompanying chorale occurs twice in the course of the work. (Carl Fischer, Inc.)

Passacaglia and Fugue in C Minor (Arr = Falcone; Hunsberger.   Pub = SO, 1969; GS, 1975.   Gr = 5.   T = 20:00.   Rec = CR-ABA-74-4, All-Japan Girls H.S., Narita)

Though one of the great organ classics, the *Passacaglia in C Minor* was not originally written for that instrument. Curiously enough, Bach first composed it for the double-manual harpsichord, later rewriting it for organ, probably while at Weimar. The nobility of its studied, yet spontaneous polyphonic structure has led to numerous transcriptions for both symphony orchestra and concert band, where the variations lend to brilliant instrumental scoring. The stately eight-measure theme is given out in unison by the lower winds, and twenty variations follow, leading to an overwhelming tutti. After a brief pause the double fugue begins, built on the first part of the passacaglia theme in combination with a counter theme in eighth notes. The work closes with a massive climax of suspended harmonies and full instrumental sonority.

JOHANN SEBASTIAN BACH

Prelude and Fugue in E Minor (Arr = Rhoads. Pub = SB, 1963. Gr = 5. T = 4:45)

This work is one of the famous *Eight Little Preludes and Fugues*. Compared with the greater preludes and fugues of Bach, this is only a miniature; yet it is a miniature perfectly drawn. It is marked by his usual satisfying chord changes and intriguing rhythms, and by the unbelievable way the music always has spoken so completely when the end is reached. The prelude serves to fix the key firmly in the listener's mind as it explores various facets of the key. Then comes the fugue which, because of the chromaticism of its subject, is particularly interesting. This piece was originally written for organ in E minor, but it has been transposed to F minor for band. (Sam L. Jones, Jr., Millsaps College)

Prelude and Fugue in G Minor (Arr = Cailliet; Moehlmann. Pub = CF, 1945; RE, 1939. Gr = 3. T = 3:00)

This selection is the sixth in a series which Bach called *The Eight Little Preludes and Fugues,* composed at Weimar between 1708 and 1717. Originally for organ these works are particularly suited to the rich sonorities of the concert band. Bach's two fugues in G minor are usually referred to as the "Great Fugue" and the "Little Fugue." The word "little" in no way means that the present work was of lesser importance; only that it was smaller in scope than the "greater" fugue.

Prelude (D Minor), Chorale and Fugue (Arr = Godfrey; Hindsley. Pub = CA, 1919; HI, ms. Gr = 5. T = 8:30. Rec = IL-57, Un. of IL. Hindsley)

An eminent musicologist has referred to the prelude to the fourth fugue of Bach's *Well-tempered Clavichord* as the "Holy of Holies—among the most eloquent things in music." It is grouped here with the famous Bach-Abert *Chorale and Fugue in G Minor*. The fugue is known as the "Great" G Minor to distinguish it from the smaller fugue in the same key. The chorale is original with Abert, who also worked it into the Bach fugue, where, presented by the brass instruments, it stands out boldly from the surrounding polyphonic structure. (Mark Hindsley, University of Illinois)

Toccata and Fugue in D Minor (Arr = Leidzen; Hindsley. Pub = CF, 1942; HI, ms. Gr = 5. T = 8:40. Rec = IL-56, Un. of IL, Hindsley; CR-MENC-78, Nat'l. H.S. Honor, Revelli)

The *Toccata and Fugue in D Minor* is one of the greatest of the masterpieces which Bach wrote for the organ. From the free and showy style of the toccata, it is rather evident that the work was not conceived for use in the church, but rather as a virtuoso concert piece. The fugue is four-voiced and includes episodes of an almost rhapsodic quality. The concluding passage is recitative, leading to a huge climax with tremendous effect. (Raymond G. Young, University of Southern Mississippi)

BURT BACHARACH

(Born in Kansas City, Missouri, 1928)

Bacharach had a cosmopolitan musical education in Montreal, New York, and California, studying with such renowned composers as Darius Milhaud and Henry Cowell. Since 1966 he has been a nominee or winner of an Academy Award several times for his songs and scoring. Bacharach was Marlene Dietrich's conductor and arranger during her triumphant musical tours of Europe and the United States and more recently has been the host in a series of television specials. Personal tours, television appearances, and sales of such records as "Switched-on Bacharach" have given him international popularity. He enjoys writing the kind of music that people can remember and finds it very rewarding whenever he hears a perfect stranger whistling one of his songs. He and collaborater Hal David won Cue Magazine's Entertainer of the Year Award for *Promises, Promises,* their first Broadway show.

Bacharach's interests range much further than music. He owns a publishing company, some real estate in Georgia, a herd of cattle, and a racing stable. He married the movie star Angie Dickinson in 1965 and the couple has a daughter, Nikki. Bacharach's friends describe him as intense, talented, and considerate of other people.

Highlights from Promises, Promises (Arr = Cable. Pub = EB. Gr = 4. T = 6:00. Rec = CR-MID-70-10, VanderCook Col., Brittain)

Promises, Promises was adapted for Broadway by Neil Simon from the screenplay, *The Apartment* by Billy Wilder and I.A.L. Diamond. The story concerns Chuck Baxter, a young office worker, who lends his apartment key to several of his office superiors for their extra-marital affairs. His generosity begins to be rewarded by rapid promotions, but Chuck finally becomes disillusioned when he learns that Fran Kubelik, the girl he secretly admires, has been rendezvousing with one of his married superiors. Chuck disgustedly resigns his position and is preparing to leave the city, but the story ends happily when he discovers that Fran really loves him. The songs in this arrangement include: "Knowing When to Leave," "I'll Never Fall in Love Again," "Whoever You Are, I Love You," and the title song. (Pamlyn Smith, New York City)

HENK BADINGS

(Born in Bandung, Indonesia, 1907)

Henk Badings was born at Bandung, on the island of Java, Indonesia, of Dutch parents, but went to the Netherlands at an early age as an orphan. He studied at the Technical University of Delft, where, after graduating with honors in 1931, he became an assistant in the laboratory of historical geology. At the same time he developed along self-taught lines as a composer, having his first symphony performed by the Amsterdam Concertgebouw Orchestra in 1930, before he finished his technical studies. After some years of scientific work in the geologic field, he decided to devote full time to music and became professor of music theory and counterpoint at various schools as well as director of the State Conservatory in The Hague. Then for many years he devoted himself principally to musical composition.

Of all contemporary Dutch composers, Badings has become the best known outside his country. Some of his works include 15 symphonies and 36 other orchestral works, 5 oratorios, 8 cantatas, 6 operas, 10 ballets, numerous piano and chamber pieces, several band compositions—some commissioned by the American Wind

Symphony—and instrumental-band concertos for flute, English horn, clarinet, sax-ophone, harp, bassoon, and three French horns. He has also written a great deal of electronic, microtonal, choral, and theater music. From 1963 to 1972 Badings was professor of composition at the Musikhochschule in Stuttgart, Germany, and from 1961 to 1977 he was professor of acoustics and information theory at the University of Utrecht in the Netherlands. He is now devoting full time to composing.

Transitions (Pub = SH, 1973. Gr = 5. T = 12:00. Rec = CR-CBDNA-73-8, Un. of IL, Begian; CR-MID-73-6, U.S. Air Force, Gabriel)

Transitions was commissioned by the College Band Directors National Association and premiered by the University of Illinois Band, with Harry Begian conducting, at the national convention in 1973. Badings believes that the essentials of a composition are to be found in the musical and psychological perceptions of the audience. The title of this work suggests different relationships, for example, the transition of thematic contours. The music begins from the preceding silence, in aleatoric bits and pieces, and is gradually transformed into complete melody. Bading's description follows:

> Vague musical shapes arise from the silence, mobile in the higher pitches, slow and dark in the lower regions. They develop to a higher grade of organization, in the lower parts to a rather grim character and in the higher parts to a shining, twinkling sound. As a consequence there is always a dramatic tension between two contrasting sound-worlds. Later a milder musical world becomes audible through the vehement sounds of the former, and their lyric shapes remain after the grim accents break off. Still later the mild melodic soundshapes are again interrupted by a new violent outburst. This material evolves into a less aggressive shape and finally into a bright, playful, pleasant tune.

(Acton Ostling, Jr., University of Louisville)

EDWIN E. BAGLEY

(Born in Craftsbury, Vermont, 1857 — Died in Keene, New Hampshire, 1922)

During Bagley's lifetime bands were usually regarded as professional groups regardless of the wide range of performance abilities among the members. Edwin Eugene Bagley and his brother Ezra both played with the professional bands of the time, including the E.N. Lafrican Band and the T.D. Perkin's Band. According to band researcher Bob Hoe, E.E. Bagley was a euphonium-trombone player who wrote marches. Some of Bagley's marches, composed while he was directing different school bands in New Hampshire, include: *The Ambassador, The Imperial, L'Agresseur (The Aggressor),* and his greatest hit of all, *National Emblem.*

National Emblem March (Pub = B3, 1906. Gr = 3. T = 2:50. Rec = RC-LSP-2688, U.S. Navy, Stauffer)

The *National Emblem March* remains one of America's most popular marches, second only to Sousa's *Stars and Stripes Forever March.* The march, written in 1906 and copyrighted by Ernest S. Williams, borrows its first principal theme from our national anthem. The contrasting second theme and the stirring trio melody have also become as well known as many popular songs. (Stuart J. Ling, College of Wooster)

JOSEPH EDOUARD BARAT

(Born in 1882 — Died in 1963)

Already a fine saxophone player, Barat began the study of harmony with Paul Vidal in 1898. Later, after entering the National Conservatory at Paris, he became a member of the composition class of Emile Pessard. He composed much music for solo winds as well as works for string quartet and for chorus. His expertise on the saxophone led to his becoming a member of a regimental band and before his retirement in 1933, he rose to the high post of director of music for the French Army.

Andante et Allegro—Trombone-Euphonium Solo (Arr = Marsteller. Pub = SO, 1964. Gr = 3/4. T = 4:10. Rec = CR-MID-76-5, Friedman w. Elk Grove, IL, H.S.)

Barat is noted for his many fine solos for various wind instruments, and the *Andante et Allegro* is one of the best. One of the traditional *solos de concours* written as test pieces for students at the Paris Conservatory, it was composed in 1935 for trombone or euphonium and piano. The style is based on conventional harmonies and makes use of typical French lyricism. The slow opening section gives the soloist ample opportunity to demonstrate expressive playing, and the allegro section provides the technical challenge. (James M. Thurmond, Lebanon Valley College)

In a 1971-72 survey of college student recital literature by Merrill Brown, *Andante et Allegro* tied with Guilmant's *Morceau Symphonique* for the most-performed work by euphonium soloists and was third highest on the trombone list. (Ed.)

SAMUEL BARBER

(Born in West Chester, Pennsylvania, 1910 — Died in New York City, 1981)

As Johann Sebastian Bach was a "conservative" composer, building on the traditions in which he was raised, so Samuel Barber was conservative, building on romantic structures and sensibilities. The most popular form of music in the late nineteenth century was the art song, and it is this genre that lies at the center of Barber's work. He was one of the few composers ever to be trained as a singer; he himself performed the solo baritone role in the recording of *Dover Beach,* based on the Matthew Arnold poem and composed when Barber was only twenty years old. Barber looked back lovingly on his childhood. He knew he possessed a fluent talent and was encouraged by generous and cultivated adults. In *Knoxville: Summer of 1915* (for soprano and orchestra), James Agee's words are those of a man who (like Barber) relives his past so intensely that the voice of his youth literally speaks through him.

While studying abroad in the 1930's, Barber was discovered by Toscanini, who conducted—in 1938—the *First Essay for Orchestra* and the *Adagio for Strings* with the NBC Orchestra in New York. Forty years later Zubin Mehta opened his first season with the New York Philharmonic Orchestra by conducting Barber's *Third Essay for Orchestra*. Institutions and committees have now certified what musicians and audiences have known. Barber has won two Pulitzer prizes, received an honorary degree from Harvard, and was elected to the Academy of Arts and Letters. During a period when many composers have felt that they had to use words to explain their scores, Barber's expression has been through the music alone. (G. Schirmer, Inc.)

Commando March (Pub = GS, 1944. Gr = 4.   T = 3:00.   Rec = TE-DG-10043, Cleveland Sym. Winds, Fennell; CR-NBA-78-6, Lakeland, TX, H.S., Miller)

Barber's second symphony—produced for the Army Air Corps in 1942—made use of an electronic instrument to imitate radio signals. In a similar wartime spirit, he completed his first band work, the *Commando March,* in 1943. This march reflects some traces of the basic style of Barber, but these characteristics are less obvious when placed within the framework of the stirring medium which is suggested in the title.   Written in quadruple meter, but with the indication to be played in "fast marchtime," the composition utilizes constant contrast of dotted and triplet rhythms, and centers around a tune which appears in a different instrumental dressing four times in the course of the work. The first performance was by the Army Air Corps Band at Atlantic City in 1943.   (Hubert P. Henderson, University of Maryland)

Intermezzo from Vanessa (Arr = Beeler. Pub = GS, 1962. Gr = 5. T = 4:00)

The opera *Vanessa* was written to a libretto by Gian Carlo Menotti and was first performed by the Metropolitan Opera Company in New York in 1958. More recently, in 1978, it was a highlight at the Spoleto U.S.A. Festival in Charleston, South Carolina. Although in the opera the "Intermezzo" is played between the scenes of the last act, it has been performed in concert by symphony orchestras throughout the world. Written within a contemporary framework, the melodic material is tonal, and the harmonies are quite post-romantic with the exception of the very opening and closing sonorities.   Extremely thin in texture, this version represents the judicious individual scoring that is so often lacking in band transcriptions. Only at the very climax of the composition is every instrument used simultaneously, and then for only six measures. This arrangement by Walter Beeler was completed in 1962. (Hubert Henderson, University of Maryland)

LIONEL BART

(Born in London, 1930)

Lionel Bart has become a prime factor in British popular music in a comparatively short time. He has written many popular songs and his lyrics for musical comedies have helped make this idiom—formerly considered exclusively American—an international proposition during the past few years. As a result of his musical comedy *Oliver*, Bart has also gained great popularity in the United States. His versatility is shown by the fact that he not only wrote the musical score to *Oliver*, but adapted the book and lyrics as well.

Highlights from Oliver (Arr = Burden. Pub = TR, 1970. Gr = 3.   T = 4:30. Rec = CR-MID-70-8, Northshore Concert, Paynter)

Lionel Bart's brilliant musical based on Dickens' *Oliver Twist* is evidence of the new strength and vitality of the British musical theater. The plot concerns the orphan Oliver who is sold to an undertaker after being considered a pest at the orphanage. Oliver runs away from the undertaker and finds promise of food and friendship with a group of young pickpockets. He is captured by the police during his first day of petty thieving, but is cleared by the rich victim and, after a series of narrow escapes from a revenge-minded group of pickpockets (whom he deserted), Oliver apparently decides to go straight. The show ends with Oliver's future seeming much more promising.

BÉLA BARTÓK

(Born in Nagy Szent Miklós, Hungary, 1881 — Died in New York, 1945)

Bartók's native village was in Hungary at the time of his birth, but it became part of Romania after World War I. Most of Bartók's teenage years however, were spent in Bratislavia, now part of Czechoslovakia. Although he studied at the Royal Academy in Budapest and learned the classical style of Beethoven and the romantic-nationalistic style of the "Russian Five," his form of composition was always colored by the gypsy songs and dances of his youth. Working with his compatriot Zoltan Kodály, Bartók developed an analytical method of folkloristic research which is still used. The two composers recorded by phonograph, or by ear, well over 6,000 Hungarian, Romanian, and Arabic folksongs.

In addition to being a composer and ethnomusicologist, Bartók was a brilliant pianist and teacher. He served on the faculty of the Music Academy in Budapest for nearly thirty years, although most of his time and energy were used in composing, concertizing, and assembling his five books of folk music research. His graded series of small pieces for solo piano, called *Mikrokosmos* ("small world"), provided music for the beginner as well as the concert artist. Among his best known concert works are three piano concertos, two violin concertos, and a viola concerto written for William Primrose—completed by his friend Tibor Serly after Bartók's death. In order to escape the Nazi influence Bartók came to the United States in 1940. He earned a bare subsistence in New York City by composing and concertizing with his youthful second wife, pianist Ditla Pastztory. He died in 1945 from an advanced case of leukemia. Like many great composers, Bartók's true genius was not recognized until after his death.

Four Pieces for Band (Arr = Suchoff. Pub = SF, 1961. Gr = 2. T = 3:05)

These four short pieces are simple in construction yet interesting enough to provoke interest in hearing more music by Bartók. The pieces were transcribed from the composer's piano collection *For Children* and contain interesting melodies, concise form, and attractive rhythms. A hint of Bartók's feeling for rhythmic contrast is heard near the opening of the first piece, Poco vivace, when the meter begins a series of alternating three and two beat phrases. The remaining three pieces are marked Allegro, Adagio, and Molto allegro.

LESLIE BASSETT

(Born in Hanford, California, 1923)

Leslie Bassett first became interested in composition while serving as trombonist and arranger with bands, orchestras, and jazz bands during and following World War II. Wartime service saw him in France and Germany with the 13th Armored Division Band, followed by study at Fresno State College, graduate work at the University of Michigan, and further study at Paris' École Normale de Musique. At Michigan he was a pupil and colleague of Ross Lee Finney, and in 1950-51, as a Fulbright Fellow in Paris, he studied privately with Nadia Boulanger and at the École Normale with Arthur Honegger. Following close association with Roberto Gerhard beginning in 1960, he worked for several months with Mario Davidovsky in electronic music.

Since 1952 Bassett has been on the faculty of the University of Michigan where he is chairman of the composition department. From 1961 through 1963 he lived in Rome as recipient of the coveted Prix de Rome. He was a Guggenheim Fellow in

1973-74 and was chosen as Distinguished Alumnus of 1978 by his California alma mater. A founding member of the university's electronic music studio and former member of the national policy committee of the Ford Foundation-MENC Contemporary Music Project, Bassett received the 1960 award from the Society for the Publication of American Music for his *Five Pieces for String Quartet*. His work has been recognized by several national music associations and he is a frequent guest on campuses and with ensembles throughout the United States. In 1966 his *Variations for Orchestra* received the Pulitzer Prize in Music, following the first American performances by the Philadelphia Orchestra with Eugene Ormandy. In 1978 Robert Reynolds and the University of Michigan Band commissioned Bassett to write another artistically descriptive band work, *Sounds, Shapes and Symbols*.

Designs, Images, and Textures (Pub = PET, 1966. Gr = 5. T = 11:00. Rec = BP-111, Un. of MI, Revelli)

This unique work for band was commissioned by and dedicated to the Ithaca (New York) High School Band, conducted at the time by Frank Battisti. On the score the composer notes that in at least one respect, *Designs, Images, and Textures* is similar to Moussorgsky's *Pictures at an Exhibition*—it invites the listener to "associate music with visual art."

The composition relates to five kinds of modern art. The first movement, Oil Painting, opens with a brilliant descending cascade of overlapping lines, followed by an ascending pyramid of sounds. Trills and numerous other textures and shapes appear but the movement stabilizes tonally as it progresses toward the close. The second movement, Water Color, opens with clusters of quiet and indistinct sounds that overlap one another. The primary figures emerge briefly and the movement ends quietly with blurred sounds. Pen and Ink Drawing, the third movement, consists of numerous independent lines which diminish in number as the content of the movement becomes clear. A Mobile (a large metallic abstract) provides the associative image for the fourth movement which begins and ends with rustling, breathy background sounds. The final movement, Bronze Sculpture, emphasizes the brasses of the band. Brilliant in sonority and extended in range and expressive means, this movement is the most incisive and rhythmically varied of the five. (C.F. Peters Corporation)

LUDWIG VAN BEETHOVEN
(Born in Bonn, Germany, 1770 — Died in Vienna, 1827)

Beethoven displayed musical talent as a child, but suffered at the hands of his father who hoped he could mold the boy into a prodigy like Mozart. The incompetence of his father finally resulted in young Beethoven becoming the sole provider for his family. His ability as a pianist, organist, violinist, and composer won him an official position at the Bonn Court from 1782 until 1792 when he left for Vienna, his home for the rest of his life. While he was first known in Vienna as a brilliant pianist, a slowly developing deafness caused him to abandon performance for composition. He was probably the first composer to receive a good income from the sale of his compositions. Even with a relatively good income, Beethoven had financial problems—often because his lack of consideration for others caused him to be evicted from his room by irate landlords who kept his rent money.

Beethoven is credited with freeing music from the restraints of classicism and leading the way to individualism and subjective feeling in composition. His works became models for many generations of composers, especially in the symphony and string quartet media. Beethoven festivals were held around the world in 1970 celebrating the 200th anniversary of the great composer's birth. His ability to speak for all mankind seems to be unlimited by time.

Coriolanus Overture (Arr = Brown. Pub = BH, 1941. Gr = 5. T = 8:00)

Beethoven's overture *Coriolanus* was composed not for Shakespeare's tragedy, but for a play on the same subject first produced in Vienna in 1807. The overture expresses the conflict in Coriolanus' heart between his inexorable resolve to attack Rome and the feeling of pity to which his mother and wife appeal, when they implore him to spare the people. Stormy contradictions within him, and his imperious gestures, give way bit by bit until pity finally wins the day over violence. The overture ends expressively and quietly. (Richard Franko Goldman, the Goldman Band)

Egmont Overture (Arr = Winterbottom; Hindsley. Pub = BH, 1924; HI, ms. Gr = 5. T = 8:30. Rec = IL-57, Un. of IL, Hindsley)

This overture clearly represents Beethoven as the political liberal, the champion of the oppressed, and the freedom fighter. Based on a tragedy by Goethe, Beethoven's work is intended as incidental music for stage performance. Taken separately the overture can be regarded as in itself a kind of programmatic music drama.

The plot concerns Count Egmont, a Flemish patriot and one of the leaders of the revolt against the tyrannical Duke of Alva, who is sent to suppress the budding secession of the Netherlands from Spain. Egmont is treacherously seized and condemned to public execution. Asleep in the prison he dreams of a vision of the Goddess of Liberty. Her face is that of his own beloved Clarchen. She tells him that in dying he will secure the eventual victory of his people and be hailed as a conqueror. He reawakens, the soldiers enter and lead him away to the scaffold. His last words are, "Fight for your hearths and homes, and die joyfully—after my example—to save that which you hold most dear."

Military March (Arr = Greissele. Pub = GS. Gr = 3. T = 5:30. Rec = DG-139045, Berlin Phil. Winds, Karajan)

The Tattoo was originally a military call sounded in the evening to signal the local tavern keepers to close shop, and the soldiers to repair to their quarters. The word seems to be derived from *taptoo,* or putting the tap to the keg and selling no more liquor that evening. In Germany, the bung *(Zapfen)* was replaced in the barrel, and a chalk line *(Streich)* was drawn across the bung by the guard so that it could not be opened without evidence of tampering.

Over the years, the tradition of the Tattoo in England and Germany has become an elaborate evening ceremony that has completely eclipsed the original function of the call. Beethoven wrote this march for the Bohemian militia in 1809, probably on commission from the Archduke Anton. Characteristic of the military bands of the period is the prominent use of the triangle, bass drum, cymbals, tambourine, and a Turkish crescent or "jingling johnny." Called Janissary music, from the tradition of the Turkish Janissary Army, this use of the percussion instruments in the band led to their incorporation into the symphony orchestra. (Raoul Camus, Queensborough Community College)

FRANK BENCRISCUTTO
(Born in Racine, Wisonsin, 1928)

Frank Bencriscutto became director of bands at the University of Minnesota in 1960. The ninth of ten children born of an Italian immigrant couple, he began formal music lessons on the saxophone at the age of ten. Within two years he was playing professionally in the jazz field—later the means of financial resources for his entire university education. Advanced study was taken at the University of Wisconsin, Northwestern University, and the Eastman School of music where he received a D.M.A. degree in 1960. His major concentration was in composition and performance, with Wayne Barlow, Bernard Rodgers, and Howard Hanson as his principal composition teachers.

Bencriscutto's background includes much professional performing, conducting, arranging, and composing. Several of his compositions were performed when the Minnesota Band toured Russia. He believes that the destiny of music education is to teach man to love music, not merely as an amusement, but for its ennobling energy, for its power to make man better by arousing in him a perception of that which is good, just, and beautiful. (School of Music, University of Minnesota)

Concertino for Tuba and Band (Pub = SH, 1971. Gr = 5. T = 10:00. Rec = UM-A-66-67, Freese w. Un. of MN, Bencriscutto)

This work was written for and dedicated to Stanford Freese, a member of the University of Minnesota Concert Band from 1963 to 1969, and later director of the Disneyland Concert Band. The solo was the vehicle for Freese's solo appearance with the band on its seven-week tour of the Soviet Union in 1969. At their request, copies of the solo have been sent to the conservatories in Leningrad, Moscow, and Novosibirsk. The *Concertino* seeks to demonstrate the melodic and technical potential of the tuba while providing readily enjoyable listening for the audience. The first theme has a touch of playful humor, and the second theme is more expressive. (Frank Bencriscutto, University of Minnesota)

Latina (Pub = S&, 1964. Gr = 3. T = 2:40. Rec = MM-1118, Un. of MN, Bencriscutto)

Latina was originally written to be performed on national TV by some ninety combined high school bands at the University of Minnesota's annual high school band day half-time show. As an exciting Latin American composition featuring the complete percussion section and the low brass, the work has become one of Bencriscutto's most popular pieces. The flowing melodies in the upper woodwinds and brasses provide a contrast with appeal for both audience and performer. (Charles H. Luedtke, Dr. Martin Luther College)

Lyric Dance (Pub = S&, 1967. Gr = 4. T = 4:05. Rec = MM-2228, Un. of MN, Bencriscutto)

Fascination with the bossa nova rhythm led Bencriscutto to incorporate it in a composition expressive of optimism and joy. The exciting pattern punctuated in low brass and colored with percussion provides a foundation over which a long, flowering principal theme is introduced. A middle section fragmenting the main rhythm and introducing a motivic interplay among woodwinds, trumpets, and horns leads back to a recapitulation. The form is ABACBA. *Lyric Dance* was premiered by the University of Minnesota Band in 1967. (Frank Bencriscutto, University of Minnesota)

Serenade for Alto Saxophone and Band (Pub = SH, 1976. Gr = 3/4. T = 4:30.
Rec = MM-1118, Krinke w. Un. of MN, Bencriscutto)

This composition seeks to reveal the melodic beauty of the alto saxophone along
with its technical agility. Rather than employing the band as a simple accompanying
unit, the composer integrates the solo and band more in the traditional manner of
the sonata; that is, the band shares principal thematic material with the solo part,
with colorful use of percussion and solo woodwind voices. (Frank Bencriscutto,
University of Minnesota)

Six Concert Fanfares (Pub = KJ, 1978, Fanfare No. 1: Gr = 4. T = 0:15.
Rec = MM-1118, Un. of MN, Bencriscutto)

These fanfares were selected by the composer from a large group which had been
used to introduce feature concert selections or to highlight marching band routines.
Instructions and suggestions for their use are included with the conductor's score
and parts. "No. 1," for example, may be used to precede *Sing u New Song* for choir
and band. In "No. 1," the jazz-rock influence is clearly evident, an ingredient
which instills both rhythmic and melodic excitement.

Symphonic Jazz Suite—Soloists and Combo Pub = KJ, 1975. Gr = 5. T − 21:00.
Rec = UM-21201, Bencriscutto, Terry, Zdechlik, Barnett, Simpson, w, Un. of MN)
Un. of MN)

This suite is divided into three movements which integrate historical jazz styles
with classic techniques of composition. The movements are titled Blues, Ballad-
Rock, and Progressive. Written to provide a vehicle for Clark Terry, the work serves
equally for any jazz soloist and combo. Optional solos are written out along with
chords allowing students to develop jazz solo skills. The composition takes advantage of the intimacy and freedom possible in a small combo along with the expanded
colors and impact of the larger concert band. Bencriscutto dedicted *Symphonic Jazz
Suite* to his wife, Jean.

DAVID BENNETT

(Born in Chicago, 1897)

David Bennett has long been considered one of America's more capable composers of band music. His compositions are characterized by ingenious rhythms,
dynamic and harmonic effects, and good taste. Bennett grew up in Chicago where
he studied at the Chicago College of Music. He is a member of the American Bandmasters Association and the American Society of Composers, Authors, and
Publishers.

Ambitious instrumentalists are thankful for the many instrumental feature composed by Bennett. Examples include: *Accordion to Hoyle, Basses Berserk, Calfskin
Calisthenics, Clarinet Royale, Cubana* (violin), *Four Hornsmen, Latinata* (alto saxophone), *Repartee* (piano), *La Rougette* (harp), *Tournament of Trumpets,* and
Trombonographic.

Clarinet Carousel—Duet (Pub = SO, 1962. Gr = 3)

Clarinet Carousel is an example of the way Bennett combines interesting and
challenging musical thoughts with his ability to write idiomatically for many in-

struments. This duet was written at the request of John Bell of Southern Music Company, and features a mixture of devices including staccato, tremolo, trill, and chromatic passages.

ROBERT RUSSELL BENNETT
(Born in Kansas City, Missouri, 1894 — Died in New York, 1980)

It is almost impossible to overestimate the importance of Robert Russell Bennett to the American musical scene, particularly the American musical theater. Not only has he enjoyed a brilliant career practicing the art of music arranging; it was he, more than any other one man, who made music arranging an art in the first place. The "Broadway sound," so world-widely admired and imitated, is not merely the sound of American tunes; it is the sound of America's best melodies as arranged for pit orchestras by Robert Russell Bennett and others whom he has influenced. To list the some 200 shows he has orchestrated is to provide a fairly complete catalogue of the biggest Broadway hits of three decades or more.

Simultaneously, as if this productivity were not enough, he has had a busy career as a composer, working in every medium from chamber music to opera, organ sonata to symphonies, movie and television background scores to works for band. They too all bear an unmistakable American sound, Bennett being as thoroughly American a composer as one can imagine.

Bennett's father was a professional musician and a baseball player; his mother, a descendant of a Massachusetts colonial governor. He grew up on a farm, studied harmony and counterpoint with Carl Busch from 1909 to 1913, and by 1916 was leading army bands, arranging, and composing in New York. In 1926 a six-year period of European study began. It included four years' work with Nadia Boulanger, this century's most influential music teacher (especially of Americans). There followed Hollywood and New York successes and many highly-deserved commissions, prizes and awards (Oscar, Christopher, Emmy), an honorary doctorate, and the highest musical citation the city of New York can offer, the Handel Medallion.

Bennett lived in New York where he was a member of "The Bohemians" Board of Governors and the National Association for American Composers and Conductors. He was long an avid baseball fan, having dedicated his *Symphony in D* to the 1941 Dodgers, and he amazed his friends with his recall of baseball statistics.

Down to the Sea in Ships (Pub = WB, 1968. Gr = 5. T = 12:30)

Commissioned by the NBC-TV network to provide the music for its epic documentary film *Down to the Sea in Ships,* Bennett chose to weave some old sea songs, which he had always loved, around the great Franz Schubert melody, "Am Meer" (By the Sea). In the suite derived from the film music, the "Am Meer' melody is heard among the waves and storms of the first movement and again in the final march. Between its appearances, listeners will recognize strains of "Blow the Man Down," "Shenandoah," "What Shall We Do with a Drunken Sailor?" and less familiar tunes including "Sally Brown," which is the basis of the Waltz of the Clipper Ships movement. The remarkable suite displays everywhere Bennett's skills as both composer and arranger, his sense of color and impeccable taste. Titles of the five movements are: The Way of a Ship, Mists and Mystery, Songs in the Salty Air, Waltz of the Clipper Ship, and the Finale, Introducing the S.S. Eagle March. (Richard Franko Goldman, the Goldman Band)

Four Preludes for Band (Pub = BE, 1974. Gr = 5. T = 12:40)

For over fifty years Robert Russell Bennett has been considered one of America's most competent arrangers of Broadway shows. During that time he was closely associated with composers George Gershwin, Vincent Youmans, Cole Porter, and Jerome Kern—among many others. *Four Preludes for Band* is his musical tribute to these composers; the preludes are titled George, Vincent, Cole, and Jerome. As a coda to each movement, Bennett has used the same tune, treating it in the same way each of his friends might. Along with his violin concerto for orchestra, he considers *Four Preludes for Band* among his principal works.

Suite of Old American Dances (Pub = CA, 1952. Gr = 4. T = 15:25. Rec = IL-35, Un. of IL, Hindsley; MG-40006, Eastman, Fennell)

This suite, composed in 1950, is an original composition for band in which the composer seeks to set the mood of a Saturday night barn dance with all the gaiety which festivity demands, recalling several of the characteristic dances remembered from childhood. The goal is achieved in a genuine piece of music—not a novelty as one might expect from such a setting. Bennett has described the music as "native American dance forms . . . treated in a 'riot' of instrumentation colors," and the composition is distinguished by superb effectiveness of instrumental writing and facile flow of musical ideas. The dances include: Cake Walk, Schottische, Western One-Step, Wallflower Waltz, and Rag. (Acton Ostling, Jr., University of Louisville)

Symphonic Songs for Band (Pub = CA, 1958. Gr = 4. T = 12:27. Rec = MG-50220, Eastman, Fennell; NE-211, Northwestern Un., Paynter)

In the words of the composer:

> *Symphonic Songs* are as much a suite of dances or scenes as songs, deriving their name from the tendency of the principal parts to sing out a fairly diatonic tune against whatever rhythm develops in the middle instruments. The Serenade has the feeling of strumming, from which the title is obtained, otherwise it bears little resemblance to the serenades of Mozart. The Spiritual may possibly strike the listener as being unsophisticated enough to justify its title, but in performance this movement sounds far simpler than it really is. The Celebration recalls an old-time county fair with cheering throngs (in the woodwinds), a circus act or two, and the inevitable mule race.

Symphonic Songs for Band was commissioned by the Kappa Kappa Psi Band Fraternity and was premiered at the 1957 national convention in Salt Lake City by the National Intercollegiate Band.

WARREN BENSON

(Born in Detroit, Michigan, 1924)

Active as a performer and educator as well as a composer, Benson was at one time a timpanist with the Detroit Symphony Orchestra. Self-taught in composition, he is a graduate in theory from the University of Michigan. He was awarded successive Fulbright Teacher Grants to Greece, where he organized the first coeducational choral group in that country. Later his Ithaca Percussion Ensemble was the first such group in the eastern United States. His book, *Creative Projects in Musician-*

ship, an outgrowth of this long involvement with the innovative Contemporary Music Project, has been translated into Spanish and Japanese. In 1967, following his tenure as a music professor and composer in residence at Ithaca College, Benson joined the faculty of the Eastman School of Music as a professor of composition.

Benson's music combines sinewy sparseness with a pervasive concern for lyricism in compositions that are varied, selective, and non-doctrinaire in their technique and style. In addition to a substantial body of pioneering works for wind ensemble and percussion groups, he has composed major works in every medium. He has conducted his own works and lectured at educational centers in the U.S., Mexico, South America, and Europe. (Carl Fischer, Inc.)

The Leaves Are Falling (Pub = EM, 1966. Gr = 6. T = 11:30. Rec = CO-2736, IN Un., Ebbs; TO-EMI-TA-72043, Eastman, Hunsberger)

In a recent study of wind band literature by Acton Ostling—one which evaluated nearly 1,500 compositions—*The Leaves Are Falling* was one of only thirty works which were both known, and considered to have serious artistic merit, by twenty highly respected conductors. Writing for *The Instrumentalist,* John Paynter calls the work, "one of the most significant band compositions in the last ten years." The composition was begun in November of 1963 (not 1964 as indicated on the score) and was motivated by an inspirational poem, "Herbst" (Autumn), from *Buch der Lieder* by Rainer Maria Rilke. (Benson recommends that the poem be used as an introduction to the music. Ed.)

Polyphonies for Percussion (Pub = EM, 1961. Gr = 4. T = 5:50. Rec = CR-MW-63, Centerville, IA, H.S., Kelly)

The *Polyphonies* presents the percussion in a mature setting which features that section while retaining an interwoven ensemble effect with the various wind sections. An emotional build-up is achieved through separate use of accelerando and crescendo in conjunction with very effective instrumental scoring. (Jack Snavely, University of Wisconsin at Milwaukee)

The Solitary Dancer (Pub = MC, 1970. Gr = 5. T = 5:50. Rec = CR-CBDNA-73, Un. of Redlands, Jorgenson)

The Solitary Dancer was commissioned by the Clarence, New York, High School Band, and is dedicated to Bill Hug. The work deals with "quiet, poised energy that one may observe in a dancer in repose, alone with her inner music," according to the brief notes on the score. It was written in the classic, one-on-a-part wind ensemble concept, although the B-flat clarinet parts, the alto clarinet, and the tuba may be doubled. Basic elements of the composition are presented in the introduction; sustained harmony by the flutes, the minor third motive stated by the soprano saxophone, the syncopation by the piccolo, and the rhythmic drive of the percussion. Piano and bass provide an ostinato for the development of thematic material. Singing and hand clapping add interesting tonal variation and rhythmic punctuation. (James Jorgenson, University of Redlands)

Transylvania Fanfare March (Pub = SH, 1964. Gr = 5. T = 3:10. Rec = IL-38, Un. of IL, Hindsley; SH-V4, Ithaca Col., Beeler)

A brass fanfare by Paul Bryan was used at the Transylvania Music Camp to signal the end of concert intermissions. Benson used a fragment of this fanfare, as well as the opening measures of Handel's "Air" from the *Water Music* (the camp's radio theme), as thematic material for this stirring march. The march was written in 1953 on commission from the Transylvania Music Camp and was dedicated to the camp band.

WILLIAM BERGSMA

(Born in Oakland, California, 1921)

Bergsma's musical interests developed very early in life; he was playing violin in an orchestra by age six. In high school he had the opportunity to conduct many of his own compositions and his ballet, *Paul Bunyon*, written when he was sixteen, had twenty-five performances. He attended Stanford University from 1938 to 1940 followed by four years at the Eastman School of Music where he studied with Howard Hanson and Bernard Rogers.

Bergsma's compositions include an opera, two symphonies, two ballets, and a variety of music in other forms. He has been awarded two Guggenheim Fellowships, the Bearns prize, and an award from the American Academy of Arts and Letters, as well as many commissions from leading organizations. From 1946 to 1963 he taught at the Juilliard School, and in 1963 he became head of the School of Music at the University of Washington.

March with Trumpets (Pub = GA, 1957.   Gr = 4.   T = 6:00.   Rec = DL-78633, Goldman, R.F. Goldman; CN-4-Cornell Un, Stith)

William Bergsma's *March With Trumpets* was the first of a series of works commissioned by Richard Franko Goldman in memory of his father, Edwin Franko Goldman, founder of the Goldman Band. E.F. Goldman set the precedent of commissioning new concert works for band from leading composers of the United States, and the Goldman Band gave first performances of these and dozens of other new works during Goldman's lifetime. Bergsma's composition is a straightforward grand march of traditional dignity and brightness. The title derives from English usage of the time of Shakespeare. (Galaxy Music Corporation)

IRVING BERLIN

(Born in Temun, Russia, 1888)

Jerome Kern once commented that "Irving Berlin has no place in American music—he *is* American music." Berlin's achievements as a philanthropist, innovator in musical theater, soldier, publisher of music and composer of film scores are by no means minor, but they fade into a role of secondary importance when compared with his forte—the invention of melodies and lyrics of simple charm and universal appeal and the genius which led to his domination of the popular song writing field and his endearment by the American public.

Irving Berlin (born Israel Baline) was the youngest of the eight children of Moses and Leah Lipkin Baline. His father was a rabbi. When young Berlin was four, all but two of the family moved to a crowded tenement on New York's lower East Side. His two years of schooling ended abruptly when his father died, and the lad sang on street corners and in cafes and developed through experience his ability to create lyrics and melodies. His years of hard work as a songwriter blossomed in 1911 with his writing of "Alexander's Ragtime Band" and the first all-Berlin show, "Watch Your Step." Then followed the Irving Berlin music publishing firm, the construction of the unique Music Box Theater, the decades of producing music for Hollywood films, and the fifty years of all-Berlin Broadway productions. (Shawnee Press, Inc.)

Irving Berlin—A Symphonic Portrait (Arr = Ades. Pub = SH. Gr = 3. T = 6:05. Rec = SH-V5-P-454, Southwestern OK St. Col., Jurrens)

Hawley Ades selected six of Irving Berlin's greatest hits for this arrangement. "There's No Business like Show Business" was written in 1946 for *Annie Get Your Gun* and was initially regarded as a "throw-away" number to be sung by the entire cast in front of the curtain during a scene change. "Say It With Music" was written in 1921 as the theme song for the proposed Music Box Theater. "Alexander's Ragtime Band" (1921) was Berlin's first international hit. The melody for "Easter Parade" was in a 1917 song called "Smile and Show Your Dimple," but was rewritten in 1933. Berlin wrote "White Christmas" for the film *Holiday Inn* in 1942 and it became a hit as the title song in the 1954 Bing Crosby film. An example of Berlin's generosity was revealed when he decided to give all the royalties from "God Bless America" to the Girl Scouts and Boy Scouts—over a half million dollars to date. (Shawnee Press, Inc.)

HECTOR BERLIOZ
(Born in la Côte-St. André, France, 1803 — Died in Paris, 1869)

Hector Berlioz was sent to medical school at the age of twenty to follow in the footsteps of his physician-father. The young man preferred music to medicine, and, despite intense parental opposition, insisted on a musical career. Dramatic and radical in his tendencies, he incurred the dislike of Maria Luigi Cherubini, head of the Paris Conservatory, who for three years withheld from the composer the Prix de Rome, and forced him to earn a meager livelihood by singing in a theater chorus. He finally gained fame and comparative wealth with his *Cantata* and *Harold Symphony*.

His trips throughout Europe were continued triumphs, whereas in Paris his compositions were received with decided apathy. Finally, election to the Academy and the Legion of Honor could no longer be denied him. He became recognized as a master of orchestral idiom. His music was stormy, like himself; his conceptions immense and original. The failure of his last opera, *The Trojans*, and the death of a son caused a complete nervous breakdown, which resulted in his death in 1869. (Carl Fischer, Inc.)

Beatrice and Benedict Overture (Arr = Henning. Pub = CF, 1937. Gr = 5. T = 7:30. Rec = CR-CRE-9009, Un. of IL, Begian)

The story concerns the difficulties encountered by Benedict—an officer in the army which as conquered the Moors in Messina—in his efforts to win the heart and hand of fair Beatrice. Berlioz said in his memoirs of his *Beatrice and Benedict:* "I had taken the book from *Much Ado About Nothing* and added the songs and episodes of the musician. Some of the Paris critics praised the music and some thought the dialogue was stupid. It is copied almost word for word from Shakespeare."

Grand Funeral and Triumphal Symphony, Op. 15 (Ed = Goldman; Whitwell. Pub = ME, Rental 1947; Whitwell, ms. Gr = 5. T = 28:00 Rec = PH-802913, London Sym., Davis)

The *Symphonie Funèbre et Triomphale* (originally *Symphonie Militaire)* was written for the tenth anniversary of the July Revolution of 1830 and the reinterment of the victims of those three days in the monument which had just been erected for them in the Place de la Bastille. Berlioz thought that a large group of wind instruments would be most suitable for the open air performance and that each movement should be descriptive of the events. The long first movement, Funeral March, recalls the combat of the three days, enveloped by the mournful sounds of a funeral march. The Funeral Oration movement is performed by solo trombone with the band answering in the manner of a chorus and was written as a final farewell to the illustrious dead at the moment their remains would be placed in the monument. The final movement develops into a marchlike hymn of glory as the tomb was to be sealed and the crowd, according to Berlioz' memoirs, "would see only the high column topped by the statue of liberty with wings outstretched, soaring toward the heavens like the souls of those who died for her."

Marche Hongroise—Rakŏczy (Tr = Smith. Pub = BL, 1957. Gr = 5. T = 4:00. Rec = CR-CRE-9005, Ithaca Col. Alumni, Beeler)

The *Rakŏczy March* is the national air of Hungary and was originally written by Michael Barna, a gypsy court musician of Prince Franz Rakŏczy, from whom this composition takes its name. The march underwent several changes. Berlioz decided to use it while he was in Budapest making arrangements for a performance of his opera, *The Damnation of Faust*. He realized the great patriotism of the Hungarians and changed his libretto to suit the situation, taking the much traveled Faust to Hungary, so that he might see the troops depart for the war, thus creating an opportunity for the playing of the *Rakŏczy March*. The success of the plan was so overpowering at the first performance in Budapest, Berlioz and others feared for their safety. (Leonard B. Smith, The Detroit Concert Band)

Roman Carnival Overture (Arr = Godfrey; Safranek. Pub = CA, 1902; CF, 1962. Gr = 4. T = 8:50. Rec = CR-NBA-78-7, U.S. Navy, Muffley)

This overture is based on themes from the opera *Benvenuto Cellini*. The opening saltarello (popular Roman dance) from the second act and Benvenuto's love theme from the first, are two of the melodies prominently featured. The opera itself was not very successful but this overture has proved exceedingly attractive ever since it was composed. Its first concert performance took place in Paris, February 3, 1844, under Berlioz' personal direction. It pleased the audience so greatly on this occasion that it had to be repeated. The chief thematic material of the overture is taken directly from the score of the opera. (Harold L. Hillyer, University of Texas at El Paso)

Symphonie Fantastique
> 2nd Movement - A Ball (Arr = Foulds. Pub = BH, 1937)
> 4th Movement - March to the Scaffold (Arr = Foulds. Pub = BH, 1937. Gr = 6. T = 5:00)
> 5th Movement - Dream of a Witches' Dance (Arr = Schaefer. Pub = WIM. Gr = 5. T = 8:30. Rec = CR-ABA-77-6, U.S. Marine, Kline)

LEONARD BERNSTEIN

Berlioz wrote his *Fantastic Symphony* during one of the most emotional periods of his life. He was deeply in love with Harriet Smithson, an Irish Shakespearean actress who did not realize Berlioz' state of mind at the time, and he allowed his imagination to run riot during the composition of the work. The symphony was first performed in 1830 and three years later Berlioz married the actress. Their marriage was anything but "fantastic" and after ten stormy years they separated. Berlioz published the following preface to his program symphony:

> A young musician of morbid sensibility and ardent imagination poisons himself with opium in a fit of amorous despair. The narcotic dose, too weak to result in death, plunges him into a heavy sleep accompanied by the strangest visions, during which his sensations, sentiments, and recollections are translated in his sick brain into musical thoughts and images. The beloved woman herself has become for him a melody, as a fixed idea which he finds and hears everywhere.

The five movements are titled Dreams and Passions, A Ball, Scene in the Fields, March to the Scaffold, and Dream of a Witches' Dance.

LEONARD BERNSTEIN
(Born in Lawrence, Massachusetts, 1918)

Leonard Bernstein is probably one of America's foremost musical geniuses. He achieved instant conducting fame when, at the age of twenty-five, with sixteen hours notice and without adequate rehearsal, he conducted a Sunday afternoon broadcast of the New York Philharmonic Symphony after the scheduled guest conductor, Bruno Walter, became suddenly ill. Equally adept in the various activities of musical performance, composition, and analysis, he has perhaps done more than anyone else to make the listening of music exciting and knowledgeable to the layman.

Bernstein attended the Boston Latin School and Harvard University where he studied composition with Edward Burlinghame Hill, A. Tillman Merritt, and Walter Piston. Later he studied orchestration with Randall Thompson, conducting with Fritz Reiner and Serge Koussevitsky, and piano with Isabella Vengerova. His first important composition, the *Jeremiah Symphony,* was composed in 1944. He has since written two other symphonies; three ballets; an opera; a film score; works for violin, chorus, and six singers, with orchestra; four Broadway musicals; and several smaller works for solo and chamber music groups. Bernstein has used the element of jazz in many of his compositions, including his *Mass* which was composed for the opening of the Kennedy Center for the Performing Arts in Washington, D.C. Two recent band transcriptions of his works include *On the Town* by Marice Stith and a concert overture, *Slava!,* by Clare Grundman.

After serving as musical director of the Philharmonic Symphony Society of New York for many years, Bernstein has more recently been devoting his time to composing, lecturing, and guest conducting. During an August, 1978 television spectacular celebrating his sixtieth birthday, William Schumann said of Bernstein: "He is an authentic American hero, a new breed of hero, an arts hero, showing that America does honor her artists."

Danzon from Fancy Free (Arr = Krance. Pub = WB, 1950-63. Gr = 4. T = 2:45. Rec = CL-MS-6677, NY Philharmonic Orch., Bernstein)

The ballet, *Fancy Free,* is concerned with young America of 1944. As the curtain rises on a scene depicting a New York street corner and bar, three sailors suddenly appear, obviously on the prowl for girls. The story of the ballet is revealed as the sailors meet the first girl, then the second, followed by a fight over the girls who are unimpressed by the action. Later, during a scene in the bar, the three sailors present competitive solo dances. The first sailor dances in an acrobatic, vaudeville style; the second changes from mock gentility to a sensuous, dance-hall style; the third—in the *Danzon*—displays an intense, emotional, Latin-American style.

The ballet became such a popular attraction of the New York Ballet Theater that its story—with a new musical score—was transformed into a Broadway musical titled *On the Town.*

Overture to Candide (Arr = Beeler. Pub = GS, 1955-62. Gr = 5. T = 4:00. Rec = CR-Mid-71-4, Lake Highlands H.S., Dallas, TX, Green)

Candide, the comic operetta based on Voltaire's work, had an unfortunately short musical life on Broadway in 1956. However its lively overture had its premiere by the New York Philharmonic Orchestra under the direction of the composer in 1957, and has become a favorite in the concert repertoire of both orchestras and bands. The work is very rhythmic, yet forceful, combining the classical and popular style into a clever and modern composition. (Carl Barnett, Will Rogers High School, Tulsa, Oklahoma)

Selections from West Side Story (Arr = Duthoit; Gilmore. Pub = GS, 1957; 1963. Gr = 4; 5. T = 8:30; 4:30. Rec = IL-36, Un. of IL, Hindsley)

West Side Story has been characterized as an American "Romeo and Juliet." With its romantic setting against a background of social and racial strife, Bernstein's music reflects the thousand and one moods which permeate Stephen Sondheim's lyrics. From a basic mood of studied nonchalance and defiance by the juvenile set, the music is at times devout and tender, or in contrasting sections, dynamic in intensity.

Duthoit's arrangement includes: "I Feel Pretty," "Maria," "Something's Coming," "Tonight," "One Hand, One Heart," "Cool," and "America." (Mark Hindsley, University of Illinois)

FREDERICK BEYER

(Born in Chicago, 1926)

Frederick H. Beyer is a native of Chicago, but his higher education and professional career have taken him to the eastern and southeastern sections of the United States. He has an A.B. degree from Harvard University, an M.A. degree in composition from Columbia University, where he studied with Otto Luening and Jack Beeson, and a D.M. degree from Florida State University, where his principal teacher was John Boda. Beyer was band and orchestra director at Largo High School in Florida for nine years and is now teaching at Greensboro College. His principal band works are *Overture for Band* (1965), *Symphony for Band* (1967), and *Ricochet for Band and Tape* (1969). He has also composed for brass ensemble and for mixed voices and was awarded the North Carolina Music Teachers Composition Commission for a 1975 work.

Overture for Band (Pub = VO, 1965. Gr = 4. T = 6:30)

The *Overture for Band* begins with a syncopated figure which is contrasted with a motive based on a triad with varying meters. The middle section follows with short solos by the flute, clarinet, and cornet, using material from the contrasting motive. After a return to the fast opening section and an increasing use of varying meters, a strong lyrical style concludes the overture. This composition won the American Bandmasters Association Ostwald Award in 1965. (C.R. Varner, College of William and Mary)

HERBERT BIELAWA

(Born in Chicago, 1930)

Herbert Bielawa is the oldest of five children. His parents were of German descent. Bielawa began piano lessons at eight, played violin in the Lindblom High School orchestra, accompanied the choir, and graduated in the top ten per cent of his class. He received B.A., B.S., and M.M. degrees in piano, music education, and composition, respectively, from the University of Illinois and continued his graduate study at the University of Southern California where he received the D.M. degree with a major in composition in 1969. He has studied with many distinguished musicians including Gordon Binkerd, Burrill Phillips, Ingolf Dahl, Halsey Stevens, David Raskin, Miklos Rosza, and Leonard Rosenmann. Bielawa has taught at Bethany College, University of Southern California, Upland College, and San Francisco State College where he is now professor of music. He has composed for a large variety of performing media including electronic music. Bielawa's wife, Sandra Soderlund, is a concert organist and the couple has two children.

Concert Fanfare (Pub = SH, 1968. Gr = 4. T = 4:06. Rec = BP-128, Clarence, NY. H.S., Good)

Although martial as the title implies, *Concert Fanfare* is symphonic in form. The composer's imagination can be observed in the development of the theme following an exciting percussion-brass introduction. Challenging in its technical demands, the work is becoming ever more popular as a curtain-raiser on contemporary band programs.

Spectrum (Pub = TE, 1967. Gr = 4. T = 6:00. Rec = BP-106, Un. of Redlands, Jorgenson)

This composition was written in 1966 for the Memorial High School Band in Houston while Bielawa was a composer-in-residence under a Ford Foundation grant. The work is for the mixed media of pre-recorded tape and live musicians and is in one movement. The tonal organization is serial, with the twelve tones of the chromatic scale divided into two motives of five notes each and one of only two notes. The rather frequent repetition of these motives makes the structure of the composition clearer than most serial compositions. The form of the entire composition is ABA with the first A section for band alone. The tape recorder enters at the beginning of the B section where the sounds were made by a mixture of piano tones and white noise (all tones of the spectrum mixed together). With the return of the A section the tape is silenced momentarily then returns with an ostinato played against different sections of the band. Here the percussionists are instructed to "wade into the ostinato," thus achieving a super-charged atmosphere for the ending. (Gene A. Braught, University of Oklahoma)

At the time *Spectrum* was written (1966), it seemed a digression from traditional compositional techniques for many band musicians and audiences. Bielawa however, pointed out on the score that the traditional aesthetic principals of "cause and effect, unity and variety, exposition and development, tension and repose all operate in *Spectrum*." (Ed.)

JERRY H. BILIK
(Born in New Rochelle, New York, 1933)

Composer and arranger Jerry Bilik attended the University of Michigan at Ann Arbor where he received the B.M.E. and M.M. degrees in music. Beginning with the *Block M March* in 1955 his compositions for band have been extremely popular with both college and high school bands. Bilik is well known for his arrangements for marching band, several collections of choir tunes, and a marching band text he has authored. After serving as the chief arranger for the West Point Military Academy Band, Bilik returned to Michigan and joined the theory faculty of the University School of Music. He now lives in Los Angeles where he devotes full time to composing and arranging. His principal composition teacher was Tibor Serly. Bilik has received many honors including two presidential commendations, is a frequent clinician and after-dinner speaker, and enjoys the sports of tennis and sailing. (John Wakefield, University of Maryland)

American Civil War Fantasy (Pub = SN, 1961. Gr − 3. T = 8:00. Rec = VA-2124, Un. of MI, Revelli)

This tone poem portrays musically the mood, music, and events leading to the Civil War. After tunes depicting daily life in the North and South, the rumblings of marching drums are heard and rallying songs fill the air. Following a meditative reflection the sounds of battle describe the conflict. After the tumult a new hope for a perpetually-united America rises from the ashes. (Jerry Bilik, Ann Arbor, Michigan)

Block M March (Pub = BE, 1955. Gr = 3. T = 3:00. Rec = MU-H80P-5838, Un. of MI, Revelli; IL-77, Un. of IL, Begian)

The *Block M* was Bilik's first published work and was written for the University of Michigan Band's annual Variety Night concert while the composer was still a student. The "Block M" is the symbol for the Michigan monogram. (Jerry Bilik, Ann Arbor, Michigan)

Concertino for Alto Saxophone and Band (Pub = JB, 1974. Gr = 4/5. T = 12:00. Rec = CR-MID-74-15, Hemke w. North Hills H.S., Pittsburgh, PA, Mercer)

The *Concertino* was commissioned to honor the retirement of Larry Teal, one of the world's leading saxophone teachers, from the faculty of the University of Michigan. The work attempts to exploit the full technical, range, and expressive capabilities of the alto saxophone within the framework of the classical concerto form. (Jerry Bilik, Ann Arbor, Michigan)

Suite Italienne (Pub = SN, 1962. Gr = 3. T = 7:00)

Bilik describes this suite as "a three-movement work depicting in miniature the life, love, and history of the Italian people." The movements are appropriately titled Tarantella, Canzone d'Amore, and Shadows of the Past.

Symphony for Band (Pub = JB, 1972. Gr = 5. T = 15:00. Rec = CR-MID-73-15, Huron H.S., Ann Arbor, MI, Downing)

This symphony is a major work for the medium and even though cast in the customary three movement form, it is somewhat unique in that the first and final movements have short interludes which both forecast and recall the other movements. For example, a short interlude introducing the basic motive material for the middle movement is heard before the first movement draws to a close. The second movement utilizes and develops this thematic material. The final movement begins with a dramatic fanfare-like motif played first by the horns. This motif recurs periodically throughout this movement. Musical statements from each of the other movements are also restated, thus creating an overall "rondo-like" summary of the complete work. Another compositional device which helps unify the entire symphony, is the system of tonal organization known as "Modus Lascivus," a system devised by Bilik's teacher, Tibor Serly, to whom this symphony is dedicated. (Wayne Pegram, Tennessee Tech)

GEORGES BIZET

(Born in Paris, 1838 — Died in Bougival, France, 1875)

Bizet's father was a singing teacher and his mother an accomplished pianist so it was natural that the young boy learned solfeggio and the piano keys before he learned the alphabet. In his ninth year he entered the Paris Conservatory where he was awarded the first prize for solfeggio at eleven, first prize for piano at thirteen, and the "Prix de Rome" for his cantata, *Clovis and Clotilde,* at twenty. He was fond of his work, admired by his teachers, and seemed destined for a brilliant career. Unfortunately the boldness of the realism of his early operas, along with a discordant newspaper press, caused the public to give a cold reception to his early works and it was not until he composed the incidental music for *L'Arlesienne* in 1872 that he was acclaimed as a leading French composer.

Bizet's skill in evoking exotic atmosphere was displayed in the three operas which followed the works of his youth. They included *The Pearl Fishers, The Fair Maid of Perth,* and *Djamileh,* each concerned with romance and ritual in areas largely unknown to the French opera audiences. He also wrote several orchestra and choral works, numerous piano pieces, and several songs. In 1875 Bizet was given the assignment of composing an opera based on Prosper Mérimee's novel of a fiery gypsy girl. The resulting work, *Carmen,* is considered by many to be the greatest French opera of the nineteenth century, and it is still one of the most popular works in the twentieth century repertory. At the time, however, the subject scandalized the audience, and the opera's reception, along with the emotional exhaustion of months of overwork, resulted in a heart attack and death of Bizet at the age of thirty-eight.

The Pearl Fishers Overture (Arr = Cailliet. Pub = SF, 1956. Gr = 4)

The Pearl Fishers, an opera concerning love and ritual in Ceylon, was written when Bizet was twenty-five. Although the libretto was not of a character to tempt a fiery and original composer like Bizet, he accepted the commission without even knowing the plot, thankful for an oppportunity to prove himself. The opera was presented for the first time in Paris in 1863 where it met with questionable success. Since that time it has never become completely accepted as an operatic standard although it was a favorite at the Metropolitan in New York during Enrico Caruso's years there. The overture demonstrates Bizet's originality in melodic and harmonic invention and the scoring, making use of the new original effects, reveals the skill of the young composer.

ARTHUR BLISS

(Born in London, 1891 — Died in London, 1975)

Sir Arthur Bliss was educated at Rugby, Cambridge, and the Royal College of Music. His musical studies were with Charles Wood, Sir Charles Stanford, Gustav Holst, Ralph Vaughan Williams, and Maurice Ravel. He was decorated for valor at the conclusion of World War I and became professor of music at the University of California in Berkeley in 1939. In 1941 he returned to London as musical director of the BBC, which position he held until 1944. He was knighted in 1950, and in 1953 was appointed Master of the Queen's Musick, succeeding the late Sir Arnold Bax. Sir Arthur received honorary doctorates of music from Edinburgh, London, and Oxford. (Jonathan Elkus, Lehigh University)

Things to Come (Tr = Godfrey. Pub = CA, 1936. T = 11:00)

Things to Come is a suite of incidental music for the London Films Production produced by Sir Alexander Korda and directed by William Cameron Menzies from the script by H.G. Wells, released in 1936 by United Artists.

The following note was written by the composer for the program of the Lehigh University Concert Band's 1959 concert:

> In the 1930's H.G. Wells wrote *The Shape of Things to Come* as a prophetic warning of what might one day happen to our world. The story starts in a great Capitol City—Wells called it Everytown—at Christmas time. Suddenly without warning an enemy launches a devastating attack from the air. This is the spark which sets alight a world conflagration. In the course of long years of war, civilization as we know it is virtually destroyed. The survivors live like men in some primitive age, deprived of any material comforts of life. From this barbarism there slowly emerges a group of men who are determined to build a new world. The film showed a glimpse into the far future when this plan is realized, and we see it, a world of order and beauty. But Wells did not believe that man ever rested on past achievements, and so in the final scene, two young volunteers, a boy and a girl, are shown setting out on a dangerous quest to reach the moon.

The Ballet for Children describes a Christmas scene at the outset of the film. The title march serves as a "motto" tune for the whole film. The Theme of Reconstruction refers to the first attempts to regain order and sanity after the world war. (Jonathan Elkus, Lehigh University)

JERRY BOCK

(Born in New Haven, Connecticut, 1928)

Jerry Bock began the study of piano when he was nine, but discontinued his music lessons before entering high school because he hated to practice. At Flushing (New York) High School, he edited the school paper and contributed articles to school journals. Working mostly on his own he also wrote text and music for a war bond show, *My Dream.* Later he studied music at the University of Wisconsin where he wrote the score for another musical, *Big as Life.* Following graduation Bock returned to New York, married, and wrote songs for television shows including the Kate Smith Hour and the Sid Caesar-Imogene Coca revues. In 1956 he wrote the score for the Broadway show, *Mr. Wonderful,* starring Sammy Davis, Jr.

In 1956 Bock teamed with Sheldon Harnick to write *The Body Beautiful;* followed by *Fiorello!* in 1959, for which they received a Pulitzer Prize; *Tenderloin* in 1960; *She Loves Me* in 1963; *Fiddler on the Roof* in 1964; and a trio of musical vignettes combined under the title of *The Apple Tree* in 1966.

Fiddler on the Roof (Arr = Burden. Pub = HN, 1972. Gr = 4. T = 6:30. Rec of Barnes ms. = CR-MENC-80-21, Perez w. Un. of KS, Foster)

The plot and the setting for *Fiddler on the Roof* are anything but glamorous. The story concerns Tevye, a Russian Jewish peasant, his shrewish wife, his guileless daughters, and his fellow townsmen who dress in rags, torn coats, and battered hats. Tevye is forever arguing with God; his skeptical piety amounts to realism. He has a wholesome nature and no illusions. He and the other peasants are vainly trying to keep traditions alive in an alien hostile world from which they are eventually forced to flee. Even though the theme is concerned specifically with impoverished Jews in Czarist Russia, the story has universal appeal. In addition to several consecutive years of playing on Broadway the show has been produced by local and road companies throughout the United States. Some of the most popular Bock and Harnick songs in the show include: "If I Were a Rich Man," the wistful "Matchmaker, Matchmaker," and the poignant "Sunrise, Sunset."

G. BONELLI

(Born in Italy)

Unfortunately little is known about the Italian composer, G. Bonelli. Concerning the composer, Leonard Falcone, former director of the Michigan State University Band, writes:

In Italy composers of marches and other small pieces were never given biographical information nor program notes concerning their music. My brother Nicholas and I played the Bonelli march with our home town band in Italy about sixty years ago (around 1915). I remember seeing the front page of the conductor score (in manuscript) and the only thing written on it was BONELLI.

Symphonic Concert March (Arr = N. Falcone. Pub = SO, 1968. Gr = 4. T = 6:30. Rec = CR-MID-68-5, Muskegon, MI, H.S., Krive)

At the mention of the word "march" most Americans naturally think of formations on parade, and our own march king, John Philip Sousa. This Italian march, however, was not intended for the parade ground, but, as its title indicates, for the concert hall. Its flowing melodies, contrasting rhythms, and contrapuntal material are too intricate for the march, and too fast for the standard military pace. Bonelli has employed themes which reappear often throughout the composition. Following the trio, the finale again returns to the motive of the introduction in resplendent form.

This arrangement is by Nicholas Falcone, an Italian who immigrated to the United States and became director of the University of Michigan Band in 1927. Forced to curtail his activities due to deafness, he continued to appear as guest conductor and make band arrangements, until his death in 1981. (Raoul Camus, Queensborough Community College)

ALEXANDER BORODIN

(Born in St. Petersburg, Russia, 1833 — Died in St. Petersburg, 1887)

Borodin was a member of the so-called "Russian Five," a group of young composers who, except for their leader, Mily Balakirev, were essentially amateur musicians. Borodin, for example, was a physician and a professor of organic chemistry at the St. Petersburg Academy of Military Medicine. He was also active in the formation of a medical college for women and became a member of its staff. He wrote several treatises on chemical subjects and played the piano and cello.

Borodin composed three symphonies (the third unfinished), a symphonic sketch, some chamber music, and a few piano pieces and songs. Compared with most professional composers, Borodin's output was not great, but many consider his *Symphony No. 2* the finest piece of symphonic music produced by any member of the "Russian Five." Most of his instrumental music was written in the traditional Western Europe pattern, but his many beautiful melodies (although original) still have the spirit of the Russian folk music.

Symphony No. 2—First Movement (Arr = Leidzen. Pub = CF, 1940. Gr = 5. T = 6:30.

Like most of the works by members of the "Russian Five," the *Second Symphony* is thoroughly Russian in character, and it is said that Borodin had in mind heroic legends of medieval Russia when he wrote it. The work was composed between 1871 and 1877 and was first performed in St. Petersburg in 1877. The first movement is full of energy and restlessness. The opening theme, of eight notes, recurs throughout the movement, often breaking into the repetition of the more lyrical second subject. The meter alternates between 2/2 and 3/2 and the instrumentation is full of color. (Leonard Smith, Detroit Concert Band)

RICHARD W. BOWLES

(Born in Rogers, Arkansas, 1918)

Richard Bowles earned degrees at Indiana University in 1940 and at the University of Wisconsin in 1950 and, in the meantime, had graduated from the Army Music School in 1944. His principal composition teachers were Robert Sanders and Cecil Burleigh. In addition to *The Saints* Bowles has over 100 published compositions and arrangements to his credit. He has received four ASCAP Standard Awards for composition, is past president of the prestigious College Band Directors National Association, and has had several articles on fishing and vacation topics published in national journals. Bowles is a professor of music at the University of Florida where he was formerly conductor of bands.

Burst of Flame March (Pub = FZ, 1955. Gr = 3. T = 3:30.)

This march, written in the mid-fifties, has been listed in *The Instrumentalist's* "100 Most Popular Marches" several times and shows promise of continuing its popularity with new generations of band members and audiences. With its unique accents and surprise entrances, along with its display of brilliant brass and melodic woodwinds, *Burst of Flame* is considered by music professor-fisherman Bowles as one of his best marches.

The Saints (Pub = CA, 1966. Gr = 3. T = 3:20)

The Saints is a two-beat jazz arrangement played at a march tempo featuring the entire trumpet section. A driving, aggressive, and exciting version of the old New Orleans favorite, *When the Saints Go Marching In,* the arrangement remains a favorite for both concert and marching bands.

LOUIS BOYER
(Born in Paris, 1864 — Died in Angers, France, 1918)

Boyer became director of music for the city of Angers, France, in 1892 after serving ten years as a musician in the French Army. While in the military service he obtained a "first prize" in oboe at the Conservatoire de Lyon and an "assistant conductor" certificate at the Conservatoire de Paris (1884).

In addition to his administrative and conducting duties in Angers, Boyer composed many overtures and fantasies for area band contests. He also wrote choral works, was director of music for the local fire brigade, and performed in the popular music theater orchestra. Boyer died at his home in Angers during the final year of World War I, survived by his widow, the former Marie Antoinette Antoine. (Information from the Bibliotheque Municipale of Angers, the Archives of Maine-et-Loire, and Gerard Gacon, Roussines, France).

Ariane Overture (Arr = Bachman and Lillya. Pub = WS, 1935. Gr = 4. T = 10:00)

According to a French legend, Ariane was the sixth wife of a sinister, medieval character named Gilles de la Val—better known as "Bluebeard." It was Ariane who tricked Bluebeard into releasing his five former wives and brought destruction upon him.

An original edition of this overture was given to Harold Bachman in 1918 by Louis Bailly who succeeded the composer as Chef de Musique of Angers, France. Bachman was the director of an American Military Band stationed at Angers during World War I. *Ariane Overture* proved to be one of the most popular concert works played by the Americans. Several years later, while Clifford Lillya was playing trumpet in Bachman's famous "Million Dollar Band," the two musicians decided to recast the instrumentation for American concert bands.

The overture is highly representative of a type of French music that is graceful, melodic, and permeated with a perpetual freshness. The work opens with an Andante minor theme, followed by an Allegro wherein the theme is developed to a climax. A subsidiary theme of broad lyric quality in a major key is introduced next followed by still another theme of particular song-like charm in six-four meter. Near the end, a marcato three-part fugue, using the original thematic material, is heard,

JOHANNES BRAHMS

(Born in Hamburg, 1833 — Died in Vienna, 1897)

Johannes Brahms, temporally of the Romantic era but artistically the successor of Beethoven, was the son of an accomplished bass player in the theater orchestra at Hamburg. Brahms' talent became evident at an early age, but his leanings toward the piano were discouraged at first by his father who felt that other instruments would prove more profitable financially. Nevertheless he studied with Cossel in Hamburg and Marxsen in Altona, and made his debut as a pianist at the age of fourteen, including on the program some variations of his own. By the time he was twenty he had met the Hungarian violinist Remenyi, with whom he toured extensively, and who is considered responsible for introducing to him the treasures of Hungarian folk music. Soon his playing and compositions attracted the attention of the great violinist, Joseph Joachim, who was to be his lifelong friend and who arranged meetings with Schumann and Liszt. Schumann's enthusiasm for the young artist was immediate, and in an article in *The New Magazine for Music* for October 23, 1853, he announced to the musical world the arrival of a new genius. His remarks were received with skepticism by some, but time soon bore out Schumann's high opinion along with tangible assistance in recommending Brahms' early works to his own publishers, Breitkopf and Hartel. After Schumann died Brahms remained a close friend of his widow, Clara, for the rest of her life.

For four years Brahms held the post as director of music for the Prince of Lippe-Detmold, a position which allowed him plenty of time to devote to composition and to the development of his artistic nature. In 1862 he established a permanent residence in Vienna, and it was there where the first performance of his monumental *German Requiem* was held on Good Friday in 1868. Brahms was forty-four when he offered his first symphony to the public. Its premiere took place at Karlsruhe in 1876. The rest of his life was marked by great activity, and during his last seven years he wrote twenty important works.

Brahms was the recipient of many honors in his lifetime, but like all great men, he was also the object of violent controversies and was much misunderstood. One of the most unfortunate of the misunderstandings was his attitude toward Wagner, for whom he had the highest regard and whose works he comprehended better than any other of Wagner's contemporaries, but whose vehicle of expression, the opera, was totally foreign to Brahms' nature as a composer.

To those who knew him best Brahms was considered a man of frankness, simplicity, and modesty combined with a wide sympathy, far-reaching intelligence, and extreme tolerance. (Carl Fischer, Inc.)

Academic Festival Overture (Arr = Safranek; Hindsley. Pub = CF, 1915; HI, ms. Gr = 5. T = 9:45. Rec = IL-51, Un. of IL. Hindsley)

Brahms wrote his *Academic Festival Overture* in 1881 as an acknowledgement of a doctoral degree which had been bestowed on him by Breslau University. The work was first performed at Breslau early in 1881, Brahms himself conducting. The overture is in reality a fantasia on four student songs. In a letter to his publisher, Brahms wrote, "I advise you to have the *Academic* arranged for military band. I should be tempted to do it myself if I knew more about it." (Mark Hindsley, University of Illinois)

HOUSTON BRIGHT

(Born in Midland, Texas, 1916 — Died in Canyon, Texas, 1968)

Houston Bright combined academically correct form with fresh and brilliant scoring. He handled the colors of the band with skill and variety, reflecting his own artistic ability as well as that of his former teachers. He received the B.S. and M.A. degrees at West Texas State College and the Ph.D. at the University of Southern California, studying with Halsey Stevens, Ernest Kanitz, and Charles Hirt. During World War II Bright served with the armed forces then returned to West Texas State, as professor of music, to direct the choir and compose. He authored a counterpoint text and composed for a variety of media. Among his earlier works were: *Marche de Concert, Four for Piano, Three Short Dances* (for woodwind quintet), and *Two Short Pieces for Brass Quartet.*

Passacaglia in G Minor (Pub = SH, 1964. Gr = 4. T = 5:00)

The classical passacaglia is generally defined as a continuous series of variations constructed upon a short, insistently repeated bass line called *basso ostinato.* This "obstinate bass" or "ground," as it is often called, usually moves downward through the minor scale in a moderate three-beat meter.

In the present work, the basses state the six-measure ground in the traditional manner, whereupon a fairly regular three-part (ABA) form gradually evolves. Each section consists of five variations throughout in which volume, tension, and excitement continually build toward the climax. At the end of the B section, the ground momentarily shifts upward to the flutes and oboes in a two-variation interlude which introduces a sudden, quiet, somewhat pastoral mood preceding the return to the A section. The work closes with a short coda consisting of a modified restatement of the original ground. (Lee A. Mendyk, Wayne State College)

Prelude and Fugue in F Minor (Pub = SH, 1960. Gr = 4. T = 6:50. Rec = SH-2)

In this work Bright made effective use of contemporary dissonances while staying within the traditional prelude and fugue form. The slow prelude is almost harsh in its dissonances while the fugue has more traditional harmonies. Thus the tension of the opening is relieved by the movement and relative consonance in the final section. The style is perfectly suited to the wind sonorities of the concert band.

JAMES H. BURDEN

(Born in St. Marys, Pennsylvania, 1923)

James Burden received both his B.S. and M.A. degrees from Pennsylvania State University where he later taught for seven years. He has also taught at the junior and senior high school level and has achieved recognition through his appearances as a clinician in both arranging and instrumental pedagogy in many colleges and universities. His experience in the professional music field includes positions as staff arranger and director of music for radio stations in Pittsburgh as well as arranger and assistant conductor of the Pittsburgh Civic Light Opera. For several years Burden was associated with both the NBC and CBS radio and television networks in New York City. He now lives in Islamorada, Florida, where he is a freelance arranger and composer.

The Ringmaster March (Pub = MG, 1975. Gr = 3. T = 2:10)

Although traditional in style this march makes more use of the softer dynamics than many of its counterparts. Interest is achieved by various sections of the band taking turns playing the melodic part, especially by the low register clarinets in the trio. Timpani and bells also play an important part in this interesting, well-scored march.

WILLIAM BYRD

(Born in Lincolnshire, England, 1543 — Died in Essex, 1623)

William Byrd lived during the unique period of musical history when England was enjoying a creative era of great unaccompanied choral literature. Byrd was best known for his superb polyphonic settings of sacred texts—he was often called the "English Palestrina." He also pioneered in music for keyboard, especially the organ and virginal, and for the string instruments. The embellishments of his keyboard style were characteristic of the ever-growing distinction between organ and harpsichord. In 1572 he combined with his teacher, Thomas Tallis, in serving as joint organist of the Chapel Royal and working under a patent granted by Queen Elizabeth for the exclusive privilege of printing music and music paper. Byrd composed both Catholic and Anglican church music, including anthems, motets, and Mass Propers, and he also wrote madrigals, solo songs, and chamber music.

The Battell Suite (Tr = Jacob. Pub = BH, 1964. Gr = 4. T = 12:00. Rec = LC-1966, Luther College)

The collected editions of William Byrd's compositions list a large variety of virginal music including a composition entitled *The Battell,* an unusually early example of a programmatic "Battle Symphony." Thirteen movements from this suite were excerpted by Gordon Jacob and freely arranged in transcription for wind band. Within the context of sixteenth century polyphony, the listener follows the progress of a "battle," highlighted by instrumental portrayal of the conflict, and the events preceding and following it.

The movements include: The Souldiers' Sommons, The Marche of Footemen, The Marche of Horsmen, The Trumpetts, The Irishe Marche, The Bagpipe and the Drone, The Flute and the Droome, The Marche to the Fighte, The Retraite, The Buriing of the Dead, The Galliarde for the Victorie, The Morris, and the Souldiers' Dance. (Boosey & Hawkes, Inc.)

William Byrd Suite (Tr = Jacob. Pub = BH, 1924-60. Gr = 4. T = 16:45. Rec = MG-SRI-75028, Eastman, Fennell)

In 1923 Gordon Jacob contributed to the tercentenary of William Byrd's death with a sensitive setting of six pieces from the *Fitzwilliam Virginal Book* which he entitled *Suite: William Byrd*. The pieces were selected from the seventy in the book because they seemed appropriate to the tonal framework of the British military band.

The first movement of the suite, Earle of Oxford's March, is taken from a collection of keyboard pieces which Byrd conceived as a single work titled *The Battell*. The stately magnificence of this steadily measured music captures the great dignity of a distinguished personage. Movement two, Pavana, slow and sustained with its long, arching lines, contains especially eloquent writing for the winds. Movement three, Jhon Come Kisse Me Now, has that harmonic charm and rhythmic vitality that is so much a part of the English madrigal and keyboard style of Byrd's time; it is a set of seven variations on an eight-bar tune. The fourth movement, The Mayden's Song, begins simply enough for a unison of brasses, then unfolds its steady contrapuntal and figurative development toward a masterful agglomeration of sounds that Jacob distributes with affectionate regard for the original. Movement five, Wolsey's Wilde, displays the suppleness that Byrd often brought to pieces of limited harmonic possibilities through skillful and imaginative play on that restriction. Jacob adds the element of instrumental texture to point out Byrd's implied dynamic contrasts. The suite concludes with The Bells (Variations on a Ground), in which a simple two-note rising figure persists without interruption and above which is unfolded, in gathering momentum, a set of variations built upon the limited sounds of bells all keyed in B-flat. (Frederick Fennell, University of Miami)

HOWARD CABLE

(Born in Toronto, Niagara-on-the-Lake, Canada, 1920)

Howard Cable is a graduate of the Royal Conservatory of Music of Toronto, first coming into prominence on Canadian radio as an arranger and conductor for the Canadian Broadcasting Corporation. The Cable Concert Band's radio broadcasts from Toronto were heard throughout the United States bringing his talent for composing, arranging, and conducting to the attention of the American public. When television commenced in Canada, he became conductor-arranger of the new network's first variety series, "Showtime," starring Robert Goulet. In the theatrical productions of the musical comedies "Sunshine Town" and "The Optimist," both starring Robert Goulet, and in the televised version of the musical, "Mr. Scrooge," starring Cyril Ritchard, Cable served as conductor-arranger.

More recently Cable became musical director of the Canadian National Exhibition's annual Grandstand Spectacular, arranging and conducting for such stars as Victor Borge, Bob Hope, and Danny Kaye. As civilian associate conductor and chief arranger of the Norad Command Band of Colorado Springs, he has appeared with the band on tour and in its annual Carnegie Hall Concerts. He has appeared frequently as guest conductor of the Toronto Symphony, has arranged for the Boston "Pops," and has composed for over thirty films. Cable is now music director of: the Royal York Hotel in Toronto and the Banff School of Fine Arts in Alberta; the Canadian National Exhibition, "Canadiana"; Canada Day Spectacular, Parliament Hill, Ottawa; and Publications for Brassworks Music, Toronto.

Stratford Suite (Pub = CA, 1964. Gr = 4. T = 12:30)

This suite is subtitled "Four Shakespearean Scenes for Concert Band." The first movement, Fanfare, Flourish and Sennet, is scored for brass and percussion and evokes the mood of the royal court as portrayed in *Richard III*. A scene from the *Merry Wives of Windsor* is the musical intent of the second movement, Masque by Herne's Oak. The third movement, Ode to Rosalind, employs only the woodwinds and percussion and is identified with *As You Like It*. The majestic style of the final movement, Elizabeth, Princess of England, is suggestive of a scene from *Henry VIII*. *(Gregg Randall, Las Cruces, New Mexico, High School)*

JOHN CACAVAS

(Born in Aberdeen, South Dakota, 1930)

John Cacavas is probably best known for his music scoring of motion pictures and television. He has gained world-wide recognition for his scoring of the CBS series, *Kojak,* for which he received an Emmy nomination in 1975. He has scored many major motion pictures (including the *Airport 1975, 77* and *79* series, and *Raising of the Titanic)*, several television movies, and three seasons of *Hawaii Five-O.* As musical director for television movies, and three seasons of arranging and conducting his hit recording of "If." Several years ago, he co-produced and composed the music for the Grammy award-winning album, *Gallant Men,* narrated by the late Senator Everett Dirksen. His songs have been recorded by artists the world over including Nancy Wilson, Roger Williams, André Kostelanetz, Sascha Distel, Ed McMahon, Les Brown, Lotte Lenya, and Guy Lombardo. As a writer in the educational field, Cacavas has over 2,000 works published by the major houses of America and Europe, and he has appeared as guest conductor with several of the major orchestras in Europe.

Cacavas was educated at Northwestern University, he was chief arranger of the U.S. Army Band, and was twice the winner of the Freedoms Foundation George Washington Honor Medal for his contribution to American music. He is also the author of a recently published arranging textbook. He lives in Beverly Hills, California, where he is a governor of the Academy of Motion Picture Arts and Sciences. In 1976 he was the recipient of Northwestern University's Distinguished Alumni Merit Award.

Burnished Brass March (Pub = CF, 1963. Gr = 2. T = 2:30. Rec = CF-BSS, Symphonic Winds, Cacavas)

This concert march features the brass, as the title indicates, but also has a melody in the trio by the woodwinds. The modern harmonies and the strong syncopations were a trademark of band works by Cacavas which have continued after this march was written. *Burnished Brass March* sounds as fresh and interesting now as it did in 1963.

Gallant Men March (Pub = CA, 1967. Gr = 2. T = 3:00.)

The *Gallant Men March* became a hit with both concert and marching bands soon after its publication in 1967. Like Alford's *Col. Bogey* and Goldman's *On the Mall, Gallant Men* was recognized as a march with a singable, repetitive, haunting theme. Unlike some of the symphonic marches however, *Gallant Men* can be performed by bands of varied instrumentation and levels of ability.

Great Themes from Great Italian Movies (Pub = EM, 1965. Gr = 3. T = 6:00.)

One of the reasons for the growing acceptance of Italian motion pictures in this country has been their wonderful music. Without question, the most outstanding score has been that written for the film, *Mondo Cane.* Its main theme, *"More,"* has become one of the most important standards of our time.

The material contained in this arrangement derives from *Mondo Cane* as well as the films, *Malamondo, 8½, Woman of the World,* and *Mondo Pazzo.* The melodic style, natural to Italian music, has provided the brilliant John Cacavas with the stimulus necessary to produce this richly textured arrangement for concert band. (Myron R. Falck, Gustavas Adolphus College)

HOAGY CARMICHAEL

(Born in Bloomington, Indiana, — Died in Rancho Mirage, CA 1981)

Hoagland Howard (Hoagy) Carmichael learned most of his piano playing on his own, although his mother was a pianist in the local movie theater. His family moved from Bloomington, Indiana, to Indianapolis when he was sixteen, and he decided to quit school and divide his time between working and playing the piano. When he was twenty he returned to high school and continued his education until he received a law degree seven years later. Meanwhile he helped meet school expenses by performing with jazz bands and writing songs. He wrote "Washboard Blues" in 1924 and the song soon became popular through a recording by Paul Whiteman's Orchestra. Even though Carmichael intended to practice law, he found himself more and more involved in music. In 1927 he wrote the classic, "Star Dust," and from then on he spent most of his time composing. Some of his best known melodies include: "Georgia on My Mind," "Rockin' Chair," "Lazy River," "Two Sleepy People," and "Ol' Buttermilk Sky."

Carmichael started a film career in 1945, and he has also been a frequent performer on radio and television. He wrote his first autobiography, *The Stardust Road,* in 1946 and the second, *Sometimes I Wonder,* in 1965.

Star Dust (Arr = Nestico. Pub = MM, 1929-66. Gr = 4. T = 4:30)

"Star Dust" is considered by many to be the best-loved song of the twentieth century. Carmichael wrote the song one evening in 1927 when he returned for a visit to Indiana University. He was sitting alone near a spot called the "spooning wall" thinking about a girl he had loved and lost. As he looked up at the star-filled sky, the first phrase of "Star Dust" came into his mind. He went to a nearby place called "The Book Nook," which had an old, battered piano, and he kept experimenting with the melody and chords until the famous song took shape. Strangely, Carmichael used a swingy, ragtime tempo at first and it was not until Victor Young made a more lyrical arrangement in 1929 that the song became popular.

CHARLES CARTER

(Born in Ponca City, Oklahoma, 1926)

Charles Carter was born in Oklahoma, but grew up and attended schools in the state of Ohio. He received his B.M. degree from the Eastman School of Music, majoring in composition. Additional graduate work in theory was taken at the Florida State University.

In 1951-52 Carter arranged for the Ohio State University Marching Band and also taught lower brass instruments at that institution. In 1953 he became arranger for the Florida State University Bands, a position he still holds. He also teaches theory, composition, and arranging while continuing to compose and arrange for various publishers and schools. His published band compositions to date number twenty-four. He presents arranging clinics and serves as guest conductor in various schools around the country.

Carter's hobby is devising new physical fitness routines. He and his wife, Sara, are the parents of two boys, Charles, Jr. and Lawrence.

Dance and Intermezzo (Pub = BA, 1967. Gr = 3. Rec = CR-CBDNA-73-1, Un. of IL, Kisinger)

Carter's artistic concept of form is evident in this attractive and exciting work. A well-blended mixture of legato and staccato styles, logical dynamic contrast, and harmonic freshness all combine to hold the listener's attention. *Dance and Intermezzo* was dedicated to Donald McGinnis and the Ohio State University Concert Band.

Overture for Winds (Pub = BO, 1960. Gr = 3. T = 5:30.)

Overture for Winds is a contemporary overture, employing the familiar three-part form. The opening section has a theme which is robust and rhythmic in character. The second theme, slightly slower and expressive, is a free form based on the original idea. The last section is a repetition of the opening thematic ideas, building to a final climax. (Blase S. Scarnati, Slippery Rock State College)

Sonata for Winds (Pub = BA, 1969. Gr = 3)

The *Sonata for Winds* demonstrates the ability of a composer to use new material in a form which has been popular for nearly two centuries and which was closely related to the earlier opera overture form. In this work Carter's fast first section is comprised of an AA'B (extended) A form, followed by the second subject at a slow tempo, the development section, the recapitulation (of first subject only), and a coda.

Symphonic Overture (Pub = CF, 1963. Gr = 3. T = 4:20. Rec = CR-MID-75-7, N. Canton, OH, Jr. H.S., Leitner; CF-BSS, Symphonic Winds, Cacavas)

Symphonic Overture is an ABA form with a lively first section and a slow second section based on a theme introduced by the first flute. At the return of the first section, the first theme is treated as a fugue, building to great heights after all four entrances are achieved. As the restatement of the first theme concludes, the contrapuntal texture gives way to a homophonic quality which closes the piece. The coda utilizes material from the first theme. The interesting melodic lines and carefully conceived counterpoint found in this overture are typical of Charles Carter's compositions.

CHARLES SIMON CATEL
(Born in L'Aigle, France, 1773 — Died in Paris, 1830)

The music of Catel is no longer familiar, although it was greatly admired in its time. Catel was one of the important musicians of France, remembered for his association with the Band of the National Guard (of which he served for a time as bandmaster) and with the Paris Conservatory, at which he was a professor and later an inspector. His treatise on harmony was for many years the accepted text on this subject. He was associated with Gossec, Cherubini, and others in important public activities on behalf of music in France. His compositions include operas, symphonies, and chamber music, as well as many works for wind instruments. (Richard Franko Goldman, the Goldman Band)

Overture in C (Ed = Goldman.   Pub = ME, 1958.   Gr = 4.   T = 5:30.   Rec = DL-78931/DL-8931, Goldman)

The *Overture in C,* composed in 1792 for the Band of the National Guard, shows the French composer, Catel, at his best. In its elegance and clarity it is characteristic of the perfection of late eighteenth-century style, and compares more than favorably with similar works by Mehul, Gossec, or Cherubini. It is one of the most delightful of all the works composed for wind band during this period. The influence of Mozart is clearly recognizable. The overture is in straightforward sonata form, with a slow introduction. It was rediscovered by Richard Franko Goldman, and edited for present-day use by Goldman and Roger Smith. (Richard Franko Goldman, the Goldman Band)

WILLIAM PARIS CHAMBERS

(Born in Newport, Pennsylvania, 1854 — Died in Newville, Pennsylvania, 1913)

W. Paris Chambers spent most of his youth in Newville, Pennsylvania, and it was there that he began to study music. His principal instrument was the cornet and, largely self-taught, he became a proficient performer in a relatively short time. He was also interested in conducting and became leader of the local band when he was eighteen. At twenty-five he assumed the position of conductor of the Capital City Band in Harrisburg, Pennsylvania, where he also taught a large number of private students. As a result of his success as a conductor, as well as a cornet virtuoso, Chambers was offered, and accepted, a similar position with the Great Southern Band in Baltimore, Maryland, in 1887.

Although recognized and praised as a conductor, Chamber's magnificent solo work with the cornet became even more admired. At one time, when he was touring through Colorado with his Baltimore band, he played a cornet solo on the summit of Pikes Peak, where, at 14,500 feet, most people have difficulty breathing. His phenomenal range extended two octaves above high C, and he was able to use beautifully controlled lip trills in the upper range while playing a simple melody. Later, while managing the C.G. Conn store in New York City, he would occasionally demonstrate his versatility for his friends by playing difficult solos with the instrument upside down, pushing the valves up with the back of his fingers. In 1905, he toured many cities in Europe and Africa playing solos.

Although Chambers wrote several cornet solos, he was best known for his fine marches, including: *Boys of the Old Brigade, Hostrauser's March, March Religioso,* and his most famous composition, *Chicago Tribune.* (Information from Robert Hoe, Jr., Poughkeepsie, New York)

Chicago Tribune March (Pub = CF, 1892-1938.   Gr = 4.   T = 3:30.   Rec = CR-MID-73-13, Texas City, TX, H.S., Renfroe)

The *Chicago Tribune March*, first published by R.F. Seitz in 1892, was written for, and dedicated to, the newspaper of the same name. Chambers repeated this procedure in 1897 when he wrote the *Detroit Free Press March.*

Although he adhered to the traditional march form with *Chicago Tribune,* Chambers added variety in his own unique way. In the second strain, for example, after twenty-four bars of fortissimo playing, he inserted two bars at a piano level, two more fortissimo a half-step higher, then two more quiet measures before continuing to the trio. In the final strain, after a quiet, hymn-like section, he changed the style of the second-strain rhythm with syncopation, and near the end he followed a chromatic scale with an unexpected rest.

CÉCILE CHAMINADE
(Born in Paris, 1857 — Died in Monte Carlo, 1944)

Cécile-Louise-Stéphanie Chaminade had a long and productive musical life. She began composing at the age of eight and began a career as a concert pianist when she was sixteen. She studied composition with Benjamin Godard and wrote a great number of piano pieces, mostly in the salon style. Her piano pieces were very popular in Europe and America, but her more serious works were never really accepted. She traveled widely and in 1908 played her *Concertstück* with the Philadelphia Orchestra. She composed over 200 piano pieces and also wrote literary articles, including a chapter on the life of Bizet for *The International Library of Music.*

Concertino, Op. 107—Flute Solo (Arr = Wilson. Ed = Wilkins. Pub = CF, 1960. Gr = 4/5. T = 8:00. Rec = CO-S-1724, Pellerite w. IN Un., Ebbs)

Concertino is a rhapsodic work in the romantic spirit featuring two principal themes. The work, written in 1910, shows a mature understanding of the flute that emphasizes the beauty and technical qualities of the instrument. The original accompaniment was for piano and the band accompaniment was scored by Clayton Wilson in 1947. The work was published with the solo part edited by Frederick Wilkins in 1960. (See William Montgomery's "Performance Checklist" in *The Instrumentalist,* May, 1978, for interpretation suggestions.)

JOHN BARNES CHANCE
(Born in Beaumont, Texas, 1932 — Died in Lexington, Kentucky, 1972)

John Barnes Chance began studying composition at the age of fifteen and received both his Bachelor and Master of Music degrees from the University of Texas. Achieving performances of his works while still in high school, he completed further study with Kent Kennan, Clifton Williams, and Paul Pisk as a university student, winning the Carl Owens Award in 1956 for the best student work of the year. Additional musical background for the composer came through performing experience as timpanist with the Austin Symphony and as arranger for the Fourth and Eighth United States Army Bands. Chance was appointed composer-in-residence with the Ford Foundation Young Composers Project from 1960 to 1962, residing in Greensboro, North Carolina.

Chance wrote music for chorus, band, orchestra, solo instruments, and chamber .groups. He was accidently electrocuted while working in the back yard of his home in Lexington on August 16, 1972. (Acton Ostling, Jr., University of Maryland)

Blue Lake Overture (Pub = BH, 1971. Gr = 4. T = 5:30. Rec = CR-ABA-73-2, U.S. Navy, Dunlop; MU, Un. of MN, Bencriscutto)

Dedicated to the Blue Lake Fine Arts Camp of Twin Lake, Michigan, this exciting overture readily demonstrates the composer's ability to develop thematic material in a remarkable number of different ways—the entire piece is developed from the initial motive heard in the horn. The highlight of the overture is the middle section in which the opening theme is repeated and given a subtle waltz-like treatment. (Boosey & Hawkes, Inc.)

Incantation and Dance (Pub = BH, 1964. Gr = 4. T = 7:30. Rec = BP-102, Luther College)

The title of this piece suggests a religious orientation, but not toward any of the established religions of a Western or Eastern culture. To the standard deities one offers prayers. Incantations are uttered in rituals of magic, demonic rites, the conjuring up of spirits evil and benign. And when the spirit comes and the worshiper is possesed, there is dancing, wild and abandoned.

The *Incantation* of Chance's piece serves formally as an introduction. It is full of mystery and expectation, wandering, unstable, and without tonality. Instruments are gradually added, but the general dynamic level remains soft, hushed, waiting.

The *Dance* also begins quietly. But percussion instruments quickly begin, one by one, building a rhythmic pattern of incredible complexity and drive. The other instruments are added and the dance grows wilder and more frenzied. The brasses hammer out ferocious snarls—the woodwinds fly in swirling scales. Here is no pretty tune but a paroxysm of rhythm, a convulsion of syncopation that drives on and on, mounting in tension, to a shattering climax of exaltation. Then—the dance is over—the worshiper is fulfilled. (R. John Specht, Queensborough Community College)

Introduction and Capriccio—Piano Solo (Pub = BH, 1966. Gr = 4. T = 7:00)

This work, which was dedicated to the composer's mother, was Chance's third composition for wind instruments. It features a delightful interplay between the solo piano and the clarinet choir in the introduction followed by a presto in rondo form. The fast section features brilliant technical passages for both piano and winds.

Variations on a Korean Folk Song (Pub = BH, 1967. Gr = 4. T = 6:30. Rec = CR-MID-76-7, East Allegheny H.S., Versailles, PA, Strange)

Variations on a Korean Folk Song was composed in 1965 winning the American Bandmasters Association Ostwald Award for the composer the following year. Chance provided the following information concerning the work in the *Journal of Band Research* for Autumn 1966:

> I became acquainted with the folk song known as Arrirang (pronounced "AH-dee-dong") while serving in Seoul, Korea, as a member of the Eighth U.S. Army Band in 1958-59. The tune is not as simple as it sounds, and my fascination with it during the intervening years led to its eventual use as the theme for this set of variations.

The work is in six sections; the opening pentatonic theme is followed by five distinct variations. The first variation features temple blocks and woodwinds and also makes prominent use of xylophone, vibraphone, and cymbals. Variation two is quiet and serene with the original melody, now inverted, played by the oboe. The third variation is a fast march, the fourth is broad and solemn, and the fifth is more involved with various sections of the band playing one of the two phrases heard in the opening pentatonic theme.

CARLOS CHÁVEZ

(Born in Mexico City, 1899 — Died in Mexico City, 1978)

Carlos Chávez was considered by many as the most eminent musician of his native country. He began his career in composition with arrangements of Mexican songs and selections for piano when he was fifteen. In 1928 he organized the Orquesta Sinfónica de México and served as its permanent conductor until 1949. From 1928 to 1934 he served as director of the National Conservatory of Mexico, and he also served until 1952 as director of the National Institute of Fine Arts. Chávez' compositions include five ballets; incidental music for Sophocles' *Antígone;* various orchestral works including six symphonies; *Toccata* (1942), the first all-percussion work to enter the international repertory; concertos for four horns, piano, violin-viola-cello, and harp; and also chamber music, piano pieces, and various songs. His principal writings were *Toward a New Mexico, Music and Electricity,* and *Musical Thought. Zandunga Serenade,* Chávez' final work for band was commissioned by Carl Fischer, Inc., and published in 1977.

In addition to introducing the music of Stravinsky, Schoenberg, Satie, Milhaud, and Varèse to audiences in Mexico, Chávez established an appreciation for Mexican music during his lectures and conducting appearances around the world. His own music is appreciated for its immense force and vitality; it is sometimes based on the folkloric elements of his native country, but more often it evokes the atmosphere of prehispanic myths and traditional rituals.

Chapultepec for Band (Pub = MM, 1963. Gr = 4. T = 8:25)

The title refers to a section of Mexico City and the work itself is a complete revision of an earlier composition for symphony orchestra, *Obertura Republicana* (1935), which represented a period of social consciousness in the composer's style and was based on three Mexican tunes, popular in the nineteenth century. Chávez considered *Chapultepec* a cancellation of his earlier work, and it is interesting to note that the new version of the suite was tested by a large Mexican band, conducted by the composer, and then revised before final publication in 1963.

The first movement, Marcha Provinciana, is based upon *Marcha Zacatecas* by Genaro Codina (1851-1901), Zacatecas being a province of Mexico. The second movement, Vals Nostalgico, is based upon *Vals Club Verde* by Rudolfo Campodonico (1866-1926), and the final movement, Cancion de Adelita, is based upon the Mexican folk song "La Adelita." (Acton Ostling, Jr., University of Maryland)

LORIS O. CHOBANIAN

(Born in Mosul, Iraq, 1933)

Loris Chobanian was born to Armenian parents in Iraq and he moved to the United States in 1960. Serious music was an everyday experience in his early childhood. His father, an amateur musician and an engineer, was a versatile performer on piano, flute, and violin; he often played in string quartets and wrote an operetta for Loris which the lad sang at age five with orchestral accompaniment.

Chobanian received his B.M. and M.M. degrees from Louisiana State University, where he studied composition with Helen Gunderson and Kenneth Klaus, and his Ph.D. degree from Michigan State University, where his composition teacher was H.

Owen Reed. He has written extensively for chamber orchestra, symphony orchestra, and wind ensemble, and his works have been performed abroad as well as in concert halls and in television studios in the United States. His principal works for band include *The Id, Capriccio for Piano and Band, Mesopotamian Festival,* and *Fugue—Homage to a Master.* Chobanian considers *Soliloquy—Testament of a Madman,* for baritone and orchestra, one of his best works outside the band medium. He has been the recipient of numerous grants and commissions and has appeared frequently as guitar soloist on television. He is a professor of composition and guitar at Baldwin-Wallace College Conservatory and also teaches lute at Oberlin Conservatory. The Chobanians have one daughter, Rita.

Armenian Dances (Pub = SH, 1977. Gr = 4. T = 13:20. Rec = SH-10, Ithaca Col., Gobrecht)

The five traditional *Armenian Dances* portray the joyous spirit of the Armenian people, comprise a balanced group, and are individually distinctive in character. The first, third, and fifth are lively, and the second and fourth are more subdued. As the dance themes are repeated, new elements of color, rhythm, and counterpoint are introduced. A descending chromatic countermelody inherent in Armenian themes appears in each dance.

In the first dance, "Nazan yar," the men of the village sing the praises of a beautiful girl named Nazan. The melody alternates between major and minor. "Noubar," the second dance, is concerned with a handsome young man to whom all the young girls are attracted. The meter in this 6/8 dance is typical of the dances in the Caucasus region; although the rhythm is obvious, the dancers use minimal body motion. "Tamzara" is a sophisticated dance coming from the city of Erzerum. With its 9/8 meter grouped 2 + 2 + 2 + 3, the theme in this movement is woven canonically with numerous rhythmic permutations. The dancers execute a slight jump on the last two beats of each bar.

The fourth dance is constructed of two distinctly complementary themes, "Goujn ara" and 'Gna gna." The slower theme provides appropriate contrast to the spritelike dance as the two alternate and change keys. 'Tsyeru bar" is the liveliest of the dances, depicting the galloping of horses. The dance develops with fragments of the theme played by different sections of the band, enhanced by coloristic punctuations from the percussion section. Some of the melodies from the other dances are used in counterpoint with the original and augmented forms of the principal theme. (Shawnee Press, Inc.)

ERIC COATES

(Born in Nottinghamshire, England, 1886 — Died in Chichester, England, 1957)

Eric Coates was noted for his works in a lighter vein. As a youngster he studied violin and composition at Nottingham, then changed his major instrument to viola. He toured South Africa with the Hamburg String Quartet in 1907, and in 1912 he became leader of the viola section in the Queen's Hall Orchestra. During this time Sir Henry Wood, the orchestra's conductor, selected several of Coates' compositions for performance. His style has been rather conservative and most of his publicly performed works have been for chamber groups or piano arrangements of his larger compositions. After 1918, when he left orchestra-performance work, he concentrated on composition. His most famous march, the *Knightsbridge,* was first published by Chappell in 1933. In addition to marches, Coates also wrote several suites and fantasies for band.

London Suite (Pub = CA, 1933. GR = 4. T = 11:45. *Knightsbridge March*: Rec = MG-GI-SRI-75099, Eastman, Fennell)

This suite, subtitled *London Every Day,* describes three areas of the city which Coates knew very well. The first, Covent Garden, is represented by a fast 6/8 tarantella. The second, Westminster (Meditation), is depicted by a slow andante movement. The final section is titled Town To-Night and sub-titled Knightsbridge March. The latter title is derived from the elegant Knightsbridge section in London where the Royal Guards' barracks and stables are situated. In this movement the listener is allowed an intimate glimpse of the pomp, pageantry, and color associated with the scarlet-coated guardsmen of Buckingham Palace.

AARON COPLAND

(Born in Brooklyn, New York, 1900)

If any one musician today can be singled out as the "dean of American music," it is Aaron Copland. Without his scores, without his generous encouragement of an entire generation of young American composers, without his unstinting labors to create and maintain an audience for music in 20th-century America, we might never have enjoyed the lively and vital musical scene we know today. Copland, born in Brooklyn in 1900, has become a classic in his time. With his ballet and theater scores on the one hand—including *Appalachian Spring, Billy the Kid,* and *Rodeo,* to name only a few—and his contributions to the orchestral and recital repertory—including notably the *Statements* and *Connotations for Orchestra,* the symphonies, *El Salon Mexico, A Lincoln Portrait,* the *Orchestral Variations,* the *Sonata for Piano,* and the *Piano Variations*—he has created, encouraged, and enriched the repertory, leading the way to a musical climate genuinely "made in America." His original works for band, which he conducts at times, are an important part of this contribution. It is a tribute to Copland the man and the musician that he is regarded by the musical public and his professional colleagues alike with admiration, respect, and above all true affection. (Richard Franko Goldman, the Goldman Band)

Emblems (Pub = BH, 1965. Gr = 5. T = 10:45. Rec = IL-42, Un. of IL, Hindsley; MG-5RI-75132, Eastman, Hunsberger)

American composer Aaron Copland to write a work for concert band, and stated the following purpose for the commission: ". . . to enrich the band repertory with music that is representative of the composer's best work and not one written with all sorts of technical or practical limitations." This was the origin of *Emblems,* Copland's first composition in the band medium. The work was completed in 1964 and received its premier performance at the CBDNA National Convention in Tempe, Arizona, that year in a concert by the University of Southern California Band, conducted by William A. Schaefer. The composer has made the following comments concerning *Emblems:*

> The work is triparite in form: slow-fast-slow, with the return of the first part varied. Embedded in the quiet, slow music the listener may hear a brief quotation of a well-known hymn tune, "Amazing Grace," published by William Walker in *The Southern Harmony* in 1835. Curiously enough, the accompanying harmonies had been conceived first, without reference to any tune. It was only a chance perusal of a recent anthology of old *Music in America* that made me realize a connection existed between my harmonies and the old hymn tune. An emblem stands for something—it is a symbol. I called the work *Emblems*

because it seemed to me to suggest musical states of being: noble or aspirational feelings, playful or spirited feelings. The exact nature of these emblematic sounds must be determined for himself by each listener.

The composition *Emblems* is unusual in presenting a "new" Copland to the listener while retaining the familiar "Americana" style and sound in alternate lyrical sections. It is a significant contribution to the repertoire for concert band. (Acton Ostling, University of Maryland)

Fanfare for the Common Man (Pub = BH, 1944. Gr = 5. T = 3:30. Rec = CL-M-30649, London Symphony Winds & Perc., Copland; CR-S-41288, Ithaca Col.)

From the concert stage to the gridiron halftime show, Copland's *Fanfare for the Common Man* has challenged the performers and excited the listeners. The fanfare was written during World War II and has been adopted by Lincoln Center for the Performing Arts as its radio "theme" music. It combines a strong lyrical brass line with accents by the percussion.

Lincoln Portrait (Tr = Beeler. Pub = BH, 1943-51. Gr = 5. T = 10:30. Rec = IL-40, Un. of IL, Hindsley, Duker)

Soon after the United States was drawn into World War II, André Kostelanetz approached three American composers with the suggestion of composing three musical portraits of eminent Americans, to express the "magnificent spirit of our country." The proposal resulted in Virgil Thomson's *The Mayor LaGuardia Waltzes,* Jerome Kern's *Portrait for Orchestra of Mark Twain,* and Copland's *Lincoln Portrait.*

The first sketches were made in February, 1942, and the portrait was finished on April 16th of that year. Concerning his work Copland wrote:

> I worked with musical materials of my own, with the exception of two songs of the period: the famous "Camptown Races" and a ballad known today as "Springfield Mountain." In neither case is the treatment a literal one. The tunes are used freely in the manner of my use of cowboy songs in *Billy the Kid.*
>
> The composition is roughly divided into three main sections. In the opening section I wanted to suggest something of a mysterious sense of fatality that surrounds Lincoln's personality. Also, near the end of that section, something of his gentleness and simplicity of spirit. The quick middle section briefly sketches in the background of the times he lived. This merges into the concluding section where my sole purpose was to draw a simple but impressive frame about the words of Lincoln himself.

The score is dedicated to André Kostelanetz who conducted the first performance at a pension fund concert of the Cincinnati Symphony Orchestra in Cincinnati on May 14, 1942. The band arrangement was made by Walter Beeler in 1951.

An Outdoor Overture (Pub = BH, 1938-48. Gr = 5. T = 9:30. Rec = VA-2115-S-348, Utah Symphony Orch., Abravanel; TO-EMI-TA-72044, Eastman, Hunsberger)

Aaron Copland composed *An Outdoor Overture* in 1938 for an entirely indoor occasion: a concert of the orchestra of the High School of Music and Art in New York City. The school's conductor, Alexander Richter, was in the process of launching a campaign to foster the writing of "American music for American youth," and the composer found the invitation to write such a work "irresistible," all the more perhaps because his music was undergoing a stylistic change. Copland was originally thought of as a kind of American Stravinsky during the period of the 1920's; tonal but boldly so, emphasizing complex and often harsh sonorities, and influenced in rhythmic language by jazz and Stravinsky himself. In the late 1930's, however, he gradually switched to almost exclusively diatonic melodic writing and simpler counterpoint. The rhythmic vitality, widely spaced textures, and hints of bitonality of his earlier style remain, to make his music more accessible, yet still distinctive. *An Outdoor Overture* was a milestone in confirming this change, since it was written for young people to play and the vague criterion of accessibility therefore mattered more to Copland than it had before. He has said that he meant the piece to sound "optimistic" and "youthful in spirit." These were not qualities associated by most with his previous works or with twentieth century music in general, and the new idiom exemplified in this work seems to reflect a desire for a more popular form of expression. This change proved crucial, of course, as the works of this period, including *Appalachian Spring* and *Rodeo* and culminating in the *Third Symphony* of 1946, have remained his best-loved and most-performed.

This version for band was made by Copland himself, several years after the original composition of the overture, at the suggestion of his publishers. The "outdoor" in the title stems from the stye of spacious chordal writing, implying that very high and very low sonorities are present throughout. (Steve Parkany, Yale University)

El Salon Mexico (Tr = Hindsley. Pub = BH, 1939-72. Gr = 5. T - 11:00. Rec = IL XCSV-126554, Un. of IL, Hindsley; CR-ABA-72-3, Lamar Un., Wiley)

El Salon Mexico was stimulated by the composer's visit to Mexico in 1932. At that time he conceived the idea of writing an orchestral work built around Mexican popular tunes. Music of the dance hall in Mexico City, Salón México, provided him with a tangible subject. "All that I could hope to do was to reflect the Mexico of the tourists. . . . Because in that 'hot spot' one felt, in a very natural and unaffected way, a close contact with the Mexican people. It wasn't the music I heard, but the spirit I felt there, which attracted me. Something of that spirit is what I hope to have put in my music."

The work has been described as one that wears its heart on its sleeve, with no elaborate analysis required to uncover for the listener its infectious tunes and rhythms. Its more carefree and uninhibited moments provide, in the slightly more than 400 bars of notation, approximately 150 meter changes and an additional 65 changes from or to duple or triple figures which must be conducted, plus many offbeat accents and changes to or from duple or triple figures without change of tempo or meter. (Mark Hindsley, University of Illinois)

Variations on a Shaker Melody (Pub = BH, 1960. Gr = 4. T = 5:45. Rec = CN-6, Cornell Un., Stith)

This set of five variations on the Shaker melody "Simple Gifts" is an excerpt from the composer's score to the ballet *Appalachian Spring*. The scenario of the ballet is a simple presentation of a Pennsylvania house-warming party in the Appalachian mountains by a Shaker man and his wife in pioneer times. The *Variations*, which is section seven of the ballet, is subtitled "Scenes of Daily Activity for the Bride and her Farmer-Husband." This setting for band was done by the composer. (Thomas Tyra, University of Eastern Michigan)

HENRY COWELL
(Born in Menlo Park, California, 1897 — Died in Shady, New York, 1965)

Henry Dixon Cowell was for many years a champion of American composers and their music. As a concert pianist and composer, he made several tours of America and Europe, becoming one of the earliest American composers to be heard abroad. At times Cowell provoked scenes bordering on riots with his extremely experimental piano music. Although tonal experimentation is not characteristic of his band music, it is nevertheless interesting to note that Cowell originated the term "tone cluster," an effect produced by playing large "bunches" of notes with the whole hand, fist, or on occasion, forearm, together with plucking or stroking the piano strings. One of the most active of modern American composers, Cowell wrote more than one thousand works of various descriptions including an opera, fourteen symphonies, numerous other orchestra works, compositions for piano and orchestra, chamber music, experimental works for percussion, and various sonatas for piano. He was one of the first American composers to turn his attention to the field of band music. There is a persistent undercurrent of folk material audible in most of Cowell's works although they vary stylistically to a great degree depending upon the particular function and instrumentation. Cowell's musical style is definitely melodic and sometimes includes the invention of new forms which he utilizes for various ensembles including voice. (Acton Ostling, University of Maryland)

Hymn and Fuguing Tune No. 1 (Pub = BE, 1945. T = 5:00. Rec = LOU-S-682, Louisville Orch.)

In addition to an interest in Asian and other cultures, Cowell was also deeply interested in American history. Inspired by the modal folk hymns of William Walker and the midwest traditions of his relatives in rural Oklahoma and Kansas, he began a long series of works titled *Hymn and Fuguing Tune No. 1, No. 2, etc.* As was customary with works of this type, the piece begins with a slow chorale-like section which leads to the faster fugal section. Cowell used many features of the originals he had heard as a boy; parallel fourths and fifths as well as occasional dissonances. Like Ives and Grainger, Cowell included the "mistakes" of the folksingers in his compositions, and he felt perfectly at home using a variety of media for works of a similar form. For example he wrote eighteen *Hymn and Fuguing Tunes* for various solo instruments and ensembles.

Little Concerto for Piano and Band (Pub = AMP, 1942. T = 12:00)

Little Concerto for Piano and Band was composed for Captain Francis Resta, at the time conductor of the United States Military Academy Band at West Point. An original and an alternate piano part are included with the work. The original part is characteristic of Cowell's experimentation with tone clusters, to the extent of utilizing the forearm for playing all white or black keys within a two-octave range. The band portion is modal, subdued, and definitely non-experimental. (Acton Ostling, University of Maryland)

Shoonthree (Pub = ME, 1940. Gr = 5. T = 5:00. Rec = BP-112, Un. of MD, Ostling)

"Shoonthree" is a Gaelic word meaning "the music of sleep." In contrast to a lullaby, the music becomes louder as sleep progresses. In *Shoonthree* the music begins softly with the entrances of solo instruments and continues to grow in intensity. Just before the end the music is suddenly softer, finally fading completely as the sleeper awakes.

PAUL CRESTON
(Born in New York City, 1906)

Few contemporary American composers of the first rank have shown more active interest in providing music for wind and percussion instruments of the concert band than Paul Creston. His ten works for band include such major contributions as *Legend* (1942), *Zanoni* (1949), *Celebration Overture (1955), Prelude and Dance* (1959), and *Anatolia* (1967). His thirty-five major works for orchestra include five symphonies, his *Symphony No. 2* having been performed by the New York Philharmonic in 1945. Creston has also written extensively for solo winds and chamber groups including concertos for saxophone, trombone, harp, accordion, and marimba. A native of New York City, he is completely self-taught as a composer. He was obliged at an early age to work for a living, but fortunately his parents recognized and sympathized with his passionate devotion to music and did not allow family hardship to interfere with his musical development. Receiving a Guggenheim Fellowship in 1939, he advanced in a very few years to the front ranks of American composers. (John Wakefield, University of Maryland)

Creston has shown a willingness to share his ideas on composition, especially the importance of rhythm, by authoring *Principles of Rhythm, Creative Harmony,* and *Rational Metric Notation.* His most recent works for band include *Kalevala, Jubilee, Square Dance '76,* and *Liberty Song.* He is a member of American Society of Composers, Authors, and Publishers; American Music Center; Kappa Kappa Psi; Pi Kappa Lambda; and Phi Mu Alpha Sinfonia. Creston now has emeritus professor status at Central Washington State College; he has two sons and five grandchildren, and includes linguistics and bowling among his hobbies. (Ed.)

Anatolia (Pub = SH, 1968. Gr = 5. T = 8:00. Rec = SD-5, Augustana Col., Lillehaug)

Anatolia is the name of that section east of Asia Minor and includes the greater part of Turkey. The work was commissioned by Eastern Illinois University in 1967 and was first performed by that university's band in 1968 with the composer conducting. *Anatolia* is in free sectional form and consists of four sections: Slow, Moderately fast, Very slow, and Moderately fast. The first section is based on an original theme; the second, on a Turkish folksong with the characteristic national rhythm, the "zeybek" (a 9/8 irregularly subdivided into 3/4 and 3/8). The third section is based on a very melancholy folksong, and the fourth section is derived from a composite of three different folk dances. (Paul Creston, Central Washington State College)

Celebration Overture (Pub = TE, 1955. Gr = 4. T = 7:30. Rec = IL-39, Un. of IL, Hindsley)

Celebration Overture was commissioned by Edwin Franko Goldman for the American Bandmasters Association in 1955. It consists of three sections: fast, slow, and fast—like the Italian Baroque overture. In style it differs considerably from its ancestor. Concerning *Celebration Overture* and his aims as a composer, Creston wrote the following:

> I was preoccupied with matters of melodic design, harmonic coloring, rhythmic pulse, and formal progression, not with limitations of nature or narrations of fairy tales. The intrinsic worth of a musical work depends on the interrelation of musical elements toward a unified whole.

The overture emphasizes melodies that are short and highly rhythmic. The harmonies are sonorous, being added to the melody in parallel to provide color and depth. The result is a bright, festive work that fulfills the promise of the title. (Duane J. Mikow, University of Alaska)

Concertino for Marimba and Band (Pub = GS, 1949-75. Gr = 4/5. T = 15:00. Rec = CR-MTNA-75-2)

This concerto, written in 1940, has gradually become accepted as one of the major works for percussionists and is now in its third printing. Creston has entitled the three movements Vigorous, Calm, and Lively; the fast-slow-fast format is traditional, but otherwise the concerto sounds very contemporary. After an opening F Major-7th chord, the harmony shifts almost as often as the rhythmic accents; a horn duet in thirds provides a short consonant interlude just before the marimba enters in the style of the introduction. The second movement challenges the soloist with four-mallet passages in some of Creston's most expressive, lush writing, and the third movement returns to the melodic, rhythmic style of the opening.

Legend (Pub = LD, 1944. Gr = 5. T = 7:00. Rec = UN-5, Un. of NE, Lentz)

Legend was composed in 1942 and was Creston's first work for band. The composer dedicated *Legend* to Richard Franko Goldman and wrote the following note on the score:

> There is no particular legend attached to this composition. It was inspired by one of the most forceful attributes of music, namely, its narrative power. It is, therefore, a purely abstract piece of music, with the modification, however, that the listener may easily create his own story.

Prelude and Dance (Pub = FC, 1960; Rental = BE, 1978. Gr = 5. T = 7:00. Rec = CR-MID-76-15, U.S. Navy, Muffley)

Prelude and Dance was commissioned by Kappa Kappa Psi and Tau Beta Sigma and was premiered by the National Intercollegiate Band in 1959 with the composer conducting. Always interested in rhythms, Creston's rhapsodic Prelude is laced with compelling accents and pulsations as it projects a long legato line above the shorter, percussive bursts of the accompaniment. The Dance is breath-taking throughout with polymeters, polyrhythms, and even a touch of tarantella. (Maurice McAdow, North Texas State University)

INGOLF DAHL

(Born in Hamburg, Germany, 1912 — Died in Fruitigen, Switzerland, 1970)

Dahl was born in Germany of Swedish parents. He studied composition with Jarnach in Cologne and Nadia Boulanger in California; conducting with Andreae, and piano with Frey, both at the Zurich Conservatory. He stayed in Zurich for two years after completing his studies then moved to the United States in 1938, becoming an American citizen in 1943. During the World War II years he was a radio conductor and arranger in Hollywood; he began teaching composition at the University of Southern California in 1945. He also conducted the school orchestra from 1945 to 1960 and 1968 to 1969. Most of Dahl's early compositions were for piano and chamber groups. His most important orchestra work, *The Tower of Saint Barbara*, was composed in 1955, and his *Elegy Concerto* for violin in 1970.

Dahl's composition students felt that he transmitted deep insights as well as techniques and that he was a man of rare vitality. He died in Switzerland in 1970 during a sabbatical leave—his wife had died only eight weeks earlier.

Concerto for Alto Saxophone (Pub = ACA, 1949.   Gr = 5/6   T = 19:00. Rec = BR-1203, Hemke; CR-CRS-4125, Timmons w. Ithaca Col., Gobrecht)

Dahl's saxophone concerto was written for Sigurd Rascher in 1949 and revised four years later. It is both a large-scale and an important work, but, because of the difficulty of the solo as well as the accompaniment, has not been performed often. The scoring of the piece is specifically for "wind orchestra," therefore implying a one-on-a-part performance.

The concerto is tonally somewhat traditional, but the treatment of rhythm is not, revealing much inspiration from jazz and the works of Stravinsky—with whom Dahl sometimes worked during this period. Dahl proves himself and his style capable of both melancholy and passionate expression in the first two movements, then a carefree wit (the kind of abandon which Beethoven called "unbuttoned") in the last; both kinds of writing well suited to the unique tone of the saxophone. In form, the concerto is unusual, forming a kind of binary unit. The first is made up of the first two movements, both of them slow, which are connected without a pause, and the second out of the more complicated rondo-finale. Near the end, in a gesture of deference to classical practice, there is a brief saxophone cadenza, leading to a brilliant prestissimo coda on the rondo theme. (Keith Brion, Yale University)

Sinfonietta (Pub = BR, 1963.   Gr = 5.   T = 17:00.   Rec = DL-719163, Eastman, Hunsberger; CR-CBDNA-75-11, CA St. Un. Long Beach, Curtis)

Sinfonietta was commissioned by the Western and Northern Divisions of the College Band Directors National Association in 1961. Although derived from a six-note row (A-flat, E-flat, C, G, D, A), the work is in the major key of A-flat. It contains many surprises and many musical references to the band's traditions. For example, the first movement opens with the band tuning note, B-flat; features off-stage trumpets; and has a dynamic march lifted from the composer's memory of his childhood in Stockholm when he watched the changing of the palace guard. The movement ends with an intricate cadenza played by the entire clarinet section in unison followed by the well-known marching band "roll-off" in the drum section.

The second movement is a nocturne which deliberately avoids the usual band sounds. It is quiet, polyphonic, with no tutti passages. It is in ternary form changing from a fugue to a waltz to a gavotte.

The third movement is a brilliant passacaglia which derives extraordinary vitality from the use of the tone row in constantly shifting keys. The movement becomes a set of dance variations which ends, contrary to the traditional band finale, as quietly and introspectively as it began. (Gale Sperry, University of South Florida)

ALBERT O. DAVIS

(Born in Cleveland, Ohio, 1920)

Davis' educational credentials include B.A. and M.A. degrees from Arizona State University as well as graduate work at the Cleveland Institute of Music and Western Reserve University. He has played both piano and French horn professionally and from 1961 to 1964 he was the staff arranger for the Air Defense Command Band at Colorado Springs. His extensive band arranging experience also includes marching band music for Arizona State University from 1948 to 1967 and Ohio State University from 1968 to 1972. Davis has been chairman of the music department at Phoenix College, composer of musical comedies, and arranger for dance orchestras during his career. Among his most popular works for band are *Norad Defenders, Desert Star, Welsh Folk Suite,* and *Ladies, Lords and Gipsies.*

From Shire and Sea (Pub = BD, 1966. Gr = 2. T = 5:00. Rec = CR-MENC-80-2, Glenridge Jr. H.S., Winter Park, FL, Kagi)

Davis' arranging experience, his love of travel, and his interest in folk music are all obvious in this setting of five folk and patriotic songs. The "shire" in the title refers to a district in England similar to a county in the United States, and the "sea" refers, of course, to the long history of sailing ships which have been so vital in the development of the British Isles. The work is divided into three short movements of moderate, slow, and march tempos. The first movement presents the songs, "Robin and the Tanner" and "Fanny Blair"; the second, the well known old ballad, "Barbara Allen" (still current in the mountainous regions of the southern U.S.A.), and the concluding movement, "The Coasts of High Barbary" and "Rule Brittania."

CLAUDE DEBUSSY

(Born in St.-Germain-en-Laye, France, 1862 — Died in Paris, 1918)

Claude Debussy was the most influential French composer of his generation and the founder of modern musical impressionism. He entered the Paris Conservatory in 1873 and remained there for eleven years, studying piano with Marmontel and theoretical subjects with Guiraud (his chief composition teacher), Lavignac, Massenet, and Durand. For a while the routine work was distasteful to him, though from time to time he won various prizes and medals for piano, for accompaniment, and for counterpoint and fugue. Finally, in 1884, he obtained the highest honor in the conservatory's awards, the *Prix de Rome,* with the cantata, *L'Enfant Prodigue.* Debussy's piano music has probably done most towards the wide extension of his fame among the general music public; it is indeed, in its mature form, typical of his genius. Debussy's finest instrumental works—the orchestral *L'Après-midi d'un faune, Nuages,* and *Fêtes,* and his string quartet—date from the decade before the outstanding piano pieces and took the lead in establishing his reputation.

For ten years (1892-1902) Debussy gave most of his attention to the composition of his highly successful opera, *Pelléas et Mélisande.* For several years he fought a gallant fight against cancer, but finally succumbed in 1918 during the long-range bombing of Paris by the Germans. (C.R. Varner, The College of William and Mary)

Fêtes (Arr = Schaefer. Pub = BE, 1959. Gr = 5. T = 7:00. Rec = CR-MID-68-8, Northshore, Wilmette, IL, Paynter)

Fêtes (Festivals) is the brilliant second of *Three Nocturnes.* His imagination, according to Debussy, dwelt on "the restless dancing rhythms of the atmosphere, interspersed with abrupt scintillations." After the exciting opening section, a procession starts as if approaching from a distance. Debussy described it as "a wholly visionary pageant, passing through and blending with the revelry; the background of the uninterrupted festival persisting; luminous dust participating in the universal rhythms.'' The music ends with a repetition of the opening measures, fading away into the distance. (William Schaefer, University of Southern California)

Marche Écossaise (Arr = Schaefer. Pub = TE, 1964. Gr = 5. T = 6:15. Rec = MA-MCBS-21360, Ithaca Col., Beeler)

Marche Écossaise, based upon the popular tune, ''The Earl of Roses March,'' was written in 1891 as a piano duet and was also orchestrated by the composer. It was arranged for band in 1964 by William A. Schaefer, director of bands at the University of Southern California. (Acton Ostling, University of Maryland)

SERGE DE GASTYNE
(Born in Paris, 1930)

De Gastyne was born in France and received his education in Hungary, France, and America. In 1950 he received a Bachelor of Arts degree from the University of Portland and later completed further study in the field of composition with Howard Hanson, followed by additional graduate work at the University of Maryland. He has been a member of the United States Air Force Band for several years and many of his compositions and arrangements have been performed by that famous group. Band works by De Gastyne include: *Symphony No. 2, Overture on American Themes, Prelude to a Play, American Rhapsody,* and *Symphony No. 4.* He has also composed works for orchestra, string quartet, string quintet, and woodwind quintet.

American Weekend March (Arr = Werle. Pub = EV, 1959. Gr = 4. T = 4:15. Rec = AC-6503, TX UIL All Region H.S.)

The *American Weekend March* was commissioned by the American Weekend Magazine and was premiered by the United States Air Force Band with George S. Howard conducting. The march opens with trumpets featured in fanfare-like figures, answered by the upper woodwinds. De Gastyne's French background seems apparent as the clarinets play a ''Parisian-in-Paris'' style theme following the introduction. Interesting counter-melodies, unusual key changes, and a brass-percussion interlude hold the listener's attention to the last note of this well-written march.

ELLIOT A. DEL BORGO
(Born in Port Chester, New York, 1938)

Elliot Del Borgo received the B.S. degree from the State University College at Potsdam, New York, the Ed.M. degree from Temple University, and the M.M. degree from the Philadelphia Conservatory, where he studied theory and composition with Vincent Persichetti and trumpet with Gilbert Johnson. He has taught instrumental music in the public schools of Philadelphia and also at the Crane School of Music, his alma mater, in Potsdam, New York. In addition to composing a number of works for band and orchestra, Del Borgo has been active as a guest conductor and as an adjudicator in the music festivals of New York. (Shawnee Press, Inc.)

Music for Winds and Percussion (Pub = SH, 1973. Gr = 5. T = 6:45. Rec = SH-6, Ithaca Col., Phillips; CR-MID-74-8, Fraser, MI, H.S., Okun)

Music for Winds and Percussion opens with a rhythmic, vigorous tutti section punctuated by the percussion. Long, agile melodic lines in a contrapuntal texture with strong and driving rhythms provide the material of the following section. Contrast is provided by lyric melodies and warm harmonies of the center portion of the piece. A return of music heard in the first section brings the work to a dramatic and vigorous close. (Shawnee Press, Inc.)

LEO DELIBES

(Born in St.-Germain-du-Val, France, 1836 — Died in Paris, 1891)

Leo Delibes entered the Paris Conservatory in 1848 at the age of twelve. In 1855 he produced an operetta, *Deux Sacs de Charbon* and when he became second director at the Grand Opera ten years later, his music for the ballet, *La Fontaine,* met with great success. His ballets, *Sylvia* and *Coppelia,* and his opera, *Lakme,* have remained among his most popular works. Delibes died in 1891, leaving a four-act opera, *Kassya,* unfinished; it was completed by Massenet in 1893. His music has been described as melodious, vivacious and elegant.

March and Procession of Bacchus (Arr = Osterling. Pub = BE, 1966. Gr = 4. T = 5:00. Rec = BE, included w. score; RC-LPM, Cities Service, Lavalle)

This march is taken from Delibes' ballet, *Sylvia,* composed in 1876. Brass flourishes amidst a pompous atmosphere characterize the first section, where, in the original ballet, the satyrs (with long, pointed ears, short horns, and the tail of a goat) enter with their javelins. Next, the maidens enter, bringing a goat for sacrifice, and followed by fauns. As indicated in the music, the revel begins with the quickening of the tempo, after which, a slow moving melody suggests the arrival of the wine drinking god, then a continuation of the pranks of the mad company.

NORMAN DELLO JOIO

(Born in New York City, 1913)

Composer, organist, pianist, jazz enthusiast, baseball player of professional standards—all these are points of emphasis in the life of Norman Dello Joio. This distinguished American composer is descended from three generations of Italian organists. His father became organist of a church in New York City in the early 1900's after his arrival in this country from Italy. Norman Dello Joio received his earliest music training from his father and soon began studies with his godfather, Pietro Yon, famed organist at St. Patrick's Cathedral.

Dello Joio studied at the Juilliard School of Music in New York City and then went to the Yale School of Music where he worked with Paul Hindemith. He states the experience with Hindemith played a major role in the development of his musical style. After these years of formal study, Dello Joio began his teaching career at Sarah Lawrence College before becoming professor of composition at the Mannes College of Music in 1958. He is presently at the School for the Arts at Boston University.

Dello Joio is traditional to the extent that his music appeals to a varied and wide public. . . Along with jazz and dance, another powerful influence in his music is

Roman Catholic liturgical chant, a result of hearing his father practice organ accompaniments for the chants used in the church at which he was organist. In his works it is often possible to find a juxtaposition of Gregorian melodies and the rhythms of jazz. His formal structure is always clear; he seems partial to variation technique. Dello Joio is well established as one of our foremost figures in contemporary American music. (Maurice Hinson, *The American Music Teacher)*

In addition to the titles below, additional works for band by Dello Joio include *Concertante, Caccia, Satiric Dances, Colonial Ballads,* and *Promises of Spring* (for chorus and band). (Ed.)

Fantasies on a Theme by Haydn (Pub = EM, 1968. Gr = 5. T = 14:00. Rec = CR-ATH-5054, W. TX St. Un., Garner)

Fantasies on a Theme by Haydn was commissioned by the Michigan School Band and Orchestra Association in 1968 and was dedicated to Leonard Falcone at his retirement as director of bands at Michigan State University. The score includes the following note by Dello Joio:

> This work for band is based on a theme from a composition for piano by Joseph Haydn. The subtly conceived theme, I concluded, offered an opportunity to fantasize in the musical language of today. The three movements are a constantly varied examination of Haydn's basic idea. The bubbling humor of the first and third fantasies flank a second, which is intensely lyric. In the final sense, it is my homage to a composer who will always remain contemporary.

(Fred Heath, University of Maryland)

From Every Horizon (Pub = EM, 1965. Gr = 4. T = 9:00. Rec = CR-ATH-5054, W. TX St. Un., Garner)

The music is a version of a score done for a film of the same title that was shown at the New York World's Fair. Dello Joio has arranged the score into three short movements which portray the hurly-burly of the commuter, the hustle of the typical New Yorker, and the weary tourist. The first movement begins and ends with a pastoral mood that prevails in the outskirts of town. In the middle, our commuter has apparently arrived in the center of town because the tempo becomes more animated and a new theme, full of bustle, appears. The second movement is nocturnal in mood, slightly reminiscent of the French horn opening in Mendelssohn's *Nocturne.* One hears isolated and stylized city sounds suggested by bits of melody, chords, trills, chimes, percussive effects, and muted tones. In the third movement we are again in the daytime bustle of the city. The piccolo, flute, oboe, and clarinet play a bright tune over bustling accompaniment. (Gene Braught, University of Oklahoma)

Scenes from the Louvre (Pub = EM, 1966. Gr = 4. T = 10:30. Rec = BP-104, Augustana Col., IL)

The band version of *Scenes from the Louvre* is taken from the original score of the NBC television special that was first broadcast nationally in November, 1964. In September, 1965, the composer received the Emmy award for this score as the most outstanding music written for television in the 1964-65 season. The five movements of this suite cover the period of the famous Paris museum's development during the Renaissance and are based on themes from composers of that period. The movements are titled: The Portals, Children's Gallery, The Kings of France, The Nativity Paintings, and Finale.

The band work, commissioned by Baldwin-Wallace College for its symphonic band, was premiered in 1966 with the composer conducting. (John Powell, University of South Alabama)

Songs of Abelard (Pub = EM, 1969. Gr = 5. T = 16:00. Rec = CR-MID-69-7, Winters, student soloist, w. Hale H.S., West Allis, WS, Blahnik; GC-CRS-4186, Un. of S. FL, Croft)

This work was commissioned by Kappa Kappa Psi and Tau Beta Sigma, national honorary band fraternity and sorority, on the occasion of the fiftieth anniversary celebration of the founding of Kappa Kappa Psi and was first performed by the National Intercollegiate Band in Stillwater, Oklahoma, in 1969, with Dello Joio conducting. The work is a symphonic synthesis taken from the music of *Time of Snow,* a dance score composed by Dello Joio and choreographed by Martha Graham.

The music is based on the tragic love story of Abelard, probably the foremost scholar of the day, and Heloise, the niece of a cleric of Notre Dame Cathedral in Paris. Their ill-fated love, which stunned the twelfth-century academic and clerical world, is still recalled by an inscription upon a small house on the Isle de la Cite in Paris:

> Heloise, Abelard, lived here. Sincere lovers.
> Precious models. The year 1118.

The optional solo voice text is based on poetic material of the period.

Variants on a Medieval Tune (Pub = EM, 1963. Gr = 5. T = 11:40. Rec = CR-CRE-1000, Cass Tech H.S., Detroit, MI, Begian)

The work was commissioned by the Mary Duke Biddle Foundation for the Duke University Band, and was first performed by that band in April, 1963 under the baton of its conductor, Paul Bryan. The theme, "In dulci jubilo," has been used by many composers, among them J.S. Bach, as the subject for a variety of musical works. After a brief introduction, the theme is clearly stated by several solo woodwind instruments. It then goes through five metamorphoses or "variants," strongly contrasting in tempo and character, and utilizing the possiblities of the band fully. (Joel Kramme, University of Missouri at Rolla)

CAMILLE DE NARDIS
(Born in Orsogna, Italy, 1857 — Died in Naples, 1951)

De Nardis was vice-director of the Naples Conservatory, director of the San Carlos Opera Theater, and conductor of the Naples Quartet Society. In addition to his reputation as a composer, he was well known as a teacher in his native country. His compositions include an oratorio, *I Turchi in Ortona,* and several operas. His dramatic, operatic style is evident in his band composition, *Universal Judgement.*

Universal Judgement (Arr = Cafarella. Pub = CF, 1934. Gr = 4. T = 9:00 Rec = CR-ABA-75-3, Lamar Un., McAdow)

This composition won first prize in a national band contest at Naples in 1878, making it one of the early works for that medium. With its dramatic nineteenth century Italian opera style, its many fugal sections, and its abrupt changes of dynamics, this symphonic poem reminds the listener of both Verdi and Beethoven. Delicate woodwind chorales and soaring romantic melodies are interspersed. A moderato section in the middle features spatially separated trumpets representing the choirs of angels. A spirited allegro brings the work to a close. (Mary Arthur, Fond du Lac, Wisconsin) .

GAETANO DONIZETTI
(Born in Bergamo, Italy, 1797 — Died in Bergamo, 1848)

Donizetti's father wanted his son to become a lawyer, but finally gave him permission to enter the Bergamo school of music where he studied voice with Salari, piano with Gonzales, and harmony with Mayr. In 1815 he changed to the Bologna Liceo Filarmonico to complete his contrapuntal studies with Pilotti and Mattei. His first opera was completed when Donizetti was twenty-one and in the next sixteen years, he wrote sixty-six dramatic works. Only one serious opera, *Lucia di Lammermoor,* and two comic operas, *L'elisir d'amore* and *Don Pasquale,* are still presented with any frequency. Besides operas, Donizetti wrote many songs, cantatas, motets, string quartets, and piano music. Much of his music contained beautiful if slightly trite melodies, but his orchestral writing was criticized when it was compared with Rossini's compositions. Donizetti was striken with paralysis in 1845 and died three years later without ever recovering his mental powers.

March for the Sultan Abdul Medjid (Ed = Townsend. Pub = ME, 1967. Gr = 4. T = 3:15. Rec = BP-111, Un. of MI, Revelli; CR-CBDNA-71-1, Un. of Houston, Matthews)

When Sultan Abdul Medjid Khan of Turkey decided to have the military music of his army revised on a basis comparable to that of Western Europe, he asked Gaetano Donizetti's brother, Giuseppe, to take over the task. Giuseppe Donizetti remained in Turkey from 1832 until his death in 1856, established an army music school which still exists today, and composed a great deal of music for his royal patron. He also commissioned two marches, one from his brother Gaetano and the other from Gioacchino Rossini. These marches were not played by modern bands until Douglas Townsend discovered the Rossini march in the library of the Conservatory of Music in Milan in 1965 and the present march by Gaetano Donizetti in the basement of the Turkish Institute in Ankara the same year. Townsend's edition follows the original scoring except for the addition of alto and bass clarinets and saxophones. (Information from Theodore Presser Co.)

CHARLES EDWARD DUBLE
(Born in Jeffersonville, Indiana, 1884 — Died in Jeffersonville, 1960)

Charles Duble wrote at least forty-five circus marches which were used by the leading tent shows during the first half of the twentieth century. In addition to his popular march, *Bravura,* he also wrote marches which required very advanced technique, including *Battle of the Winds* and *Wizard of the West.* Duble played trombone with various circus and minstrel bands for twenty-three years. He started with the Sun Brothers Circus and continued with circus bands of John Robinson, Barnum and Bailey, Hagenbeck-Wallace, Sells-Floto, Sparks, Downie Brothers, and finally with Ringling Brothers and Barnum and Bailey's Combined Shows. Merle

Evans, famous director of the latter group has described Duble as "a fine musician and a unique character." He maintained a home in Jeffersonville, Indiana, during his years on the road, and he died there in 1960. (Information by Robert Hoe, Jr., Poughkeepsie, New York)

Bravura March (Pub = TP-JC, 1918. Gr = 4. T = 2:45. Rec = DL-78451, Barnum and Bailey's Circus, Evans)

Although the introduction and first strain of this march are in a minor key, it has a solid, bravura, rhythmic sound that is meant for marching, not just listening. Being a trombonist, Duble made sure that the lower brass had their share of interesting soli sections, for example the last four bars before the repeat to the beginning; interestingly enough, he wanted the introduction played twice. The upper woodwinds have their fun at the trio. Although *Bravura* was written for the circus; the rodeo bands, the street parade bands, and the football bands also claim the march as their own.

PAUL DUKAS

(Born in Paris, 1865 — Died in Paris, 1935)

Paul Dukas has been considered a glittering ornament of French modern music and his name has been linked with the revolt of contemporary composers against artistic formalism.

From his earliest childhood he showed a singular bent for music. His family was too poor to provide instruction, but he tinkled the keys of a neighbor's piano whenever the chance afforded. He entered the Paris Conservatory in 1882, where his musical appetite, according to his instructors, was enormous. He soon became an outstanding student, for he studied and practiced night and day. Like all young Frenchmen of military age, he had to give up the Conservatory for a time for the life of the field and garrison. But he always considered this a valuable period, for he had leisure to study the scores of the classics, page by page, thereby gaining a new insight into composition.

After a stint in the army Dukas began work on an overture, *Polyeucte,* his first composition to be performed publicly. But his renown became international with the performance of *The Sorcerer's Apprentice.* He composed two operas, *La Péri* and *Ariadne and Bluebeard.* The latter, on a text of Maeterlinck, has been described as "second only to *Pelléas* in French opera of the twentieth century." *(Great Orchestral Music* by Julian Seaman)

Fanfare from La Péri (Pub = DUR-TP. Gr = 5. T = 1:00. Rec = CR-CRE-9004, Un. of IL, Begian; LO-STS-15022, L'orchestre de la Suisse Romande, Ansermet)

La Péri, composed in 1912 when Dukas was forty-seven, was his last important work. He did write a few large compositions during the remaining twenty-three years of his life, but decided to burn these and all other manuscripts a few hours before his death, apparently because he felt they did not meet the standard which he had set by his earlier works.

The composer called *La Péri a poème dansé*—a symphonic poem for dancing. "Peri" was originally a Persian word meaning "genie" or "elf," though it has been taken unchanged into many western languages. The fanfare precedes the dance proper in the manner of an overture, although there is no thematic similarity between the two sections. Strikingly demonstrated here is the sound of pure brass in one of the most famous fanfares in twentieth century literature.

The Sorcerer's Apprentice (Arr = Winterbottom; Hindsley. Pub = BH, 1923; HI, ms. Gr = 6. T = 10:30. Rec = IL-46, Un. of IL, Hindsley)

The basis of this "scherzo" (a term used deprecatingly by Dukas to describe this work) was a ballad by Goethe, based in turn on a tale by the Greek poet Lucian (120-180 A.D.). The ballad concerns a magician's apprentice who experiments with his master's magic formula and transforms a broomstick into a "robot" which begins drawing water from the well and filling all the pitchers in the house. Unfortunately, the broom overdoes it, the room is flooded and the apprentice forgets the stopping formula. In desperation, he splits the broom in two, but now both parts begin carrying water and the flooding increases. The apprentice screams for help, the sorcerer returns, speaks the magic word, and the calamity is averted.

Although Dukas was anything but enthusiastic about this work, he played the manuscript for some of his musical friends on a piano in Brussels, and they were so impressed by the pictorial quality and animation of the music that they persuaded the composer to orchestrate it for performance. *The Sorcerer's Apprentice* was premiered by the Société Nationale in Paris in 1897. Its popularity has continued to increase ever since on concert programs, records, and even films; Disney's classic, *Fantasia*, and his cartoon with Mickey Mouse in the title role, have made this "scherzo" one of the most widely known of all symphonic classics.

ANTONIN DVOŘÁK

(Born in Nelahozevas, Bohemia, 1841 — Died in Prague, 1904)

Antonin Leopold Dvořák was the eldest son of Frantisek Dvořák, the local butcher and innkeeper. The boy grew up healthy and high-spirited. The only person in the village capable of giving him the rudiments of a musical education was the Czech cantor, Josef Spitz, an excellent organist. Learning first the basic elements of violin-playing well enough to help his father in his capacity as village musician, the boy finally went to live with an uncle in a nearby village. There he learned German and carried on his music. In his sixteenth year, he undertook systematic study at Prague, profiting greatly by contact with Smetana and Bendl and struggling heroically onward until, in 1875, he gained financial assistance from the Viennese government. After completing his studies at Prague, Dvořák joined the Komzak Concert Band and later was incorporated with this band into the National Theater Orchestra.

His *Slavonic Dances* established his reputation as a composer, although a previous patriotic cantata brought him to the attention of musicians. The success of this work was striking, for in it he first made use of the national idiom. But the popularity of the dances spread his name far and wide among the lay public.

The friendship at this time of several famous musicians helped his career immeasurably. Among them was Brahms, who had been one of the judges to pass upon works submitted for an annual pension. The duets of Dvořák fascinated him and enlisted his immediate enthusiasm. He soon kindled the interest of the other judges to such an extent that Dvořák won the prize.

In 1892 Dvořák was invited to become director of the National Conservatory of New York. He accepted and filled the position until 1895. He passed two summers in a Bohemian colony in Iowa, where a good part of the *"New World"* Symphony was composed, also some chamber music, and songs. He returned to Bohemia and headed the Prague Conservatory. He died there suddenly on May 1, 1904. (*Great Orchestral Music* by Julian Seaman)

ANTONIN DVOŘÁK

Finale from Symphony No. 5 in E Minor (Arr = Leidzen; Hindsley. Pub = CF, 1935; HI, ms. Gr = 5. T = 10:30. Rec = CR-ABA-79-3, Hardaway H.S., Hindsley)

During the time that he was in the United States as director of the National Conservatory, Dvořák was greatly interested in developing a nationalistic music in this country; music based on native melodies. There have been many arguments as to what extent Dvořák himself has used such themes in his "New World" symphony. H.T. Burleigh, a prominent Negro musician and pupil of Dvořák, believed that "Swing Low, Sweet Chariot," which he sang many times for the composer, was quoted in the symphony. Dvořák said at one time, "The influence of America must be felt by anyone. . .."; at another time, "I tried to write only in the *spirit* of those national American melodies."

The final movement recapitulates the material of the other movements of the symphony. The principal theme is announced in the brasses after a brief introduction. A lively bridge passage leads to the second theme, which is much quieter and more song-like in character. During the development echoes of the themes of preceding movements are heard and the work finally reaches a thunderous climax.

Arguments concerning the "nationality" of this work continue among music historians. All seem to agree, however, that it was actually Dvořák's ninth symphony and that it was written in 1893. Whether a person hears "Three Blind Mice" or the Czech folksong, "Weeding Flaxfields Blue," in the finale, probably depends on his frame of reference. Along with many other comments on the symphony, Dvořák did say at one time, "None of it would have been written just so if I hadn't seen America."

Serenade, Op. 22 (Arr = Moehlmann. Pub = VO, 1967. Gr = 3. T = 6:15. Rec = PH-839706, London Sym. Strings, Davis)

The term "serenade" has been used since the eighteenth century to indicate lighter multimovement music for winds or strings. This work, written in 1875 for strings and now arranged for band by Moehlmann, gives the wind group a chance to display its sensitive side. The expressive, passive melody of the beginning is effectively contrasted in the middle section by a lilting dotted-note melody played first by the brass and later by the woodwinds. The material of the beginning returns to unify the movement. which is brought to a quiet close on a full ensemble chord marked "very, very softly." (Ray C. Wifler, Fond du Lac, Wisconsin, Community Band)

Serenade in D Minor, Op. 44 (Arr = Johnson. Pub = CF, Rental. Gr = 4. T = 17:00. Rec = LO-6594, London Sym., Kertesz)

Dvořák composed this work in two weeks, the first movement being written in one day. It was written in 1878 and was premiered that same year in Prague with the composer conducting. With its instrumentation of ten winds and two strings and the charm of its melodies, it is reminiscent of the Mozart serenades written a century earlier. The minuet is an example of the native influence on Dvořák's compositions. Its trio is a "furiant," which is a "Czech dance in quick triple time with syncopation," and this provides a marked contrast to the surrounding minuet sections of the movement. Also noteworthy is the return of the opening first movement theme toward the end of the final movement, leading into a grand conclusion of the piece. This opus is truly one of the masterpieces for wind ensemble. (David Nelson, University of Michigan)

JOHN EDMONDSON

(Born in Toledo, Ohio, 1933)

John Edmondson received his B.A. degree from the University of Florida and his M.M. degree in composition from the University of Kentucky where he studied with Kenneth Wright and R. Bernard Fitzgerald. His interest in band music is shown by the fact that all of his published compositions have been for band; many of his works, for example, *Fantasy on a Fanfare, Song for Winds,* and *Winchester March,* are playable by elementary and junior high school bands. He and Paul Yoder co-authored the well known *Fun-Way Band Method,* and, like Yoder, Edmondson has arranged a great deal of music ranging from sacred to Broadway and pop tune style. From 1970 to 1979, Edmondson was educational editor with Hansen Publications, Inc. He is a member of the ASCAP from which he has been the recipient of several annual awards, and he and his wife, Anne McGinty, live in Wauwatosa, Wisconsin.

Pageantry Overture (Pub = BA, 1970. Gr = 3. T = 5:12. Rec = OH-1972, OH State Un., McGinnis; CR-ABA-74-5, Motokaga, Japan, Elementary, Tomura)

Pageantry Overture was originally composed for the Belmont Junior High School Band of Winchester, Kentucky, while Edmondson was the director there. The title describes the overture, and the work is essentially monothematic, that is, the various sections are based on or built from a single theme which is stated in the opening few measures by the brass. Inspiration for the piece came from the composer's conviction that very little good music was being written at the time for young junior high ensembles. Since its publication in 1970, *Pageantry Overture* has been selected for contest listings in several states.

EDWARD ELGAR

(Born in Broadheath, England, 1857 — Died in Worcester, 1934)

Sir Edward William Elgar was the first English composer to obtain international recognition in more than two hundred years. His father was organist of the Roman Catholic church in Worcester and young Elgar learned to play the piano, the violin, and the bassoon. By the time he was twenty he realized that his dreams of being a virtuoso violinist would not materialize so he turned to conducting a band, then a glee club, and eventually began composing for both groups.

Elgar loved the English heritage and became the unofficial musician-laureate of the late Victorian and Edwardian eras. He had the idea that music was in the air and only needed to be notated. What he wrote made much sense to his countrymen and eventually to the entire world. His oratorio, *The Dream of Gerontius,* the *Enigma Variations,* and his *Violin Concerto* were among his major works.

Elgar married in 1889 and his wife encouraged him with much intelligent advice, criticism, and understanding. When she died in 1920 he gave up composing until 1929 when he composed a hymn of prayer for King George V, who was ill. After that time he wrote the *Severn Suite* for brass band, his fifth *Pomp and Circumstance March* and a *Nursery Suite* for the Duchess of York. By 1932 the composer seemed to be taking a new lease on life and began plans for a symphony and an opera. However he became seriously ill in 1933 and died in February, 1934.

Enigma Variations (Arr. = Slocum. Pub = SH-TE, 1965. Gr = 5. T = 15:30. Rec = CR-ABA-75-2, Un. of TN, Fred; IL-84, Un. of IL, Begian)

The *Enigma Variations* were written for orchestra in 1899 and bore the dedication, "To My Friends Pictured Within." The theme and fourteen variations belong to that period in which Elgar developed the style that placed him in the front rank of English composers. The immediate success of the opus can be attributed in part to its programmatic characteristics, but the fact that the work has lived and continues to bring enjoyment to audiences is due to the contrasting moods and to Elgar's masterful writing for instruments. Earl Slocum has selected six variations to transcribe.

The theme is pliable, plastic and expressive in itself, tender and noble. Variation I (C.A.E.) is a study of the composer's wife, Caroline Alice. Variation II (W.M.B.) marches in with the furious energy of the country squire, William M. Baker. Variation III (R.P.A.) takes as its subject a son of Matthew Arnold. Variation IV (G.R.S.) is George R. Sinclair, organist of Hereford Cathedral. Variation V is called Nimrod. Nimrod is the great hunter of the Bible; "hunter" in German is "Jaeger." So the subject is A.J. Jaeger, publisher. Variation VI (E.D.U.) is the nickname for Elgar known only to his close friends. Said to depict his strugglings and energies, the work is nevertheless concluded nonprogrammatically so that it caps the series of variations in a broad, triumphant presentation of the original theme in major. (Harold L. Hillyer, University of Texas at El Paso)

DUKE ELLINGTON
(Born in Washington, D.C., 1899 — Died in New York City, 1974)

Edward Kennedy (Duke) Ellington had a scholarship to study art at New York's Pratt Institute after graduating from high school in Washington, D.C., but he decided to play piano for the customers in an ice cream parlor where he worked instead. By the time he was nineteen he had organized a small jazz band and was playing for dances. In 1927 he started a five-year engagement with a twelve-piece band at the Cotton Club in New York and the world of jazz has never been quite the same since.

In addition to performing with his band, Ellington also became well known for his motion picture appearances, his ability to discuss jazz at music clinics, his arrangements, and perhaps most importantly, his many compositions—beginning with "The Soda Fountain Rag" in 1923 and continuing into the 1970's with symphonic jazz, movie, jazz-sacred, and ballet scores. In spite of a host of worldwide honors and degrees, Ellington remained a modest man, a tireless composer and performer, until his death in 1974.

An Ellington Portrait (Arr = Werle. Pub = MM, 1965. Gr = 4. T = 7:00)

Duke Ellington was one of the few jazz artists whose style never seemed to become dated. He was always able to blend his own art with new influences and trends. Songs he wrote as long as forty-five years ago still sound fresh and many of the most up-to-date jazz musicians continue to play them. Floyd Werle's setting of *An Ellington Portrait* includes eight—but by no means all—of his best ones: "It Don't Mean a Thing," "Sophisticated Lady," "Mood Indigo" (his first "hit"), "Azure," "I Let a Song Go Out of My Heart," "Solitude," "Caravan," and "In a Sentimental Mood." (Raoul Camus, Queensboro Community College)

FRANK ERICKSON
(Born in Spokane, Washington, 1923)

The name of Frank Erickson has been prominently associated with quality compositions for school bands since the 1950's. *Overture Jubiloso, Black Canyon of the Gunnison, First* and *Second Symphony for Band,* and nearly 100 other original band works have brought Erickson national recognition afforded few other composers.

Erickson graduated from high school in Spokane, Washington, where he played trumpet and wrote his first concert piece for band, *The Fall of Evening.* During World War II he arranged for army bands and, following the war, worked as a dance band arranger while studying composition with Mario Castelnuovo-Tedesco. He entered the University of Southern California in 1948, studied composition with Halsey Stevens, and arranged for the U.S.C. Band while working toward the B.M. and M.M. degrees. He later taught at U.C.L.A. and San Jose State College, served as musical editor for Bourne, Belwin, and G. Schirmer, and in 1970 organized the firm of Summit Publications.

Erickson has acted as guest conductor, lecturer, and clinician in over thirty states, has had over 150 compositions published, and is a member of the American Bandmasters Association, Phi Mu Alpha Sinfonia, and Kappa Kappa Psi. He now lives in Kansas City, Missouri, and is a consultant for Belwin-Mills Publishing Corp.

Air for Band (Pub = BO, 1956. Gr = 3. T = 3:15. Rec = TT-Golden Gate, TN Tech. Un., McGuffey)

Several generations of band members have developed their ability to play a sustained line, to listen for the moving part, and to improve their intonation while playing this work since it was first published in 1956. While not difficult to play technically, *Air for Band* takes careful rehearsing to get the results the piece deserves. The composition begins softly and in a minor key, and by gradually adding instruments and increasing the dynamics and range, the climatic section is reached approximately half way through. Erickson then uses the opening melody to create interesting rhythms and dialogues between sections on the way to a modulation to a major key and another crescendo leading to a maestoso ending.

Balladair (Pub = BO, 1958. Gr = 3. T = 3:00. Rec = TT-Golden Gate, TN Tech. Un., McGuffey)

Balladair is written in a style similar to the AABA modern dance form. However, another section is added after B, resulting in an AABCA form. The harmonies are fairly traditional, with the exception that certain jazz chords and progressions have been utilized. Written in 1958, this piece is one that "wears well"; it continues to be programmed and enjoyed.

Citadel March (Pub = BE, 1964. Gr = 2. T = 2:00)

This march is an example of a piece which is easy to play and is still interesting. Written in 1964, it has continued to gain in popularity and is played very often as a warm-up march by junior high school bands at music festivals as well as during school and public concerts.

Double Concerto for Trumpet, Trombone, and Concert Band (Pub = BO, 1956. Gr = 5. T = 11:30)

Erickson has contributed many works for band, especially in the lyric and folk song style. Most of his works are excellent for use by high school band and his keen knowledge and effective use of scoring has made his work interesting to audiences and players alike. The *Double Concerto* is a departure from his usual flowing and sonorous style, utilizing more of the modern dissonances and rhythms. (L. Bruce Jones, Louisiana State University)

Fantasy for Band (Pub = BO, 1955. Gr = 3. T = 4:00.)

By definition a "fantasia" or "fantasy" allows the composer to use his "free flight or fancy" rather than adhere to a conventional form such as an overture or march. In this work the mood is constantly shifting from a mood of joy to one of solemnity; from a chorale style to a more rhythmic style. The title is well chosen.

First Symphony for Band (Pub = BO, 1961. Gr = 5. T = 12:00)

The *First Symphony for Band* was conceived as a complete symphony in one movement and written without the restriction of a composition geared for public school use. In this atmosphere of complete freedom of expression, Erickson produced an ambitious work of major significance as an addition to the intellectually respectable repertoire for the modern concert band. The music is tonally and rhythmically complex, the scoring is brilliant, and the entire composition abounds in sonority. The opening Allegro is rhythmic, the Andante con moto is smooth and transparent, the second Allegro is contrapuntal, the Lento is chordal and very romantic, and the closing Allegro contains first a return to the contrapuntal style, then the rhythmic brilliance of the opening.

The work was completed in 1953 with major revisions the following year. The first performance was at the University of Washington with the composer conducting. (Hubert P. Henderson, University of Maryland)

Second Symphony for Band (Pub = BO, 1958. Gr = 4. T = 17:00.)

The *Second Symphony* was a monumental contribution to the field of music education when it was composed in 1958. Here was a complete symphony, from a contemporary composer, that was conceived with the idea of being well within the performing possibilities of many of our nation's fine high school bands. The work is certainly one of Erickson's most mature compositions. His idiomatic scoring and clear understanding of wind sonorities make for an interesting, effective, and powerful piece of music.

Toccata for Band (Pub = BO, 1957. Gr = 4. T = 5:15. Rec = TT-Golden Gate, TN Tech. Un., McGuffey)

Frank Erickson's *Toccata for Band* has been extremely popular among high school and college bands ever since it was published. Essentially two ideas are expressed in the Allegro non troppo and Andante con moto sections. The first, featuring the trumpets and clarinets, is quick and rhythmic; the second, featuring a horn solo, is slow and lyrical. (John Mitchum, DeKalb College)

MANUEL DE FALLA

(Born in Cadiz, Spain, 1876 — Died in Cordoba, Argentina, 1946)

Manuel de Falla was a leading Spanish composer of the early twentieth century. His early works were imbued with the melodic and rhythmic qualities of Spanish popular music and his later compositions showed the maturity resulting from a lifetime of analyzing music of all periods and associating with composers like Debussy, Ravel, Dukas, and Felipe Pedrell, his composition teacher for three years.

Falla's mother taught him piano, and he later studied piano with Jose Trago in Madrid; but his primary ambition was to be a composer not a virtuoso performer. In 1904 he won a prize offered by the Academy of Fine Arts in Madrid for the best lyrical drama by a Spanish composer with his two-act drama, *Life is Short.* In 1907 he left for a "seven-day" excursion to Paris and stayed there for seven years. In spite of financial poverty Falla learned much from the French composers, and his reputation began to grow with his work for piano, *Four Spanish Pieces,* dedicated to the Spanish composer Isaac Albeniz in 1908. In 1914 Falla made a setting of seven folk songs then returned to Madrid where he produced one of his most successful works, the ballet-pantomime, *El Amor Brujo*, in 1915. His only concert piece for orchestra, *Night in the Gardens of Spain,* was impressionistic—similar in style to Debussy's *Nocturnes.* In 1919 his ballet, *The Three-Cornered Hat,* was produced by Diaghilev, with sets by Picasso. His last extensive work, considered by many to be his most mature composition, was the *Harpsichord Concerto* completed in 1926.

Falla became disenchanted with the Spanish regime and moved to Argentina in 1939. He died in Alta Gracia, Cordoba, Argentina, in 1946.

Ritual Fire Dance from El Amor Brujo (Arr = Greissle; Morrissey. Pub = EM, 1952, 1966. Gr = 5. T = 4:15. Rec = CL-ML-5479, Verrett w. Philadelphia Orch., Stokowski)

El Amor Brujo had its world première in Madrid in 1915 and its American première in 1922 with Leopold Stokowski conducting the Philadelphia Orchestra. Falla's scoring for orchestra was of classical proportions, without trombones or tubas. The band arrangement uses the full instrumentation for the climaxes, but much of the work is thinly scored as in the original composition.

Of the thirteen movements of Falla's *El Amor Brujo* (Love Bewitched), the *Ritual Fire Dance* is probably the best known. With sudden changes, in dynamics and mood the composer captures all the excitement of the Andalusian folk dance. Although considered a pure folklore product by many, the ballet does not contain a single authentic folk tune.

The subject of *El Amor Brujo* was taken from folk legend and concerns Candélas, the beautiful Spanish heroine who is in love with handsome Carmelo, the bullfighter. However, she cannot approach him because of the constant intervention of a ghost representing a curse on the family. In desperation, she turns to sorcery, and as the clock strikes midnight, does the *Ritual Fire Dance* in an effort to banish the evil spirit which is ruining her life.

GILES FARNABY

(Born in Truro, England, 1560 — Died in London, 1640)

Farnaby lived in England during the so-called "Golden Age" of composition. A few of the outstanding among this galaxy of composers are William Byrd (1543-1623), Thomas Morley (1558-1603), John Wilbye (1574-1638), and Orlando and Orlando Gibbons (1583-1625). Like the others Farnaby wrote madrigals, motets, psalms, other sacred music, and a large group of pieces for virginal. Fifty-two of these keyboard pieces were included in the *Fitzwilliam Virginal Book* collection.

Farnaby grew up in Cornwall in the southwest coastal region of England, graduated from Oxford University when he was thirty-two, and later moved to London, where he remained until his death. One of his madrigals, "Come, Charon," may be seen in manuscript in the Royal College of Music, and part of another is in the British Museum.

Giles Farnaby Suite (Tr = Jacob. Pub = BH, 1969. Gr = 4. T = 19:00. Rec = CR-MID-70-14, North Hills H.S., Pittsburgh, Mercer)

The material for this beautifully conceived work was selected from the *Fitzwilliam Virginal Book,* a manuscript collection of nearly 300 pieces for virginal dating from approximately 1560 to 1610. The music is frequently modal and often contrapuntal, with good mixtures of full band and transparent scoring. The skill and musicianship of the transcriber, Gordon Jacob, are apparent throughout the suite. The eleven movements (with Middle English spelling in some instances) include: Fantasia, The Old Spagnoletta, Giles Farnaby's Dreame, Farnaby's Concert, His Rest, His Humour, Tell Mee Daphne, Rosasolis, A Toye, Loth to Depart, and Tower Hill.

PAUL FAUCHET
(Born in 1858 — Died in Paris, 1936)

Paul Fauchet was a church organist and an assistant to Paul Vidal at the Paris Conservatory. Little is known of his other musical activities, except that he conducted the chorus at the Opera-Comique in Paris. In 1897 the Folies-Dramatique presented a three-act comic opera by Fauchet entitled *La Carmagnole.*

Symphony in B-Flat (Arr = Gillette and Campbell-Watson. Pub = WS, 1926-49. Gr = 5. T = 30:15. Rec = IL-5, Un. of IL, Hindsley)

Fauchet's *Symphony in B-Flat* was given its first performance by the French National Guard Band in 1926. In 1933 it was performed in America by the Carleton College Symphony Band conducted by James R. Gillette. Since then it has been rescored for American band instrumentation by Gillette and Frank Campbell-Watson and published in an American edition.

Fauchet's symphony is not strictly a symphony, but more properly a suite of four movements (Overture, Nocturne, Scherzo, and Finale) symphonically related in progression. The music itself is fresh, buoyant, and richly melodic with well-defined texture and harmonic interests. It is one of the more significant of earlier works composed directly for the concert band. (Mark Hindsley, University of Illinois)

HENRY FILLMORE
(Born in Cincinnati, Ohio, 1881 — Died in Miami, Florida, 1956)

Henry Fillmore was the most colorful bandman of his time, and that era stretched across fifty vibrant years during which time he probably wrote, arranged, and edited more band music than any other composer/bandmaster in history. According to

Paul Bierley, Fillmore composed under a total of eight names, including Gus Beans, Harold Bennett, Ray Hall, Harry Hartley, Al Hayes, Henrietta Moore, and Will Huff—there was a real Will Huff, however, whose works were published by the Fillmore Bros. A list of Henry Fillmore's music covers ninety-six double-spaced pages! His background in his family's publishing house in Cincinnati led him down a variety of productive paths as a composer, including those of the hymn, popular overture, fox-trot, waltz, and his particularly lucrative specialty (for his own instrument)—the trombone novelty, with titles such as *Lassus Trombone, Bones Trombone,* and *Shoutin' Liza Trombone.*

Fillmore conducted the Syrian Temple Shrine Band in Cincinnati from 1921 to 1926 and organized his own professional band in 1927. This group, famous into the 1930's as a Cincinnati radio band, was among the last in a long line of great professional bands that provided America with their particular combination of music and entertainment. Henry Fillmore himself was "great entertainment"—the last of the minstrelmen. As a conductor he was the showman supreme, able to control any musical forces in front of him regardless of size, but able as well to reach and to thrill audiences which always responded enthusiastically to whatever he did. His friend, Harold Bachman, said ". . . he used certain little gestures which delighted the spectators. . . . No one enjoyed his performances more than Henry himself." Other bandmasters always gave him a very wide berth.

Fillmore never toured with his bands in the same sense as did Sousa, for example. He did attend the national Shrine conventions in various cities with his Shrine Band, and on the way home the group made some interesting side-trips; at one time, on the way home from Los Angeles, they went sight-seeing to Alaska. His professional band only played a few spot engagements in Cincinnati and surrounding towns in addition to their regular WLW broadcasts.

In 1938 heart problems forced Fillmore to give up his career in Cincinnati and move to Miami where he intended to retire. He soon forgot his illness however, and began to assist with the University of Miami Band, judge music festivals, and guest conduct all over the United States. Before he died in 1956, Fillmore willed the bulk of his estate and his ever-continuing band music royalties to the University of Miami. (Frederick Fennell, University of Miami; Carl Fischer, Inc.; additional information from Paul Bierley, Columbus, Ohio)

Americans We March (Pub = FI, 1929; CF, 1958. Gr = 3. T = 2:50. Rec = MG-GI-SRI-75, Eastman, Fennell; CR-CRS-4112, Un. of IL, Begian)

This march, dedicated by Fillmore, "to all of us," is an example of the exuberance in his music which was also in the composer. The expertise of his writing served to guide others as well, in a day when classes in band arranging and composing did not exist. Paul Yoder, a close friend of Fillmore's wrote that ". . .he was my inspiration in trying to write music for the band. I had taught in junior high with young beginners and would stand in the back of the class and play along on cornet or clarinet in teaching the tunes in the famous *Bennett Band Books* (one of Fillmore's pseudonyms). I could play about as well as the kids and so I learned how he put these tunes together. . .; he once told me that he wrote music to make people happy." (Frederick Fennell, University of Miami; Carl Fischer, Inc.)

The Circus Bee March (Pub = FI, 1908. Gr = 3. T = 3:00. Rec = MG-GI-SRI-75087, Eastman, Fennell; CR-CRS-4096, Un. of IL, Begian)

Whenever circus band musicians or followers get together for a talk session (for example the Windjammers Unlimited convention), they invariably discuss, among other things, whether or not the present-day circus bands are playing music which is too "commercial," and also what music should be played for which circus acts--the overture, the clowns, the leopards, the performing dogs, etc. According to the *Circus Fanfare,* the Windjammers' magazine, Fillmore's marches (under his own name or pseudonym) are high on the circus band popularity list. *The Circus Bee March* is one work which seems to capture all the excitement of the "big tent" whether it is performed by a six-piece band at the circus or a sixty-piece band on the concert stage.

The Footlifter March (Pub = FI, 1935. Gr = 3. T = 3:00. Rec = CR-CRS-4112, Un. of IL, Begian)

This march was written in 1929, during the time Fillmore was conducting his professional band in area concerts and radio broadcasts from Cincinnati, Ohio. From the opening trumpet fanfare, the march encourages the listener to "lift his feet" and enjoy the music. If Fillmore were still living, he would probably be writing music to jog by now.

His Honor March (Ed = Fennell. Pub = FI, 1933; CR, 1978. Gr = 3. T = 3:15. Rec = MG-SR-90105, Eastman, Fennell; CR-CRS-4112, Un. of IL, Begian)

Many of Fillmore's marches, overtures, and novelty pieces were composed especially for his own band of professional musicians, organized in 1927 in Cincinnati. One of these, *His Honor March,* proved to be a favorite of band members and audiences alike. The title referred to, and was dedicted to, the mayor of Cincinnati.

Technically, the march is more challenging than many of Fillmore's marches. When the chromatic passages in the first strain are played accurately, the dynamic changes in the trio are observed, and the syncopated sections in the break strain are played with precision, *His Honor March* honors above all, its composer, Henry Fillmore.

In his recent edition, Fennell writes that "in the tradition of its composer, infinite varieties of format are open to the imaginative conductor." The version played by the University of Miami Band is then explained as a possible performance procedure.

The Klaxon March (Pub = FI, 1929; CF, 1959. Gr = 3. T = 3:15. Rec = CR-CRS-4112, Un. of IL, Begian)

Paul Bierley, who has written two highly researched books on John Philip Sousa and his music, is now beginning the seventh year of his research concerning Fillmore. Among many interesting sidelights he has learned that even though Fillmore did use the pseudonym Gus Beans, the oft-repeated story that he picked this name at random from a Cincinnati telephone book, is apparently false—there was no Gus Beans in the Cincinnati telephone book at that time. The story concerning the dedication of *The Crosley* to the memory of one of the first compact cars is also "a little remote," according to Bierley. Fillmore actually wrote the march for Powell Crosley, owner of station WLW, who was manufacturing radios at the time and was a personal friend of the composer. At any rate, the account concerning Fillmore's dedication of *The Klaxon* to the Klaxon automobile horn has not been disputed—yet!

Rolling Thunder March (Pub = *FI, 1916. Gr = 4.* T = 2:30. Rec = CR-ABA-73-4, U.S. Marine, Slater; CR-CRS-4112, Un. of IL, Begian)

Mature band members who have grown up with the *Arban, Klose,* etc. instrumental method books (and metronomes) love to play this march; and at a fast tempo. At the circus or rodeo it's used to generate excitement. On the concert stage it's known as a "show stopper." After all, who wants to hear any more music—or read any more program notes—after the *Rolling Thunder March?*

JOHANN FISCHER

(Born near Schlackenwerth, Bohemia, 1665 — Died in Rastatt, Germany, 1746)

Johann Kaspar Fischer was an important composer for keyboard instruments whose works predated and apparently influenced the compositions of J.S. Bach. Fischer served as house musician to the Margrave of Baden during the period 1696 to 1716. He wrote ballets, airs, harpsichord suites, organ pieces, sacred music, and a collection of preludes and fugues for organ in twenty keys. The latter set, composed in 1715, foreshadowed Bach's first set of preludes and fugues by seven years. As a young man Fischer earned his living by playing violin and also by copying music for the renowned Jean-Baptiste Lully. By incorporating many of the innovations of the French school, Fischer was able to exert a great influence on German instrumental music.

Le Journal du Printemps, Suite No. 3 (Tr = Wilson. Pub = AMP, 1951. Gr = 4)

The titles to Johann Fischer's early works were in French, the middle group were in Latin, and the final compositions were mostly in German. He published as opus one, in 1695, the year before he moved to Baden, Germany, a group of eight suites under the title *Le Journal du Printemps* (diary, or book, of spring). An approximate translation of the sub-title is "consisting of airs and ballets for five parts with trumpets ad lib." No definite instrumentation was given for the five parts. Each of these eight suites consists of a French style overture; a slow, dotted rhythm introduction, followed by a faster imitative section, and concluding with a series of slower dance movements. The music is in the style of Lully; elegant, soothing, and delightful. The parts to this suite are titled Overture, Menuet, Gavotte, and Chaconne.

TREVOR J. FORD

(Born in Tasmania, Australia, 1931)

Trevor John Ford was born in Australia but has lived most of his life in England and Norway. His family moved to Oxford when he was three years old and he lived there until he joined the Royal Band Service at sixteen. He played the oboe in the Royal Marine Band for thirteen years followed by five years as bandmaster of the home fleet. His teaching experience with the Royal Marine School of Music proved valuable as preparation for his present position (since 1964) as inspector for the Norwegian Band Federation—he is now responsible for all music education in Norway. Ford has adjudicated music contests in several European countries and in 1978 was a member of the adjudication panel for the World Music Contest in Kerkrade,

Holland. He has guest conducted in America, England, Sweden, and Holland. Among his most popular compositions for harmonie (wind band) are *Four Contrasts for Wind, Nordisk Rhapsody, Tribute to Youth,* and *City of Spires.* Ford has written several theory books, is a regular broadcaster over Norwegian radio, and is European chairman for the National Band Association. He and his (Norwegian) wife and daughter live in Bjornemyrsvingen, Norway.

Four Contrasts for Wind (Pub = MOL, 1975. Gr = 3. T = 7:30. Rec = MO-MBS-5, Molenaar's Harmonieorkest, Lijnschooten; MA-MC-5117)

As the title indicates, this suite offers contrasts in all three elements of harmony, melody, and rhythm. The first movement features the upper woodwinds in a sophisticated, French-like melody; the second is a slower 12/8 section with dialogues between upper woodwinds and lower brass; the tempo of the third movement increases to a Moderato with a sprightly melody on each side of a low brass technical exercise; the final movement, Alla Marcia, continues to make use of different timbres building to a majestic close. The piece is an example of mature writing by a composer with varied musical experiences.

Tribute to Youth (Pub = BD, 1976. Gr = 3. T = 5:20. Rec = MA-MC-5117; CR-OM-75-11B)

Ford's "tribute" to the young people is a very appropriate musical composition which features different sections of the band and includes solo parts for various instruments. Percussion and wind sections are both used to bring out the rhythmic elements in a march-like section following an expressive saxophone solo. The general optimism of most youth is reflected in this work by a composer who writes that he is "very happy with life and looking toward the future."

LELAND E. FORSBLAD
(Born in Kingsburg, California, 1922)

Leland Forsblad is a prolific composer of works for band. In the 1978 edition of *Band Music Guide* he was credited with a total of sixty-six separate titles. He has also written several choral compositions, and he is the director of the Fresno Women's Choir. Forsblad is a teacher in the Fresno city school system and also manages to do some farming. His education credentials include degrees from California State University at Fresno and the University of Southern California where he studied with Ingolf Dahl, Ernst Kanitz, Halsey Stevens, and Miklos Rosza. His principal works for band include *Compendium, Elektra, Imperatives, Andante e Presto,* and *Litany and Alleluia.* Forsblad is active in the Fresno Community Band, and he and his wife are the parents of one daughter.

Four Freedoms Overture (Pub = HL, 1975. Gr = 3. T = 3:00. Rec = CR-MID-76-11, Bedford Jr. H.S., Temperance, MI, Salvo)

The overture opens with a majestic introduction followed by the main theme played marcato by the first trumpet. In the middle, more expressive, section the solo flute plays a melody which is based on the main theme. Once again the brasses enter with thematic material and the overture gradually slows to an impressive finale. The work is an example of interesting and worthwhile music which is not technically difficult to play.

ARTHUR FRACKENPOHL

(Born in Irvington, New Jersey, 1924)

Arthur Frackenpohl received his B.M. degree from the Eastman School of Music in 1947 and subsequently earned his master's degree at the Rochester University and his doctorate at McGill University. His principal composition teachers were Bernard Rogers, Darius Milhaud, and Nadia Boulanger. Since 1949 he has taught piano, composition and theory at the Crane School of Music in Potsdam, New York. He has received several honors including a Ford Foundation grant, several ASCAP awards, and four faculty research fellowships from the State University of New York Research Foundation. In addition to many works for band Frackenpohl has written several instrumental solo and ensemble pieces, a cantata, and music for strings and for orchestra.

American Folk Song Suite (Pub = SH, 1973. Gr = 3. T = 7:45. Rec = SH-6, Ithaca Col., Phillips; CR-ABA-74-2, Un. of HI, Neilson; CR-ABA-75-3, Lamar Un., Dunlop)

The *American Folk Song Suite* is based on four songs which use "blue" notes—the flatted third, sixth, and seventh degrees of the major scale. "He's Gone Away" is an Appalachian folk song, originally from Scotland which tells a sad tale of parting and loneliness. "John Henry" is a "hammer" song about a powerful epic hero, a steel-drivin' man who wins a contest with a steam drill but at the cost of his life. "Go 'Way from My Window" is a tender love lament from the Ozarks. "Mama Don't Allow" is a fast swinging song about all the things which mama don't allow, from trombone playin' and bass slappin' to fancy swingin' and two-step danccin'; but which are done anyhow. (Shawnee Press, Inc.)

Variations for Tuba and Winds (Pub = SH, 1973. Gr = 4/5. T = 5:30. Rec = SH-7, William Kinne w. Ithaca Col., Gobrecht)

Following a short introduction, the solo tuba plays the well-known theme, "The Cobbler's Bench," ("Pop, Goes the Weasel"). Originally a seventeenth century dance tune, this melody became a popular square dance tune in America. (The "weasel" refers to the pressing iron which the tailor often pawned in order to buy the material for a suit. He "popped" the weasel out of the pawn shop when he made a payment. Ed.)

Variation I features octave skips and scalewise runs. Variation II is legato and in a slower tempo. Variation III is a fast waltz using cross rhythms and the interval of the third. Variation IV is a funeral march in minor. Variation V uses syncopations in a fast 2/4 and leads into a solo cadenza. The composition concludes with a codetta similar to the introduction. (Shawnee Press, Inc.)

CÉSAR FRANCK

(Born in Liege, Belgium, 1822 — Died in Paris, 1890)

It would seem unfortunate for a boy named after a ruler of the entire known world not to achieve some degree of fame and accomplishment. The rise of César August Franck, however, was not based on military and political conquest. The son of a rather austere banker, he demonstrated a talent for music very early in life. This pleased the father who then set about to "accrue" the maximum benefits for his son's natural endowment. Private study of piano, organ, and theory led to matriculation in the Paris Conservatory. At the age of nineteen, the young Franck confounded his professors in a scholarship competition. In piano he transposed the contest piece at sight to a key a third lower. In organ he was given two themes to improvise a sonata and a fugue. Sensing the possibilities of the two themes, he combined them spontaneously. The judges were so upset they disqualified him and then reconsidered to give him second prize.

After many years of teaching and playing, especially at the organ in the Basilica of St. Clothilde in Paris, Franck, at the age of fifty, seemed to find himself from the standpoint of composition. From then on his writing reached the full fruition of intellect and inspiration. During this period he produced *The Beatitudes,* an oratorio; *Symphony in D-Minor; Symphonic Variations;* and additional works for solo, chorus, and orchestra. Finally, after a lifetime of humble, saintly devotion to God, to his art, and to his beloved students, Franck was just beginning to receive a bit of recognition. At sixty-eight he was struck by an omnibus on a street in Paris. He lingered awhile but never recovered. His compositions are now among the top ranks of musical literature. (George Kreamer, Lake Charles, Louisiana, Civic Symphony)

Panis Angelicus (Arr = Harvey; Wilson.   Pub = EV, 1943; CF, 1943.   Gr = 3.   T = 3:00)

César Franck was a religious man for whom music was an act of faith. In his works there is a spirit of deep sincerity that, while reserved in its utterance, is of a highly personal nature. Franck wrote the *Panis Angelicus* (nation's prayer) in 1872 for tenor voice, organ, harp, cello, and double bass. Russell Harvey transcribed this beautiful religious meditation for band in 1943.

Psyché and Éros (Arr = Harding.   Pub = KJ, 1952.   Gr = 4.   T = 5:30.   Rec = DG-2530771, Orchestra of Paris, Barenboim)

Psyché and Éros, completed in the same year as the famous *D Minor Symphony,* was a symphony for orchestra with chorus in its original form. Published in 1900 as an orchestral suite, "Psyché" appeared as the last movement of the suite.

According to classical myth, Psyché is borne to the garden of Éros, her celestial lover, where she imprudently wishes to pierce the mystery which surrounds him. Failing, she falls to earth and wanders aimlessly as she sings of her woes. Éros finally forgives her, and together they soar back to their celestial home. The undulating course of the music, rising from low sonorities through successive climaxes to a tranquil close in the high woodwinds, artistically parallels the verbal program.

Symphony in D Minor, First Movement (Arr = Malone.   Pub = GS, 1950.   Gr = 5.   T = 8:00)

This symphony was first produced at the Paris Conservatory in 1889. Music critics and other composers of the period were most critical of Franck's symphony, especially of the use of English horn and the mixture of trumpets and cornets in the brass section. A few admitted that it was an interesting work, but certainly not a "symphony" by any stretch of the imagination. Time has been on the side of the composer of the *Symphony in D Minor.* Although the work was Franck's only symphony, it has remained one of the most popular symphonies of the entire Romantic Period.

The first movement is constructed of three musical ideas; first, a three-note motive of upward inflection; second, a lyrical, scale-like melody of quiet beauty; and finally, a theme which begins and constantly returns to a central pitch.

GIROLAMO FRESCOBALDI
(Born in Ferrara, Italy, 1583 — Died in Rome, 1643)

Frescobaldi was the most eminent organist of the first half of the seventeenth century. When he was appointed organist at St. Peter's in Rome in 1603, 30,000 people were reported to have witnessed his first performance. His style of organ playing was passed on to future generations by his pupils, notably the German, Johann Froberger. Except for the period 1628-33, when he served as the court organist at Florence, Frescobaldi was the organist at St. Peter's from 1608 until his death in 1643. He was known to his Baroque contemporaries as "the miracle of his epoch."

Frescobaldi composed many five-part madrigals in addition to his works for organ. Breitkopf and Hartel published a total of sixty-eight of his compositions. Still existing is a copy of his *Fiori musicali* of 1635 which is signed with the name of its proud owner, "J.S. Bach, 1714."

Preludium and Fugue (Arr = Brunelli. Pub = CA, 1969. Gr = 3. T = 4:50. Rec = BM-Third Series)

The *Preludium* was originally a prelude from Frescobaldi's work for organ entitled *Toccata in D Minor* and the *Fugue* was taken from his *Fugue in G Minor for Organ*. In arranging the works for one concert band piece, Louis Brunelli has followed a tradition which goes far back into musical history. Brunelli teaches at the Manhattan School of Music and is also the program coordinator for Italy's Festival Musicale at Salerno.

Toccata (Arr = Slocum. Pub = MM, 1956. Gr = 4. T = 5:20. Rec = CR-CBDNA-73-1, Un. of IL, Kisinger)

A toccata is a rhapsodic form of instrumental music. Originally written for the organ, it was essentially a solo piece which was improvised. The name "toccata" indicates that it was conceived as a "touch piece" characterized by rhapsodic sections with sustained chords, scale passages, and broken figuration. The present toccata consists of three sections with tempos of slow, fast, and slow. The rhapsodic beginning and closing sections enclose a quick middle section, featuring French horns, based on a development of a tuneful fanfare motive. The subject is treated antiphonally and is varied continually through the addition of new counter-subjects and accompaniments. The movement concludes with a short, fast coda. (Gene Braught, University of Oklahoma)

JULIUS FUČIK
(Born in Prague, Czechoslovakia, 1872 — Died near Berlin, 1916)

Julius Ernst Wilhelm Fučik was born in Prague where he studied at the conservatory from 1885 to 1891 with, among others, the noted Anton Dvořák. He later served in the 49th Austro-Hungarian Regimental Band at Krems with J.F. Wagner (composer of *Under the Double Eagle March),* then returned to Prague to play bassoon in two local orchestras. In 1897 he began his career as a bandmaster with the 86th Regiment Band in Sarajevo, Yugoslavia, and later returned to his country to lead the 92nd Regiment Band at Theresienstadt. He retired as a bandmaster in 1913 and settled in Berlin where he organized an orchestra and started his own music publishing firm, Tempo Verlag.

Fučik was a prolific composer. His 400 works included operettas, chamber music, masses, songs, and a symphonic suite. Of his more than 100 marches, the *Entry of the Gladiators* and *Florentiner March* are probably the best known and most recorded. (Robert Hoe, Jr., Poughkeepsie, New York)

Entry of the Gladiators March (Pub = CF, 1901. Gr = 4. T = 2:35. Rec = DL-78451, Barnum & Bailey's Circus, Evans; MG-SRI-175087, Eastman, Fennell)

When Fučik wrote this famous march, also known as *Thunder and Blazes,* he may have been thinking of the Roman gladiators who lived nearly 2,000 years ago, or he may have had the pre-World War I Austrian soldiers in mind. However in America, "gladiators" can refer to the heroes and heroines under the circus big top, or to the daring riders at the rodeo, or even to the participants on the gridiron. Regardless of the association no one knows better than the band members that it takes an extremely "athletic" musician to play this march up to tempo.

Florentiner March (Arr = Lake. Pub = CF, 1916. Gr = 4. T = 4:50. Rec = LO-TW-91459, Netherlands Marine, Lijnschooten; DG-2721-077, Berlin Phil. Winds, · van Karajan; TO-EMI-TA-72043, Eastman, Hunsberger)

Although Julius Fučik has been remembered by American audiences for his *Entry of the Gladiators March* more than any other composition, recent popularity polls among band directors indicate a preference for his *Florentiner March,* sub-titled *Grande Marcia Italiana.* The length and content of this march lead one to believe that, like Sousa with his *Free Lance March,* Fučik must have tried to condense an operetta into a march. The march opens with a short bugle fanfare, then proceeds directly into a strain of repeated notes which sound like a flighty Florentine signorina chattering to her gentleman friend from Berlin who only has time to answer a (two-note) "ja-wohl" occasionally. The march continues with another fanfare; a light, floating trio melody; an interlude; and a triumphant repeat with a challenging piccolo part.

If this march is typical of Fučik's other music, it might be worth a trip to Prague during the next Carnival season to hear the Czech Philharmonic and other groups play the overtures, waltzes, and more marches by this master of melody.

GEMBA FUJITA
(Born in Tokyo, 1937)

Fujita was born in Tokyo and received his education in Japanese schools. He has become interested in the native folk songs and in the possibilities which exist for using these traditional melodies in instrumental settings. His instructions for the performance of his works, which accompany the score, reveal an excellent knowledge of the wind and percussion instruments, and also the close relation which exists between the physical make-up of chords and the feelings expressed by the music.

Japanese Folk Song, "Itsuki no Komoriuta" (Pub = ON. Gr = 4. T = 3:30)

This lullaby, traditionally sung in the area around Itsuki Village, Kumamoto in central Kyushu, has become extremely popular. It originated during ancient times when a serf system was in practice.

The lyrics relate the past experiences of a young girl, brought up in a poor family, who was compelled to become a maid and work constantly for the others. In this state she sings a sad lullaby to a baby strapped on her back. Fujita's arrangement conveys this feeling of sadness and tension through most of the piece, concluding with a more relaxed impression at the end.

JACOB GADE

(Born in Vejle, Denmark, 1879 — Died in Copenhagen, 1963)

Jacob Gade was a Danish violinist, conductor, and composer. From 1919 to 1921 he lived in the United States, playing violin in the New York Symphony Orchestra, then he returned to Copenhagen and became very active there as a conductor. Most of Gade's compositions were of a light nature, but he also composed several symphonic poems, including *Don Sidste Viking* and *Leda and the Swan*.

Jalousie (Arr = Krance. Pub = MP, 1967. Gr = 4. T = 6:30. Rec = CR-MID-68-10, VanderCook Col., Brittain)

Jalousie is reported to have been inspired by an actual drama of passion, with a fatal outcome, which occured in Copenhagen in 1925. The work was performed for the first time in Copenhagen in connection with a film entitled *Don Q,* starring Douglas Fairbanks.

After hearing the "gypsy" qualities in *Jalousie,* listeners are usually surprised to learn that its composer was Danish. However the abandon and frenzy of the gypsy violinists were traits which were well known to late nineteenth-century violinists throughout Europe—as, for example, Brahm's *Hungarian Dances.* In this arrangement, John Krance has captured the inherent gypsy qualities of the piece and at the same time has used the tonal colors of the wind and percussion instruments in a highly imaginative manner.

THOM RITTER GEORGE

(Born in Detroit, 1942)

Thom Ritter George began the study of violin and composition while still in elementary school in Detroit. He majored in composition at the Eastman School of Music earning the B.M. degree (with distinction) in 1964 and the M.M. in 1968. At Eastman George studied violin with Millard Taylor and composition and orchestration with Louis Mennini, Wayne Barlow, John La Montaine, and Bernard Rogers. As a student of composition he was awarded the George Eastman Honorary Scholarship, the Edward B. Benjamin Award, and two Howard Hanson prizes.

Having begun to compose at the age of ten, George's compositions now number more than 280, ranging from simple songs to symphonic compositions. In addition to many works for orchestra, string quartet, woodwind quintet, instrumental duets and solos, George's catalogue also includes such major band works as *Hymn and Toccata, Western Overture,* and *Proclamations.* He has also written music for the documentary film, *the American Dreadnaught.*

From 1966 to 1970, George served as composer-arranger for the United States Navy Band in Washington, D.C. Since 1970 he has been music director and conductor of the Quincy (Illinois) Symphony Orchestra. His work there has been nationally noted for the promotion of contemporary music. George and his wife Patricia, a flutist, have one daughter, Samantha.

Proclamations (Pub = BH, 1968. Gr = 4. T = 7:00. Rec = CR-MID-68-5, Muskegon, MI, H.S., Krive)

Proclamations, Thom Ritter George's second work for band, was written in late 1965 while the composer was living in Rochester, New York. The score is dedicated to Floyd K. Grave, a musicologist and a friend of the composer.

The title is derived from the nature of the music, rather than from any specific programmatic idea. The score consists of three large sections, each of which is devoted to a musical "proclamation."

The first section, Allegro, features writing for brass in a brilliant style, with syncopated woodwind backgrounds, and forceful percussion scoring. Largo, the second part, demands mature sostenuto playing from the ensemble—the music is poetic and lyrical in expression. Antiphonal effects between woodwinds and brasses are used in the middle of the slow section. The ending Allegro section is cast in a tight sonata-allegro design. The woodwind writing offers many opportunities for technical display—the brass writing is generally chordal, either staccato or sustained. Near the end, themes from the opening of *Proclamations* are brought back and combined with the music of the finale. These ideas are closely interwoven and give the composition a unified and powerful ending. (Thom Ritter George, Quincy, Illinois)

GEORGE GERSHWIN
(Born in Brooklyn, New York, 1898 — Died in Hollywood, CA, 1937)

George Gershwin (born Jacob Gershvin) occupies a unique place in the history of American music. A gifted writer of popular songs, musical comedies, a folk opera, and other art music, he was able to combine the styles of Tin Pan Alley and Carnegie Hall music in a way which seemed perfectly clear to him, but never quite right to many music critics.

Gershwin grew up in Brooklyn where he attended the public schools, took piano lessons, and began composing. When he was sixteen he was hired by the Remick Publishing Co. to "plug songs" for potential buyers. When he was eighteen, he wrote "Pretty Lady," which was interpolated into the Sigmund Romberg score for *Passing Show,* and when he was twenty-one, Gershwin wrote the score for his first Broadway show, *La La Lucille.* When Al Jolson began singing "Swanee," (written in fifteen minutes), Gershwin's fame and fortune began to increase rapidly. With his brother Ira as lyricist, he wrote over a dozen successful music comedies between 1919 and 1933. Gershwin died in 1937 after an unsuccessful brain tumor operation. Since that time his opera *Porgy and Bess,* his symphonic piece *Rhapsody in Blue,* and his piano concertos have been performed around the world, proving his prediction that jazz and art music really could be combined.

An American in Paris (Arr = Krance. Pub = WB, 1929-59. Gr = 4. T = 5:45. Rec = CR-4022, Ithaca Col., Beeler)

Gershwin, best known as a writer of entertainment for the entertainment market, made several excursions into the realm of art music. One of these was the result of a European journey in 1928. Gershwin himself called this piece "a rhapsodic ballet." His own description follows:

> I have not endeavored to present any definite scenes in this music. The rhapsody is programmatic in a general impressionistic sort of way, so that the individual listener can read into the music such episodes as his imagination pictures for him. The opening section is followed by a rich "blues" with a strong rhythmic undercurrent. Our American friend, perhaps after strolling into a cafe, has suddenly succumbed to a spasm of homesickness. The blues rises to a climax followed by a coda in which the spirit of the music returns to the vivacity and bubbling exuberance of the opening part with its impressions of Paris.

Amusing to the listener is the use of taxi horns on various pitches which contribute picturing of the street noises and French atmosphere. (William A. Schaefer, University of Southern California)

Porgy and Bess, Selections (Arr = Bennett. Pub = CA, 1942. Gr = 4. T = 12:00. Rec = CR-4022, Ithaca Col., Beeler)

Gershwin's folk opera *Porgy and Bess* climaxed his brief but spectacular career as both a popular and serious work. He had read DuBose Heyward's *Porgy* in 1926 and was immediately interested in tranforming the novel into an opera, but it was almost eight years before arrangements were completed for Gershwin to begin writing the music. It was first performed by the Theatre Guild in Boston and New York in 1935 by an all-negro cast with Todd Duncan as Porgy and Anne Brown as Bess. The opera ran 124 performances in New York, a flop by Broadway standards. However it was revived in 1942, almost five years after Gershwin's death, and the show had the longest run of any revival in Broadway musical history. Between 1952 and 1956, *Porgy and Bess* toured the major cities around the globe, including those behind the Iron Curtain, and in 1959 was made into a lavish movie starring Sidney Poitier, Dorothy Dandridge, and Sammy Davis, Jr. During all of the presentations for its first forty years of existence the show was never given it its entirety. Finally, in 1975, it was presented completely in a concert format in Cleveland, and the following year was given its first complete stage presentation by the Houston Grand Opera Company.

Gershwin's folk opera has been criticized as being between serious opera and musical comedy, but the beauty of the music and the expressive content which is so right for the occasion, has an immediate and complete appeal between the composer and the audience which overshadows the criticism. This arrangement by R.R. Bennett, includes: "Summertime," "A Woman Is a Sometime Thing," "I Got Plenty o' Nuttin'," "Bess, You Is My Woman," "It Ain't Necessarily So," "Picnic Parade," and "Oh Lawd, I'm On My Way."

Rhapsody in Blue (Arr – Grofe. Pub = MP, 1924-38. Gr = 4/5. T = 22:00. Rec = CR-CRS-41288, Mary Ann Covert w. Ithaca Col.)

Rhapsody in Blue was first performed by the Paul Whiteman orchestra at a concert in New York's Aeolian Hall on February 19, 1924. Gershwin had written the score several weeks previously (at Whiteman's request), and the famous arranger Ferde Grofe had orchestrated it page by page as it came from the pen of the composer. It was written for piano and jazz orchestra and at the concert Gershwin played the piano part himself. He hadn't as yet scored the music for the piano and played the part, as he said, "from the music in my mind." The work scored such a success that it has been performed repeatedly ever since. (James M. Thurmond, Lebanon Valley College)

Second Prelude (Arr = Krance. Pub = MP, 1927-64. Gr = 4. T = 4:00)

This very popular and familiar prelude is the second of Gershwin's three preludes for piano. John Krance's colorful arrangement defies the belief that piano music cannot be transcribed well for the concert band. The arranger makes excellent use of the variety inherent in the band with several solo passages and an emphasis in the low-reed register.

Summertime (Arr = Krance. Pub = GE, 1935-59. Gr = 3)

Summertime is one of the superb songs from Gershwin's folk opera, *Porgy and Bess.* The opera united the traditions of opera and musical comedy to convey a realistic impression of southern Negro life in the 1930's. Many critics have described the opera as one of the finest dramatic compositions by an American. Gershwin considered *Porgy and Bess* his greatest achievement. After attending one of the early rehearsals, he was heard to say, "I always knew that *Porgy and Bess* was wonderful, . . . I tell you after listening to that rehearsal today I think the music is so marvelous I really don't believe that I wrote it."

VITTORIO GIANNINI
(Born in Philadelphia, 1903 — Died in New York, 1966)

Vittorio Giannini began his music career by taking violin lessons with his mother at their home in Philadelphia. At the age of nine he was awarded a scholarship to the Royal Conservatory in Milan, Italy, where he studied composition with Trucco. He returned to New York in 1917 where he completed his graduate studies at the Juilliard School, studying violin with Hans Letz and Albert Spaulding, and composition with Rubin Goldmark. From 1939 to 1965 he served as professor of composition at the Juilliard School of Music, the Manhattan School of Music, and the Curtis Institute. He was a guiding force in the founding of the North Carolina School of Arts and served as its first president.

Giannini's compositions include eleven operas, several large choral works, songs, motets, madrigals, numerous works for piano, chamber music, two melodramas for soprano and orchestra, and numerous orchestral works including five symphonies. A highly gifted and superbly trained musical craftsman, Giannini has explained his philosophy of composition as follows: "The composer's duty is to express what is in him with utmost sincerity, with no thought of whether it is 'original' and no desire to make an impression by doing startling things." His works for band reveal his sincerity and ability and are considered by many as being on a par with those of Hindemith, Persichetti, Gould, and Creston.

Fantasia for Band (Pub = FC, 1963. Gr = 4. T = 7:00. Rec = IL-42, Un. of IL, Hindsley)

Fantasia for Band, published in 1963, was commissioned by the Northern Westchester and Putnam County Music Teachers Association in New York, and was Giannini's third work for the medium of the concert band. The *Fantasia* is romantic in spirit and is less technical than the composer's previous band works, *Praeludium and Allegro* and *Symphony No. 3.* The *Fantasia* opens with dissonance between the melody and harmonic structure, moves on to a moderately fast section with alternating triplet and eighth note rhythms, and closes with full sonorities at a slow tempo, emphasizing length of melodic line. (Hubert Henderson, University of Maryland)

Praeludium and Allegro (Pub = RC, 1959. Gr = 5. T = 7:30. Rec = GC-Revelli Years, Un. of MI, Revelli)

The *Praeludium and Allegro* was commissioned in 1958 by Richard Franko Goldman in memory of his famous father, the founder of the Goldman Band. The music is characteristic of Giannini's fine craftsmanship and sensitivity for dramatic chord shifts. Almost ponderous as it moves in legato style, the opening part contrasts sharply with the brilliant fast section in which an angular and unlikely musical fragment is tossed around the band against a rhythmically clever bass line. (Hubert Henderson, University of Maryland)

Symphony No. 3 (Pub = RC, 1961. Gr = 5. T = 23:00. Rec = IL-33, Un. of IL, Hindsley; BP-112, Un. of MI, Revelli)

The *Symphony No. 3* follows no program. The first movement, in sonata-allegro form, offers a victorious opening. Its fundamental germinating force is the interval of a fourth, which is heard immediately in the first theme. The second movement takes advantage of the lyric woodwind sound of the band and in ABA form presents a quiet, restful section of great beauty. The third movement, ABAB, is an example of rhythmic playfulness. Here, the kaleidoscopic shifting pulses of 6/8 and 3/4 meters rebound over and upon one another in intriguing fashion. The final movement, in sonata-allegro form, is announced by a tremendous woodwind sweep. Its pure excitement gives a thrilling emotional climax to the work. (James D. Pritchard, University of South Carolina)

Variations and Fugue (Pub = FC, 1967. Gr = 5. T = 14:30. Rec = GC-Revelli Years, Un. of MI, Revelli)

Variations and Fugue was Giannini's fifth work for band and was not published until several months after his death. All five band works were written during the last ten years of his life. Despite its chromaticism and obvious melodic romanticism, this work is relevant to our times. Its massive sonorities and long melodic lines are combined to provide a nostalgic look at the past, but the piece ends in a mood of optimism and hope. It is a mature work from a mature artist who retained his creative powers and enthusiasm to the very end of his life. (Gale Sperry, University of South Florida)

DON GILLIS

(Born in Cameron, Missouri, 1912 — Died in Columbia, South Carolina, 1978)

The name of Don Gillis on a program leads audiences to expect tuneful, picturesque music, descriptive of various American scenes. Born in Missouri, educated in Kansas, a college band director and music department head in Texas, musical director for NBC radio during a long series of Toscanini broadcasts, a promoter for the National Music Camp—these are a few of the activities which have influenced the compositional styles of Don Gillis.

Gillis received the B.A., B.M., and honorary Mus. D. from Texas Christian University, and the M.M. degree from North Texas State University. In addition to composing for a variety of choral and instrumental ensembles, he has guest-conducted bands and orchestras in the United States and in Europe. Some of his better-known scores include: *The Man Who Invented Music, The January February March, Alice in Orchestralia, The Coming of the Kings, Symphony for Band, Ballet for Band, Saga of a Pioneer, Tulsa, Symphony 5½,* and *Symphony X (Big "D")*. His works, which number over 200, have been performed in thirty-five countries. Before his death in January, 1978, Gillis was the director of the Center for Media Arts Studies and composer-in-residence at the University of South Carolina.

Symphony No. 5½ (Arr = Ford. Pub = BH, 1967. Gr = 5. T = 15:00)

Many of Gillis' titles are in a whimsical vein, for example the fraction in this symphony's title (composed between his fifth and sixth symphonies), and its subtitle, "A Symphony for Fun."   The four movements are named Perpetual Emotion, Spiritual?, Scherzofrenia, and Conclusion. The Spiritual? features tone color and expressive performance whereas rhythmic variety and tempo are important in the other three movements. The slow movement was first transcribed for band by Glenn Cliffe Bainum. The present version was transcribed from the orchestra score by Maurice Ford. The work contains square dances, blues, swing, and even ragtime, but all treated in typical Don Gillis fashion.

Tulsa (Tr = Ford. Pub = MM, 1957. Gr = 5. T = 10:25. Rec = CR-SMENC-79, Lenoir City, TN, H.S., Best)

Tulsa was commissioned by the First National Bank and Trust Company of Tulsa, Oklahoma, for H. Arthur Brown and the Tulsa Philharmonic Orchestra. The score was completed July 7, 1950. Gillis describes the composition as follows:

> *Tulsa* is a symphonic poem in four sections, the first of which is a pastoral movement depicting the land before the settling of the white man. This moves without pause into a rather violent struggle for possession of the land. This struggle, filled with the energy and passion of frontier civilization, ends in victory as the land is transformed from wilderness to homestead and thence to a modern city. The third movement attempts to "bring in" an oil well, and is graphic in its portrayal of the violence of a "gusher." The final section is a celebration in which the whole population joins in a shirt-tail parade and square dance in the street.

Variations on a Kitchen Sink (Pub = IP, 1959. Gr = 3. T = 4:00)

Most of Gillis' music for band, orchestra, and choir is of a serious nature. This piece is for fun; it is nevertheless very well written with interesting melodies, modulations, and rhythms throughout. Using a variety of unusual "kitchen" instruments (pots, pans, washtub, etc.) along with the more traditional snare drum, maracas, and woodblocks, this piece gives the percussion section an opportunity to finally enjoy working with a "kitchen sink."

ALBERTO GINASTERA

(Born in Buenos Aires, Argentina, 1916)

Much of Ginastera's music draws inspiration from folklore. Written in a variety of forms, his music has been described as being compact and harmonically advanced. His works range from the ballets *Panambi* and *Estancia,* written in 1940 and 1941 respectively, to the *Piano Concerto No. 2,* which was given an exciting world premiere performance by Hilde Somer with the Indianapolis Symphony Orchestra in March, 1973.

Ginastera graduated from the National Conservatory of Music in his native Argentina in 1938. In 1946 he came to the United States on a Guggenheim Fellowship and in 1953 he became professor of composition at his alma mater in Buenos Aires. His third opera, *Beatrix Cenci,* was given its first performance in New York in 1973 at the same time that Ginastera's wife, Aurora Natola-Ginastera, was being featured as cello soloist with the Berlin Philharmonic Orchestra. Like many of his earlier works the opera has music which is both savage and hypnotic and yet is brilliantly and logically constructed. Ginastera's interest in percussion instruments was climaxed in 1961 with his *Cantata para America Magica,* for dramatic soprano and percussion ensemble of fifty-three instruments.

Since about 1960 Ginastera's style has changed from a nationalistic orientation to that of more advanced idioms. His more recent works have made frequent use of twelve-tone, microtonal, and aleatory techniques, and he has concentrated on the larger works such as cantatas, operas, and concertos.

Danza Final from Estancia (Tr = John.   Pub = BH, 1965.   Gr = 4.   T = 4:00. Rec = CR-MID-76-15, U.S. Navy, Phillips; MS-13, Morehead St. Un., Hawkins)

Estancia was commissioned in 1941 for the American Ballet Caravan, but the troupe subsequently disbanded and the work was not performed as a full ballet until 1952. In the meantime, Ginastera extracted the four-movement suite which was premiered by the Teatro Colon Orchestra in 1943. The work soon became well-known as an orchestra piece and also as a band transcription, played from manuscript by the U.S. Navy Band.

Estancia is the Argentine word for ranch and the work reflects many aspects of Argentine ranch life. As the story unfolds, a city boy finds difficulty in winning a ranch girl who considers him a weakling and unable to compete with the athletic gauchos on the ranch. The city boy is finally successful in the courtship through a series of events in which he demonstrates that he can emerge victorious in the gaucho environment. The ballet suite *Estancia* contains music from four scenes: The Land Workers, Wheat Dance, The Cattlemen, and Final Dance, "Malambo." The malambo is a lively, exciting, and often lengthy dance tournament between two gauchos. (Acton Ostling, University of Maryland)

CAESAR GIOVANNINI
(Born in Chicago, 1925)

Caesar Giovannini began piano lessons at the age of five at the Chicago Conservatory of Music. In 1938, he was the winner of the Chicago Conservatory Silver Medal in its annual piano competition. He joined the U.S. Navy in 1943 where he was soloist with the Navy Band in Washington, D.C. Giovannini resumed his studies at the Chicago Conservatory after his release from the navy in 1946, and he graduated with an M.M. degree in composition in 1948. He joined the National Broadcasting Company Staff Orchestra as a pianist in 1949, appearing as a soloist in various radio and television shows. During the years 1956 and 1957, he was the music director of the "Kukla, Fran and Ollie" television show, after which he joined the American Broadcasting Company Staff Orchestra in 1958. Giovannini moved to Los Angeles in 1959 and is currently active as a free-lance pianist and composer for motion picture and television films. (Belwin-Mills Publishing Corporation)

Alla Barocco—Folk Rock (Sc = Robinson.   Pub = SF, 1969.   Gr = 4.   T = 5:30)

Alla Barocco represents a happy union of baroque elements with one of the purest forms of "pop" music, Folk-Rock. The "pop" feeling is created not only by the dance drums but also by the sophisticated accents found in the active woodwind passages and the brass punctuations. The work is organized in a loose rondo form. (Charles Luedtke, Dr. Martin Luther College)

Chorale and Capriccio (Sc = Robinson.   Pub = SF, 1965.   Gr = 4.   T = 5:30. Rec = SF-Comp., Concert Cacavas)

Chorale and Capriccio is in two movements played as one, beginning with an ostinato "G" which is heard in various registers and in four different guises. The chorale is immediately stated by the brasses in a sonorous and expressive manner. After the introduction of a secondary theme and its development, the first theme is restated. The chorale closes with a full, rich ensemble.

After a short bridge passage for percussion, the capriccio enters, establishing a rather satirical mood. This alternates with fanfare-like brass figures; the entire movement then draws to a triumphant conclusion. (Sam Fox Publishing Company)

Jubilance (Pub = SF, 1971.   Gr = 4.   T = 5:45.   Rec = CR-NBA-78-7, U.S. Navy, Muffley)

People of all times and places have experienced both joy and despair; for all of us there have been times of exultation and of depression. *Jubilance* is Caesar Giovannini's musical portrayal of our happier moments, in uniquely contemporary terms. The music has an insistent drive, a restless energy that speaks especially of the hectic life of the modern world. This impression of unceasing energy is achieved through a lack (though subtle) of a clear structure and by a parade of ideas and themes which hurry by without being logically fulfilled.

The one exception to the general restlessness is the broad, singing melody in the middle of the piece; first in the flutes and clarinets and then in the horns and saxophones. The various percussion instruments are also very prominent, serving to give a kenetic, rhythmic thrust that propels the listener through the piece. *Jubilance* does affirm the optimistic life view. Even in our own day, with all its restlessness and dead ends, man finds reason to rejoice. To rejoice, to jubilate, to energize, each in his own way and for his own reasons. (R. John Specht, Queensborough Community College)

Overture in B-Flat (Sc = Robinson.   Pub = SF, 1966.   Gr = 4.   T = 4:50. Rec = BP-127, West York, PA, Area H.S., Wyand)

The *Overture in B-Flat* is a spirited composition written in a contemporary manner and in one tempo throughout. The opening sounds are those of energetic brass fanfares answered by legato woodwind passages. This is followed by a brief developmental section ending in transitional material which leads to the first thematic statement. (Sam Fox Publishing Company, Inc.)

Sonatina for Band (Sc = Robinson.   Pub = SF, 1969. Gr = 4. T = 9:05. Rec = CR-MID-74-12, Indian Trails Jr. H.S., Addison, IL, Palmer)

The *Sonatina for Band* is a concert work in three movements of symphonic proportions. The thematic materials are subjected to all of the composer's compositional skills emerging in a multi-faceted symphonic structure. Both the composer and scorer have utilized the vocabulary of contemporary music to create a vehicle teeming with kaleidoscopic moods and dramatic tensions—the vigor, humor, lyricism, and, above all, the humanity, make for a significant listening experience. (Harold L. Hillyer, University of Texas at El Paso)

REINHOLD GLIÈRE

(Born in Kiev, Russia, 1875 — Died in Moscow, 1956)

Reinhold Moritzovitch Glière was one of the most influential Russian composers during the transition from Czarist to Soviet Russia. He was a pupil of Taneyev, Arensky, and Ippolitov-Ivanov at Moscow where he was an excellent student, winning a gold medal for composition. He used the folk idioms of the Asiatic national groups within the Soviet Union in a romantic, colorful style and later showed considerable regard for modern techniques in composition. He was extremely prolific, producing operas, ballets, symphonies, symphonic poems, overtures, chamber music, songs, and piano pieces. His most important works included the symphonic poem, *The Sirens,* the *Third Symphony, Ilya Murometz,* and the ballet, *The Red Poppy.* Glière became a professor at the Moscow Conservatory in 1920 and trained two generations of Soviet composers, including Khatchaturian, Miaskovsky, and Prokofiev.

Russian Sailors' Dance from The Red Poppy (Arr = Leidzen. Pub = CF, 1937. Gr = 5. T = 3:00. Rec = CR-ABA-73-6, U.S. Interservice, Stauffer)

The ballet *The Red Poppy* was written in 1927 (revised 1949). It deals with an uprising on board a Chinese ship and the successful intervention of Russian sailors. The *Russian Sailors' Dance* is the best-known excerpt from the ballet, and is founded on the popular Russian folk tune titled "Yablochka" (Little Angel). The dance takes the form of a series of variations on this striking song (Richard Franko Goldman, The Goldman Band)

Symphony No. 3—Ilya Murometz (Arr = Bainum. Pub: 1st mvt = PD, 1958; 2nd mvt = KJ, 1968. Gr = 4; 5. T = 8:30; 7:00. Rec = EX-CR-MID-68-8, Northshore, Bainum)

Glière's colossal *Symphony No. 3* is based upon the legendary tales of a mighty warrior, Ilya Murometz. In the first movement Ilya, the peasant's son, has apparently accomplished nothing for the past thirty years. Two wandering pilgrims, with mystical powers, convince him that he is destined to become a famous warrior. Ilya goes forth seeking the mighty hero Sviatogor, who befriends him and gives him much wise advice before lowering himself into an immense coffin to die, leaving his heroic force to Ilya.

In the second movement, Ilya passes through a dense forest, home of the terrible brigand, Solovei, who has the power to strike men dead by his grotesque imitating of the trilling and twittering of birds. Solovei tries his powers on Ilya, but instead Ilya wounds Solovei with an arrow of glowing iron, ties him to his stirrup and rides away, passing a bevy of wood nymphs whose song is heard through the ever-present singing of the forest birds.

EDWIN FRANKO GOLDMAN

(Born in Louisville, Kentucky, 1878 — Died in New York, 1956)

Edwin Franko Goldman was born in Kentucky where his father was a member of the legal profession and also an amateur musician. His mother was an excellent pianist who, with her brother, had been an inspiration in the early career of John Philip Sousa. When Edwin was nine his father died and it was necessary for the two Goldman boys to enter the Hebrew Orphan Asylum in New York while their mother established herself as a piano teacher. Edwin was very popular with the other students at the orphanage; he learned to play cornet in the band and was also fond of baseball. Later he received a scholarship to the National Conservatory of Music, then under the direction of Antonin Dvořák. By the age of seventeen, Goldman was playing with the Metropolitan Opera Orchestra and had established himself as a virtuoso cornetist. In 1905 he began his career as a conductor, and in 1911 he founded The New York Military Band, which became known as The Goldman Band a few years later. By 1924 the band's summer concerts were being underwritten by the Guggenheim Foundation so that Goldman could concentrate on the musical, not the financial, aspects of the enterprise.

Under Goldman's direction his band became one of the greatest in history. His pioneering of new repertoire and his care in maintaining the highest standards of musical performance have influenced bands throughout the world. His personal visits to schools and colleges during the last twenty years of his life helped raise the standards of bands and band music everywhere. Goldman was a prolific composer as well, with over 100 published marches and many miscellaneous pieces including cornet solos. His influence is still being felt wherever band music is heard.

Chimes of Liberty March (Pub = B3, 1937. Gr = 3. T = 3:00. Rec = NW-266, Goldman Band, R. Goldman; RC-LSP-2687, U.S. Marine, Schoepper; CR-ABA-73-6, U.S. Inter-Service, Harpham)

The year 1937 was a good one for Goldman marches; he wrote eight that year, including *Chimes of Liberty*. Richard Franko Goldman writes that he "doesn't know any 'story' connected with the march, but it has always been an audience favorite." However, like Sousa, many of Edwin Franko Goldman's march titles were patriotic—for example *Builders of America, America Grand March, George Washington, Abraham Lincoln, Freedom Forever,* and *Old Glory Forever* were all written just before or during the early part of World War II. With Italy having invaded Ethiopia in 1935, civil war in Spain in 1936, and Hitler's *Panzer* divisions preparing to invade Czechoslovakia in 1937, Goldman was not the only American who was wondering how long the chimes of liberty would continue to ring in this country.

Jubilee March (Pub = B3, 1937. Gr = 3. T = 3:00. Rec = RC-CAL-125, Goldman; SC-109, S. CA Directors)

Goldman wrote marches out of necessity as well as musical inspiration. The Goldman Band played sixty concerts on successive nights without repeating a program and a large and varied repertory was essential. The *Jubilee March,* written in 1937 to "fill the march spot," is even more popular now than it was in the thirties and forties.

Kentucky March (Sc = Leidzen. Pub = TP, 1949. Gr = 3. T = 3:00)

Goldman was asked by the University of Louisville to compose a march for their band concert in April of 1950. As Goldman was a native of Louisville, he was happy to oblige with the *Kentucky March*. A strain from "My Old Kentucky Home" was used in the trio.

On the Mall March (Sc = Lake. Pub = CF, 1923-38. Gr = 3. T = 3:15. Rec = RC-CAL-125, Goldman; CR-ABA-79-4, U.S. Air Force, Mahan; MG-GI-SRI-75004, Eastman, Fennell)

This march, almost as popular as Sousa's *Stars and Stripes Forever March* was written in 1923 for the dedication of the Elkan Naumburg bandshell in Central Park. Richard Franko Goldman notes that his father "did not think much of the march at that time, and was astonished that it became the most popular of all of his compositions."

RICHARD FRANKO GOLDMAN
(Born in New York City, 1910 — Died in New York City, 1980)

Richard Franko Goldman, composer, conductor, and critic, son of the late Edwin Franko Goldman, represents the third generation of professional musicians in the Goldman and Franko families. Born in New York City in 1910, he was educated in the New York public schools and at Columbia College, from which he graduated with honors in 1930. During the years following his graduation, he studied under a special Columbia Fellowship in Fine Arts and Archaeology. He studied music privately in the United States and abroad, working with Ralph Leopold and Clarence Adler in piano, and Pietro Floridia, Nadia Boulanger, and Wallingford Riegger in theory and composition.

In his position as conductor of the Goldman Band (from 1956 to 1979) Richard Franko Goldman introduced to American audiences many new works for band by leading contemporary composers. Many of these were written at his request and on commission from him, and have been maintained in the band's repertoire since their premier performances. He also helped to revive many historic band works from the eighteenth and nineteenth centuries.

Goldman was chairman of the Theory Department at the Juilliard School of Music from 1946 to 1960, and he also taught conducting, orchestration, and advanced chamber music. He lectured extensively at various universities and from 1968 to 1977 was president of the prestigious Peabody Institute in Baltimore and director of the Peabody Conservatory of Music. He was the author of several books, including: *The Band's Music, The Concert Band, The Wind Band—Its Literature and Technique,* and *Harmony in Western Music.*

Goldman's compositions have been performed by orchestras, bands, ensembles, and soloists throughout the United States, Europe, Japan, and South America. His most popular band marches include *The Foundation, National Band Association* (the official march of the N.B.A.), and *Seaside Park.* He received many honors including honorary doctorate degrees from Lehigh University, University of Maryland, and Mannes College of Music.

The Foundation March (Pub = ME, 1959. Gr = 3. T = 3:30. Rec = FS-LPS-1231, Northwestern Un., Paynter)

Richard Franko Goldman wrote *The Foundation March* in 1958 in appreciation for the support provided for the Goldman Band concerts by The Daniel and Florence Guggenheim Foundation. It was his first march, as he did not wish to write in this form during his father's lifetime. Goldman programmed the march with the National Intercollegiate Band not long after it was written and the members of the band helped to popularize the march throughout the United States. Written in typical march form, *The Foundation March* can be used successfully by both concert and marching bands.

A. CARLOS GOMEZ

(Born in Compinas, Brazil, 1839 — Died in Para, Brazil, 1896)

Antonio Carlos Gomez was a highly talented boy of Portugese descent, and was sent to Milan at an early age, where he received his musical education at the Brazilian government's expense. His claim to fame rests chiefly upon the opera, *Il Guarany*, but he composed other important works, including one each for the Philadelphia Centennial and the Columbian Exposition at Chicago. He received an appointment as director of the conservatory at Pará, Brazil, but death cut short his work there.

Gomez' operas usually have their locale in the composer's native South America. They are spirited and picturesque, if somewhat imitative of Verdi's style. Gomez received unusual recognition of his artistry from the Brazilian government in the issuance of a postage stamp bearing the opening measures of *Il Guarany*. (Carl Fischer, Inc.)

Il Guarany Overture (Arr = Clarke. Pub = CF, 1914. Gr = 5. T = 7:00. Rec = CR-ABA-72-5, U.S. Army, Loboda; CR-ABA-77-1, FL A&M Un., Wilson; CR-ABA-74-9, Sam Houston St. Un., Bynum)

This overture is one of the most brilliant in the repertory of the concert band. Local Brazilian color is obtained by the use of Amazon Indian melodies. The themes of the overture are largely drawn from the opera itself and each has its place in the action. The majestic opening subject accompanies the invocation to the sun god by a wild tribe of Indians called the Aimores. The melody played in octaves by clarinet and bassoon is the one associated with a scene between the hero and heroine in the camp of the Aimores. The broad, expressive melody following later provides the instrumental background for the plotting of Gonzales and his henchmen. Among the other interesting musical passages is a beautiful melody sung by the principal characters as a love-duet in the opera. The overture closes with a shortened version of the invocation to the sun god. (Carl Fischer, Inc.)

FRANÇOIS JOSEPH GOSSEC

(Born in Vergnies, Belgium, 1734 — Died near Paris, 1829)

Gossec is but one of many composers of the Classical Period who have been relegated to the ranks of lesser-known musicians. This unfortunate position did not come about altogether through the inferiority of his musical compositions but as a result of having history view him in the same time period with Haydn, Mozart and later, Beethoven.

Gossec was a choirboy in the Cathedral of Antwerp until he was fifteen and was largely self-taught in composition. At the age of seventeen he went to Paris and through the assistance of Jean Philippe Rameau, became conductor of the private orchestra of Alexandre de la Poupliniere. Eleven years later he became the conductor of the orchestra of the Prince Conti at Chantilly. In addition to serving in various conducting positions, Gossec wrote seventeen operas, twenty-six symphonies, several choral works and many smaller orchestral numbers.

In 1789 a group of forty-five wind and percussion players, gathered together by a young musician named Sarrette, formed the band of the National Guard. A year later the band had increased to seventy members with Gossec as bandmaster and Charles Simon Catel as his assistant. Gossec's interest in the wind band was demonstrated by three symphonies, several marches, and many dignified hymns for choir and winds which he wrote while living in Paris. He introduced clarinets and horns into the opera orchestra and was influential in founding the Paris Conservatory in 1795.

Classic Overture in C (Arr = Goldman-Smith. Pub = ME, 1955. Gr = 4. T = 5:00. Rec = DL-78633, Goldman; CR-CBD-69-4, Un. of Sn. MS, Drake)

This overture (written in 1794-95) is one of the many works of the Classical Period written for the wind band. The wind band had become immensely popular in the revolutionary period of French history and occupied an important place in the many festivals, parades, and rallies held by the revolutionaries. The overture shows the wind band at its best. The tripartite structure is simple and unadorned, without lengthy codas or extended developments. It remains throughout a work of beauty and charm that is thoroughly idiomatic of the group for which it was composed. (Robert Weatherly, Southeastern Louisiana University)

Military Symphony in F (Arr = Goldman-Leist. Pub = ME, 1950. Gr = 3. T = 5:00)

Gossec's *Symphonie Militaire* was written in 1793-94 during the French Revolution for the Band of the National Guard. Writing in the *Journal of Band Research* (Vol.6, No.1), David Swanzy proposes that this work has a fourth movement for choir and band, thus pre-dating Beethoven's choral symphony by a full thirty years. He indicates that "perhaps Gossec should be given credit as the 'father' of the choral symphony."

The first movement of this symphony is spirited and majestic and is written in the key of F—a common key for the period because of the preponderance of brass instruments built in F and restricted to upper partial tones. The second movement is a short, melodic Pastorale in a slow 6/8 meter. The third movement is fast and exciting even though the tonality of C major may seem a bit inconclusive.

LOUIS MOREAU GOTTSCHALK

(Born in New Orleans, Louisiana, 1829 — Died in Rio de Janeiro, Brazil, 1869)

Louis Moreau Gottschalk was the first American composer and performer to gain international recognition. Many contemporary musicians and concertgoers question the validity of his compositions, but few doubt the brilliance of his technique and the emotional effect of his playing. A highly gifted piano virtuoso, Gottschalk adopted many of the mannerisms of Franz Liszt and was highly acclaimed in Europe, South America, and the United States before Lincoln was elected President. During most of the American civil war, he lived with his mother and younger brothers and sisters in Paris, where his home became a mecca for the musicians, writers, and authors of the time.

Gottschalk was born in New Orleans of British and Creole parents who recognized their son's musical ability at an early age. He studied piano in Paris from 1841 to 1846, was refused admittance to the Paris Conservatory, and was composing pieces by the time he was sixteen. Most of his works were rhythmic, often with an Afro-Caribbean flavor, and all were entertaining—especially when played or conducted by the composer. He wrote two operas, two symphonic poems, about twelve songs, and over 100 piano pieces. Because of his popularity as a concert idol, Gottschalk became very wealthy; he just as quickly lost his wealth because of his generosity and extravagant life style. He died of yellow fever in Brazil when he was forty, on the eve of what was to have been his greatest triumph, the première of his symphony and his *Marche Triomphale.*

Tournament Galop (Arr = Boyd; Butler. Pub = SH, 1975; CF, 1976. Gr = 4. T = 3:00. Rec = SH-7, Ithaca Col., Gobrecht)

Few of Gottschalk's 100 or so piano pieces are still performed, although the 1976 bicentennial observance did rekindle an interest in his music. Among those which are still performed are *Tournament Galop, The Banjo, Souvenir de Porto Rico, Danza,* and a sentimental, improvisatory piece titled *The Last Hope.* The *Tournament Galop* seems to be more appropriate for band than piano, although Liszt's galops for piano probably influenced Gottschalk's choice of medium at the time. This exciting band arrangement begins fast and ends even faster; the conductor's instructions for the finale are "Marcato—fast as possible."

MORTON GOULD

(Born in Richmond Hill, New York, 1913)

Morton Gould showed signs of musical talent at a very early age. He began to play the piano when he was four years old, published a composition at the age of six, and was engaged to play piano over radio station WOR when he was seven. He was only eighteen when he joined the musical staff of the Radio City Music Hall. At twenty-one he became conductor and arranger for his own program with a large orchestra over the WOR-Mutual network, leading to the creation of many works which have since been played by the top professional orchestras.

Gould's music freely employs advanced harmonic usages while emphasizing, American themes as evidenced in such works as the four *American Symphonettes* and *A Lincoln Legend.* Band works include *Jericho* (1941), *Ballad* (1946), *Symphony for Band* (1952), *St. Lawrence Suite* (1959), and *Prisms* (1961). He has also composed for musical comedy, television, and motion pictures. His ballet scores include those for Jerome Robbins, George Balanchine, and Agnes de Mille. He has appeared both in this country and Europe as guest conductor, composer, and soloist.

American Salute (Arr = Lang. Pub = MM, 1943. Gr = 4. T = 5:00. Rec = CN-18, Cornell Un., Stith; CR-ABA-79-3, Hardaway H.S., Foster; IL-76, Un. of IL, Begian)

Morton Gould's music is unique in its Americanism and in the seemingly endless wealth of creativity displayed by the composer. Like much of his music, *American Salute* is semi-serious in nature, and reflects Gould's uncanny skill in thematic development. Using only "When Johnny Comes Marching Home Again" for melodic resources, he contrives a brilliant fantasy. Originally written for orchestra and transcribed for band, *American Salute* has become a program favorite for both bands and orchestras.

Ballad for Band (Pub = GS, 1946. Gr = 4. T = 8:10. Rec = CR-NCBDNA-78-2, Un. of WI, Milwaukee, Fennell; MG-GI-SRI-75086, Eastman, Fennell)

The *Ballad for Band* is a one movement work in ABA form. The slow and lyrical first and third sections are contrasted by a faster middle section. The piece has many examples of beautifully scored ninth and thirteenth chords. Gould wrote the composition in 1946 and it was premiered by the Goldman Band the same year.

Jericho Rhapsody (Pub = MM, 1941. Rental = BE. Gr = 5. T = 11:00. Rec = CRE-9010, Un. of IL, Hindsley; RC-LSC-2229, Gould Sym. Band)

The Biblical story of Joshua and the Battle of Jericho is a familiar one. In *Jericho Rhapsody* Gould uses jazz rhythms and modern chords, antiphonal trumpets, and heavy percussion to emphasize the various programmatic episodes. Moving without pause, the rhapsody begins with the Prologue, continues with the Roll Call, Chant, Dance, March and Battle, Joshua's Trumpets, The Walls Came Tumblin' Down, and concludes with a victorious Hallelujah.

Symphony for Band (Pub = GS, 1952. Gr = 5. T = 20:00. Rec = MG-SRI-75094, Eastman, Fennell; BP-131, Sam Houston St. Un., Mills; RC-LSC-2229, Gould Sym. Band)

This symphony was written for the West Point Sesquicentennial celebration at the request of Francis E. Resta of the West Point Academy. It was first performed in 1952, with the composer conducting.

This symphony was written for the West Point Sesquicentennial celebration at the request of Francis E. Resta of the West Point Academy. It was first performed there in 1952, with the composer conducting.

The first movement, Epitaphs, is an elegaic fantasy referring to absent femininity. Its quiet and melodic opening statement of the main theme leads directly into a broad and noble exposition of one of the motifs, becoming a passacaglia based on a martial theme first stated by the tuba. After a series of variations which grow in intensity, the opening lyricism, combined with the passacaglia motif and an allusion to "Taps," make a quiet but dissonant closing to the first movement.

embellishments and rhythmic variations. At the beginning of the movement and in later sections as well, the wind instruments play figures which suggest typical snare drum rhythms. After numerous transformations of the principal marching motive the work ends in a virtuoso coda of martial fanfares and flourishes. (Robert E. Fleming, Youngstown State University)

CHARLES GOUNOD

(Born in Paris, 1818 — Died in Saint-Cloud, France, 1893)

Charles Francois Gounod's father was a talented painter and his mother an accomplished pianist. He received his early musical training from his mother and entered the Paris Conservatory in 1836 where he studied with Halevy, Paer, and Lesueur, obtaining the Grand Prix de Rome for his cantata *Fernand* in 1839. While in Rome he studied the music of the church composers, especially Palestrina, and composed a Mass for three equal voices and orchestra which was performed in 1841. He returned to Paris in 1844, became organist at the Foreign Missions Chapel, and for several years contemplated becoming a priest. However, through the intervention of Madame Viardot, a celebrated singer, Gounod was persuaded to compose an opera on the text of *Sappho* by Emile Augier. From that time on he knew that music would be his life work although most of his early works had experienced little success. From 1852 to 1860 Gounod conducted the Orpheon, a union of choral societies, obtaining valuable knowledge of the voice and its use in choral effects. Later he wrote three oratorios, several Masses, and three Requiems.

Ballet Music from Faust (Arr = Godfrey. Pub = CA, 1918. Gr = 4. T = 18:50. Rec = CL-MS-7415, New York Phil. Orch., Bernstein)

Like many other works famous today, *Faust* was at first received with indifference. Produced first in Paris in 1859, the opera had its New York premiere in

1863. Since that time *Faust* has probably had more productions than any other opera—more than 2,000 performances at the Paris Opera alone. The complete *Ballet Music* from the opera was first arranged for band about 1880 and later became known across the United States through the performances of the Bohumir Kryl Band. Contemporary American bands use either the arrangement by Godfrey or the more recent arrangement by Laurendeau.

The ballet is divided into seven parts as follows: 1. Valse for the Corps de Ballet; 2. Helen and Her Trojan Maidens, and Cleopatra and Her Nubian Slaves; 3. Entry of the Nubian Slaves; 4. Dance of Cleopatra; 5. Entry of the Trojan Maidens; 6. Dance of Helen; and 7. Bacchanale and Entry of Phyrne.

CLAUDIO S. GRAFULLA
(Born in Minorca, 1810 — Died in New York, 1880)

Grafulla was born on the island of Minorca, which is off the coast of Spain; he moved to the United States when he was twenty-eight. He became a member of the Lothiers brass band in New York, which was part of the famed Seventh Regiment Band. As director of that band, he became known nationally; he also became known as a composer and arranger of military music. He served as the regiment's bandmaster for twenty years without salary. Newspapers in Washington and New York frequently referred to the band's skill and to the gifted musicianship of its conductor. Many receptions, weddings, and society balls featured appearances by the regimental band. While best known during his life as an arranger, Grafulla wrote many marches, waltzes, schottisches, and galops. His arrangements were mostly of national and operatic selections by such composers as Balfe, von Suppe, and Rossini. Several years ago many of the works and arrangements of Grafulla's were found in the Library of Congress, in the *Port Royal Band Books,* and recorded with authentic Civil War instruments. More recently, several of his marches were recorded by the Coast Guard Band under the sponsorship of Robert Hoe.

Grafulla was a quiet, unassuming man who never married. His whole life centered around music. The results of his inspired devotion are now beginning to be known and appreciated—a century after his death. (Information from Jon Newsome and Raoul Camus)

Washington Grays March (Arr = Reeves.   Pub = CF, 1905.   Gr = 4.   T = 3:50. Rec = CR-CBDNA-71-7, U.S. Air Force, Gabriel; CR-ABA-73-2, U.S. Army Field, Bierley)

This work has been called a march masterpiece, a band classic, and the father of the concert-type march. It has also been called some uncomplimentary names by band members who have had problems coordinating the tongue and the fingers at the proper tempo. The march shows the German influence stylistically with just the proper balance of melodic and technical passages.

Grafulla wrote *Washington Grays* in 1861, the first year of the American Civil War. This arrangement was made by G.H. Reeves (whose real name was Louis Laurendeau) and published in 1905.

PERCY GRAINGER

(Born in Brighton, Australia, 1882 — Died in White Plains, New York, 1961)

Percy Aldridge Grainger first studied piano with his mother, a professional teacher; later, with Louis Pabst in Melbourne. At the age of ten he gave a series of recitals which financed his study in Germany. In 1900 he first started his career as a concert pianist, with sensational successes in such widely separated places as England, Australia, and South Africa. In 1906 his playing so impressed Grieg that the latter invited him to his home in Norway. They spent the summer of 1907 preparing for the premiere of the *Grieg Concerto* due to be conducted by the composer later that year in Leeds, England. Grieg died before the performance, but Grainger's rendition established him as one of the concerto's great interpreters. He came to America in 1915, winning acclaim for his playing. At the outbreak of World War I he enlisted as an army bandsman (an oboist) soon being promoted to the Army Music School. He became a United States citizen in 1919, and again made many worldwide concert tours. For some time he was professor and head of the music department at New York University. (Carl Fischer, Inc.)

Grainger's position as a relative unknown in the ranks of twentieth century music is difficult to assess. He was a remarkable innovator, using irregular rhythms before Stravinsky, pioneering in folk music collection at the same time as Bartok, writing random music in 1905 and predating Varese in experimentation with electronic music. Possible explanations for his lack of favor include his use of a basically nineteenth century harmonic pallette, lack of compositions in large scale symphonic forms, and his popular reputation as an extraordinary but eccentric pianist and arranger of folk music. However it now seems that the contributions of Grainger are beginning at last to be recognized. For example, Benjamin Britten and Peter Pears have regularly featured his music at their Aldeburgh festivals since 1948. At Yale, in-depth recorded interviews with Grainger's contemporaries, a comprehensive collection of his recordings, and performing materials for wind band used during his guest conducting ventures have been collected.

Grainger's inventiveness in musical composition was occasionally matched in his life style. He was married (to the former Ella Viola Strom, a Swedish poet and actress) in the Hollywood Bowl before 22,000 people during the intermission of a concert. Grainger conducted the first half, which included his *To a Nordic Princess* for his bride, and appeared as soloist in the second half. Ella Grainger has survived her gifted husband and still lives in White Plains, New York, where she devotes her time to the promotion and care of her husband's music. (Keith Brion, Yale University)

Children's March, Over the Hills and Far Away (Rev = Erickson.   Pub = GS, 1933-71.   Gr = 3.   T = 7:00.   Rec = DL-8633, Goldman; CRE-9012, Un. of IL, Hindsley)

In this work, cast in a sunny, care-free mood, the composer has carried into practice certain theories with regard to scoring for the military band. Grainger was of the opinion that it is in the lower octaves of the band and from the larger members of the reed families that the greatest expressivity is to be looked for, and consequently we find in his *Children's March* a more liberal and more highly specialized use of such instruments as the bassoons, English horn, bass clarinet, contra-bassoon, and the lower saxophones than is usual in writing for military band. The march was first performed by the Goldman Band in 1919 and was recorded in its original form by the same band with the composer at the piano. (Richard Franko Goldman, the Goldman Band)

Colonial Song (Pub = CF, 1962. Gr = 4. T = 6:00. Rec = CR-CBDNA-77-2, West VA Un., Wilcox; IL-"Over the Hills," Un. of IL, Begian)

Grainger used no traditional tunes in this piece which was written for and about the people in his native Australia. He expressed the wish to "voice a certain kind of emotion that seems to me not untypical of native-born colonials in general." Concerning colonials he wrote the following:

> Perhaps it is not unnatural that people living more or less alone in vast virgin countries and struggling against natural and climatic hardships (rather than against the more actively and dramatically exciting counter wills of their fellow men, as in more thickly populated lands) should run largely to that patiently yearning, inactive sentimental wistfulness that we find so touchingly expressed in much American art; for instance in Mark Twain's *Huckleberry Finn,* and in Stephen Foster's songs. . . . I have also noticed curious, almost Italian-like, musical tendencies in brass band performances and ways of singing in Australia (such as a preference for richness and intensity of tone and soulful breadth of phrasing over more subtly and sensitively varied delicacies of expression) which are also reflected here.

(Keith Brion, Yale University)

Handel in the Strand (Arr = Goldman. Pub = GA, 1962. Gr = 3. T = 3:35. Rec = IL-32, Un. of IL, Hindsley)

This composition was originally titled *Clog Dance.* A close friend of Grainger's, William Gair Rathbone (to whom the piece is dedicated) suggested the present title because the music seemed to reflect both Handel and English musical comedy—the Strand in London is a street which is the home of English musical comedy. According to Grainger his composition sounded "as if old Handel were rushing down the Strand to the strains of modern English popular music." (Thomas Giles, Mankato State College)

Hill Song No. 2 (Pub = LD, 1950. Gr = 5. T = 4:30. Rec = CR-CBDNA-77-5, Eastman, Fennell)

Grainger's first *Hill Song,* written in 1901, reflected his early interest in wind instruments. In an effort to learn more about band scoring in 1904 he had an agreement with Boosey of London to borrow a different wind instrument each week. The practical results of this interest may be noted in both *Hill Songs* as well as in subsequent works for wind ensembles and bands.

Many of Grainger's compositions were part of a back-to-nature urge. He said that his *Hill Songs* arose out of "thoughts about, and longing for, the wildness, the freshness, the purity of hill-countries, hill-peoples, and hill-musics. . . In a letter to Frederick Fennell, Grainger wrote of a visit to Scotland in 1900:

> I was entranced by the sound of the bagpipe and . . . felt a great urge to weave these fierce nasal sounds into a polyphonic welt. The result was my *Hill Song No. 1,* . . . which consisted of both fast and slow elements. . . . Wishing to write a bagpipe-like hill song that consisted only of fast and energetic elements, I wrote my second *Hill Song* in the period 1901-1907. This time the scoring for twenty-four solo wind instruments was mainly for a mixture of double reeds and single reeds. This is probably the first time in known music that such a large body of solo winds was brought together in chamber music.

Irish Tune from County Derry and *Shepherd's Hey* (Arr = Kent. Pub = CF, 1918-48. Gr = 3-4. T = 3:30-2:15. Rec = CR-CRE-9001, Un. of IL, Begian)

This work is based on a tune collected by a Miss J. Ross of New Town, Limavaday, County Derry, Ireland, and published in *The Petrie Collection of Ancient Music of Ireland* in 1885. Grainger's setting was written in 1909 and was dedicated to the memory of Edward Grieg. The "perfect" melody and the rich sonorities of the arrangement have kept the *Irish Tune* in a favored position for decades. (Carl Fischer, Inc.)

The air on which *Shepherd's Hey* is based was collected by Cecil J. Sharpe. In some agricultural districts in England teams of "Morris Men," decked out with jingling bells and other finery, can still be seen dancing to such traditional tunes as "Shepherd's Hey," which are played on the fiddle or on the "pipe and tabor" (a sort of fife and drum). (Richard Franko Goldman, The Goldman Band)

Lincolnshire Posy (Pub = GS, 1940. Gr = 5. T = 15:00. Rec = MG-75093, Eastman, Fennell; IL-"Over the Hills," Un. of IL, Begian)

As the composer himself has written, this is a "bunch of musical wildflowers" based on folksongs collected in Lincolnshire, England, in 1905-06. Grainger was a picturesque nationalist who tried to retain something of the original flavor of British folk songs and their singers by strict observance of peculiarities of performance such as varying beat lengths and the use of "primitive" techniques such as parallelism.

The first movement, "Lisbon Bay," is a sailor's song in a brisk 6/8 meter with "plenty of lilt." The song is presented several times with changing accompaniment. The second song is entitled "Horkstow Grange," or "The Miser and His Man, a Local Tragedy." The accents shift constantly throughout as the number of quarter notes in a measure changes from four to five to three and back again. The third song, "Rufford Park Poachers," is the longest and most complex of the settings. The instrumentation emphasizes the piccolo in a high register playing with the solo first clarinet three octaves lower. This tune is accompanied by itself in canon by the E-flat clarinet and bass clarinet. It is a unique musical sound and idea.

The fourth song, "The Brisk Young Sailor," is rather simple in contrast to the previous song. The fifth song, "Lord Melbourne," begins in free time, "heavy and fierce." The conductor is instructed to vary his beat lengths as folk singers do. The sixth and last song, "The Lost Lady Found," is the most conventional setting of all. It is in straight 3/4 meter, with usual accompaniment patterns. (Gene Braught, University of Oklahoma) (See May, Sept., and Oct., 1980, *Instrumentalist* for an analysis by Frederick Fennell, Ed.)

The Power of Rome and the Christian Heart (Pub = MM, 1947. Gr = 5. T = 12:00. Rec = CR-CBDNA-77-3, Un. of MD, Gardner)

Grainger described his thoughts concerning this work as follows:

> Just as the early Christians found themselves in conflict with the power of ancient Rome so, at all times and places, the Individual Conscience is apt to feel itself threatened or coerced by the Forces of Authority—and especially in wartime. Men who hate killing are forced to be soldiers, and other men, though not unwilling to be soldiers, are horrified to find themselves called upon to fight in the ranks of their enemies. The sight of young recruits doing bayonet practice in the First World War gave me the first impulse to this composition which, however, is not in any sense program music and does not portray the drama of actual events. It is merely the unfoldment of musical feelings that were started by thoughts of the eternal agony of the Individual Soul in conflict with the Powers That Be.

Ye Banks and Braes O' Bonnie Doon (Pub = GS, 1949. Gr = 2. T = 3:00. Rec = CR-MID-75-15, Lake Highlands H.S., Dallas, TX, Green)

Grainger considered the folksingers the "kings and queens of song. . . lords in their own domain—at once performers and creators." He once described concert singers as slaves to tyrannical composers. It was for the wind band, a "vehicle of deeply emotional expression," that Grainger made some of his most memorable folk song settings, several of which are now cornerstones of band repertoire. "Ye Banks and Braes O' Bonnie Doon" is a slow, sustained Scottish folk tune. Grainger's original setting of this was done in 1901 for "men's chorus and whistlers," and the present version for band was published in 1901. (David Nelson, University of Michigan) (See September, 1981, *Instrumentalist* for an analysis by Frederick Fennell, Ed.)

CLARE GRUNDMAN
(Born in Cleveland, Ohio, 1913)

Clare Ewing Grundman is one of the most prolific and highly respected composers for band on the American scene today. He is represented in one publishers's catalogue with nearly fifty works for band, in addition to other media.

Grundman grew up in Ohio earning both B.S. and M.A. degrees at Ohio State University. From 1937 to 1941 he taught arranging, woodwind, and band at Ohio State and during World War II he was a member of the U. S. Coast Guard. He credits Manley R. Whitcomb with first encouraging him to write for band and Paul Hindemith with providing practical techniques for composition.

Grundman's activities also include scores and arrangements for radio, television, motion pictures, ballet, and Broadway musicals. His arrangements have been used by many well-known entertainers including Carol Channing, Marge and Gower Champion, Sid Caeser, and Victor Borge. He has taken a special interest in composing for school bands, and his works have been performed by school and college bands throughout the country. Some of Grundman's most recent band works include *Norwegian Rhapsody* (1979), *Overture on a Short Theme* (1978), *American Folk Rhapsody No. 4* (1977), and *Tuba Rhapsody* (1976).

American Folk Rhapsody No. 2 (Pub = BH, 1959. Gr = 3. T = 5:00. Rec = BH, Cassette Tape)

Dedicated to Manley Whitcomb and the Florida State University Band, this rhapsody was composed in 1959. American folk tunes included are "Billy Boy," "Skip to My Lou," and "Shenandoah." The form generally followed is that of a short introduction, statement of the folk tunes with variations, and a short but stately coda. (Boosey & Hawkes)

American Folk Rhapsody No. 3 (Pub = BH, 1970. Gr = 3. T = 6:30. Rec = BH-SNBH-5000, FL St. Un., Whitcomb)

As in the first two *American Folk Rhapsodies* Grundman's purpose here was to give a fresh and interesting treatment to some familiar, yet not hackneyed, American songs—songs that have persisted through our history as a nation, and which have improved with age. The first is "Colorado Trail," followed by "Git Along, Little Dogies." Then the poignant ballad, "Careless Love," precedes the lively and more familiar "Turkey in the Straw," a classic barn-dance tune. The *Rhapsody* closes with a reprise of "Careless Love" interspersed with other songs. (Boosey & Hawkes, Inc.)

The Blue and the Gray (Pub = BH, 1961. Gr = 3. T = 9:00. Rec = CR-MID-73-12, Jonesboro, GA, H.S., Creamer)

This suite was written for the centennial observance of the American Civil War. Nearly all of the songs were composed and published during war years except for "The Battle Hymn of the Republic" which was written a few years before and was first popular in southern camp meetings. "The Battle Cry of Freedom" and "Marching Through Georgia" were popular in the North, while "Dixie," "The Bonnie Blue Flag," and "The Yellow Rose of Texas" were whistled, played, and sung by the Confederates. "Kingdom Coming," "Tenting Tonight," and "Aura Lee" were sung and loved by both sides.

Fantasy on American Sailing Songs (Pub = BH, Gr = 3. T = 5:30)

Fantasy on American Sailing Songs was dedicated to the Michigan School Band and Orchestra Association. This lively and robust medley of sailing songs includes "Hornet and Peacock," "Lowlands," "What Shall We Do With a Drunken Sailor?," and "Rio Grande." Each song is clearly stated then effectively developed with appealing melodic and harmonic treatment. (Boosey & Hawkes)

An Irish Rhapsody (Pub = BH, 1971. Gr = 3. T = 6:50. Rec = BH-SNBH-5000, FL St. Un., Whitcomb)

This setting for symphonic band contains six songs of Ireland—some familiar and some which have not been heard often enough. First is "The Moreen" (also called "The Minstrel Boy"), then the ballad, "I Know Where I'm Going," followed by the typical jig tune, "Shepherd's Lamb Reel." The well-loved "Cockles and Mussels" precedes the spirited, "The Rakes of Mallow," which in turn leads into the love song, "Kathleen O' More," presented simply at first, and then accompanied by a jig-reel figure. The coda returns to "Cockles and Mussels" and the tempo broadens as the horns and woodwinds add their countermelodies in an impressive ending. (Boosey & Hawkes)

Two Moods Overture (Pub = BH, 1947. Gr = 3. T = 3)

This overture, well known to bands and audiences in the late 1940's, seems to be making a comeback. The work was written immediately following the composer's discharge from the U.S. Coast Guard in 1946. According to Grundman, the piece "expresses a certain amount of restrained exuberance in two moods—the first meditative and the second more jaunty and buoyant."

ALEXANDRE GUILMANT

(Born in Boulogne, France, 1837 — Died near Paris, 1911)

Guilmant's early musical training was received from his father whom he replaced as church organist at St. Nicholas in Boulogne in 1857. Later he studied with Lemmens in Paris where he inaugurated several new church organs, notably those of St. Sulpice and Notre Dame. Through numerous concert tours in England and America he established himself not only as a virtuoso of first rank, but as the head of the modern French school of organ composers. Guilmant helped establish the Schola Cantorum where he became professor of organ and he also taught at the Paris Conservatory. His works include twenty-five sets of pieces in various styles, two symphonies for organ and orchestra, and many pieces for liturgical use.

Morceau Symphonique—Trombone Solo (Arr = Shepard. Pub = PO, 1966. Gr = 4/5. T = 6:00. Rec = CR-RE-7001, Falcone, Solo)

Morceau Symphonique, as the title implies, is intended as a "bit" or a "piece" of something symphonic for the trombone. Guilmant was basically a composer for organ, but in this contribution to wind instrument literature he exhibits an unusual command of idiomatic writing for trombone. Exploring the extremes of expressive legato and powerful staccato, this composition has now become a recognized standard for the legitimate solo trombonist.

The work is divided into two sections—an expressive Andante sostenuto and a rhythmic Allegro moderato. A brief reminder of the opening theme is heard near the end, and the solo concludes in a brilliant flourish of scales and arpeggios. The work is definitely romantic, yet it exhibits a conservative style in its chromatic changes. It explores the complete range of the instrument, and it is only the advanced trombonist who finds success in an artistic performance of this composition. (Hubert Henderson, University of Maryland)

In a survey of 273 members of the National Association of the Schools of Music in 1971-72, Merrill Brown found that this solo was the second most highly-performed piece for both trombone and euphonium. (Ed.)

Prelude and Allegro (Arr = Hubbell. Pub = FE, 1977. Gr = 3. T = 4:40. Rec = CR-78-6, South Lyon, MI, Centennial Middle Sch., Kochalko)

The opening section of this work is written in a sustained manner at a moderate tempo with a decrease in volume as the movement ends. The Allegro section is much more rhythmic with important articulations required of the performers. The arranger has scored only two parts for the sections which are usually arranged for first, second, and third parts. The result is a cleaner, lighter sound than many works of this level.

R.B. HALL

(Born in Bowdoinham, Maine, 1858 — Died in Portland, Maine, 1907)

Robert Browne Hall inherited his love of music from his mother who played the piano and the violin, and from his father who played the cornet. His father gave young Hall his first instrumental lessons—on E-flat cornet—and the boy made rapid progress. At the age of eighteen he was solo cornetist with a summer band at Old Orchard, Maine, and at twenty-four he shared the solo cornet chair with Alessandro Liberati in the famous Baldwin Cadet Band of Boston. Although Hall studied with several teachers, he was especially grateful for the help he received from Melvin Andrews of Bangor, Maine. One of Hall's early marches, *M.H.A.,* was dedicated to Andrews. Many of Hall's early marches were lost, but of the over 200 which he wrote, sixty-two were published; some selling for as little as five dollars. Several of his marches became so popular in England that many people thought he was a native of that country. Actually, his health was never good, and he apparently never traveled far from the New England area. He conducted bands in Richmond, Maine, which he considered his home town; Waterville and Bangor, Maine; and Albany, New York—with considerable success in each instance. Hall's most popular marches include *New Colonial, Independentia, Officer of the Day, S.I.B.A.,* and *Tenth Regiment.* (Information from Thomas C. Bardwell, Vineyard Haven, Massachusetts)

New Colonial March (Pub = JC/TP, 1901. Gr = 3. T = 2:45. Rec = PO-2383-302, H.M. Royal Marines, Mason)

This march is usually found on any list of "best" or "most popular" marches. Audiences, band members, and conductors all appreciate its singable melodies and countermelodies and appreciate the fact that it was obviously written by a gifted musician who knew how to write for the various instruments. *New Colonial* has been played for military reviews and concerts in England for so long that it is often mistaken for an English march.

S.I.B.A. March (Pub = CF, 1895. Gr = 3. T = 2:15)

This march is dedicated to the Southern Illinois Band Association and was published by Fischer in 1895. Although it is not known if Hall visited the Mid-west, the members of the band association obviously knew of his excellent reputation. This is a march that sounds fine with a large symphonic or marching band, but was written so that even a six to sixteen piece town band could still play all the parts.

Tenth Regiment March (Pub = CF, 1897. Gr = 3. T = 3:15. Rec = CR-4073, Ithaca Col., Beeler)

Hall dedicated this march to the Tenth Regiment Band of Albany, New York, presumably while he was conductor of that band. He had been invited to Albany for the specific purpose of reorganizing the regimental band—in which he was very suc cessful—and he continued to compose while he was there. In 1901 the management of the Pan-American Exposition at Buffalo, New York, invited twenty-two of the finest bands in the country (including the bands of Sousa, Brooke, and the Canadian 48th Highlanders) to provide continuous music at the exposition. One of the highlights of Hall's career came with the invitation for his Tenth Regiment Band to perform with the nation's best at the exposition.

The *Tenth Regiment March* is so widely played in England and Europe that it has received another title, *Death or Glory.* (Information from Robert Hoe, Jr., Poughkeepsie, New York)

GEORGE FRIDERIC HANDEL
(Born in Halle, Germany, 1685 — Died in London, 1759)

Handel was a compatriot of Johann Sebastian Bach, although the two never met, and shares with him the distinction of bringing the "baroque" era to a close. Unlike Bach, Handel was a cosmopolitan composer who added to his German heritage a firsthand knowledge of Italian, English, and French style. His travel and his personality made it possible for him to cope with many temperamental operatic performers, but did not keep him from being involved in endless conflicts with managers and his public.

Handel was somewhat of a musical prodigy although his father was bitterly opposed to any musical training until, during a visit to Duke Johann Adolf's residence, he was made to realize (by the duke) that young Handel was extremely gifted and deserved the opportunity to take music lessons. After studying organ, oboe, and harpsichord as well as counterpoint and fugue with Friederich Zachow in his native city of Halle, he assumed the position as assistant organist at the age of twelve. Following his father's wishes, Handel began the study of law but quit when he was eighteen, went to Hamburg and became associated with opera. In 1706 he went to Italy where he became successful as a composer of Italian opera and dramatic oratorios, learning much at the same time from Scarlatti, Corelli, and Pasquini. In 1710 he returned to Germany as court conductor (in Hanover), but left the same year for England and with the exception of a year or two, lived the remaining fifty years of his life in London.

From that time on Handel was occupied with teaching, directing the English Royal Academy of Music, composing, presenting operas, and traveling. He knew triumph and disappointment, financial security and bankruptcy, excellent physical health and extreme illness during his life in England. His principal compositional area was that of opera until 1741, when, finally realizing he could not stop the decline of Italian opera in England, he turned to the composition and production of oratorios. He wrote over forty operas, a huge number of other vocal forms such as anthems, masques, cantatas, and vocal ensembles and solos, but he achieved lasting fame with one of his twenty-seven oratorios, *The Messiah*. He also was a prolific composer of instrumental compositions including concerto grossi, harpsichord suites, organ concerti, chamber music for strings, winds, and keyboard, and large orchestral works. He has been credited with setting the form which has ruled oratorio and cantata in English-speaking countries for the last two hundred years.

Concerto Grosso, Op. 6—Two Flutes and Clarinet (Arr = Malin. Pub = MP, 1952. Gr = 4. T = 12:45. Rec, Allegro = UN-6-1972, Un. of NE, Lentz)

Originally written for two solo violins and cello, this work is one of twelve grand concertos by Handel. The opening and closing Allegro movements display both tonal beauty and technique of the solo flutes and clarinet. The middle section, Largo, though brief, adds color and effects captured by Malin in this transcription for concert band.

Unlike most Baroque concertos which were written for performance as separate entities at public concerts or for private concerts of the wealthy and noble, the twelve grand concertos were written to provide musical interludes between the sections of large choral works. Each concerto, including this one, was written in one day (in the fall of 1739) and was advertised for sale at Handel's home by an ad in the *London Daily Post*.

Royal Fireworks Music (Arr = Hindsley; Mackerras & Baines; Sartorius. Pub = HI, ms.; OX, 1960; MP, 1942. Gr = 5. T = 15:00-21:00. Rec = IL-46, Un. of IL, Hindsley; TE-5030, Cleveland Sym. Winds, Fennell; VA-S-289, Mackerras Ens.)

Handel's *Royal Fireworks Music* was composed in 1749 for a mammoth festival proclaimed by King George II to celebrate the Peace of Aix-la-Chapelle following the war of the Austrian succession. In the outdoor setting of Green Park a large wooden building was erected with broad wings and a huge musicians' gallery. On it were figures of Mars and Neptune and above, a bas relief of King George handing Peace to Britannia. Amid the splendid setting, Handel's music was to be the feature attraction, followed by a tremendous display of fireworks. The performance of the music was accorded with great acclaim and was followed by cannon and ordnance shots, but the fireworks proved fitful and erratic. In the grand finale the entire building was set on fire and burned to the ground, enraging the King whose image crumbled and fell in flames. Only Handel's reputation remained unscathed, for the music brought him a governorship and the lasting favor of the King.

Like the *Water Music* this work was scored for a large wind band consisting of forty trumpets, twenty French horns, sixteen oboes, sixteen bassoons, eight pairs of kettle drums, flutes, fifes, and a serpent. In this edition for the modern wind band, the work has been arranged in concerto grosso with small and large groups. (John Paynter, Northwestern University)

Water Music Suite (Arr = Harty & Duthoit; Kay. Pub = CA, 1929-43; TP, 1950. Gr = 4. T = 13:00-17:00. Rec = MG-75005, London Sym., Dorati; AN-S-36173, Bath Festival Orch., Menuhin; GC-The Revelli Years, Un. of MI, Revelli)

Shortly after the accession of George I to the English throne, Handel was requested to compose some music for the occasion of an aquatic festival given by the King. This festival was held August 22, 1715, on the River Thames. For the occasion Handel wrote a suite of twenty-odd pieces which were performed by a band of musicians under his direction. It is interesting to note that he composed the music for a group of wind instruments. Thus, we may regard the suite as an original band work. The musicians were seated upon a barge immediately following that of the King, and played continuously during the voyage from Limehouse to Whitehall.

The Allegro makes use of the concerto grosso principle of alternating between a larger body of instruments (concerto) and a smaller body (concertino). The familiar, graceful Air, with its characteristically baroque dotted rhythm, is divided into two main sections, the first beginning with woodwinds, the second with brass. Each element of the first section is repeated before going on to subsequent material, giving a total pattern of AABBAB. (Charles H. Luedtke, Dr. Martin Luther College)

HOWARD HANSON

(Born in Wahoo, Nebraska, 1896 — Died in Rochester, New York, 1981)

Howard Hanson is one of the most important figures in the American music world. He has exerted widespread influence as a composer, conductor, and educator. Born in Wahoo, Nebraska, in 1896, Hanson studied music at Luther College, at the Institute of Musical Art (Juilliard School of Music) in New York, and at Northwestern University. At the age of twenty, he accepted an appointment as dean of the Conservatory of Fine Arts, College of the Pacific in San Jose. In 1921 he was the first composer to enter the American Academy in Rome, having won its Prix de Rome. Upon his return to the United States in 1924, he became the director of the Eastman School of Music, a position he held until 1964. In 1936 he was elected to membership in the National Institute of Arts and Letters in New York, and in 1938 to fellowship in the Royal Academy of Music in Sweden. In 1944 he received the Pulitzer Prize for his *Symphony No. 4*. In 1945 he won the Ditson Award, followed in 1946 by the George Foster Peabody Award, and in 1951 by the Award of Merit of the Alumni Association of Northwestern University. He holds thirty-six honorary doctorates from American colleges and universities, in addition to many other honors and distinctions received both in this country and abroad.

Hanson's major works include his opera, *Merry Mount*, six symphonies, many choral and chamber works. Among his principal works for band are *March Carillon, Dies Natalis, Young Person's Guide to the Six-Tone Scale,* and *Laude.* Hanson's style is romantic, tonal (although enhanced by euphonious dissonances), with asymmetric rhythms at times, and a preference for the low instrument registers. He explains his compositional practices, as well as those of other contemporary composers, in his theoretical treatise, *Harmonic Materials of Modern Music: Resources of the Tempered Scale.*

Chorale and Alleluia (Pub = CF, 1955. Gr = 4. T = 5:20. Rec = MG-50084, Eastman, Fennell; BP-125, AR Polytech. Col., Witherspoon; FAMU-ABA-77, FI A&M Un., Fennell)

Chorale and Alleluia was completed in January, 1954, and is Hanson's first work for symphonic band. It was given its premiere on February 26, 1954, at the convention of the American Bandmasters Association at West Point with William Santelmann, leader of the U.S. Marine Band, conducting.

The composition opens with a fine flowing chorale. Soon the joyous "Alleluia" theme appears and is much in evidence throughout. A bold statement of a new melody makes its appearance in the lower brasses in combination with the above themes. The effect is one of cathedral bells, religious exaltation, solemnity, and dignity. The music is impressive, straightforward, and pleasingly non-dissonant. Its resonance and sonority are ideally suited to the medium of the modern symphonic band. (Carl Fischer, Inc.)

Merry Mount Suite (Arr = Garland. Pub = CF, 1964. Gr = 4. T = 9:30. Rec = CR-MID-70-14, North Hills H.S., Pittsburgh, Strange)

Merry Mount is an opera based on Nathaniel Hawthorne's short story, *The Maypole of Merry Mount*. Hawthorne's story has an historical basis in conflict between the Puritans and Cavaliers, which in recently-settled New England resulted in the conflict between the settlers of Plymouth and the Cavalier group led by Thomas Morton, who had established Merry Mount at what is now Quincy, Massachusetts. Hanson's score reflects the modal quality inherent in the music of that time as we are given musical portrayals of the somber religiosity of the Puritans as opposed to the carefree gaity of the Cavaliers, shown in their maypole revels. (Harold Hillyer, University of Texas at El Paso)

JOHANNES HANSSEN
(Born in Ullensaker, Norway, 1874 — Died in Oslo, 1967)

Johannes Hanssen was one of Norway's most active and influential bandmasters, composers, and teachers during the first fifty years of the twentieth century. He was born in Ullensaker, a small town near Oslo, and played in a military band in Oslo as a young boy. His principal teachers were Gustav Lange and Catharinus Elling. He was bandmaster of the Oslo Military Band from 1926 to 1934 and from 1945 to 1946. He also taught music theory for several years and wrote a theory text titled *Practical Music Handbook*. Hanssen received many honors in his lifetime including the King's Order of Merit in Gold and King Haakon VIII's Jubilee Medal. He was an honorary member of the Norwegian Musicians' Association and was chairman of the Oslo Music Association. During his long life as an instructor for various boys' and amateur bands, Hanssen composed many works. His principal compositions for band are *Valdres March, Østerdal Rhapsody, Norwegian Bridal March, Festival March,* and *Bear Dance.* (Information from Oslo University Library)

Valdres March (Arr = Bainum. Pub = BH, 1963. Gr = 4. T = 3:25. Rec = RC-Int-CL-40024, King's Guard, Norway, Nöddelund; CR-MENC-80-24, U.S. Army, Morlan; SD-VIII, Augustana Col., Lillehaug)

Hanssen began writing this march in 1901, but it was not completed until 1904. After the premier performance, during an open air band concert in Oslo, the composer (who was playing in the band) heard only two people applaud—his two best friends. Later he sold the march to a publisher for twenty-five Kroner; about five dollars. Today the march is popular with bands and audiences around the world.

The title has both a geographical and musical reference. Valdres is that region in Norway which is just north of the halfway point on the train ride between Oslo and Bergen—one of the most beautiful regions on earth. The first three measures in

Valdres March contain the old signature fanfare for the Valdres Battalion, which is based on an ancient lur melody (the lur, or lure, in this instance was a straight wooden trumpet, long enough that the player could play from the third to the sixth partial—the same range used by modern amateur buglers). Other melodies in the march suggest folksongs and in the Trio a characteristic trait of Norwegian music— the drone bass—is heard beneath a simple tune based on the pentatonic scale. Hanssen's march is a charming and inspiring masterpiece in miniature. (Information from Egil Gundersen, Skien, Norway)

WALTER HARTLEY
(Born in Washington, D.C., 1927)

Walter S. Hartley studied composition at the Eastman School of Music from which he holds B.M., M.M., and Ph.D. degrees. While at Eastman he studied with Bernard Rogers and Howard Hanson. He is one of America's more prolific composers with over one hundred works to his credit. In addition to *Sinfonia No. 4,* Hartley's most popular works for band include the *Concerto for Twenty-three Winds* (1957). He began writing for winds during his student days and has continued to produce instrumental solo and ensemble works of outstanding value.

Hartley has taught piano and theory at the National Music Camp, was chairman of the music department at David and Elkins College in West Virginia, and is currently a professor of theory and composition at State University College, Fredonia, New York. His three most recent band works are *Symphony No. 2, Concertino for Tenor Saxophone,* and *Sinfonia No. 5.*

Concerto for Twenty-three Winds (Pub = ACC, 1957. Gr = 6. T = 16:00. Rec = CR-ABA-72-4, Un. of TX Austin, Reynolds)

Hartley composed this work for the Eastman Wind Ensemble in 1957 and it was premiered by that group during the Eastman School's annual Festival of American Music in 1958. Hartley sent the following comments to conductor Frederick Fennell concerning the *Concerto:*

> The work is in four movements roughly corresponding to those of the classical symphony or sonata in form, but it is textually more related to the style of the Baroque concerto, being essentially a large chamber work in which different soloists and groups of soloists play in contrast with each other and with the group as a whole. The color contrasts between instruments and choirs of instruments are sometimes simultaneous, sometimes antiphonal; both homophony and polyphony are freely used, . . . The first and last movements make the most use of the full ensemble; the second, a Scherzo, features the brass instruments, the slow third movement, the woodwinds. The harmonic style is freely tonal throughout. There is a certain three-note motif (ascending G-A-D) which is heard harmonically at the beginning and dominates the melodic material of the last three movements.

(Frederick Fennell, Eastman School of Music)

Sinfonia No. 4 (Pub = MC, 1967. Gr = 6. T = 10:00. Rec = MA-MM-1116, St. Un. Col., Fredonia, Hartman)

Sinfonia No. 4 was commissioned by Frank Battisti and the members of the Ithaca High School Concert Band and was first performed in May, 1966. The work was composed during the previous year while the composer was on sabbatical leave in Great Britain and Europe. Hartley described the composition as follows:

> The *Sinfonia,* in four movements, is written in condensed classical forms of the rondo type, contrasting in tempo; each movement is designed in its own way to exploit the various facets of the modern wind-percussion ensemble in line and color. There is much antiphonal writing between the choirs, many solo passages for a wide variety of instruments, and a general reliance on pure colors with little doubling (except for voices at the octave). The style is tonal (with free dissonance frequently producing bitonal effects) with a constant opposition of chordal and contrapuntal textures. The last two movements are lighter in mood than the first two, especially the finale, which is almost but not quite a march.

Reviewing the work in the April, 1968, edition of *The Instrumentalist,* John Paynter wrote:

> Walter Hartley has been uniquely successful in creating new ways of expressing himself with the traditional forms of scales, chords, and instruments, while preserving his self-esteem and the respect of musicians. Far from being a traditionalist, his music manages to sing, to disturb, to laugh, and to emote afresh in a vocabulary that intrigues without offending . . . Particularly noteworthy are the numerous solo passages, the tasty writing for percussion, and the overall compactness of the music that could hardly be titled other than "Sinfonia."

KOH-ICHI HATTORI

(Born in Yamagata, Japan, 1933)

From the North Country (Pub = ON, 1967; BH, 1971. Gr = 3. T = 5:00)

From the North Country was composed at the request of the All Japan Band Association in 1967. It was used that year as a required work for junior high school bands in the All Japan Band Contest.

Hattori has used some folk song melodies from his native Yamagata Prefecture, an area some 300 miles north of Tokyo, in this "north country" overture. An example is played by the trumpets at the beginning after a two-bar percussion introduction. A quiet middle section, Lento expressivo, provides contrast by using the darker woodwind and horn qualities and a most unusual (for Western ears) folk melody in the clarinets. A return to the opening allegro con brio tempo concludes the overture.

FRANZ JOSEPH HAYDN

(Born in Rohrau, Austria, 1732 — Died in Vienna, 1809)

Franz Joseph Haydn was born in a lowly peasant cottage, the son of Matthias and Maria Haydn. He was the second of twelve children and showed signs of musical ability at a very early age. When he was five, young Haydn was sent to live with a distant relative, Johann Frankh, who taught the boy elementary rudiments of music. He joined the St. Stephen's boys choir when he was eight and remained with the group until his voice began to change some nine years later. He was turned out into the street, destitute and starving, but he managed to survive by becoming a street musician, singing under windows, playing at taverns, and giving lessons to children.

After several more years of hardship Haydn gradually became recognized for his compositions and in 1761, when he was twenty-nine, he was hired by the wealthy Prince Esterhazy as his private music master—a position he kept for nearly thirty years. During this time he composed most of his symphonies, quartets, trios, and wind ensemble works. In 1790 the British impresario, Johann Peter Salomon, visited Haydn and persuaded him to visit London and conduct six new symphonies. His stay in England lasted over a year and he returned to Vienna a wealthy and famous musician. Haydn composed two great oratorios, *The Seasons* and *The Creation,* after he was sixty-five.

Unlike Mozart, Haydn began composing concertos in his youth. After he joined the Esterhazy household many of his concertos were written to display the virtuosity of some of the court musicians, especially Thaddaus Steinmuller (horn), Joseph Weigl (cello), and Luigi Tomasini (violin). The only concertos from Haydn's mature years were written for cello, piano, toy organ, and finally (in 1796), the trumpet. The trumpet concerto has been described as Haydn's most perfect concerto, a work of art by a master craftsman.

Concerto for Trumpet (Arr = Duthoit   Pub = CA, 1948.   Gr = 3/4,   T = 14:30. Rec = IL-23, John Haynic w. Un. of IL, Hindsley)

Haydn's concerto marked an important stage in the development of the trumpet. For several decades the use of the instrument had declined from its position of greatness during the baroque "golden age of brass." The baroque trumpet was limited by its lack of valves to the natural harmonics of the upper register and it remained for Anton Weidinger, a trumpeter in the Viennese court, to invent a trumpet with keys which could play a chromatic scale. Haydn wrote the concerto for Weidinger in 1796 and the trumpeter-inventor is credited with the first performance by a program which may be seen in the Kunsthistorisches Museum in Vienna.

Typical of the period the first movement has two expositions, the first of which is performed by the accompaniment. Near the end of the movement the soloist is allowed to express himself with a cadenza, either original or "borrowed." The andante second movement demonstrates the romantic sound of the trumpet and the finale combines rondo and sonata forms in a skillful and climactic manner. This work, written at the zenith of Haydn's compositional period, has been described as his "most perfect concerto."

Orlando Palandrino Overture (Arr = DeRubertis.   Pub = RE, 1938,   Gr = 3. Rec = VA-71126, Vienna Fest. Orch., Janigro)

Written for one of Haydn's largely unknown nineteen operas, this overture nevertheless demonstrates his ability as a mature composer. Written in abridged symphonic first movement form, there is no development section between the exposition and the recapitulation. However, he has taken a minimum of melodic material and expanded it through use of motivic variation and modulation to distant keys—techniques usually reserved for the development. It is interesting that Haydn, whom we consider the father of classical form, so frequently "breaks" the rules of form that we attribute to him! (Mary Arthur, Fond du Lac, Wisconsin)

St. Anthony Divertimento (Arr = Wilcox. Pub = GS, 1965. Gr = 3. T = 11:00. Rec = MAC-S-9087, Vienna Wind Sym.)

This transcription of a suite for an octet of wind instruments adds a fascinating composition to the repertoire of the modern concert band. Between 1780 and 1800 Haydn wrote, and later revised, this most famous of six *Feldpartiten* (suites to be played in the open) for the military band of Prince Esterhazy. It was originally for two oboes, two horns, three bassoons, and a serpent—an obsolete bass cornet built in the shape of a snake. The second movement is an adaptation of an old Austrian pilgrims' song, and was used by Brahms nearly a hundred years later as the theme for his *Variations on a Theme of Haydn, Opus 56.* Karl Geiringer, in *Haydn, A Creative Life in Music,* pointed out the close melodic relationships among the four movements; three of them are really variations on the second movement, the *St. Anthony Choral.* In form and style the four movements follow the traditional classical symphony except that the work is technically unpretentious and comparatively short. (James Wilcox, Southeastern Louisiana University)

HERBERT HAZELMAN

(Born in Topton, North Carolina, 1913)

Herbert Hazelman has combined a long and distinguished career as a band director with those of a composer of works for band and orchestra and a professional photographer. He received his education in his home state, earning B.A. and M.A. degrees from the University of North Carolina at Chapel Hill and an M.E. degree from the University of North Carolina at Greensboro. Lamar Stringfield was his principal conducting and composition teacher. Hazelman is presently coordinator of instrumental music in the Greensboro Public Schools.

Hazelman's principal compositions for band include *A Short Ballet for Awkward Dancers, Dance Variations on an Obscure Theme, Gallic Galop,* and *Dance for Three.* He also composes for orchestra. Hazelman has received the Benjamin Restful Music Commission from the North Carolina Symphony Orchestra, and is a member of several national professional fraternal and service organizations. His favorite hobbies include model trains, cabinet making, golf, and traveling.

A Short Ballet for Awkward Dancers (Pub = TE, 1966. Gr = 4. T = 5:40)

As might be suspected from the title, this work is pure satire to be performed tongue-in-cheek. The first movement, March for Two Left Feet, is played in a strict march cadence except for the occasional measures which lack one-half beat. The jerky rhythm which results is remindful of the awkward marcher who is constantly skipping steps in an attempt to stay in step with his cohorts. The second movement, Waltz for People with Slipped Discs, is a lugubrious solo for trombones complete with smears, slides, pedal tones, and other comic effects of which that noble instrument is capable.

The third movement, Twelve Tone Rag, is built on three twelve-tone rows, one serving as a basso ostinato line, another for afterbeats, and the third for the melody. The bounce section is performed in the style employed by most dance bands in the late 1920's. The final movement, Four-Footed Galop, moves with reckless abandon and closes with a resounding crash from the percussion section. (Shawnee Press, Inc.)

J.C. HEED

(Born in Hackettstown, New Jersey, 1862 — Died in Newark, New Jersey, 1908)

John Clifford Heed, known as the "March Wizard," had a brief but productive career as composer, arranger, and performer. During the post-Civil War years of his boyhood, bands and band music flourished in hundreds of northern and midwestern towns. Heed joined the newly formed Hackettstown Cornet Band at the age of nine or ten and in a few years became the group's director. In addition to cornet, he also played the piano, the violin, and most of the other wind instruments. This performance experience proved extremely helpful in later years when he was composing for a variety of instruments and instrumental groups. Heed never received any formal instruction in composition although a professor of music in the area, Charles Grobe, may have assisted him with some music theory and in the practical business of getting his works published—beginning in 1881.

Heed became director of the George Herrick's Band in Providence, Rhode Island, at the age of seventeen. From about 1886 to 1891 he lived in Worcester, Massachusetts, where he taught music, performed in local groups, composed, and became married. In 1891 he went to Newark, New Jersey, to accept a position as solo cornetist with the famous national guard group known as Voss' First Regiment Band. During the 1890's Heed's musical career flourished, but the turn of the century brought a change in his fortune; he contracted tuberculosis and died in a Newark hospital in 1908. Heed's compositions included four overtures, several cornet solos, a number of polkas and schottisches, and more than sixty marches. His best known marches are *In Storm and Sunshine, Regimental Pride, Metronome,* and *Clipper.* (Information from Robert Hoe, Jr., Poughkeepsie, New York)

In Storm and Sunshine March (Pub = FI, 1905; CF, 1973. Gr = 4. T = 2:30. Rec = CR-ABA-77-1, FL A&M Un., White; MG-50360-SR90360, Eastman, Fennell)

In Storm and Sunshine was written in 1885, when the compser was twenty-three; it was published that same year by the Squire Publishing Firm and in 1905 was published by Fillmore Brothers. Although nearly all of Heed's sixty-plus marches were written after this march, it has remained the most popular to the present time. *In Storm and Sunshine* has all the ingredients for a great march: a strong, attention-getting introduction; dynamic contrast from fff down to a bar of silence; technical melodies for both treble and bass instruments; and a melody in the last strain that everyone can remember. Whether Heed had the circus in mind when he wrote this march is not known, but it has been a big-top favorite, as well as a concert highlight, for most of the twentieth century.

JERRY HERMAN

(Born in New York City, 1933)

Jerry (Gerald) Herman is one of Broadway's most talented and successful composer-lyricists. In 1964, he won a Tony Award and both of Variety's "Best Composer" and "Best Lyricist" awards for his work in *Hello, Dolly!* The following year he was selected by the U.S. Junior Chamber of Commerce as one of the nation's "Ten Outstanding Young Men."

Herman is a native New Yorker. His father owned a children's camp and his mother taught school. He began piano study at an early age, attended schools in New York, and graduated from the University of Miami in 1954 with a degree in drama. His first musical, *I Feel Wonderful*, was produced in New York the same year. After a year in the armed forces Herman returned to New York and began writing for a variety of performers including Garry Moore, Jane Froman, and Tallulah Bankhead. In 1960, Herman became the only lyricist-composer to have three musicals on Broadway. In recent years he has received additional honors, including two Grammy Awards, Drama Critics Circle Award, and the Order of Merit from the University of Miami. In addition to *Hello, Dolly!* and *Mame*, Herman's other most popular musicals are *Dear World, Mack and Mabel,* and *The Grand Tour.*

Highlights from Hello, Dolly! (Arr = Cacavas; Lang. Pub = EB, 1964; 1969. Gr = 3. T = 6:00-8:00)

The musical comedy, *Hello, Dolly!,* was based on a book by Michael Stewart, suggested by Thornton Wilder's play, *The Matchmaker.* Jerry Herman wrote both lyrics and music, Gower Champion directed and choreographed the show, and Carol Channing starred in the opening production in 1964. Based on an old-fashioned concept that people come to the theater for entertainment, not lectures, "Dolly" became a resounding hit, earning $8,000,000 on an original investment of $350,000.

The story reaches back to New York in 1898. Dolly Levi, the widow of a dry goods merchant, becomes a marriage broker. Working on a deal to find a wife for wealthy Horace Vandergelder, she decides to win him herself. She arranges for Vandergelder to take her to her favorite restaurant, the Harmonia Gardens, where the employees welcome her back with the uproarious title song. After various distractions, Van finally proposes, is accepted, and the curtain falls.

In 1967 the show was presented with an all-Negro cast starring Pearl Bailey and Cab Calloway, and again "Dolly" was a smashing success.

Highlights from Mame (Arr = Krance. Pub = EB, 1966. Gr = 4. T = 9:00)

Before *Mame* became one of Broadway's most successful musicals of the middle 60's, it scored first as a novel, then a Broadway play, then a movie starring Rosalind Russell. Embellished with songs, dances, beautiful settings, and stunning performances by Angela Lansbury, the Broadway musical was described by a Variety critic as "the whopping musical-comedy hit that everybody has been waiting for. . .a song and dance block buster."

In the show, Mame is a delightful, egocentric, and boisterous lady who suddenly inherits an orphaned nephew, Patrick Dennis. The play moves through the years 1928 to 1946 and Mame attempts to fit Patrick into her crazy scheme of life. After a period of financial depression in the early thirties, Mame marries a wealthy southerner, who is killed while on a skiing expedition in the Alps. By now, Patrick is a young man, he marries the right girl, after getting involved with the wrong one, and the show finally ends with Mame preparing to take their young son on a trip around the world.

Included in this arrangement by John Krance are the five top tunes from the show: "Open a New Window," "If He Walked Into My Life," "My Best Girl," "We Need a Little Christmas," and, of course, "Mame."

RALPH HERMANN

(Born in Milwaukee, Wisconsin, 1914)

Ralph J. Hermann began studying piano at an early age. Before the age of fourteen he played professionally with local theater and dance bands and made a series of guest appearances with symphony orchestras in and around Milwaukee. Subsequently his attention turned to composition and with this in mind, he studied virtually all of the instruments, later receiving a formal education in composition at New York's Juilliard School of Music with Vittorio Giannini. During World War II he served two years with the Army Air Corps and one year with the Infantry as the musical director of Gen. Bradley's 12th Army Orchestra. Upon returning to New York he embarked upon a career which included membership with Toscanini's NBC Orchestra and with Paul Whiteman's Orchestra, engagement as an arranger, composer, and conductor with the National Broadcasting Company and later with the American Broadcasting Company.

Hermann has arranged for such famous orchestras as Percy Faith's and Andre Kostelanetz' and for such popular radio and television shows as the *Hit Parade*, *Jackie Gleason Show*, and *Show of Shows*. Considered an outstanding contemporary American composer for symphony orchestra and chamber ensemble as well as concert band, Ralph Hermann has continued as radio and television arranger and more recently as arranger-conductor for the *Super Circus* television productions in New York City.

Ballet for Young Americans (Pub = PD, 1956. Gr = 4. T = 13:00. Rec, 1-2-4 = DL-8264, American Sym. Band of the Air, Revelli)

Hermann's five-movement work is a musical representation of the fast pace and active lives led by most teenagers. Teenage Overture describes the rapid pace of the Teen-Ager. . .constantly on the move with legs and arms flying wildly. . .time out for a soda and sandwich. . .and back to the fast moving energy of the Teen-Ager. Day Dreaming pictures the Teen-Ager seated in the classroom on a warm afternoon. . . outside the bees are buzzing, the birds chirping. . .the Teen-Ager is dreaming. In First Driving Lesson, our Teen-Ager gets to drive the family car. . .after two unsuccessful attempts at starting the motor he moves slowly into traffic. . .he picks up speed with courage. . .he does quite well until he comes to the big corner. He takes courage and pulls into the traffic. . .all is successful until he nears home. . .the girl next door watches him as he pulls into the driveway and piles into the other car with a tremendous crash. Prom Night is that important night. . .the best girl. . .the first tuxedo. . .the first formal. . .the first orchid. . .the rhythmic music of the band as they dance away into the corner. . .out of sight of the chaperone. Finally, Graduation March, with the teachers wishing him well. . .marching down the aisle to the music of that familiar graduation march. . .(Podium Publishing Co.)

Concerto for Horn (Pub = PD, 1964. Gr = 4. T = 8:50)

An important addition to the repertoire for French horn the *Concerto* was written for James Chambers and first performed in 1958 at the convention of the American Bandmasters Association. The composition follows the classical concerto form of three movements. The slow second movement makes good use of the horn's lovely lyrical qualities, while the first and third movements illustrate the technical facility of the instrument. (William E. Rhoads, University of New Mexico)

Nocturne (Pub = CF, 1959. Gr = 3.   T = 4:40. Rec = OS-9207, Spencerport, NY, H.S.)

Nocturne was composed for the Tri-State Band Festival of 1958 and dedicated to the host school, Phillips University of Enid, Oklahoma. Hermann conducted the Phillips University Band in the première of the work. *Nocturne* is a composition of contrasting moods—suggesting the night's quiet darkness, then brilliant flashes of the starry sky—but pervaded throughout by the rich harmonies and textures characteristic of the composer's works. (Blase S. Scarnati, Slippery Rock State College)

North Sea Overture (Pub = EMS, 1955. Gr = 4. T = 8:00)

The North Sea, perhaps the most feared body of water on earth, has for centuries claimed the lives of countless seamen. In this descriptive composition the composer has rendered a picture of the never-ending battle between man and the North Sea. The opening theme depicts the challenge of the sea to the men and their ships. The second theme dramatically portrays the violent sea striking the vessels with all her fury. The thoughts on the minds of the "men of the sea" as they momentarily think of their homes and loved ones is told in the third theme. The contest mounts and expands to grandiose proportions building to a tremendous climax, ending in a note of triumph—this time a triumph for man over the defiance and the assault of the North Sea. (L. Bruce Jones, Louisiana State University)

PAUL HINDEMITH

(Born in Hanau, Germany, 1895 — Died in Frankfurt, 1963)

Paul Hindemith began to show interest in music at the age of eleven by playing the violin. By the time he was twenty, Hindemith was concertmaster of the Frankfurt Opera (1915-23) and after making the viola his specialty toured Europe with the Amar Hindemith Quartet.   About 1936 he became interested in the musical *Jugendbewegung,* a movement devoted to the furtherance of active music-making among amatuers. Hindemith's continuing interest in composing *Gebrauchsmusik—* music for practical use rather than music for art's sake—stemmed from this association. In 1927 Hindemith was appointed professor of composition at the Academy of Music in Berlin and out of this teaching experience grew his famous theoretical work, *The Craft of Musical Composition,* published in 1937, the most comprehensive theory of harmony ever devised. In 1940, Hindemith was appointed to the Yale University School of Music faculty. Later he took up residence in Switzerland and made frequent visits to the United States until his death in 1963.

In addition to operas, symphonies, and numerous other orchestral works, Hindemith has written much music for chamber groups, keyboard instruments, and choral combinations. His sonatas for each of the wind instruments have long served as exemplary material for advanced performers. (Hubert Henderson, University of Maryland)

According to Merrill Brown's 1971-72 survey of 173 members of the National Association of Schools of Music, Hindemith's sonatas for various wind instruments rated in recital popularity as follows: Flute, 2nd; Oboe, 2nd; English Horn, 2nd; Bassoon, 2nd; Clarinet, 1st; Alto Saxophone, 13th; Trumpet, 3rd; French Horn, 5th; Trombone, 1st; and Tuba, 1st.

Guy Duker has recently transcribed two of Hindemith's orchestral masterpieces for band, *Mathis der Maler* and *Concert Music, Op. 10.* (Ed.)

Concert Music for Band, Op. 41 (Pub = S&C. Gr = 5. Rec = MU-SM-0003, Un. of MI, Reynolds)

Hindemith's interest in the combined sound of wind instruments probably motivated the writing of this opus. The work was composed for a small German band with an instrumentation including saxhorns. The first movement is titled Concert Overture; the second, a satire of the typical German band, is called Six Variations on the song, "Prince Eugene the Noble Knight"; and the final movement is titled March.

March from Symphonic Metamorphosis on Themes by Carl Maria von Weber (Tr = Wilson. Pub = BE, 1972. Gr = 4. T = 7:30. Rec = CR-MID-73-6, U.S. Air Force, Gabriel; OS-8101, U.S. Marine; CR-NEC, New England Conserv., Battisti)

Hindemith wrote this work in 1943, during his tenure as a professor at the Yale School of Music. He felt strongly that the "Metamorphosis" should be available in a band version and asked his colleague Keith Wilson to do the transcription. Not until 1960 was permission received from Hindemith's publishers, and then the work, regarded by Wilson as his largest and most significant transcription, took one and a half years to complete. The March is the fourth and final movement of the work and it reveals Hindemith's knowledge of wind combinations and timbral contrasts.

The most important part of the march theme is a little two-bar fragment which begins in the brass at the very outset. This reappears and is developed at different points of punctuation throughout the movement. There is also a more lyrical "trio" theme which is repeated and developed, fortissimo, featuring most notably a stunning crescendo passage in the horns. The burden of the melodic writing shifts from the woodwinds in the initial presentation of the themes to the brass in the last half of the piece. The form is somewhat different than that of a standard march. (Keith Brion, Yale University)

Symphony in B-Flat (Pub = AMP, 1951. Gr = 6. T = 16:50. Rec = SE-S-60005, Philharmonia Orch. Winds, Hindemith; MU-SM-0003, Un. of MI, Reynolds; MG-SRI-75057, Eastman, Fennell; CR-CRE-1000, Cass Tech, Begian)

The *Symphony for Concert Band* was composed at the request of Lt. Col. Hugh Curry, leader of the United States Army Band, and was premiered in Washington, D.C. on April 5, 1951, with the composer conducting. The three-movement symphony shows Hindemith's great contrapuntal skill, and the organized logic of his thematic material. His melodies develop ever expanding lines, and his skill in the organization and utilization of complex rhythmic variation adds spice and zest to the strength of his melodies.

The first movement is in sonata allegro form in three sections, with the recapitulation economically utilizing both themes together in strong counterpoint. The second and third movements develop and expand their thematic material in some of the most memorable contrapuntal writing for winds. The second movement opens with an imitative duet between alto saxophone and cornet, accompanied by a repeated chord figure. The duet theme, along with thematic material from the opening movement, provides the basic material for the remainder of the movement. The closing section of the third movement utilizes the combined themes while the woodwinds amplify the incessant chattering of the first movement. The brass and percussion adamantly declare a halt with a powerful final cadence. (James Jorgenson, University of Redlands)

The *Symphony in B-Flat* rivals any orchestra composition in length, breadth, and content, and served to convince other first-rank composers—including Giannini, Persichetti, Creston, and Hovhaness—that the band is a legitimate medium for serious music. (Hubert Henderson, University of Maryland)

GUSTAV HOLST

(Born in Cheltenham, England, 1874 — Died in London, 1934)

Gustav Holst, one of England's most prominent composers, was also a professional trombonist and a teacher of composition and organ. His music includes operas, ballets, symphonies, chamber music, and songs. His most popular work was an orchestral suite, *The Planets,* in which planets are depicted as astrological symbols. In addition to astrology Holst was also deeply interested in folk music and in the orient. During the first World War he was placed in command of all English Army Bands, organizing music among the troops under the Y.M.C.A. Army and Education program. His *First Suite in E-Flat* was written for military band in 1909 marking a new epoch in band literature and being rarely, if ever, equalled by the composers who imitated it. The *Second Suite in F for Military Band*—military band being the English term for a wind group with a complete instrumentation, as opposed to the British brass band—written in 1922, and *Hammersmith, Prelude and Scherzo* (1930), reflect a creative ability and high quality of craftsmanship assuring Holst an honored position for three truly significant contributions to band repertoire. (Acton Ostling, Jr., University of Maryland)

First Suite in E-Flat (Pub = BH, 1921-48. Gr = 4. T = 10:00. Rec = TE-5038, Cleveland Sym. Winds, Fennell; CRE-9005, Ithaca Col. Alumni, Beeler)

British composers have produced several exceptionally fine works for the concert band. Of all these, the *Suite in E-Flat* is generally regarded as the cornerstone. Written in 1909 it is one of the few band originals that has been transcribed for symphony orchestra.

The opening theme of the Chaconne is repeated incessantly by various instruments as others weave varied filigrees about the ground theme. In the middle of the first movement the principal theme is inverted for several repetitions. The Intermezzo is based on a variation of the Chaconne theme, presented first in an agitated style, then in a cantabile mood, the two styles alternating throughout the movement. The two themes of the March, one dynamic and the other lyric, are also taken from the Chaconne theme, the first being something of an inversion, whereas the lyric theme is "right side up." Eventually the two are combined in a thrilling counterpoint leading to the coda. (Charles H. Luedtke, Dr. Martin Luther College)

(See April, 1975, *Instrumentalist* for an analysis by Frederick Fennell. Ed.)

Hammersmith—Prelude and Scherzo (Pub = BH, 1956. Gr = 4. T = 12:45. Rec = MG-SRI-75028, Eastman, Fennell; TE-5038, Cleveland Sym. Winds, Fennell)

This work seals Holst's unique position as the wind band's first great champion among composers of the first rank. He was commissioned in 1930 by the British Broadcasting Corporation to write a work for its military band, and although it had been twenty years since he had written for this challenging instrumental combination, he immediately seized upon this commission to write a major work designed for performance by the best professional players in England. This source of Holst's commission was a vital factor in scoring the composition for band, for he spared nobody in fashioning a work of uncompromising technical and musical demands. However, the expected first performance by the BBC military band never took place, so when Holst died four years later (after having transcribed the opus for orchestra). he had never heard a public performance of the work in its original form. The work was prémiered by the U.S. Marine Band, conducted by Captain Tayler Branson, at the American Bandmasters Association convention in Washington, D.C., on April 17, 1932—Holst had been scheduled to conduct, but was ill and could not appear. (See May, 1977 *Instrumentalist* for an analysis by Frederick Fennell. Ed.)

this work by Frederick Fennell may be found in the May, 1977, issue of *The Instrumentalist*. Ed.)

Holst lived and worked in the west metropolitan borough of London, called Hammersmith, for thirty years. The sharply contrasted elements that he observed as life there unfolded about him were dominant factors in his philosophy as well as the basic ingredients underlying his choice of the Hammersmith area as the subject for his BBC commission. As Cantrick observed (see *Journal of Band Research, Vol. 12, No. 2):* "In *Hammersmith* Holst turned to the band to express musically a profound philosophic problem, one which was deeply rooted in his nature all his life; the paradoxical interplay of the humane and the mystical in man's experience. He did this at the height of his artistic maturity under the most favorable creative conditions of his career. . . . This tension never resolved itself in Holst's personal life. . .but this very unresolved tension is the essence of *Hammersmith*. Here he finally found adequate musical means for expressing the paradox in a one-movement work—the mood of the Prelude other-worldly, non-human, self-contained and inward looking; the mood of the Scherzo raffish, vulgar, worldly, excited, warm, emotional, and extroverted; the artistic union of the two achieved without elevating either to superior status over the other." (Frederick Fennell, University of Miami; Mercury Records)

Moorside March (Arr = Jacob. Pub = BH, 1960. Gr = 4. T = 4:00. Rec = CR-ABA-72-3, Lamar Un., Wiley)

Moorside March, arranged for concert band by another well known British composer, Gordon Jacob, is taken from Holst's *Moorside Suite,* written in 1928 as a brass band contest piece. The march is begun by a rising, four-note motive which leads into a vigorous theme, noteworthy because of its six-bar phrases. A second theme, in a major key, employing more normal eight-bar phrases, is first introduced by the saxophone, and it is followed by a brief return to the main theme. The Trio which follows is reminiscent of the great ceremonial marches of Elgar and Walton in its pomp and dignity. After a brief modulatory section based on the opening motive, the first two themes are restated. The march concludes with a coda containing material from the Trio. (Fred Heath, University of Maryland)

The Planets:

Jupiter (Pub = BH, 1924. Gr = 3. T = 9:30. Rec = CR-CBD-69-2, North TX St. Un., McAdow)

Mars (Pub = BH, 1924. Gr = 5. T = 7:30. Rec = UN-1, Un. of NE, Lentz)

The Planets, composed for orchestra in 1915, is a suite of seven tone poems, each describing symbolically a different planet. The work has insistent odd meters of five and seven beats, thick streams of parallel triads, and an opulent instrumentation. The entire suite was first performed for a private audience in 1918 and in public, without *Venus* and *Neptune,* in 1919.

Jupiter—The Bringer of Jollity is introduced by a genial, syncopated dance, appropriately so since a happy and festive mood is maintained throughout this movement. Holst's love of English folk song and dance is readily demonstrated here. The middle section presents a surprising contrast—a majestic flowing melody in 3/4 meter which Holst later used for a patriotic song. (Boosey & Hawkes, Inc.)

Mars—The Bringer of War was complete in the composer's mind in the early summer of 1914, when the First World War was but an emerging threat. The work is dominated by a relentless hammering out of a 5/4 rhythm which suggests the relentless destruction of war. The opposition of harmony and rhythm is skillfully used to produce a startling aural and emotional effect. This movement was transcribed for band by the composer in 1924. (Boosey & Hawkes, Inc.)

Second Suite in F (Pub = BH, 1922. Gr = 4. T = 14:00. Rec = IL-24, Un. of IL, Hindsley; CR-NCBDNA-78-3, MI St. Un., w. soprano soloist, DeRusha)

The *Second Suite*, composed in 1911, uses English folk songs and folk dance tunes throughout, being written at a time when Holst needed to rest from the strain of original composition. The suite has four movements, each with its own distinctive character.

The opening march movement uses three tunes, set in the pattern ABCAB. Tune A is a lively morris dance, a type of dance that was very popular in the Renaissance, and was commonly danced in England as part of the May games. There were two groups of six male dancers each, plus several solo dancers, often including a boy with a hobby-horse. In Holst's setting, the tune's opening five-note motive is heard twice as an introduction, and then the tune itself begins. Tune B, a folk song called "Swansea Town," is broad and lyrical, played first by the baritone. This statement is followed by the entire band playing the tune in block harmonies—a typically English sound. The third tune, "Claudy Banks," is distinctly different from the other two having a lilting, swinging feeling derived from its compound duple meter.

The second movement is a slow, tender setting of an English love song, "I'll Love My Love." It is a sad tune, heard first in the oboe, with words which tell of two lovers separated by their parents, and of the deep love they will always have for each other.

"The Song of the Blacksmith" is complex rhythmically, much of it being in septuple meter. It demonstrates Holst's inventive scoring with a lively rhythm being played on the blacksmith's anvil.

"The Dargason" is an English country dance and folk song dating at least from the sixteenth century. Its peculiar property is that it does not really have an end but keeps repeating endlessly, almost like a circle. After "The Dargason" is played seven times, and while it continues to be played, Holst combines it with a well known tune, "Green Sleaves," a love song which later acquired different words and became a Christmas carol. With a complex combination of 6/8 and 4/5 meters, "The Dargason" alone "winds down" to the final chord of the suite. (R. John Specht, Queensborough Community College)

ALAN HOVHANESS
(Born in Somerville, Massachusetts, 1911)

Alan Scott Hovhaness is an American composer of Armenian descent. He received his collegiate musical training at the New England Conservatory of Music and his career includes teaching composition and conducting the student orchestra at Boston Conservatory, and performing as organist at nearby St. James Church in Watertown, Massachusetts. The list of compositions by Hovhaness is impressive, especially in consideration of the fact that the composer destroyed nearly a thousand of his works in 1940. The listing which dates from this time is still very large, including eighteen compositions for orchestra as well as a large number of chamber compositions, violin pieces, and piano works. While studying traditional techniques of composition, Hovhaness has also become involved in oriental musical systems which he embodies in his works, creating effects of impressionistic exoticism.

The music of Alan Hovhaness is unlike any composed in modern times, and usually revolves around two or three notes rather than being tonal in the key sense. It often has the effect of returning to a point of rest on the dominant, and utilizes sonorities which most nearly approach the expressive content of Asiatic music. Many of his compositions have characteristics of tranquility and gentleness which contrast with our contemporary age of dissonance. (Acton Ostling, Jr., University of Maryland)

Hovhaness has written music for almost every conceivable combination including one most unlikely, a work for orchestra and recorded songs of whales, *And God Created Great Whales,* his third commission from the New York Philharmonic. He has received a remarkable number of commissions from other sponsors also, as well as three honorary doctorates, fellowships from the Guggenheim Foundation, and an award from the National Institute of Arts and Letters. Of even greater impact is the effect his music has had upon listeners and critics. Following a performance of the *Mysterious Mountain* with the Boston Symphony Orchestra, conducted by Robert Shaw, critic Rudolph Elie said: ". . .Alan Hovhaness stands almost alone today among Americans as a composer born with the mantle of genius. . . . *Mysterious Mountain* . . .is the musical expression of a man of enormous integrity and enormous talent." (Oliver Daniel, Broadcast Music, Inc.)

Hymn to Yerevan (Pub = PET, 1968. Gr = 3. T = 4:00. Rec = MAC-S-9099, North Jersey, Brion)

The ancient city of Yerevan, at the foot of majestic, towering Mount Ararat, is the home of Armenians who found refuge there from many massacres.

The music, composed in the ancient fifth mode ('kim-tza') of the Armenian church, is in Sharagan or Armenian hymn style. A solemn contrapuntal motet expresses sorrow, strength, and spiritual resurrection. A middle section, in free rhythmless chaos of bells and roaring trombones, celebrates a dauntless defiance of tragedy. The solemn contrapuntal hymn returns, heroic and triumphal. (Alan Hovhaness, C.F. Peters Corporation)

Suite for Band (Pub = PET, 1968. Gr = 3. T = 10:00)

The *Suite for Band* is a series of solemn festival pieces in religious style—sometimes of Armenian character, sometimes of renaissance spirit. The composer has juxtaposed movements influenced by chant featuring one section of the band with contrapuntal movements utilizing the whole band. The music is an evocation of pageantry and splendor. (Max Planck, Eastern Michigan University)

Symphony No. 4 (Pub = PET, 1959. Gr = 4. T = 18:00. Rec = CN-CUWE-3, Cornell Un., Stith; MG-90366, Eastman, Roller)

Symphony No. 4, composed in 1958, includes three movements. The first, Andante-Allegro, is constructed of a hymn and two fugues, and contains six sections which the composer notates as "phrases." Trombones in a choir are followed by solo bass clarinet, trombones and horns, solo contrabassoon (contrabass clarinet), and is almost entirely performed by percussion instruments. Extensive solos for marimba, vibraphone and xylophone, are amplified by solo oboe, flute, bassoon, and English horn. The third movement, Andante-Allegro, includes two hymns and fugues. A crescendo of clashing bells in free rhythm is unleashed at one point, and the composer has commented that instead of using the "spineless glockenspiel, chimes, and vibraphones," he would prefer to "ring all the bells in the thousand towers of the lost Armenian city of Ani in wildly clashing free rhythm." The full instrumentation is not used until the final Allegro. (Acton Ostling, Jr., University of Maryland)

Tapor No. 1 (Pub = PET, 1968. Gr = 3. T = 5:00. Rec – IL-55, Un. of IL, Hindsley)

Tapor is the Armenian word for a processional of religious character. One can imagine an ancient church processional with banners led by priests blessing the four corners of the earth. This pagan, solemn festival mood should be felt in the performance of this music. The melody is original with the composer—not of folk, not of church origin, but a new offering to the style of majestic pagan splendor of the Armenian church. (Alan Hovhaness, C.F. Peters Corporation)

JAMES H. HOWE
(Born in Durham, England, 1917)

Most of James Howe's professional career has been a combination of military service and music. He attended the Royal Military School of Music and also studied at the Royal Academy of Music and the Royal College of Music. From 1959 to 1974 he was the musical director for the H.M. Scots Guards and from 1970 to 1974 was the senior director of music for the Household Division. His extensive conducting experience includes concerts for the BBC and in London's Royal Albert Hall, as well as in several other countries. Howe has also spent some time promoting concerts during his career. Two of his most treasured honors include an Award for Service to Military Music and the Member of the British Empire Award. Among his march compositions are *Pride of Princes Street, Corner Flag, Pentland Hills,* and *Men of Steel*. Light band concert pieces include *Traffic Tangle* and the *Medley of Robert Burns Songs*. Howe is a staff member of the International Education Institute of Oak Park, Illinois; he and his wife are parents to one daughter and two sons, and he relaxes from his musical responsibilities by working in his garden.

Pentland Hills March (Pub = SO, 1965. Gr = 3. T = 2:20. Rec = IL-88, Un. of IL, Begian)

This march is named after the range of hills near Edinburgh, Scotland, where it was composed. It is based on three Scottish airs; "The Lass O' Gowrie," "John Anderson, My Jo'," and "Rowan Tree." The march is very popular with the British bands and is featured by H.M. Scots Guards on the ceremony of "Trouping the Colour." (Major James Howe, Surrey, England)

JOHANN HUMMEL
(Born in Pozsony, Hungary, 1778 — Died in Weimar, Germany, 1837)

Johann Nepomuk Hummel was born in Hungary but lived as a boy in Vienna where his father, Joseph Hummel, became conductor at Schikaneder's Theater. As a young man Hummel drew much attention to his piano playing and for two years lived in the home of Mozart, with whom he studied and under whose direction he made his debut in Dresden in 1787. As a child prodigy Hummel appeared in concert in cities throughout Europe and upon his return to Vienna in 1793 began the study of composition with Albrechtsberger and Salieri. In 1804 he succeeded Haydn as Kapellmeister of the Esterhazy court chapel at Eisenstadt and in 1819 became the Kapellmeister at Weimar, a position held a century before by J.S. Bach. In addition to being a student of Mozart and a protege of Haydn, Hummel was a close friend of Beethoven, Weber, and Chopin, and a teacher of Czerny and Hiller. One of the greatest pianists of his era, Hummel was a prolific composer of Masses, operas, ballets, cantatas, chamber music, and music for the piano. Though immensely popular in his own time, his music has suffered almost total—and sometimes undeserved—neglect by succeeding generations. (Hubert Henderson, University of Maryland)

Concerto for Trumpet (Arr = Corley. Pub = RK, 1960. Gr = 4/5. Rec = MH-746, Maurice André w. Lamoureux Orch., Mari; AN-S-40123, Timofey Dokschitzer w. Moscow Cham. Orch., Barshai; NO-H-71270, Edward Tarr, w. Consortium Musicum Orch., Lehan)

The Hummel concerto, like the Haydn concerto, was composed for the Viennese trumpeter, Anton Weidinger. The composition was completed on December 8, 1803, and performed on January 1, 1804, in Esterhazy Castle. For the performance Weidinger used the same style trumpet he had invented for the first performance of the Haydn concerto in 1796. The keyed trumpet (not bugle) was a specially-constructed instrument with keys resembling those of a modern saxophone and could play chromatically between the open harmonics of the natural trumpet. Unlike the baroque C trumpet with its eight-foot length of tubing, the keyed trumpet resembled somewhat the shape of the modern cornet. (Copies of Weidinger's trumpet are again being manufactured and sold in Europe and America.) The tone of the instrument has a more veiled, romantic sound than most of the modern trumpets. The Hummel concerto was originally in E major rather than the commonly-preferred E-flat major.

KAREL HUSA

(Born in Prague, 1921)

Husa studied at the Prague Conservatory in his native Czechoslovakia and at the Paris Conservatory where his teachers were Arthur Honegger and Nadia Boulanger. He was widely respected as a composer and conductor before coming to the United States in 1949. Many of his compositions illustrate the successful amalgamation of twelve-tone technique with Czech melody, rhythm, and brilliant colors. He was awarded the Pulitzer Prize in Music in 1969 for his *String Quartet No. 3,* one of a long list of compositions written for a variety of musical media. Husa's *Music for Prague 1968,* (written as a result of the Soviet invasion of his native city) has won much praise in performances throughout the world. A more recent work, *Divertimento for Brass and Percussion,* is a tonal piece illustrating the Czech dance rhythms and melodies in a contemporary setting. Husa presently teaches composition and conducts the orchestra at Cornell University.

Apotheosis of This Earth (Pub = AMP, 1971. Gr = 6. T = 25:00. Rec = CR-S-4134, Un. of MI, Husa; MS-8, Morehead St. Un., Hawkins)

The composition of this work was motivated by the present desperate stage of mankind and its immense problems with everyday killings, war, hunger, extermination of fauna, huge forest fires, and critical contamination of the whole environment. Man's brutal possession and misuse of nature's beauty, if continued at today's reckless speed, can only lead to catastrophe. The composer hopes that the destruction of this beautiful earth can be stopped, so that the tragedy of destruction—musically projected here in the second movement—and the desolation of its aftermath (the "Postscript" of the third movement) can exist only as a fantasy, never to become reality.

In the first movement, Apotheosis, the Earth first appears as a point of light in the universe. Our memory and imagination approach it in perhaps the same way as it appeared to the astronauts returning from the moon; the Earth grows larger and we can even remember moments of tragedy—as illustrated by the xylophone near the end of the movement. The second movement, Tragedy of Destruction, deals with the actual brutalities of man against nature, leading to the destruction of our planet, perhaps by radioactive explosion. The Earth dies, a savagely, mortally wounded creature. The last movement is a Postscript, full of the realization that so little is left to be said—the Earth has been pulverized into the universe, the voices scattered into space. Toward the end, these voices—at first computer-like and mechanical—unite into the words, "this beautiful Earth," simply said, warm and filled with regret. . . and one of so many questions comes to our minds: "Why have we let it happen?" (Karel Husa, Cornell University)

Concerto for Alto Saxophone and Concert Band (Pub = AMP, 1967-72. Gr = 5. T = 20:00. Rec = CR-CBDNA-71-2, Fred Hemke w. Un. of TX, Moody; CN-CUWE-3, Sigurd Rascher w. Cornell Un., Stith—premier performance)

This concerto was commissioned by the Cornell University Wind Ensemble and its conductor, Marice Stith, in 1968. Sigurd Rascher was the soloist for the first performance. In the three movements—Prolog, Ostinato, and Epilog—new possibilities for solo saxophone as well as new effects and colors for wind ensemble are explored. The solo part requires subtle and delicate shadings as well as technical virtuosity.

Music for Prague, 1968 (Pub = AMP, 1969. Gr = 5. T = 18:30. Rec = CR-4134, Un. of MI, Husa; CR-MENC-78-18, Nat'l H.S. Honor, Revelli; CR-CRE-9007, Un. of Northern IA, Holvik)

Three main ideas bind the composition together. The first and most important is an old Hussite war song from the fifteenth century, "Ye Warriors of God and His Law," a symbol of resistance and hope for hundreds of years, whenever fate lay heavy on the Czech nation. It has been utilized by many Czech composers, including Smetana in *My Country*. The beginning of this religious song is announced very softly in the first movement by the timpani and concludes in a strong unison (Chorale). The song is never used in its entirety.

The second idea is the sound of bells throughout. Prague, named also the "City of Hundreds of Towers," has used its magnificently-sounding church bells as calls of distress as well as calls of victory.

The last idea is a motif of three chords first appearing very softly under the piccolo solo at the beginning of the piece in flutes, clarinets, and horns. Later it reappears at extremely strong dynamic levels, for example, in the middle of the Aria.

Different techniques of composing as well as orchestrating have been used in *Music for Prague, 1968* and some new sounds explored, such as the percussion section in the Interlude and the ending of the work. Much symbolism also appears: in addition to the distress calls in the first movement (Fanfares), the unbroken hope of the Hussite song, sound of bells, or the tragedy (Aria), there is also the bird call at the beginning (piccolo solo), symbol of the liberty which the City of Prague has seen only for moments during its thousand years of existence. (Karel Husa, Cornell University)

Music for Prague, 1968 was commissioned and premiered by the Ithaca College Concert Band. The first performance was given for the Music Educators National Conference in Washington, D.C. in 1969, with Kenneth Snapp conducting. Over 4,000 known performances of the work have been given since its première. (Ed.)

CHARLES IVES

(Born in Danbury, Connecticut, 1874 — Died in New York City, 1954)

Charles Ives, the son of a Civil War bandmaster, is regarded as the first truly American composer of the twentieth century. Encouraged by his father, Ives experimented with all kinds of music and acoustic sounds. A church organist at thirteen, he later entered Yale University, studying composition with Horatio Parker, but became an insurance executive instead of a professional musician. On making this decision Ives wrote, "Assuming a man lives by himself with no dependents, he might write music that no one would play prettily, listen to, or buy. But—but if he has a nice wife and some nice children, how can he let the children starve on his dissonances?" Far in advance of the then-current style, Ives employed techniques such as polytonality, atonality, polymetric patterns, tone clusters, and microtones. Mixed with these innovations were hymn tunes, patriotic melodies, and ragtime, all mixed together in a style which was both imaginative and daring.

Ives had to hire musicians and conductors occasionally so he could hear his works performed. His *Symphony No. 3*, written in 1911, was not performed until 1947—then it won the Pulitzer Prize. Composing outside of "business hours" Ives managed to write four symphonies and other large orchestral pieces, fifteen choral pieces, nearly two hundred songs, two quartets, four violin sonatas, and countless other fragments. There was little recognition for his compositions until late in life and after his death in 1954. According to the *BMI Orchestral Survey* of works performed by American symphony orchestras, "the 1963-64 season showed only 25 performances of compositions by Ives. By 1966-67, the figure had expanded to 82, and a season later to 192. By 1972-73, Ives' performances had climbed to 467, eclipsing all other American composers and such European notables as Bartok, Hindemith, Shostakovich, Prokofiev, et al."

Ives was undoubtedly a genius in many ways. For example, he retained clearly every single childhood memory into his last years. In his music he could recall each particular note and its location. In 1929, the year before his retirement from his insurance business, the company added $48,000,000 worth of new business; Ives however, reckoned up what he considered his moral share of the wealth and took only that much with him into retirement. In his biography of Ives, Henry Cowell wrote, "The style of his finest music is a style of richness and an outpouring of warmth and largess. It is humanitarianism applied to sound." Perhaps the same description could apply to the style of his life.

Country Band March (Arr = Sinclair. Pub = TP, 1974. Gr = 5. T = 4:00. Rec = CN-17, Cornell Un., Stith)

This march was composed in 1903 and arranged for full band in 1973 by James Sinclair of Yale University. The piece displays some of Ives' most distinguishing characteristics, particularly the use of quotations of tunes which were popular in his childhood. Unlike other composers who make use of similar material, Ives sought deliberately to capture the inaccuracies of rhythm and intonation which he usually heard in amatuer performances. The results can be wildly humorous and raucous, and affectionately nostalgic, often at the same time. *Country Band March* later became part of larger works by Ives: the *Symphony No. 4* and the Putnam's Camp movement of *Three Places in New England*. (Richard Franko Goldman, The Goldman Band)

Finale from Symphony No. 2 (Arr = Elkus. Pub ≃ PI, 1974. Gr = 4. T = 11:00.
Rec = CR-MID-74-11, VanderCook Col., Zajec) ·

The finale of the *Second Symphony* is a reworking of the lost *American
Woods*—a kind of overture—played partly as a shorter piece by Charles Ives'
father's orchestra in 1889 and by the Danbury, Connecticut, Band. Concerning this
work Ives wrote the following in his *Memos:*

> Some of the themes in this symphony suggest Gospel Hymns and
> Steve Foster. . . . Some nice people, whenever they hear the words
> "Gospel Hymns" or Stephen Foster," say "Mercy Me!," and a little
> high-brow smile creeps over their brow—"Can't you get something bet-
> ter than that in a symphony?" The same nice people, when they go to a
> properly dressed symphony concert under proper auspices, led by a
> name with foreign hair, and hear Dvorak's *New World Symphony,* in
> which they are told this famous passage was from a negro spiritual, then
> think that it must be quite proper, even artistic, and say "How
> delightful!"

Besides evoking the spirit of Foster in its French horn theme ("while over it the old
farmers fiddled a barn dance with all of its jigs, gallops, and reels"—*Memos),* the
movement works up to a rousing climax on "The Red, White and Blue" ("O Columbia, the Gem of the Ocean"). In the 1940's Ives changed the last three measures
of the movement from conventional harmonies to a wildly dissonant flourish, apparently as a joke. (James Sinclair, Yale University)

Variations on America (Tr = Rhoads. Pub = TP, 1969. Gr = 5. T = 7:00. Rec = CR-
ABA-72-4, Un. of TX, Moody)

Variations on America is a witty, irreverent piece for organ which was composed
in 1891. According to Ives' biographers, Henry and Sidney Cowell, it was played by
Ives in organ recitals in Danbury and in Brewster, New York, in the same year. His
father would not let him play some of the pages at the Brewster concert because they
had canons in two and three keys at once that proved to be unsuited to performance
in church; they made the boys "laugh out and get noisy." This is the earliest surviv-
ing piece using polytonality. William Schuman wrote a remarkably effective orchestra transcription of this work in 1964 and it is this version upon which William
Rhoads based his equally effective band transcription. (Franko Colombo Publications)

Variations on Jerusalem the Golden (Arr = Brion. Pub = AMP, 1974. Gr = 4.
T = 4:00)

Charles Ives is thought to have written at least ten pieces specifically for band. Of
these, only the marches *Omega Lambda Chi* and *Intercollegiate* exist in a completed
form. Except for a portion of *Runaway Horse on Main Street,* the original versions
of the others are thought to be lost. *Fantasia on Jerusalem the Golden* is one of the
lost manuscript pieces.

This arrangement uses another of Ives' works, *Variations on Jerusalem the
Golden,* to re-create the fantasia. The *Variations* was probably composed for organ,
although some of the passages appear unplayable on that instrument. The music was
thought to have been composed in 1888 when Ives was fourteen, and the possibility
exists that the score was a sketch for a missing band piece. The tune "Jerusalem the
Golden," is typical of the New England hymn tunes that were part of the fabric of
Ives' musical vocabulary. The band of Ives' day used a group of small bore nineteenth century instruments, less full-sounding in the middle and bass than the

concert band. In this arrangement, a small village brass band is contrasted in concerto grosso style with a modern concert band, whose scoring approximates the fuller sound of Ives' symphonies. (Keith Brion, Yale University)

GORDON JACOB

(Born in London, 1895)

Gordon Jacob, a native of London, was educated at the Royal College of Music, and since 1926 has been a teacher of counterpoint, orchestration, and composition at the college. As a composer his orchestral and choral works include a ballet, a concert overture, two symphonies, numerous concertos for wind and string instruments, many pedagogic works for piano and for chorus, a variety of chamber works, songs, and film music. Jacob ranks as one of the foremost contributors to the expanding repertoire of original works for band through his compositions for military band—the English term for a wind group of complete instrumentation as opposed to the British brass band. Two notable works are *An Original Suite for Military Band,* which is a worthy companion to the Holst suites and the Vaughn Williams suite for band, and a monumental work, *Music for a Festival,* commissioned by the Arts Council of Great Britain for the Festival of Britain in 1951. In addition, he has arranged the keyboard music of William Byrd for band in two delightful works, *William Byrd Suite,* and *The Battell.* (John Wakefield, University of Maryland)

From 1928, when he composed *An Original Suite,* to the present period of commissioned works, Jacob's band compositions have spanned a period of over fifty years. Recent pieces for band include: *Giles Farnaby Suite, Symphony for Band "A.D. 78," Tribute to Canterbury, Fantasia for Euphonium and Band, Miscellanies for Alto Saxophone and Band,* and *Cameos for Bass Trombone and Band.* In addition to composing, teaching, writing, and conducting, Jacob continues his interest in several societies including the *Incorporated Society of Musicians* and the *Worshipful Company of Musicians.* He married the former Margaret Gray and the couple has a son and a daughter. (Ed.)

Concerto for Band (Pub = BH, 1969. Gr = 4. T = 12:30. Rec = CR-MID-70-8, Northshore Concert, Wilmette, IL, Paynter)

This major composition shows the craft and musicianship that is Gordon Jacob's hallmark. The style is very much that of the English folk song which he enriches by adding meter changes. With important solos for each instrument, the work is almost a "multi-instrument concerto." The composition is constructed solidly on classical formal lines though its musical language is that of the twentieth century. The first and third movements are lively and dramatic while the center movement is more chorale-like. A mixture of old and new, Jacob's *Concerto for Band* is an impressive original work.

Flag of Stars (Pub = BH, 1956. Gr = 5. T = 11:00. Rec = IL-36, Un. of IL, Hindsley)

The symphonic overture *Flag of Stars,* a salute to America, was commissioned by Pi Omicron Band Fraternity at the University of Kentucky. Jacob included the following program reference:

> The overture was written during the end of 1953 and the beginning of 1954 and is intended as a gesture from an inhabitant of the Old World to those of the New. The introductory fanfare and the slow section which

follows it recall the sacrifices made by your country in both world wars in the struggle with dark forces of destruction. The allegro is prompted by thoughts of the energy, vitality, and cheerfulness of the American people—young, optimistic, and full of faith in their destiny. The second subject in 3/4 time might perhaps suggest a sort of national song and right at the end there is a brief quotation from the "Star Spangled Banner."

(Acton Ostling, Jr., University of Maryland)

Music for a Festival (Pub = BH, 1951. Gr = 5. T = 26:00. Rec = IL-49, Un. of IL, Hindsley)

This work, consisting of eleven movements, was commissioned by the Arts Council of Great Britain for the Festival of Britain in 1951. The general structure of the composition is an alternation of movements between brass choir and full band. The writing for brass calls on their several resources; brilliance, fullness, and at times delicacy, and choral style. The sections for band are written in a refreshing vein and serve as a contrast to the other sections. The suite is reminiscent of the classical suite both in arrangement and in the style of several of the movements. (William A. Schaefer, University of Southern California)

An Original Suite (Pub = BH, 1928. Gr = 4. T = 9:15. Rec = CR-CBDNA-77-2, West VA Un., Wilcox)

An Original Suite was Jacob's first work for the band medium, having been completed in 1928. Presumably the word "original" in the title was to distinguish the composition from the transcriptions which made up the bulk of the band's repertoire at that time. The composer may also have wanted audiences to know that the "folk song" sections were original. The suite is divided into March, Intermezzo, and Finale movements.

LOUIS E. JADIN

(Born in Versailles, France, 1768 — Died in Paris, 1853)

Louis Emmanuel Jadin became interested in music as a page in the household of Louis XVI. Later, when France was undergoing a political and social change during the revolutionary decade of 1789 to 1799, almost every type of music except the "aristocratic" opera continued unabated. Robespierre and the other leaders of the revolution realized the value of music, especially the gigantic band and choir festivals, in building *esprit de corps* among the people. Jadin, along with Gossec, Mehul, Catel, and other leading French composers of the time, wrote music for wind band and also for the more traditional instrumental, keyboard, and choral media. In 1789, Bernard Sarrette assembled a forty-five member National Guard Band which became, and continues to be 200 years later, one of the world's great bands. Jadin, impressed by the musicianship of the players (many of whom were virtuoso instrumentalists from the closed opera houses), joined the famous group in 1792 and composed many excellent pieces for various combinations of wind instruments—some of which have only recently been re-discovered. In 1802, Jadin became a professor of piano at the newly established Paris Conservatory, succeeding his brother, Hyacinthe Jadin. Most of the teachers at the conservatory (headed at first by Sarrette) were former members of the National Guard Band which was disbanded for a time. Jadin's orchestral overture, *La Bataille d'Austerlitz,* was one of the more popular patriotic pieces during the Napoleonic wars.

Symphonie for Band (Ed = Schaefer.   Pub = SH, 1963.   Gr = 3.   T = 5:40. Rec = SH-2)

During the French Revolution, and in the period immediately following, the many outdoor ceremonial functions led to a concentration of works for band. Many of these were in the key of F due to the use of natural trumpets in that key. The instrumentation included the serpent (a wooden, serpent-shaped bass instrument with an ivory cup mouthpiece), in addition to the familiar instruments.

Written in 1794, the symphony is cast in a single movement and suggests the form of an overture. It was found in the archives of the National Library of Paris, and rescored for modern symphonic band by William A. Schaefer. (Shawnee Press)

ROBERT JAGER
(Born in Binghamton, New York, 1939)

Robert Jager received his music education at Wheaton College and at the University of Michigan. He served four years in the U.S. Navy as staff arranger at the Armed Forces School of Music. He has received a number of awards for his music, including the American Bandmasters Association Ostwald Award in 1964, 1968, and 1972. He received the National School Orchestra Association Roth Award in 1964 and 1966. In 1973 he was named Tennessee Composer of the Year and also received Kappa Kappa Psi's Distinguished Service to Music Medal the same year. Jager has received twenty-three commissions to date from various high school and college music groups. In 1976 he received the ASBDA Volkwein Award.

In addition to the titles described below, some of Jager's more popular compositions include: *Variations on a Theme of Robert Schumann* and *The Tennessean March* for band; *Concerto Grosso for Jazz Band and Symphony Orchestra; Concerto for Alto Saxophone, Brass, and Percussion;* and a tuba trio titled *Variations on a Motive by Wagner.* In one year (1978), Jager's published works included: *Jubilate, Symphony No. 2, Pastorale and Country Dance, Cliff Island Suite, Apocalypse,* and *Caucasian Sketches.*

Jager is a member of ASCAP, Phi Mu Alpha Sinfonia, and Kappa Kappa Psi. He is the director of composition and theory at Tennessee Technological University in Cookeville. He and Mrs. Jager have two children, Kathleen and Matthew, and his hobbies are gardening and camping.

Diamond Variations (Pub = VO, 1968. Gr = 5. T = 12:00. Rec = BP-125, Un. of IL, Hindsley; UN-4, Un. of NE, Lentz)

Diamond Variations was composed to celebrate the seventy-fifth anniversary of the University of Illinois Band. The Trio of *Illinois Loyalty* is used as the basis for the variations, although the theme as such never appears in the set of five variations. After a short introduction based on the phrase, "Alma Mater," the fragments of the march theme undergo various settings and alterations. The first variation is a grotesque dance; the second is more mysterious and sinister; the third is full of driving figures and rhythmic punctuations; the fourth is more peaceful and almost romantic; and the fifth gives almost every instrument in the band a chance to have its say about the theme. The theme almost appears in the brass near the end in an augmented, quasi-waltz setting. *Diamond Variations* won the American Bandmasters Association's Ostwald Award in 1968. (Robert Jager, Tennessee Tech University)

March Dramatic (Pub = SO, 1969. Gr = 4. T = 2:30. Rec = CR-MID-70-5, Ft. Hunt H.S., Alexandria, VA, Wickes)

This march is rather traditional in form, harmonic structure, and melody, but novel in its use of unexpected accents and dynamic contrast. All sections of the band are challenged at times with the basses especially busy in the break strain. *March Dramatic* was commissioned and premiered by the Perrysburg (Ohio) High School Band.

Second Suite (Pub = VO, 1965. Gr = 4. T = 10:00)

The *Second Suite* places much emphasis on tone color in the band. The opening fanfare of restrained dignity contrasts the higher instruments with the lower. The second movement is based on a lyrical theme played first by English horn. The final movement is a brilliant and driving scherzo with solos in percussion, bassoon, and euphonium. Following a dynamic build-up of the main theme, the opening fanfare returns in abbreviated form before the work concludes with a final presto. (Donald A. Stanley, Mansfield State College)

Sinfonia Nobilissima (Pub = EV, 1968. Gr = 3. T = 8:00. Rec = CR-MID-68-7, Fenton H.S., Bensenville, IL, Lewis)

This overture is a work in a neo-romantic style and is in three sections. After a short introduction, a dramatic and syncopated fast section begins. Then after several false climaxes, as well as a brief fughetta, the slow, more emotional middle section begins. In the final part of the work, a fast, syncopated style abruptly returns, and the overture ends with several deceptive, then complete chords. (Robert Jager, Tennessee Tech University)

Stars and Bars March (Pub = VO, 1965. Gr = 4. T = 2:30.)

This march has the traditionally accepted ingredients for a standard march, but the scoring and the rhythmic drive combine to convince the listener that the work is unique. A piccolo solo in the Trio, active trumpet parts, a powerful break strain, and a sudden half-step modulation in the last half of the Trio hold attention to the final chord. Jager's experience in arranging for the military service bands is most obvious in this challenging, attractive march.

Symphony No. 1 for Band (Pub = VO, 1965. Gr = 4. T = 18:00. Rec = TT, TN Tech, Pegram)

Symphony No. 1 was dedicated to Gilbert Mitchell, former director of the U.S. Army Band. For its composition, Jager was the 1964 recipient of the American Bandmasters Association's Ostwald Award. The first movement of the four-movement work is ternary in form, opening with a dramatic "motto" theme that is the basis of the entire symphony and appears in every movement. The second movement is a march and, except for one change of dynamic level in the middle, is to be performed with one continuous crescendo to the end. The third movement is a slow, ballad-like movement, and the fourth part returns more obviously to the "motto" theme of the opening, developing it further before ending in a joyous manner. (Robert E. Jager, Tennessee Tech University)

Third Suite (Pub = VO, 1967. Gr = 4. T = 8:05. Rec = CR-CBDNA-71-7, U.S. Air Force, Gabriel; BP-2nd Series)

Third Suite was written for the Granby High School Band of Norfolk, Virginia. The first movement is a march which is altered rhythmically by the use of alternating meter signatures. The second movement is a waltz which continues the meter alteration idea and features oboe, flute, bassoon, and brass sections. The Rondo is full of fun and bright tunes which are developed near the end followed by a quick coda stating the main theme once again.

ARMAS JÄRNEFELT

(Born in Vyborg, Finland, 1869 — Died in Stockholm, 1958)

Armas Järnefelt studied with Wegelius and Busoni at the Helsinki Conservatory then continued his music study in Berlin and Paris. He was an opera coach in Germany in 1896 and 1897, first at Magdeburg, then at Düsseldorf. In 1898 he returned to Vyborg where he conducted for a time, but he spent most of his professional life (1907-32) as conductor of the Stockholm Opera. He did return to Finland, however, in 1932, to conduct the Helsinki Opera for four years and the Helsinki Municipal Orchestra from 1942 to 1943. Much of Järnefelt's music is reminiscent of the Finnish folksong style. His orchestra works, *Berceuse* and *Praeludium*, were his most popular compositions.

Praeludium (Arr = Slocum. Pub = SH, 1967. Gr = 4. T = 2:40. Rec = SH-4, Ithaca Col. Gobrecht; CR-MID-68-11, Brownsville, TX, H.S., Becker)

This short prelude was composed for chamber orchestra and premiered in 1901 in Vyborg, Finland (now Russia—not to be confused with Viborg, Denmark), with Järnefelt conducting. In this tasteful arrangement by Slocum the work opens with a short introduction which leads to a brisk march theme by the oboe with a light, brass quintet accompaniment. Later the woodwinds introduce new melodic material over a drone bass followed by a return to the principal theme and important solos by flute, oboe, and horn. The piece ends with a series of quiet, staccato eighth notes.

JOSEPH W. JENKINS

(Born in Philadelphia, 1928)

Joseph Willcox Jenkins received a pre-law degree at St. Joseph's College before deciding upon a musical career. He studied composition with Persichetti at the Philadelphia Conservatory of Music and with Thomas Canning and Howard Hanson at the Eastman School of Music. He received his Ph.D. degree at the Catholic University of America and is now chairman of the theory and composition department at Duquesne University. Active in conducting as well as composing, Jenkins works with church choirs and is the conductor of the Diocesan Nun's Choir of Philadelphia. He has received the ASCAP Serious Music Award each year for the last fifteen years and was commissioned by the University of Eastern New Mexico in 1973 to write *Sinfonia de la Frontera*.

Jenkins' most popular band work is *American Overture*, but his *Cumberland Gap*, *Charles County Overture*, *Cuernavaca*, and *Three Images* are also widely performed. His works for other media include two symphonies, a string quartet, carols, songs, and other chamber music. Recent commissions include music for a musical comedy; a biblical tone poem for organ, *Thin Small Voice;* and a symphonic work for strings and winds for the Australian Broadcasting Corporation. In addition to his administrative responsibilities and his dedication to composition, Jenkins also conducts the orchestra and choir at Duquesne. He is married, has two sons, and his hobbies include railroading, meteorology, astronomy, and cartography.

American Overture for Band (Pub = TP, 1956. Gr = 4. T = 5:00. Rec = IL-48, Un. of IL, Hindsley; CR-MID-77-12, Clark H.S., Winchester, KY, Campbell)

This overture was written for the U.S. Army Field Band and dedicated to its conductor at the time, Chester E. Whiting. The piece is written in a neo-modal style being flavored strongly with both Lydian and Mixolydian modes. Its musical architecture is a very free adaptation of sonata form. The musical material borders on the folk tune idiom although there are no direct quotes from any folk tunes. The work calls for near-virtuoso playing by several sections, especially the French horns, and is a favorite of advanced high school and university bands. Although *American Overture* was Jenkins' first band piece, it remains his most successful work, and in his words, he is "hard-pressed to duplicate its success."

Toccata for Winds, Op. 104 (Pub = HL, 1978. Gr = 5. T = 8:00. Rec = CR-MID-78-8, North Hills H.S., Pittsburgh, Mercer)

Toccata for Winds was commissioned by the North Hills High School Band of Pittsburgh, and its conductor, Warren Mercer. As described by the composer, the work is intended to be a "showpiece" for the better high school and college bands. The piece opens with a percussion soli followed by the trumpets playing the first main theme in the Lydian mode. A contrasting subject is then played by the clarinets accompanied by a timpani ostinato. The middle section features a calmer treatment of the theme before a recapitulation of previous material and a presto coda bring the work to a strong finish.

SCOTT JOPLIN

(Born in Texarkana, Texas, 1868 — Died in New York City, 1917)

Scott Joplin grew up in a musical home where he learned to play piano, later studying with Louis Chauvin who included ragtime in the boy's music instruction. Later he was a pianist in several cafes in St. Louis, an orchestra leader at the 1893 World's Fair in Chicago, and a ragtime performer in Sedalia, Missouri. His compositional ability was soon recognized by a local publisher, John Stark, who began publishing Joplin's rag pieces in 1899. His most famous piece, "The Maple Leaf Rag," was published the same year and was followed in the next eighteen years by over fifty rags, a primer in ragtime performance, ten songs, and two operas. He died in a mental hospital in 1917.

Ragtime Dance (Arr = Elkus. Pub = SN, 1975. Gr = 4. T = 4:30)

At its prime, ragtime was listened to, danced to, sung to, and marched to—and these uses demanded that it be scored for various instrumentations. Thus, the most popular tunes appeared in band and orchestra arrangements, among which was the classic *Red Back Book,* a collection of some fifteen favorite rags by Joplin and others, arranged for a small, practical combination that might play in theatre pits as well as on the dance floor. Joplin's great song with choreography, "The Ragtime Dance," originally appeared in 1902 for singer, piano, and dancers. A subsequent shorter arrangement for piano solo appeared in 1906. This arrangement of *Ragtime Dance,* by Jonathan Elkus, was premiered by the Yale University Band in 1973. (Keith Brion, Yale University)

DMITRI KABALEVSKY

(Born in St. Petersburg, Russia, 1904)

Although not as well known as Shostakovich and Prokofiev, Dmitri Kabalevsky is one of Russia's highly-gifted composers. His style is in the Tchaikovskian idiom with appropriate modern trimmings—which is another way of saying that his music has great and immediate appeal for the average listener.

Kabalevsky was fourteen when he and his family moved from St. Petersburg to Moscow, where he attended the Scriabin School of Music from 1919 to 1925. In 1925 he entered the Moscow Conservatory where he studied composition with Miaskovsky, who apparently had the greatest influence on Kabalevsky's early works. He later developed his own style, marked by clear tonality and energetic rhythms. He is presently composer and professor of composition at the Moscow Conservatory. (Franko Colombo, Inc.)

Colas Breugnon Overture (Arr = Beeler; Hunsberger. Pub = SH, 1967; MC, 1967. Gr – 4. T = 4:30. Rec = CR-S-4077, Ithaca Col., Beeler; CR-NBA-78-7, U.S. Navy, Muffley; BP-105, W. TX St. Un., Garner)

This overture is a brisk, brilliant, and high-spirited piece, written as the curtain raiser of Kabalevsky's opera based on Romain Rolland's lusty novel of life in French Burgundy during the sixteenth century. The hero of the story has something in him of both Robin Hood and François Villon (a French lyric poet who was banished from Paris in 1463), and Kabalevsky has written music admirably fitting this character. Band transcriptions have been made by Beeler, Hunsberger, and Harding. (Everett Kisinger, University of Illinois)

Suite in Minor Mode (Arr = Siekmann & Oliver. Pub = MC, 1968. Gr = 2. T = 4:00. Rec = CR-MID-69-6, Waukegan, IL, Grade School, Stiner)

This suite is well arranged with interesting parts for all players. The first movement, Dance, is fast and in a minor key as would be expected from the suite's title. The second movement, A Little Song, is slower and expressive, and the last movement, Horseman, is spirited like the first and also in minor. The descriptive titles help the performance style of the musicians and also make for more enjoyable listening.

BASIL KALINNIKOV
(Born in Orlov, Russia, 1866 — Died in Yalta, 1901)

Basil Sergeivitch Kalinnikov, a contemporary of Tchaikovsky, was an unusually brilliant composer. His works are characterized by great artistic refinement, and there seems no doubt that, but for his premature death at the age of thirty-five, he would have won a place in the top rank of Russian composers.

Kalinnikov was an assistant conductor to the Italian Opera Company in Moscow for the 1893-94 season, but had to relinquish the post because of consumption brought on by early privations. During his remaining years he composed a cantata, two symphonies, a string quartet, and various orchestral pieces. (William Swor, Louisiana State University)

Finale from Symphony No. 1 (Arr = Bainum. Pub = PD, 1958. Gr = 4. T = 8:30. Rec = CR-4015, Ithaca Sym. Winds, Beeler; CR-MID-69-5, Pioneer H.S., Ann Arbor, MI, Bordo)

Kalinnikov's first symphony is an inspired work, national in style. It is highly melodious and beautifully written and is generally considered to be the composer's freshest and most popular work. The transcription of the vigorous finale was made by Glenn Cliffe Bainum.

BIN KANEDA
(Born in China, 1935)

Kaneda earned his B.A. degree in composition from the University of Tokyo in 1958. In 1956 and 1957 he won first prize at the Mainichi Newspaper composition contest with his chamber and orchestra music works. He was commissioned to write the required composition for the All Japan Band Contest in 1964, 1967, and 1972. Since 1971 Kaneda has been an associate professor in the music department at Gifu University.

Divertimento for Band (Pub = ON. Gr = 5. T = 7:30. Rec = CB-CBS-SONY-20AG-399, HANKYU Dept., Suzuki)

This work was commissioned by the All Japan Band Association as required music for the high school band division of the national contest in 1967. In keeping with the traditional definition of the title, this divertimento is divided into separate movements—in this instance three—titled Toccata, Chorale, and Fugue.

Elegy for Symphonic Band (Pub = ON, 1974. Gr = 5. T = 8:10. Rec = JC-GS-7052)

This composition, commissioned by the Komazawa University Band, was completed in 1974 and first performed by that band in June the same year.

The theme played by the horn at the beginning dominates the entire composition. Short motives, taken from the opening theme, are augmented or diminished at various times. In addition to rhythmic and tonal modification, a gradual increase and decrease of intensity provide additional expressive interest.

According to Kaneda the elegiac (mournful) quality of the work is meant to be interpreted personally by each listener. No other meaning was intended.

Japanese Folk Song Suite, Warabe-Uta (Pub = SH, 1974. Gr = 3. T = 7:30. Rec = SH-V8-P-544, Ithaca Col., Gobrecht)

This suite consists of three songs for children—*Warabe-Uta*—from old Japan. The first movement is based on a tune, "Where Are You From?"—Antagata-Dokosa—which is a simple, lively tune that often accompanies the children's game of bouncing a ball. The movement is played by the brass and percussion sections.

The second movement is based on perhaps the best known lullaby in Japan, Komori-Uta, expressing the joys and sorrows of child care, and is played by the woodwind and percussion sections.

The third movement is based on the tune "An Ancient Priest in a Mountain Temple"—Yamadera-No-Oshosan—and is also a song that children sing while bouncing a ball. The words to the song are humorous.

Kaneda has used a variety of compositional devices, including tone clusters, triadic and quartal harmony, and various percussive sounds, to create this effective setting of folk songs. (Shawnee Press, Inc.)

Passacaglia for Symphonic Band (Pub = ON, 1971. Gr = 4. T = 6:04. Rec = JC-GS-7014; CR-ABA-80-8, Komazawa Un., Ueno)

This work was commissioned in 1971 by the Ongaku No Tomo Sha Corp. (Tokyo music publisher, "musical friend") to commemorate its thirtieth anniversary. In writing the passacaglia Kaneda wanted to create something both playable and enjoyable for junior and senior high school bands.

The passacaglia is built from phrases with various figures following one after another while the theme, comprising twelve different tones, is augmented and diminished through eighteen repetitions. Although the theme uses all twelve notes without repetition, the work is not based on the twelve-tone system; neither is there a major or minor key, although a tonality centering on E-flat may be heard.

Symphonic Moment for Band (Pub = ON, 1975. Gr = 5. T = 9:27. Rec = TO-EMI-TA-72043, Eastman, Hunsberger)

Symphonic Moment was commissioned by the Japanese Yamaha Band in 1974 and completed the following year. In this work the composer hoped to demonstrate the symphonic capabilities of the concert band and to also show some of the deep emotion that can be expressed through music. The title refers to the length of time required to perform the music—in reality only a slight moment in the life span of the average listener.

MASARU KAWASAKI

(Born in Tokyo, 1924)

Masaru Kawasaki is well known in Japan as a composer, conductor, and author. After receiving his diploma from the Tokyo Academy of Music he became the conductor of the Tokyo Symphonic Band. He has composed opera music, solo and ensemble music, and several excellent works for band including *The Sketch of Pastoral Scenery, Warabe-Uta,* and *March Forward for Peace.* Kawasaki has written an arranging book for band and has also contributed to band journals. He is a professor of composition and instructor of flute at Tokoha College.

Fantasy for Symphonic Band (Pub = ON. Rec = CB-20AG-179. Gr = 5. T = 7:09)

Fantasy for Symphonic Band was commissioned by the Ongaku No Tomo Sha Publishing Corporation to commemorate the thirtieth anniversary of its founding. The composer has attempted to "draw Japanese feelings into the music" in this piece as well as in two previous works for band. A ballad-like theme unifies the three parts which are marked Largo con sentimento, Allegretto feroce, and Tempo I. In this ternary arrangement the climax is found in the middle section, and a variation on the opening theme leads to a tranquil closing. (Masaru Kawasaki, Tokyo)

GERALD KECHLEY

(Born in Seattle, Washington, 1919)

Kechley received both B.A. and M.A. degrees from the University of Washington where he now teaches composition and conducts the University Madrigal Singers. His principal teachers were George McKay and Aaron Copland. Previously he taught at Centralia Junior College and at the University of Michigan.

Among Kechley's commissioned works are: *The Dwelling of Youth* for chorus, band, and orchestra; *Psalm 150* for men's voices, brass, and organ; and *Processional Music for Brass and Percussion.* In addition to *Antiphony for Winds,* Kechley's principal band compositions are: *Mosaic for Winds, Andante and Scherzo,* and *Suite for Concert Band.* Other honors include Guggenheim Fellowships in 1949 and 1951, and ASCAP's Serious Music Award.

Kechley is married and has four children, two of whom are also composers.

Antiphony for Winds (Pub = CF, 1958. Gr = 4. T = 5:00. Rec = IL-24, Un. of IL, Hindsley)

The plan for *Antiphony for Winds* features an antiphonal interchange between woodwinds and brasses. The piece, conceived originally for wind instruments, exploits their characteristic flavor, using both woodwind and brass as independent choirs, and in various combinations as well. The drive and crispness of the opening section contrasts with the choral-like middle section, increasing in intensity to the climax in the maestoso coda. (Carl Fischer, Inc.)

KENT KENNAN

(Born in Milwaukee, Wisconsin, 1913)

Kent Wheeler Kennan studied piano and organ before entering the University of Michigan in 1930. He received his B.M. degree from the Eastman School of Music in 1934 and his M.M. degree from the same school two years later. After winning the Prix de Rome in music, he lived in Europe from 1936 to 1939 and studied briefly at the Accademia di Santa Cecilia in Rome. For most of his teaching career Kennan has been at the University of Texas in Austin, where, although officially retired, he continues to teach one course each semester. He is the author of two widely used texts, *The Technique of Orchestration* and *Counterpoint.*

Kennan's compositions reveal the same high degree of instrumental expertise shown in his orchestration text. He has composed *Scherzo, Aria, and Fugato* for oboe and piano, *Nocturne* for solo viola and orchestra, *Il Campo dei Fiori* for solo trumpet and orchestra, *Sonata for Trumpet and Piano,* several preludes for piano, and other works for orchestra. In addition to his famous *Night Soliloquy* for flute, Kennan has also written *Concertino* for piano and wind ensemble.

Night Soliloquy—Flute Solo (Pub = CF, 1962. Gr = 4. T = 4:00. Rec = CO-S-1724, Pellerite w. IN Un., Ebbs)

Night Soliloquy was written originally for flute and piano in 1936 while Kennan was living at the American Academy in Rome. Later, in an arrangement for flute, strings, and piano, the work was performed by most of the major orchestras in the United States including an unforgettable concert by the Philadephia Orchestra in 1955, featuring William Kincaid in his farewell performance.

In 1962 the composer arranged the accompaniment for wind ensemble, thus allowing a much larger audience to enjoy this delightful and challenging work for flute soloists.

ARAM KHACHATURIAN

(Born in Tiflis, Georgia, Armenia, 1903 — Died in Moscow, 1978)

Khachaturian is probably best known outside of Russia for his *Concerto for Piano and Orchestra* (1936), the *Concerto for Violin and Orchestra* (1940), and the "Saber Dance" from his ballet *Gayane* (Happiness, 1942). His incidental music and music for films have made him well known and popular in his native land. His music is deeply rooted in Armenian folklore and several of his themes have become Armenian national songs.

Khachaturian began his study of music at age nineteen at Gnessin's Music School in Moscow, where he studied cello and composition. In 1929 he transferred to the Moscow Conservatory, where he studied with Miaskovsky and Vassilenko. Khachaturian played an important part in the musical life of his country with his conducting, composing, and position as professor at the Moscow Conservatory. Contrary to the expressed opinion of some of his Soviet contemporaries, he believed in the free expression of all creative individuals.

Armenian Dances (Tr = Satz. Pub = MC, 1945. Gr = 4. T = 6:00. Rec = PH-PC 16 3, Eastman, Fennell)

The two *Armenian Dances* are among several works for military band by Aram Khachaturian. The dances were written originally for a Red Army Cavalry Band in 1943 and were adapted for modern band instrumentation by the gifted American musician and scholar Ralph Satz. Tempo markings on the two dances are Allegro Moderato and Allegro. (John Wakefield, University of Maryland)

Three Dance Episodes from *Spartacus* (Arr = Hunsberger. Pub = MC, 1969. Gr = 5. T = 13:00. Rec, 1st mvt = CR-MID-69-11, Clovis, NM, H.S., Molenaar; LO-6322, London Orch., Khachaturian)

Khachaturian was well known for his ballets, especially *Spartacus* and *Gayane*. In arranging these three dances for band, Hunsberger has shown a complete knowledge of scoring for wind and percussion instruments. Excellent players are required on the solo parts as well as in the tuba, horn, and percussion sections. The first dance is divided into Dance of a Greek Slave, Entrance of the Merchants, Dance of a Roman Courtesan, and General Dance. The second section, in a slower tempo, has two parts; Dance of Phrygia, and Dance of an Egyptian Girl. The fiery finale is titled Sword Dance of the Young Thracians. The ballet, *Spartacus*, was composed between 1950 and 1956.

KARL L. KING

(Born in Paintersville, Ohio, 1891 — Died in Fort Dodge, Iowa, 1971)

Karl King began his long career in music by buying a cornet with money earned by selling newspapers. He was born in Paintersville, Ohio, but his family moved to Canton, Ohio, in 1902 and it was there that he bought a cornet, exchanged it later for a euphonium which he played in the local Thayer Band, and by the time he was seventeen, had his first composition published. At the age of nineteen he began playing in circus bands, including the Robinson, Sells-Floto, and Barnum and Bailey Bands. For two seasons (1914-15) he directed the combined Sells-Floto and Buffalo Bill's Circus Band. He then returned to Canton to start a publishing business and direct the Grand Army Band of Canton, but two years later he moved his business to Fort Dodge, Iowa, and became director of the municipal band there—conducting it for over fifty years. During his long tenure the Fort Dodge Municipal Band became one of the nation's best known bands, giving two concerts each week during the summer and playing at almost every Iowa State Fair since 1920.

King had almost 250 published works to his credit, including serenades, overtures, waltzes, and galops, as well as his famous marches. Among his many honors was an honorary doctorate from Phillips University, and the naming of a state highway bridge in Fort Dodge after its favorite adopted son. King used the name Carl Lawrence for his works published with the J.E. Agnew Company as he was under contract with another publisher at the time—for less money.

In an interview with Karl Holvik *(Journal of Band Research, III-2)*, King said that "whatever I learned in composition or conducting or anything else (it was) mostly by imitation, by experimentation, and by listening to good men and watching good men. I think that's one of the best ways of getting an education."

Barnum and Bailey's Favorite March (Pub = BA, 1913. Gr = 4. T = 2:30. Rec = CR-4096, Un of IL, Begian; CR-NBA-78-7, U.S. Navy, Muffley; CR-MID-72-14, Cicero, NY, H.S., Codner)

King wrote this march for the Barnum and Bailey Circus Band in 1913 at the request of its director, Ned Brill. King was twenty-two at the time and was preparing to join the band as a euphonium player. The euphonium part in this march (and in most of King's other marches) shows his love for the instrument—he liked to hear the euphonium "romping around." His use of the word "favorite" in the title was a good choice. It is still one of the most popular marches played—in or out of the circus.

The Big Cage Galop (Pub = KK, 1934. Gr = 3. T = 1:30. Rec = CR-4096, Un. of IL, Begian; MG-GI-SRI-75087, Eastman, Fennell)

King gave up trooping with circus bands in 1915, but he continued to write marches and galops for the circus for many years. One interesting example is *Atta-Boy March* which he published in 1926, then re-published in 1961 as *Center Ring March*. *The Big Cage* was written in 1934 and dedicated to Clyde Beatty who was as famous as a lion trainer at that time as Gunther Williams is now.

The galop, as a musical form, has increased in tempo considerably from its nineteenth century, European origin as a ballroom dance. Then, it was a moderately fast hop-glide dance step; now, it is a fast and furious contest between the tigers and the musicians to see who can "finish their act first."

JOHN KINYON

(Born in Elmira, New York, 1918 — Died in Coral Gables, Florida, 1980)

John Kinyon spent a lifetime in the field of music education, much of it in directing school bands at various levels, and in all types of communities including rural, suburban, and city. His methods, compositions, and arrangements for elementary and junior high bands number in the hundreds and are listed in the catalogs of nearly ever major educational publisher. Kinyon held degrees from the Eastman School of Music (1940) and Ithaca College (1949). and was for many years director for Warner Bros. Music. He was a member of ASCAP and had for several years received one of their awards for prestigious composition. His conducting textbook, *The Teacher on the Podium*, has recently been released by the Alfred Publishing Company.

Kinyon was active as a writer, clinician, and guest conductor, and was a professor of music education at the University of Miami. (Alfred Publishing Company)

Monterey Jack March (Pub = CF, 1969. Gr = 3. T = 2:15)

Imagination is the only means of supplying some bit of legend for this title. "Jack" may have been that type of hero who was a seaman, a woodsman, or an outlaw. . .a rough-and-tumble sort given to living by the sword, axe, or pistol and, of course, meeting his demise through the same means. (Carl Fischer, Inc.)

The march adheres to an ABA form and in part, is based on three-measure phrases with an underlying jazz harmonic structure. Although written as a concert march, it shows possibilities for a "six-to-five" marching band interjecting a few steps of "eight-to five" when the 6/8 meter changes to 2/4. (Ed.)

Royal March (Pub = AL. Gr = 2. T = 2:00)

This is the most popular work in Kinyon's *Mini-Score Series*. As the title implies, the music suggests a visit to one of the many castles of Europe—the dazzling Schonbrunn Palace in Vienna; the countless castles along the Rhine River between Mainz and Koblenz, as seen from the deck of a river boat; or the "Tower" of London with its history displayed in every building within its ancient walls.

Scarborough Fair (Pub = AL. Gr = 2)

This English folksong has a haunting melody which contributes to its popularity with succeeding generations of young people. The American duo of Paul Simon and Art Garfunkel helped to popularize the song in this country with their recording in 1966 and their background music for the film, *The Graduate,* in 1968. Kinyon's arrangement, taken from his *Mini-Score Series,* retains the flavor of the folksong and is still not difficult to play.

GEORGE T. KIRCK

(Born in Mount Vernon, New York, 1948)

George Kirck has conducted the concert bands at Northern Illinois and Millikin Universities. His professional teaching experience includes working with instrumental ensembles and creative/electronic music at all levels. Kirck received his B.M. and

135

B.M.E. degrees from Hartt College of Music and his M.M. degree from Northern Illinois University. He is currently working toward a doctoral degree in composition at the University of Illinois. (Shawnee Press, Inc.)

Renaissance Triptych (Pub = SH, 1978. Gr = 3. T = 6:00. Rec = CR-MID-79-5, Hale H. S., West Allis, WI, Blahnik)

This three-part work is based on a dance and two songs from the rich literature of 1300-1600 Western music. "Douce Dame Jolie" is an example of the medieval virelai by Guillaume de Machaut, the leading composer and poet of the fourteenth century French Ars Nova. This 600 year old monophonic dance alternates repeated sections between soloist and chorus. This alternating pattern is preserved in this setting with the use of soli and tutti textures. "Lirum Bililirum," a love song by Rossinus Mantuanus, is representative of the northern Italian frottola form of poetry and music popularized at the courts of Verona, Padua, Venice, and most notably Mantua, near the turn of the sixteenth century. The frottola is essentially a chordal composition in three or four parts, characterized by simple harmonic progressions, short repeated sections, and the melodic-like prominence of the highest voice—quite often the only voice with text. Due to the prominence of the highest voice, it is believed these secular works were frequently performed as solo songs with instrumental accompaniment.

"Riu, Riu Chiu" is a Spanish Christmas song comprised of several stanzas linked by a refrain. It is a musical setting of a popular fifteenth century Spanish poetic form called the villancico, and was generally set in a chordal texture. This arrangement was dedicated to and premiered by the 1977 Bloomfield, Connecticut, Junior High School Band (John Erskine, conductor) at the 1977 eastern division meeting of the Music Educators National Conference. (Shawnee Press, Inc.)

KIYOSHIGE KOYAMA
(Born in Nagano, Japan, 1924)

Kiyoshige Koyama is one of Japan's most popular composers of music for band. He has been highly successful at portraying various facets of Japanese culture with the traditional international instrumentation of the concert band. Koyama graduated from Nagano Teachers College in 1933 and in 1941 moved to Tokyo. In 1946 he won the prestigious Nainichi Newspaper composition contest and in 1954 he began devoting all of his time to composing. Since 1969 Koyama has been a professor of music at Kobe Yamate Girls Junior College.

Daikagura for Band (Pub = ON, 1971. T = 6:00. Rec = TO-TA-9301 by members of NHK Sym. Orch., Yamada)

The music was composed at the request of the Tokyo Music College in 1971 and premiered the same year by the Tokyo Music College Symphonic Wind Ensemble conducted by Chiaki Murakawa. Some of the thematic material in the piece was taken from a "Kagura-bayshi" (Shinto music and dance), traditional folk music from Yawata Village in Nagano Prefecture.

The performance of the "Kagura-bayashi" consists of a dance with lion's mask or comical acting with humorous masks of "Okame" (a moon-faced woman) and "Hyottoko" (a clown) during the playing of flutes, drums, gong, etc. The tinkling of the bells in unison at the end of the piece represents the composer's memories concerning the traditional dances. (Kiyoshige Koyama, Kobe Yamate Girls Junior College)

Echigo Jishi (Pub = ON, 1970. Gr = 5. T = 6:00. Rec = TO-TA-9301 by members of NHK Sym. Orch., Yamada)

Echigo Jishi was composed at the request of the Ongaku No Tomo Sha in 1970 and performed in Tokyo the same year by members of the NHK Symphony Orchestra conducted by Kazuo Yamada. The title refers to the "Lion of Echigo," originally a masterpiece of Japanese traditional music in the style of "nagauta." It was composed by Rokuzaemon Kineya the 9th in 1811.

"Nagauta" developed as background music accompanying the kabuki dance. Since the kabuki dance was inserted into a tragic scene of the kabuki play for a change of mood, the accompaniment is usually flamboyant in style. The performance of "nagauta" traditionally consists of a chorus in conjunction with instrumentalists playing flutes and hand-drums. This arrangement features part of the original work and is characterized by violent changes in tempo. (Kiyoshige Koyama, Kobe Yamate Girls Junior College)

Kobiki-Uta (Pub = ON, 1962-70. Gr = 5. T = 10:00. Rec = TO-TA-9301 by members of NHK Sym. Orch., Yamada)

Kobiki-Uta is a work song sung by lumberjacks while cutting wood. This piece is a set of variations based on a "kobiki-uta," a folksong of Kyushu in southern Japan. The first movement, Theme, begins with the song of the lumberjacks and ends with temple bells portraying the end of the day. Bon-odori (Bon dance) takes place during the hot summer. A prelude of vigorous flute and drum sounds is followed by humorous lyrics which lead to a climax. Asa No Uta conveys the refreshing mood of the morning. Written in a fast five meter, the movement features the melodic percussion and piano playing a variation of the theme. In the Finale all of the instruments join in a frenzy of excitement before repeating the opening tenor saxophone solo, and the work concludes with the sounds of the gong and the bass clarinet.

The composition was arranged from an earlier orchestra work and was first performed by the Tokyo Kosei Band conducted by Kazuo Yamada in 1970. (Kiyoshige Koyama, Kobe Yamate Girls Junior College)

Mogura-Oi (Pub = ON, 1970. Gr = 5. T = 2:15. Rec = TO-TA-9301 by members of NHK Sym. Orch., Yamada)

"Mogura-Oi" (mole-hunting) and "Tori-Oi" (bird-hunting) are performed early in the morning on January 15 each year as a tradition originating many years ago among the children in Nobusato Village, Nagano Prefecture, where the composer was born. This annual event for the children has elements of a magic rite. A wooden pail is placed in the yard and the children rub the brim with a Tembinbo carrying-pole to charm away such vermin as moles, snakes, and centipedes. During the screeching sounds caused by the rubbing (imitating the wailing of moles), some of the shrieking children beat the ground with wooden poles. Because of the programmatic connotation of the composition, rhythmic elements are emphasized.

The Ongaku No Tomo Sha commissioned *Mogura-Oi* in 1970 and it was first performed by members of the NHK Symphony Orchestra conducted by Kazuo Yamada in Tokyo that same year. (Kiyoshige Koyama, Kobe Yamate Girls Junior College)

Otemoyan (Pub = ON, 1971. Gr = 5. T = 2:00. Rec = TO-TA-9301 by members of NHK Sym. Orch., Yamada)

The folksong, "Otemoyan," originated among the people of Kumamoto Prefecture and is now well known throughout Japan. It has a universal appeal as it retains its Japanese flavor even after it is adapted to Western instrumentation. The most salient feature of the tune is its humorous character, for example the dissonant intervals heard intermittently throughout the work.

The Ongaku No Tomo Sha commissioned Koyama to arrange *Otemoyan* in 1970. A public recording performance was presented during the same year at the Fumonkan Hall in Tokyo by members of the NHK Symphony Orchestra conducted by Kazuo Yamada. (Kiyoshige Koyama, Kobe Yamate Girls Junior College)

JOHN KRANCE

(Born in Bridgeport, Connecticut, 1935)

John Krance received his formal training at the Eastman School of Music. Presently residing in New York City, Krance has served as music director of radio station WPAT in New York, has arranged and conducted motion pictures, and has also arranged and orchestrated music for a number of conductors and recording artists—among them Morton Gould, Henry Mancini, and Frederick Fennell. During his service with the armed forces he was chief-arranger for the U.S. Army Field Band of Washington, D.C.—the traveling "showcase band" of the U.S. Army.

Krance has spent a labor of love for bands and band music. His compositions and arrangements for concert band have received wide acclaim and numerous performances and recordings both here and abroad. All of which attests his special affinity with and unique insight into this medium. (Edwin H. Morris and Co.)

Broadway Curtain Time (Pub = EB, 1968. Gr = 4. T = 9:00. Rec = CR-MID-69-8, Northshore Concert, Wilmette, IL, Paynter; CR-MID-14, Plymouth, MI, Centennial Park H.S., Griffith)

The American musical theater has come a long way from the flimsy revues of the twenties and early thirties. It has developed into a distinguished and highly sophisticated art form. Some of the most popular, endearing, and imaginative music this country has produced was composed specifically for the Broadway stage. In recent years there have been a number of brilliantly successful Broadway musical productions which have captured the imagination of people everywhere: *Hello, Dolly!* and *Mame,* both with music and lyrics by Jerry Herman; *Bye Bye Birdie* and *All American,* both with music by Charles Strouse, and lyrics by Lee Adams; *Wildcat* (which starred Lucille Ball), music by Cy Coleman and lyrics by Carolyn Leigh.

In arranging *Broadway Curtain Time* for concert band, John Krance captures and projects the excitement, spirit, and feeling of the show from which each tune comes—casting the whole into an embodiment of today's recording, television, and film sound. Included are six great tunes—all six of which have become what is known in the trade as "standards"—from the above mentioned shows: "Hello, Dolly!", "Put On a Happy Face," "If He Walked Into My Life," "Mame," "Once Upon A Time," and "Hey, Look Me Over." (Edwin H. Morris and Co.)

ERNST KRENEK

(Born in Vienna, 1900)

Ernst Krenek began his musical studies with Franz Schreker at the Vienna Academy of Music when he was sixteen years of age. Subsequently, as a student or opera coach, he lived in Berlin, Paris (briefly), Kassel and Wiesbaden, Germany. In 1928 he returned to Vienna where he became a correspondent for the *Frankfurter Zeitung* and also learned the intricacies of twelve-tone technique through his personal friendship with Alban Berg and Anton Webern. He was married for a brief time to Anna Mahler, daughter of Gustav Mahler; he is now married to Gladys Nordenstran, also a composer. He credits both his studies and his life experiences with being the determining influences in the different stages of his career as a composer. Charles Boone (in *Dictionary of Contemporary Music, 1st Ed.)* lists the following five periods of Krenek's compositions: (1) atonal, 1921-23; (2) neoclassic, 1924-26; (3) romantic, 1926-31; (4) twelve-tone, 1931-56; (5) serial, since 1957.

Krenek's most successful stage work, the opera *Jonny spielt auf* (1925-26), enabled the young composer to devote full time to composing. Included among his over 200 works are twenty operas, seven string quartets, five symphonies, and a variety of instrumental, vocal, and electronic works for different combinations. Hindemith's influence may be seen in his choice of some instrumental combinations. Krenek immigrated to the United States in 1938 teaching first at Vassar College then at Hamline University. He has lived in Palm Springs, California, for the last several years and has continued his composing and writing. Krenek holds three honorary doctorates from American universities and is the recipient of meritorious awards from the Federal Republic of Germany, Austria, and the cities of Vienna and Hamburg.

Dream Sequence, Op. 224 (Pub = EAM, 1978. Gr = 5. T = 15:00. Rec = CR-CBDNA-77-6, Baylor Un., Krenek)

The *Dream Sequence* was Krenek's first composition for large symphonic band, although he had written works for smaller wind groups, including *Symphony for Winds and Percussion, Op. 34* and *Three Merry Marches, Op. 44,* in the early 1920's. *Dream Sequence* was commissioned by the College Band Directors National Association, with H. Robert Reynolds as contracting chairman (see *The Instrumentalist, Jan., 1978),* and was premiered at the 1977 CBDNA convention by the Baylor University Band (Richard Floyd, conductor) with the composer conducting. Krenek describes the work as follows:

> The title of *Dream Sequence* hints at the imagery that may loosely be associated with the music. It does not mean that the music describes any particular dreams or narrates any story. The titles Nightmare and Pleasant Dreams indicate the general character of the first two movements. Puzzle, the third movement, is a strictly constructed serial piece (perhaps more the result of a sleepless night than of any dream).
>
> The five movements of the piece are each subdivided into five segments. Every segment in a movement has a different characteristic ending, but these same endings are used—in a different order—in all the other movements. The endings change their order of succession according to the pattern 12345, 51423, 35214, 43152, 24531, similar to the sestina pattern of medieval poetry. Each segment consists of two statements of a 12-tone row (using 24 tones plus the repetition of the first tone), which at the same time is the first tone of the row-form used in the following segment. The last movement is evocative of the sentiments that accompany the familiar *Dream about Flying.*

HOMER C. LAGASSEY
(Born in Amesbury, Massachusetts, 1902)

LaGassey began his musical career at the piano when he was eight and later studied with prominent teachers in both the United States and Europe. He graduated from Cass Technical High School in Detroit and subsequently earned the M.M. degree at the Detroit Institute of Musical Art followed by the M.E. degree at Wayne State University. He served in the Detroit public school system as teacher, head of fine arts, and supervisor of music education from 1920 until his retirement in 1962. In 1944 he was choral director for the Ford Sunday Evening broadcasts; in 1954 he was program director at the Interlochen National Music Camp; he conducted the Detroit Federation of Musicians Parks Band and the Detroit Faculty Symphony Orchestra for several seasons; he served as adjudicator in many music festivals in the midwest area. His best-known band compositions are *Sequoia* and *Sea Portrait*. LaGassey now lives in a retirement home in Lighthouse Point, Florida.

Sequoia (Pub = KJ, 1941. Gr = 4. T = 6:00.)

LaGassey's tone poem *Sequoia* was originally written for orchestra and later transcribed for band by the composer. It was performed by several major orchestras including the Detroit Symphony and the San Francisco Symphony. As a transcription the work utilizes the unique sonorities and tonal grandeur of the symphonic band. Much of this richly-scored composition is reminiscent of the film scoring of the World War II era.

WILLIAM P. LATHAM
(Born in Shreveport, Louisiana, 1917)

William Peters Latham attended Asbury College before earning the B.S., B.M., and M.M. degrees in trumpet, composition, and theory at the Cincinnati Conservatory where his composition teachers were Sydney Durst and Eugene Goosens. He then studied with Herbert Elwell and Howard Hanson at the Eastman School of Music while he completed his Ph.D. requirements. During World War II Latham served first as a cavalry bandsman and later as an infantry officer in Germany where he was wounded in action. After the war Latham began his teaching career at the University of Northern Iowa (in 1946) and nineteen years later joined the faculty as professor of music and coordinator of composition at North Texas State University. He was appointed director of graduate studies in 1969 and in 1978 was promoted to the rank of distinguished professor of music—the eighth faculty member at the large university to be so honored.

Latham has composed almost 100 works—about half of which have been published—for orchestra (beginning with *The Lady of Shalott,* premiered by the Cincinnati Symphony in 1941), band, choir, wind instrument concertos, and chamber works. Most of his early band works were tonal and traditional in form, but his *Dodecaphonic Set* of five 12-tone pieces (published in 1967) began a gradual trend toward the use of more avant garde techniques. Fortunately, Latham has the aesthetic perception to use such techniques toward a musical result. Examples include *Prayers in Space,* which is published; and *Fusion, Revolution!, Prolegomena, Dilemmae,* and *Concertino for Alto Saxophone and Wind Ensemble,* which are available from the composer. These are challenging compositions for band.

Latham's sense of humor and his wide knowledge of literature are often expressed in his works. His wife is also a composer and one daughter is a flutist. Another daughter teaches Latin and their son is a physicist.

Brighton Beach March (Pub = SB, 1954. Gr = 3. T = 3:15)

Written in 1954, this concert march has numerous dynamic contrasts as well as unusual scoring of the woodwind parts. The forward-moving rhythmic patterns and the fully harmonized melodies combine to make this march a welcome change of pace.

Court Festival (Pub = SB, 1957. Gr = 3. T = 5:30. Rec = OS-8806, Fourth All-American Bandmasters)

Court Festival is a suite in the style of instrumental dance music of the late sixteenth and seventeenth centuries, used at various European court festivals and other ceremonies. The opening Intrada has a festive or march-like character; the Pavan and Galliard are both based on dance music known through Europe from the early part of the sixteenth century—the pavan is a stately dance in duple meter, the galliard a gay dance in triple meter. The concluding "The Horses" Branle is in the style of another popular sixteenth-century dance. The branle was danced everywhere—in the country and at the court—and included singing, swaying movements of the body and hands, and pantomime. (Donald L. Panhorst, Edinboro State College

Proud Heritage March (Pub = SB, 1956. Gr = 3. T = 4:00. Rec = CR-MID-75-12, Oconomowoc, WS, Jr. H.S., Reul)

An excellent processional or concert march, *Proud Heritage* makes use of the legato tone quality of the reeds and baritones in their lower range. The French horns also share the spotlight. Climaxes are powerful and brilliant and the use of brass choir alone for several measures provides an interesting tone color change.

Serenade for Band (Pub = SH, 1967. Gr = 3. T = 5:00)

Serenade for Band is one movement of a suite, entitled *Escapades,* which was commissioned by the Mid-American Intercollegiate Band for its Fifth Annual Festivel held in Cedar Rapids, Iowa, in 1965. The composition has no specific verbal or pictorial meaning. It is simply a calm interlude.

Three Chorale Preludes (Pub = SB, 1956. Gr = 3. T = 6:30. Rec = MU-H-80-P-5837, Un. of MI, Revelli; CR-ABA-76-2, AZ St. Un., Strange)

Although these preludes are written in early eighteenth-century style and are based on familiar chorale melodies, they are not arrangements, but are original compositions for band. "Break Forth, O Beauteous Heavenly Light" is a tune by Johann Schop, first published in Rist's *Himmlische Lieder* in 1641. It has been used by many composers, including J.S. Bach, in his *Christmas Oratorio*. "My Heart is Filled with Longing" is best known as the "Passion Chorale," or "O Sacred Head Now Wounded." The melody was originally that of a love song, "Mein G'mut ist mir Verwirret," by Hans Leo Hassler, and as such, appeared in his collection of secular songs *Lustgarten Neuer Deutscher Gesang* in 1601. Bach used this melody several times in the *St. Matthew Passion,* and there have been numerous polyphonic settings by other composers, including Brahms. "Now Thank We All Our God" first appeared in Johann Cruger's *Praxis Pietatis Melica* in 1647. Bach used this chorale in his *Cantata for Reformation Sunday*. (Cecil Wilson, Case Western Reserve University)

MICHAEL LECKRONE
(Born in North Manchester, Indiana, 1936)

Mike Leckrone is chairman of the band department and professor of music at the University of Wisconsin. A native of Indiana, Leckrone received his B.M. and M.M. degrees from Butler University in Indianapolis. His experience includes professional work as a conductor, composer, arranger, and performer; he is continuously active as a clinician. (Studio P/R, Inc.)

Analogue (Pub = PR, 1978. Gr = 3. T = 5:10. Rec = PR-R-7801)

The term "analogue" can be defined as "a compound structurally similar to another but differing often by a single element." This entire work is based on a four-note motive which is first stated simply in the flutes and then expands into a highly rhythmic version utilizing mathematical combinations and permutations. *Analogue* was written for the Wisconsin Music Association. (Studio P/R, Inc.)

Avatara (Pub = PR, 1974. Gr = 3)

Leckrone composed this work for the Wisconsin and Indiana band contests, and it has since become very popular in several other states for both contest and concert use. *Avatara* is contemporary in style and reveals the experience and originality of its composer. In Hindu mythology "avatar" refers to a descent, as of a deity to earth in bodily form.

Here's the Band (Pub = PR, 1977. Gr = 4. T = 5:00. Rec = PR-R-7801)

This work features seven different sections of the band and is based on the popular folk classic, "Mama Don't Allow." It also highlights various styles for each variation, including dixieland, hillbilly, and jazz.

PIERRE LEEMANS
(Born in Schaarbeek, Belgium, 1897)

Pierre Leemans is not only the composer of the world famous *March of the Belgian Parachutists;* he is a musician who has had a great influence on Belgian music—especially band music. He studied piano, harmony, orchestration, and composition with J. Sevenants, M. Lunssens, and Paul Gilson between 1919 and 1922 after having taught at the Etterbeek Music Academy (near Brussels) since 1917. He served in the army for a year when he was twenty-two, taught music again until 1932, then resigned to become pianist-conductor-program director for the N.I.R. (the official broadcasting company—now B.R.T.-R.T.B.). In 1934 he won the composition contest for the official march of the 1935 Brussels World Exhibition.

In 1940 Leemans founded the Schaarbeek High School Choir, and in 1943 he won a composition contest for school songs. In 1945 he wrote a prize-winning dirge for the fallen heroes of World War II, and two years later he was selected as the Belgian delegate to the Geneva congress for standardizing music notation. From a group of 109 anonymous composers, Leemans' works were selected for first and second prize for the 1958 Brussels World Fair. He has written for various media including choirs, bands, orchestras, chamber groups, and motion pictures. Among his many works for band are *Light Aviation* (an official regimental march), *Belgian Air Force, Symphonic Divertimento, and Ghost Dance.* Leemans still lives in the area which he knows best, Brussels, Belgium. (Francis Pieters, Kortrijk, Belgium)

March of the Belgian Parachutists (Arr. Wiley. Pub ≐ TN, 1975. Gr = 4. T = 2:50. Rec = TE-DG-10043, Cleveland Sym. Winds, Fennell; CR-MENC-78-18, Nat'l H.S. Honor, Revelli)

As the original title, *Marche des Parachutistes Belges,* indicates, the listener expects to hear a march with a European flavor. The thin scoring (for example two piccolos and two oboes on the introduction and bass clarinet and bassoon on the first melody) and the folk song idiom of the first strain soon confirm the European origin. At the trio the same tune reappears as a counter-melody to a smooth-flowing melody. The march was first heard on a recording by members of the Lamar University Band. Finding no music available in this country, assistance was eventually received through the American Embassy in Belgium, and a copy of the march was sent to Charles Wiley, the Lamar band director, who rearranged the march to fit American (and Texas!) band instrumentation.

Leemans wrote this work in 1945 after a dinner with a group of Belgian paratroopers. As their commander, Major Timmerman, drove him home that night, the march melody came to mind and he finished the other parts after reaching his home. As Leemans explained, "Like all successful music, this tune came from my pen as water out of a fountain."

ERIK LEIDZEN
(Born in Stockholm, Sweden, 1894 — Died in New York, 1962)

Erik Leidzen, well known composer, conductor and arranger, was born in Stockholm, and received his musical training at the Royal Conservatory of Music there. He came to the United States at the age of twenty and later became an American citizen. During most of his life he was associated with the Salvation Army's music programs, and he wrote many compositions and arrangements for the use of Salvation Army groups. He contributed substantially to the repertoire of bands throughout the country through his many well known original compositions and arrangements. Leidzen was closely associated with Edwin Franko Goldman for many years and a large number of his arrangements were made for the Goldman Band. Some of his most popular original works for band include *Nordic March, E.F.G. March* (for Edwin Franko Goldman), *Swedish Rhapsodies Nos. 1 and 2,* and *Overture Springtime.* (Mills Music)

First Swedish Rhapsody (Pub = MM, 1950. Gr = 4. T = 7:30)

Four contrasting melodies form the thematic material of this composition, and the introduction is based on the first of these; a nostalgic song of home. Then follows a typical Scandinavian folk-tune, after which comes a students' song, emphasizing the "sweet idleness" between classes. The quiet pastorale is suddenly interrupted by martial strains leading to a march-like folk melody, the development of which brings the rhapsody to a sonorous ending. This original band work was dedicated to Josef Toft, a friend of the composer. (Mills Music)

MITCH LEIGH
(Born in Brooklyn, New York, 1928)

Mitch Leigh studied composition with Paul Hindemith at the Yale School of Music and played first bassoon in the Yale Concert Band. After gaining B.A. and M.A. degrees, he went to New York, and in 1957 he founded and organized Music Makers, Inc., an enormously successful commercial production house that has won numerous awards for radio and television commercial music. Leigh writes in a variety of forms from jazz to opera, and he is at home in almost any musical style. He has been represented on the Broadway stage as composer of the incidental music for the plays, *Too True to Be Good* and *Never Live Over a Pretzel Factory*. *Man of La Mancha,* his first Broadway musical, had a New York run of 2,328 performances, was produced around the world, and was made into an award-winning motion picture.

Man of La Mancha (Arr = Erickson; Yoder. Pub = SF, 1966; 1967. Gr = 4/3. T = 4:30; 1:45)

The Cervantes classic, *Don Quixote,* has been fashioned into one of the most successful musical plays of all time—*Man of La Mancha*. Composer Mitch Leigh has produced a musical score unique in the annals of the Broadway musical in that it was originally written for wind instruments. The production has received numerous awards in recent years. Ranging in style from severe classical Spanish models to the free guitaristic and flamenco influences, the score presents a musical profile of the knight, Don Quixote, which is kaleidoscopic in character, reflecting on one hand the ardent suitor in "Dulciana" and on the other, the exalted defender of chivalry in "The Impossible Dream." (Ralph Wahl, University of South Carolina)

HENK VAN LIJNSCHOOTEN
(Born in The Hague, Holland, 1928)

Henk van Lijnschooten attended the School of Music in The Hague, Holland, where he was born and later played in the Royal Netherlands Military Band for twelve years. He graduated from the Royal Netherlands Conservatory of Music with special distinction in 1956. From 1957 to 1964 Lijnschooten was the director of the Royal Netherlands Marine Band which became famous as a concert and recording group under his direction. He has since become director for wind instruments at the Rotterdam School of Music and professor of band conducting at Rotterdam Conservatory. He is one of the leading composers of band works in Europe; most of his compositions have been for "harmony band" (woodwinds, brass, and percussion), but he has also written pieces for "fanfare band" (saxophones, brass, and percussion), and "brass band" (brass and percussion). He has also composed much music for films and television. Working with musicians from other countries, including Paul Yoder (U.S.A.), Joseph Moerenhout (Belgium), Robert Svanesoe (Denmark), Desire Dondeyne (France), and Albert Haberling (Switzerland), Lijnschooten (with his expertise in French, German, Dutch, and English) has been instrumental in promoting an international instrumentation for band—a concept advocated for many years by Raymond Dvorak, William Revelli, Herbert Johnston, Herbert Hazelman, Manley Whitcomb, John Paynter, and others in the United States.

Rhapsodie Française (Pub = MOL. Gr = 3. T = 6:10. Rec = MO-11, Militaire Kapel, Lijnschooten)

This French rhapsody is a collection of folksongs which are familiar to all or most French people and should be familiar to other nationalities also. The best known tune in the rhapsody is probably "Alouette," which is heard near the beginning after a soft introduction and a rhythmic percussion-bass interlude. Lijnschooten balances the simplicity of the melodies with a variety of contrasting styles; changing meters, different solo and soli timbres, a fugue, and even a drone bass against a melody à la bagpipe. The rhapsody diminishes in volume near the end and suddenly stops with four strong, marcato beats.

Rhapsody from the Low Countries (Pub = MOL-1967-78. Gr = 3. T = 6:00)

When this rhapsody was first distributed in the United States by Hansen Publishers, the instructions in five languages and alternate instrumentation for bands in various countries were novel to say the least. Now, a decade later, thanks to television, foreign trips, and worldwide band festivals, the problems of an international band instrumentation are beginning to be understood. Meanwhile this rhapsody has now "gone home" to Holland where it is distributed by Molenaar's Muziekcentrale. The "low countries" in the title refer to the Benelux nations of Belgium, Netherlands, and Luxembourg, and the melodies of the rhapsody originated in those picturesque, low-lying areas of western Europe.

FRANZ LISZT

(Born in Raiding, Hungary, 1811 — Died in Bayreuth, Germany, 1886)

Franz Liszt learned the rudiments of playing the piano from his father, a musical amateur, and gave his first public concert at the age of nine. Acclaim as a genius brought him sponsorship for a musical career beginning with studies under Czerny, Salieri, and others At about the age of thirteen he toured the Continent and England performing as a pianist. At fourteen he made his first serious attempt at composition. He continued to travel extensively but settled periodically at Weimar, Rome, and Paris. Liszt received wide acclaim as a performer, composer, editor, and teacher during his lifetime, and his memory has been honored throughout the world. His compositions include sixty-five sacred choral works, eighteen secular choral works, twenty-five orchestral pieces, seventy-two songs, and three hundred ninety-eight piano works. As if this were not enough, Liszt has often been called the greatest of all pianists.

Les Préludes (Tr = Duthoit/Brown; Hindsley. Pub = BH, 1936; HI, ms. Gr = 6. T = 14:00. Rec = IL-48, Un. of IL, Hindsley; MS-8, Morehead St. Un., Hawkins)

Franz Liszt was a legend—even in his own time. According to the written reports of the critics and concert-goers who heard his performances at the piano, he combined his genius as a virtuoso with a style of showmanship not too far removed from that of some present-day rock "artists." Liszt apparently borrowed some of his mannerisms from the Italian violinist, Niccolo Paganini, who was rumored to be in league with the devil. When Liszt titled some of his works *"Faust" Symphony,* *"Dante" Sonata,* and *"Mephisto" Waltz,* he only confirmed the suspicion by some that he also had demonic powers.

By 1847, when he was still at the height of his performing ability, Liszt had made the decision to give up paid concerts (he still played command performances for the Pope in Rome and an occasional charity concert in Budapest), and concentrate on composing. In 1848 he moved to the tiny German province of Weimar, where he had a court orchestra and a court opera at his disposal, and he gained a thorough knowledge of orchestration as he experimented and composed. Liszt's inspiration for *Les Preludes* came from the poetry of Alphonse Lamartine (1790-1869), an aristocratic French author and diplomat. When Liszt read the lines, "What is life? Only a series of preludes to that unknown song whose first solemn note is tolled by death," he had the title for his most famous symphonic poem. Liszt's composition approximates the succession of images in Lamartine's poem—the mysterious opening, the crescendo to the first transformation of the theme, the tranquil version of the opening phrase, another crescendo to "the tragic storm that cuts short the illusions of youth," a calm interlude, and the final triumphal sounds which signal that "the soul has proved itself in battle"—the music sums up the temper of the mid-nineteenth century in a manner no historian can equal.

ALEX LITHGOW

(Born in Glasgow, Scotland, 1870 — Died in Launceston, Tasmania, 1929)

Alex Lithgow was born in Scotland, but his family moved to Invercargill, New Zealand, when the boy was six years old. New Zealand had been made a crown colony in 1841, and gold was discovered in 1861; the two events attracted many immigrants from England and Scotland who took their band instruments and music with them to their new homes. Both Alex and his brother Tom were tutored in music and both played in bands. Alex was admitted to the Invercargill Garrison Band when he was only eleven; he became the principal cornet soloist at sixteen and the leader of the band by the time he was twenty. In 1894 Alex Lithgow became director of the St. Joseph's Band in Launceston, Tasmania (an island off the south coast of Australia), and in 1898 he founded the Launceston Orchestral Society. In the years that followed he composed many works for band, orchestra, piano, and voice although many of the manuscripts which he sent to Germany were lost during the outbreak of World War I. In addition, many of his pieces were not copyrighted, and others were protected only within the British Empire. Determined to continue composing, Lithgow worked as a printer by day and composed his music at night. The strenuous existence took its toll on his health, and he died in 1929, leaving his widow and three children.

Invercargill March (Arr = Laurendeau.   Pub = CF, 1913.   Gr = 4.   T = 2:15. Rec = FS-LPS-1250, New Zealand National, Thorn)

After Alex Lithgow moved from Invercargill, New Zealand, to Launceston, Tasmania, to conduct the St. Joseph's Band, his brother Tom became leader of the band in Invercargill. In 1909 Tom Lithgow requested that Alex write a march for an approaching band contest. The composer responded with a march he had already finished, but which had been rejected by a publisher. The march was named *Invercargill* in honor of the city of his youth. Because of the success of the march Lithgow became known as one of the band world's greatest composers. Carl Fischer still lists six other Lithgow marches, all published after *Invercargill* and none as famous. (Information from Robert Hoe, Jr., Poughkeepsie, New York and James A. Perkins, Chatfield, Minnesota)

FREDERICK LOEWE
(Born in Vienna, 1904)

Frederick Loewe was born in the musical city of Vienna where his father was a famous tenor in the operettas. Regarded as a prodigy, Loewe was the youngest pianist to solo with the Berlin Symphony Orchestra; he was thirteen. At eighteen he won the Hollander Award, after studying composition with Ferruccio Busoni and piano with Eugène d'Albert. "Katrina," a song that he wrote when he was fifteen, sold a million copies. In 1924, hoping to become a concert pianist, he migrated to the United States, but his difficulties with the English language and music style forced him to work as a bus boy, riding instructor, boxer, cowboy, and even gold prospector. In the early thirties Loewe returned to his piano playing and began writing songs. He met Alan Lerner in 1942 and the resulting Broadway stage productions and films have won him many awards for the team. Loewe's major works include music for *Brigadoon, Paint Your Wagon, My Fair Lady, Camelot,* and *Gigi.*

Gigi (Arr = Bennett. Pub = CA, 1958. Gr = 3. T = 8:00)

The tunes heard in this arrangement are "Gigi," "The Night They Invented Champagne," "I Remember It Well," "Thank Heaven for Little Girls," "I'm Glad I'm Not Young Anymore," and "If Ever I Should Leave You." Very few Broadway composers have enjoyed the success of having their show tunes, such as these, remain popular over a period of years as have Lerner and Loewe. Maurice Chevalier and others sang the melodies from *Gigi* in this country and abroad long after the film's popularity had waned.

My Fair Lady, Selections (Arr = Bennett; Herfurth; Cacavas. Pub = CA, 1956. Gr = 3. T = 9:00. Rec = CR-MID-69-7-Cacavas arr., Hale H.S., West Allis, WI, Ncau)

Few musical comedies in recent years have been as eagerly awaited as *My Fair Lady,* the incontestable champion of the 1955-56 season. A musical adaptation of Bernard Shaw's *Pygmalion,* it has delighted even dedicated Shavians with an extraordinary mixture of wit, movement, and color. Produced by Herman Levin with book and lyrics by Alan Jay Lerner and music by Frederick Loewe, *My Fair Lady* is a joyous experience, brimming with melody and laughter. Heard in this selection, which was transcribed for band by Robert Russell Bennett, are the following popular songs: "With a Little Bit of Luck," "Wouldn't It Be Loverly?", "Get Me to the Church on Time," "I've Grown Accustomed to Her Face," and "I Could Have Danced All Night." (Everett Kisinger, University of Illinois)

Paint Your Wagon (Arr = Cacavas. Pub = CA, 1970. Gr = 3. T = 10:00. Rec = CR-MID-70-11, Oconomowoc, WI, Jr. H.S., Reul)

Lerner and Loewe's spectacular 1951 Broadway production, produced two decades later in a film version by Paramount, is set in the 1853 gold rush atmosphere of California. It traces the history of a mining camp from its change as a rugged boom town to a ghost city. The effect of a woman's touch on the rough and tough life of a gold panner is the basic motif upon which the story is built. This arrangement by John Cacavas includes "There's a Coach Comin' In," "Wand'rin' Star," "I'm On My Way," "I Still See Elisa," "I Talk to the Trees," and "They Call the Wind Maria."

ROBERT LOGAN

(Born in Beatrice, Nebraska, 1926)

Robert Logan grew up in the state of Nebraska and majored in music education (B.M.E. and M.M.E.) at Drake University in Des Moines. His principal composition teacher at the time was Francis Pyle. He taught in public schools from 1953 to 1955 before becoming music director at Clear Lake, Iowa, Junior College in 1955. He has combined originality with practical knowledge of wind and percussion instruments to produce a variety of works for concert band.

Two of Logan's published band works are for solo instruments with band accompaniment. The first, *Have Horn, Will Travel,* is a light-hearted novelty number for trumpet, and the other, *Presto Chango,* is for any one of a variety of wind instruments. His two most popular concert works are *Joi* and *Dimension.*

Joi (Pub = S&, 1966. Gr = 3. T = 5:00)

Logan has sub-titled this work "A Contemporary Selection" and it is modern in sound, but not with the dissonance that many listeners associate with the music of the last decade or two. The work has unusually interesting rhythms and exciting sounds which make for a joi-ful listening experience. Originally published in 1966, *Joi* has been a popular selection on the contest selection lists for several states.

NEWELL H. LONG

(Born in Markle, Indiana, 1905)

Newell Long earned his first degree in mathematics at Indiana University, then changed his major to music and completed the requirements for the M.A. and Ed.D. degrees at the same school and the M.S. degree in music education at Northwestern University. His principal composition teachers were Winfred Merrill and Robert Sanders. He became a professor of music at Indiana University in 1935 and retired from teaching in 1975. His music experience with bands ranges from several years as an associate director at his university to conductor of the Bloomington Community Band in 1978. Additional administrative experience includes the presidency of both the Music Educators National Conference (North Central Division) and the National Association of College Wind and Percussion Instructors.

Examples of Long's varied interests in composition may be shown by his *Bravos for Benny* (orchestra), *Journey Toward Freedom* (chorus and orchestra), and *Royal Clambake* (trombone quartet). Among his most popular band works are *Lincoln Lyric Overture, Symphonic Variations on Yankee Doodle, The Wise Owl* (for young bands), and *Art Show.* The latter work is a gentle satire on some examples of contemporary art and serial music (using a 12-tone row throughout), but it turns out being as worthwhile a composition as it is fun to play and hear. Most of Long's "retirement" time is now devoted to working on new commissions, but he still maintains an active interest in a variety of hobbies including railroads.

Concertino for Woodwind Quintet and Band (Pub = SO, GL, 1963. Gr = 4. T = 7:30. Rec = BP-107, Un. of IL, Hindsley)

Concertino was written at the suggestion of Philip Farkas, noted hornist, who pointed out the need for a work which would exploit the tonal resources of the woodwind quintet in conjunction with those of the modern concert band. It follows the scheme of recent multiple concerti rather than that of the Baroque concerto grosso in that the five solo instruments as a unit do not alternate with the band frequently and antiphonally, although they are heard as an unaccompanied quintet in several passages. The five featured winds are heard singly, in pairs, and in various combinations, sometimes with band or sections of it, sometimes without. The various themes are shared by the quintet and the band, and the musical material is organized in extended sonata-allegro form. The flute and bassoon each have a cadenza, but the oboe and clarinet have short dialogues instead.

Concertino for Woodwind Quintet and Band was composed at the Huntington Hartford Foundation in California and was first performed in October of 1961 at the University of Illinois under the direction of Mark H. Hindsley. (Leblanc Publications, Inc.)

RONALD LO PRESTI

(Born in Williamstown, Massachusetts, 1933)

Ronald Lo Presti is a graduate of Eastman School of Music and a former Ford Foundation composer-in-residence. He has taught at Texas Technical University, Indiana State College (Penn.), and is presently a member of the music faculty of Arizona State University. *Tundra,* a recent work for symphonic winds, received its first performance at the College Band Directors National Association convention at Ann Arbor, Michigan. Lo Presti has been the recipient of several Ford Foundation grants to young American composers.

Elegy for a Young American (Pub = TP, 1967. Gr = 4. T = 5:30. Rec = CR-ABA-80-9, AZ St. Un., Hines)

Elegy for a Young American was written in 1964 and is dedicated to the memory of John F. Kennedy. The Indiana Wind Ensemble, with Daniel DiCicco conducting, premiered the work in April of that same year. Except for a ten measure allegro near the end, the tempo of the entire work is a slow adagio. Contrast and balance are achieved by solo instruments alternating with small sections of instruments and with the sound of the full band.

Pageant Overture (Pub = TP, 1963, Rental. Gr = 4. T = 6:30)

Pageant Overture was first published in 1963 and dedicated to Frederick Fennell, conductor of the Eastman Wind Ensemble at the time. The overture is written in a fast-slow-fast form with some broadening of the tempo near the end. Although dissonant chords abound in the quicker sections, the Andante near the middle begins with a flowing melody and sustained tonal accompaniment. The same thematic material is developed in a variety of ways before the second Allegro recapitulates the opening material a whole step lower, drops dynamically to a whisper near the end, then crescendos to a powerful fortissimo with the lower brass repeating the same fast three-note motive heard at the very beginning.

ZDENĚK LUKÁŠ

(Born in Prague, Czechoslovakia, 1928)

Zdeněk Lukáš studied music theory with Kabeláč in Prague for a time, but he is largely a self-taught composer. From 1955 to 1965 he lived in Pilsen, Czechoslovakia, as a choral conductor, composing during the same period. Although his writing lacked technical skill during this first creative period, Lukáš gained important practical experience while composing several solo and chamber works and concluding with his *Symphony No.1* in 1960. During his next period of composition, Lukáš wrote a tremendous number of works. His *Symphony No. 3* was written entirely in the modal system and his earlier technical problems were no longer evident. Although his music has become even more enriched by original and novel sound quality and expression in recent years, his basic style has not changed. Lukáš has written for a variety of media including *Sonata Concertata* for piano, winds, and percussion (1966), three string quartets (1960-65-73), a wind quintet (1969), and *Thou Shalt Not Kill,* an electronic oratorio for chorus, instruments, and tape (1971). A true and spontaneous musicianship is evident throughout all these works. (Information from Stanley DeRusha, Michigan State University)

Musica Boema (Ms. = MIS, 1978. Gr = 5. Rec = CR-NCBDNA-78-3, MI St. Un., DeRusha)

Musica Boema was commissioned in 1977 by Stanley DeRusha while he was director of bands at the University of Wisconsin at Milwaukee. The work is in two movements and is typical of the style of Lukáš. The first movement, a large ABA form, is repetitive in presenting the first two themes; the solo trumpet plays the opening theme and the woodwinds play the second theme. The middle section begins with an extended harp and percussion soli which gives way to a saxophone solo, then continues with a recapitulation of the opening themes to end the first movement. The second movement is in an ABA' form with the first section beginning in a highly energetic and polyrhythmic manner, and closing, in the opposite way, with less and less intensity. The B section demonstrates Lukáš' great love of melody; the piccolo, soprano saxophone, and baritone saxophone are the first to play the melody (which is continually interrupted by an outburst in the brass playing the last five notes of the melody just played). The return of the opening section is changed somewhat but still recognizable as the motive which began the second movement. As the motive gains intensity a two measure ostinato gains its own momentum, reminiscent of the bells of Prague. The work closes with a characteristically brassy coda, restating the opening theme in a bright major tonality. Czech folk tunes, irregular in length and modal in tonality, are used in both movements. (Information from Stanley DeRusha, Michigan State University)

W. FRANCIS McBETH

(Born in Lubbock, Texas, 1933)

W. Francis McBeth has written extensively in the areas of orchestral, chamber, and band music. He received his B.M. degree at Hardin-Simmons University, his M.M. degree at the University of Texas, and did his doctoral study at the Eastman School of Music. McBeth studied with such composers as Clifton Williams, Kent Kennan, Wayne Barlow, Bernard Rogers, Macon Summerlin, and Howard Hanson.

He has been at Ouachita University since 1957 and is now the chairman of the department of theory-composition and resident composer. In addition to teaching and composing, McBeth has guest-conducted all-state and honor bands in the United States, Canada, and Japan. He was appointed composer laureate for the state of Arkansas in 1975 by the governor.

Cantique and Faranade (Pub = SO, 1967. Gr = 3. T = 7:00. Rec = SO-McBeth-V-1, TX Tech., McBeth)

Cantique and Faranade was commissioned in 1966 by the Arkansas School Band and Orchestra Association and premiered the next year by the all-state band.

The two movements of the work have contrasting tempos, but have certain stylistic elements in common. As McBeth's general approach is developmental, his melodies exist not so much for what they are, but rather for what they can become. The listener's attention is held by their transformation and development. Using the same techniques developed by masters of the classical sonata form, McBeth breaks the melodies into short motives of a few notes then manipulates them in various ways.

The first movement of this work is slow and solemn, moving in a great arch from a quiet beginning, to a climax in the middle, and back to a soft and calm conclusion. Tension is often created by dissonance between the chords and the melody, but this is resolved as the two periodically join in a common harmony.

The second movement is considerably faster and follows a general ABA form. The return of A is highly varied both in instrumentation and in the handling of motives from the main theme. Near the end the percussion combine with the winds in a dramatic, "molto rallentando" conclusion. (R. John Specht, Queensborough Community College)

Canto (Pub = SO, 1978. Gr = 2. T = 4:30. Rec = CR-MID-78-6, South Lyon Centennial M.S., MI, McBeth)

Canto was commissioned by and dedicated to the All-Japan Band Association on the occasion of their fortieth anniversary. It was commissioned for the national contest as a required work for the Japanese junior high school bands. The composition is loosely based on the melody "Sakura," which is well known to all Japanese children. The hand-clapping part by different sections is vital to the rhythmic movement of the piece and also much fun for the participants.

Chant and Jubilo (Pub = SO, 1963. Gr = 3. T = 7:00. Rec = SO-McBeth-V-1, TX Tech, McBeth)

This work was commissioned by the Four States Bandmasters Convention in Texarkana, Texas, and first performed there in 1962.

The *Chant* opens softly, with a single, simple melodic line which recalls the melodies of Gregorian chant. The chant has three phrases plus a fourth phrase which concludes the opening section. After a somewhat longer section of development, a snare drum roll leads into the opening trumpet fanfare of the *Jubilo* where the mood is jubilation, praise, and joy. The fanfare theme is then subjected to multiple variations before the activity is resolved in affirmation, a call to joy, a closing hallelujah. (R. John Specht, Queensborough Community College)

Drammatico (Pub = SO, 1970. Gr = 4. T = 7:40. Rec = SO-McBeth-V-1, TX Tech, McBeth)

Drammatico was commissioned by Dan Gibbs and the Monahans (Texas) High School Band. It is scored in a brilliant contemporary vein and utilizes the modern wind band extremities in dynamics, tempos, and tonal colors. Although McBeth has been credited with numerous worthy band compositions, the *Drammatico* is thought by many conductors and educators to be one of his most outstanding. (Harold Jackson, Southwest Baptist College)

Joyant Narrative (Pub = SO, 1966. Gr = 4. T = 7:23. Rec = SO-McBeth-V-1, TX Tech, McBeth)

Joyant Narrative is dedicated to Col. Harold Bachman and was written for him because of his help and friendship to the composer during the early years of his career. The work is based on the first national anthem of the Republic of Texas, titled "Won't You Come to My Bower That I Have Shaded For You," later known as the *San Jacinto Quick Step*. The tune is heard intact in the slow movement, although it is slightly altered in mode. (W. Francis McBeth, Ouachita University)

Kaddish (Pub = SO, 1977. Gr = 4. T = 7:00. Rec = SO-McBeth-V-2, TX Tech, McBeth)

Kaddish (rhymes with Schottische) is the Jewish prayer for the dead. It is said by the bereaved each morning and evening for eleven months, then on the anniversary of the death thereafter. The composition was written as a memorial to J. Clifton Williams, noted composer and former teacher of McBeth at the University of Texas. The work was commissioned by Howard Dunn and the Richardson (Texas) High School Band.

(See May, 1981, *Instrumentalist* for an analysis by the composer, Ed.)

Masque (Pub = SO, 1968. Gr = 4. T = 7:15. Rec = SO-McBeth-V-2, TX Tech, McBeth)

Masque (pronounced "mask") was commissioned in 1967 by the State College of Arkansas for the dedication of the Fine Arts Center and was premiered there by the college band in 1968.

This music is in a contemporary idiom familiar to followers of concert band music—not unusually experimental but nevertheless making use of twentieth century devices. For example *Masque* uses a variety of percussion instruments, has non-traditional harmonies, and makes use of short motives for melodic interest. Two motives serve as the basic material for the entire piece; one is rhythmic, being heard only in the fast (first and third) sections, and the other is a melodic three-note motive which is developed during the entire course of the work.

In England during the sixteenth and seventeenth centuries a masque was a very elaborate stage spectacle attended by the nobility. There were actors and singers, elaborate ballets, and spectacular scenery. McBeth's score reflects the general air of festivity of the early masques without any specific musical relationship. (R. John Specht, Queensborough Community College)

Mosaic (Pub = SO, 1964. Gr = 5. T = 8:00. Rec = SO-McBeth-V-2, TX Tech, McBeth)

Commissioned by the Fayetteville, Arkansas, High School Band and premiered by that organization in 1964, the work is an organic variation of the four note "fate" motive from the last quartets of Beethoven. The economy of material is one of its outstanding features. (Harold Hillyer, University of Texas, El Paso)

To Be Fed By Ravens (Pub = SO, 1975. Gr = 6. T = 11:35. Rec = SO-McBeth-V-2, TX Tech, McBeth)

To Be Fed By Ravens was dedicated to and commissioned by the Texas Music Educators Association on the occasion of its fiftieth anniversary. The work is in two contrasting movements, each with a dedication of its own. The first movement is an elegy to Marion B. McClure (1909-1973), and the second movement is dedicated to each individual Texas bandmaster. Materials used in the second movement are fragments of the "Texas Ranger Song," the "Mexican Deguella," and "Green Grow the Lilacs."

The title was inspired by a passage from the oratorio *Elijah* by Mendelssohn: "Elijah! Get thee hence; depart, and turn thee eastward: thither hide thee by Cherith's brook. There shalt thou drink its waters; and the Lord thy God hath commanded the ravens to feed thee there: So do according to His word." (1 Kings 17:3-4)

GUSTAV MAHLER

(Born in Kalischt, Austria, 1860 — Died in Vienna, 1911)

Gustav Mahler was born of Jewish parents, the second of a family of twelve. At the age of fifteen he was sent to the Conservatory at Vienna where he studied with Epstein, Fuchs, and Krenn. After concluding his formal studies he began to work unremittingly as an opera conductor in Austria and Germany. He continued serving in various positions as a symphony or opera conductor throughout his life. In 1907 he moved to the United States and became the conductor of both the Metropolitan Opera House and the New York Philharmonic Society. After two seasons, his hectic schedule sapped his strength and he returned to Europe, his health shattered. Mahler composed ten symphonies, the last unfinished, and numerous songs. In his use of counterpoint and knowledge of texture Mahler ranks with the great composers of the last two centuries.

Symphony No. 3, Finale (Arr — Reynolds. Pub = BII, 1971. Gr = 3. T = 7:00. Rec = CR-MENC-78-18. National H.S. Honor, Revelli)

The symphony on which this arrangement is based was the sixth movement of the work completed in 1895, the year Mahler became a Roman Catholic. It was entitled "Was mir die Liebe erzahlt" (What Love Tells Me).

The movement can best be described in Mahler's own words—"the peak, the highest level from which one can view the world. I could almost call it 'what God tells me,' in the sense that God can only be comprehended as love." (Shawnee Press, Inc.)

MARTIN MAILMAN

(Born in New York City, 1932)

Martin Mailman earned the B.M., M.M., and Ph.D. degrees from the Eastman School of Music. He was a composition student of Louis Mennini, Wayne Barlow, Bernard Rogers, and Howard Hanson. Professional affiliations include the U.S. Naval School of Music, composer-in-residence under a Ford Foundation Grant for the Music Educators National Conference, composer-in-residence and professor of music at East Carolina University, and professor of music at North Texas State University. He has won numerous awards as a composer and writes prolifically for a variety of performance media.

Geometrics No. 1, Op. 22 (Pub = SO, 1973. Gr = 4. T = 6:00. Rec = CR-ATH-5056. Capital Un., Suddendorf)

The *Geometrics No. 1* of Martin Mailman, written while he had a Ford Foundation Grant, is characterized by frequent shifts in the metric pattern and extensive exploitation of the initial motif. From a calm, almost monotonous beginning, the piece builds to a forceful, dissonant climax and then returns to a feeling of relaxation and repose. (Thomas J. Anderson, DeKalb College)

Liturgical Music for Band (Pub = BE, 1967. Gr = 4. T = 10:00. Rec = CR-MID-68-7, Fenton H.S., Bensenville, IL, Brittain)

In this composition, Mailman attempts to capture the essence of a worship experience. In the first movement, Introit, we hear a joyful church processional accompanied by bells, chimes, and triangle. The second movement, Kyrie, symbolizes the prayer, "Lord have mercy upon us." The mood of this movement is dark and somber, with the rhythms based on speech inflections taken from the first word of this traditional Latin prayer, "Kyr-i-e." The third section, Gloria, represents the exultation of the words, "Glory to God in the highest." The last movement, Alleluia, expresses the jubilance of man's faith, with sustained brass chords set against an ascending theme in the woodwinds, representing man's heavenly aspirations. (Roger L. Beck, Sioux Falls College)

ANDREAS MAKRIS
(Born in Salonika, Greece, 1930)

After graduating as a prize student from the National Conservatory in Greece, Andreas Makris continued his studies at Phillips University, Kansas City Conservatory, Mannes College of Music, Aspen Music Festival and in Fontainebleu, France. He is a recipient of the Exchange Student Scholarship, Damrosch Grant, National Endowment for the Arts Grant, and the Martha Baird Rockefeller Award. He holds the honor of being the first contemporary composer to be performed at the Kennedy Center Concert Hall with the National Symphony Orchestra under the direction of Antal Dorati. Mstislav Rostropovich, conductor of the National Symphony Orchestra in which Makris performs as a member of the first violin section, recently appointed Makris to the post of Composer-in-Residence with the orchestra and advisor to Rostropovich in selection of new works for performance.

Andreas Makris' compositions have been performed in almost every major city in the United States and many cities abroad. His major works include: two string quartets, *Quintet for Soprano and String Orchestra, Concerto for Strings, Viola Concerto, Anamneses* (for orchestra), *Aegean Festival Overture* (for orchestra or symphonic band), *Concertino for Trombone and Strings, Efthymia* (for orchestra), *Fantasy and Dance for Saxophone, Mediterranean Holiday* (for concert band), and *Chrometekinesis* (for orchestra).

Aegean Festival Overture (Pub = GA, 1971. Gr = 5. T = 10:00. Rec = CR-CBDNA-71-7, U.S. Air Force, Gabriel)

The work was written in 1967 as an orchestral overture for the Washington National Symphony and was premiered by that group under Howard Mitchell a year later at Constitution Hall. Its immediate success then and on tour occasioned the collaboration between Makris and Albert Bader of the United States Air Force Band to arrange the overture as a concert piece for band. It has since been premiered and featured on tour by the USAF Band under the direction of Arnald Gabriel. From its first hammering dotted eighth rhythms, the *Aegean Festival Overture* reflects the Greek origin of its composer. The driving energy of the fast section with its restless 5's and 7's and the lyric plaintiveness of the contrasting middle section, all molded into a symphonic form, epitomize the musical style of Makris—a blend of classic form and Greek folkloristic elements. (Galaxy Music Corporation)

RICHARD MALTBY

(Born in Evanston, Illinois, 1914)

Richard Maltby graduated from Evanston Township High School, then attended the Music School at Northwestern University. He continued his studies with Leo Sowerby. Turning to the practical aspects of music, he played with and arranged for many of the outstanding dance bands including those of Benny Goodman, Artie Shaw, and Tommy Dorsey. Later, Maltby became staff arranger for CBS, Chicago, and for the Blue Network. Moving to New York, he joined the American Broadcasting Company music staff under the direction of Paul Whiteman. Subsequently, he founded his own band as well as the Richard Maltby Music Productions. Later, he turned to symphonic works which included his *Threnody (An Elegiac Tribute to the Memory of John F. Kennedy)*. His success lies not only in his great versatility, but in his unusual musical invention in creating works which have immediate mass appeal. (Carl Fischer, Inc.)

Jazz Waltz (Pub = CF, 1968. Gr = 4. T = 5:00)

The jazz waltz, a popular idiom for instrumental performers during the sixties, is among the more sophisticated and novel popular music sounds of that decade. Designed for enjoyable and relaxing listening, this composition by Maltby flows at a moderately rapid rate. Skill and dexterity are required for its proper performance.

SIMONE MANTIA

(Born near Palermo, Italy, 1873 — Died in New York, 1951)

Simone Mantia immigrated to the United States from Italy as a young boy, and during his lifetime he was considered (along with Herbert L. Clarke and Arthur Pryor) as one of the greatest brass players of the century. Mantia's instruments were the euphonium and trombone and he displayed a dazzling technique on both—he even substituted on trombone for Arthur Pryor at times, when both were playing in the Sousa Band. Mantia began playing trombone when he was twelve and by the time he was seventeen, he was playing in the orchestra of the Grand Opera House in Brooklyn. He played euphonium most of the time during the twenty-five years he played with Arthur Pryor's Band and the seven years he was with Sousa's Band. He played trombone with Victor Herbert's Orchestra for a time and was personnel manager and first trombonist with the Metropolitan Opera Orchestra from 1907 to 1944. During that time he directed his own little symphony at Asbury Park, New Jersey (1921-25), and in 1940 he was a member of the New York World's Fair Band. Two of Mantia's euphonium solos, *Endearing Young Charms* and *Original Fantasie,* are still performed, as is *Priscilla,* a trombone solo. Mantia also wrote a widely used method book, *The Trombone Virtuoso Method.*

Endearing Young Charms—Euphonium Solo (Arr = Brasch.   Pub = HT, 1970.
Gr = 5.   T = 4:30.   Rec = BL-SABC-7R, Earle Louder w. Detroit Concert, Smith;
MS-XII, Louder w. Morehead St. Un., Hawkins)

The original "Believe Me, If All Those Endearing Young Charms," is an old Irish
melody with words by Thomas Moore.   In Brasch's arrangement of Mantia's
euphonium solo, the melody is still familiar, but the variations are another story.
Like *Carnival of Venice* for the cornet and *Blue Bells of Scotland* for trombone,
Endearing Young Charms challenges the soloist to "sing" the melody with expression, and "play the notes off of the page" during the variations.   Mantia's original
arrangement was published in 1908 by the Dixie Music House of Chicago.

JULES MASSENET

(Born in Montaud, France, 1842 — Died in Paris, 1912)

Jules Massenet was born with an unusual gift for music and he received his earliest
training with his mother, a piano teacher.   He was accepted at the Paris Conservatory at the tender age of eleven and encountered continual success, eventually obtaining the Prix de Rome in 1863 with his cantata *David Rizzio*.   Generally favored
by his musical contemporaries and the public, Massenet enjoyed the rare privilege of
recognition during his entire lifetime. He was appointed professor of advanced composition at the Paris Conservatory in 1878, where he served until his death, and he
was the youngest member ever to be elected to the Académie des Beaux-Arts.
Decorated by the Legion of Honor, he became Grand Officer in 1899.

Meditation from Thaïs—Flute Soli (Arr = Harding.   Pub = KJ, 1952.   Gr = 4.
T = 5:00.   Rec = CR-MID-72-11, G.P. Babb Jr. H.S., Forest Park, GA, Wilkes; GC-
Revelli Years, Un. of MI, Revelli)

Thaïs, written in 1894, was the most popular of Massenet's many operas.   The
scene is laid in Egypt in the stormy period when Christianity was battling with
paganism for supremacy and the plot concerns the monk Athanel's attempts to con-
vert the Egyptian priestess, Thaïs, to Christianity.   He succeeds in his mission, but
tragedy results for both when the monk falls in love with Thaïs.

This setting for band was made by A.A. Harding, the former director of bands at
the University of Illinois.   The entire flute section plays the traditional violin solo in
unison.

Phedre Overture (Arr = Cailliet.   Pub = SF, 1965.   Gr = 4.   T = 9:30.   Rec = SD-III,
Augustana Col., Lillehaug)

The idea of composing a concert overture, unassociated with either an opera or a
play, for orchestra performance apparently had its origin with Mendelssohn's
Hebrides, first played in London in 1830.   Subsequent composers have written
dozens of such individual works for orchestra, usually in sonata-allegro form and
typically pitting a lyrical long-spanned melody against an energetic, rhythmic theme.
This pattern describes the plan of the overture, *Phedre*, which was written in 1873
and still occupies a place in the symphonic repertoire.   In transcribing the principal
themes as solos for clarinet and flute and making judicious use of the tutti band, the
arranger achieves remarkable clarity of both form and sonority and provides a
brilliant vehicle for wind playing. (Acton Ostling, Jr., University of Maryland)

F.W. MEACHAM

(Born in Buffalo, New York, 1856 — Died in New York City, 1909)

Frank W. Meacham is known principally for his American Patrol, but information found recently in an 1886 Brooklyn newspaper indicates he composed a great deal more music. Meacham was born in Buffalo, but his family moved to Brooklyn when he was two and he apparently lived there most of the rest of his life. He was very interested in music as a child and when he was ten he wrote a song titled "Come Over the Sea," which was published by Chandler in Brooklyn. Although his first song, and several others which followed, did not sell very well, he finally made a hit with "Down in the Cotton Fields." Meacham gradually turned his attention toward arranging music of other composers and by 1885 he was considered one of the best ballad arrangers in the United States.

Meacham's first hit for band was a set of waltzes titled *Happy Life,* written for the Gilmore band. The waltz was so popular that three editions were published and, at Gilmore's second request, he wrote the *Columbus March*—in an hour's time. The first edition of 4,000 copies was quickly sold and a second edition was printed. With the exception of *American Patrol,* composed in 1885, most of Meacham's subsequent works were for the piano or voice. The majority of his vocal compositions were ghost written for other people—another reason why Meacham has not received the credit he deserves. (Information from J.C. Sweet, Jr., New Canaan, CT)

American Patrol (Pub = CF, 1891-1919. Gr = 3. T = 4:00. Rec = MG-SRI-75004, Eastman, Fennell; IL-6, Un. of IL, Hindsley)

A simple drum cadence is heard as if a band were approaching from afar. The first melody begins, heard softly at first, and increasing in sound level as the band approaches. This first tune, the composer's own, is followed by a medley of well-known patriotic tunes—"Columbia, the Gem of the Ocean," "Dixie," and "Yankee Doodle." The band marches past the parade-watching crowd with exciting strains and passes on with the music fading away. A final burst of martial music concludes the piece.

FELIX MENDELSSOHN

(Born in Hamburg, 1809 — Died in Leipzig, 1847)

Felix Mendelssohn was, like many composers, a child prodigy. At nine he made his first appearance as a concert pianist; by 1820, it is believed, he had composed over fifty movements for different media. In 1829, after three years study at the University of Berlin, he undertook music as a career. In that year he conducted Johann Sebastian Bach's *Passion According to St. Matthew,* which started a revival of interest in Bach's music that had been dormant for many years. Also in this year he started a three-year tour of Europe and made his first appearance in England where for many years he was a popular favorite as composer, conductor, and pianist. As conductor of the famous Gewandhaus Orchestra of Leipzig, he brought it to great heights, and restored much great music to its repertoire. His most popular compositions include the oratorio *Elijah,* the *Violin Concerto in E Minor,* and the *Scotch* and *Italian Symphonies.* He also wrote many chamber, piano, and vocal works. (Carl Fischer, Inc.)

FELIX MENDELSSOHN

Concerto in G Minor, Op. 25—Piano Solo (Arr = Dahnert. Pub = SU, 1954. Gr = 4. T = 6:30. Rec = MH-4057T, Johnson w. Royal Phil. Orch., Freeman)

The *G Minor Piano Concerto, Opus 25* is the best known of five works written by Mendelssohn in this medium. Although it may not approach the great beauty of his *Violin Concerto,* it has real intrinsic value along with historical importance. A complete break with classical tradition is found in the absence of long tutti sections for orchestra and cadenzas.

A short introduction building to a brilliant crescendo is followed by the statement of the first theme of dynamic power in octaves by the piano. The second theme is more serene and poetic in nature. Scale passages and arpeggiated sequences abound throughout the work which ends with a brilliant cadenza-like passage for the solo instrument.

Fingal's Cave Overture (Arr = Seredy. Pub = CF, 1946. Gr = 4. T = 10:00. Rec = MH-3630W, Leipzig Gewandhaus Orch., Mazur)

This concert overture, virtually a tone poem, was written in 1832 and is still as popular as ever. After a busy concert season in London, Mendelssohn made a pleasure tour through Scotland, where he was greatly impressed by the wild and beautiful scenery, and there he conceived the idea of the *Fingal's Cave Overture,* one of the works in which his poetic imagination found happiest and most flawless expression. The ocean-washed cave on the Isle of Straffa, in the Hebrides, and the ruins of a vast, fantastic castle are suggested with eerie sights and sounds making up the dramatic thoughts of the overture.

Overture for Band (Arr = Greissle; Zurmuhle. Pub = GS, 1948; MOL, 1965. Gr = 4. T = 7:00. Rec = CR-ABA-72-2, Un. of TN, Fred; MH-4327, Vienna Wind Ens., Klöcker)

The original edition of Mendelssohn's *Overture for Band* included an instrumentation not too different from those of contemporary wind ensembles. The following note is included with the score of the current edition:

> Mendelssohn composed this *Overture in C Major for Wind Band* in the summer of 1824 during his stay at the fashionable seaside resort of Doberan on the shores of the Baltic. The bathing establishment there boasted of a very acceptable wind band, so acceptable that the young composer (who was never happier than when he had any excuse to compose) felt prompted to write a composition for the group to perform at one of its concerts. The work was published by Simrock in 1826 as *Ouvertüre für Harmoniemusik, Opus 24.* (G. Schirmer, Inc.)

Ruy Blas Overture (Arr = Roberts-Kent. Pub = CF, 1946. Gr = 4. T = 12:00. Rec = RC-AGLI-2703, London Symphony, Previn)

Ruy Blas is one of Victor Hugo's super-charged romantic tragedies, the tale of a lackey who gains great political power and finally sacrifices himself to save a queen's life. In February, 1839, representatives of the Theatrical Pension Fund at Leipzig asked Mendelssohn to write "an overture and a romance" for a charity performance of Hugo's *Ruy Blas.* Mendelssohn found the task onerous but consented to supply them with their overture which he tossed off in two days. It has virtually nothing in common with Hugo's play (e.g., the play ends tragically, the overture is a blaze of triumph). But considered as a piece of absolute music, it reveals all of Mendelssohn's compositional characteristics. (Harold L. Hillyer, University of Texas at El Paso)

PETER MENNIN

(Born in Erie, Pennsylvania, 1923)

Peter Mennin is one of America's most gifted composers. A native Pennsylvanian of Italian extraction, Mennin received his musical training at the Oberlin Conservatory and the Eastman School of Music from 1940 to 1945. He became a faculty member of the Juilliard School of Music in 1947 and held that position until 1958 when he was appointed director of the Peabody Conservatory of Music in Baltimore. Mennin returned to New York City to become president of Juilliard School of Music in 1962. His compositions include seven symphonies; works for chamber orchestra, chamber winds, and string orchestra; concertos for violin and piano; cantatas, choruses, and songs. Cast in a neo-Classical mold, the music of Mennin is at its best in purely instrumental works, and is formally compact with a strong sense of purpose in its thematic development. (John Wakefield, University of Maryland)

Allegro Tempestuoso from Symphony No. 5 (Arr = Bencriscutto, ms. Gr = 5. T = 8:00. Rec – MG-75020, Eastman-Rochester, Hanson; UM, Un. of MN, Bencriscutto)

According to the composer, the basic aim of *Symphony No. 5* was expressivity. As a result great emphasis was placed on the broad melodic line, and there was little use of color for its own sake. The colors might be considered primary rather than pastel in quality. Hence, the work as a whole is direct, assertive, and terse in communication

The *Allegro Tempestuoso* (final) movement is one of rapid and bare linear writing set off by brass and percussive punctuation. It demands great virtuosity from the band. The basic girder of the movement is an idea in canon which has numerous variations in rhythm and mood. The closing sounds are similar to those which Mennin used in the first movement.

Canzona (Pub = CF, 1954. Gr = 5. T = 5:00. Rec = AC-6577, N. TX St. Un; MG-50084, Eastman, Fennell)

Mennin composed his *Canzona* as a part of the continuing series of commissions from Edwin Franko Goldman in cooperation with the League of Composers, and it was first played by the Goldman Band. The concept of the "canzona" as set forth here is not that of lyrical song implied by the name, but rather that of the early baroque "canzona" so brilliantly exploited by Gabrieli (1555-1612) at the Cathedral of St. Mark in Venice to display contrasting wind and string sonorities together with rhythmic-polyphonic virtuosity. Using the reeds and brasses of the band in alternate tonal blocks, Mennin has created a stunning essay of the same type in the twentieth-century manner. (Frederick Fennell, Eastman School of Music)

(See September, 1980, *Instrumentalist* for an analysis by Donald Hunsberger, Ed.)

GIAN CARLO MENOTTI

(Born in Cadegliano, Italy, 1911)

Gian Carlo Menotti, the sixth of ten children, began composing at the age of five. In 1928 he came to America to study at the Curtis Institute of Philadelphia where he completed his first published opera *Amelia Goes to the Ball*. Menotti, who made the opera "box office on Broadway," is a librettist, a dramatist, and a director, as well as a composer. He founded the Festival of Two Worlds in Spoleto and has received two Pulitzer Prizes and numerous commissions, including one from the Opéra Comique of Paris for *The Last Savage*. (Educational Record Reference Library, Belwin-Mills)

Overture and Caccia (Arr = Lang. Pub = FC, 1966. Gr = 5. T = 7:30. Rec = BP-102, Un. of MI, Revelli)

Menotti continues the tradition of over three centuries of Italian opera and brings to the medium a unique grasp of singable melody, clear textures, and lucid forms. It is clear in listening to Menotti's music that he is fully aware of the styles of his Italian predecessors in opera. He avoids complicated metrical tricks, contrived contrapuntal designs, and mechanical methods of composition. His music reflects the Italian love of beautiful, entertaining music of a rather melodramatic and passionate nature. *Overture and Caccia* was originally written for the opera *The Last Savage.* The function of the overture is, of course, well known but the "caccia" is less familiar. It originally was a fourteenth-century Italian form of vocal music that rather realistically represented a "chase" as implied in its name. Menotti, however, uses the device so freely, it is doubtful whether it would be recognized by a fourteenth-century Italian.

Sebastian Ballet—Excerpts (Arr = Lang. Pub = RC, 1961. Gr = 5. T = 7:45. Rec = BP-107, Un. of Houston, Matthews)

This arrangement by Philip Lang makes exciting concert fare for band, requiring mature players in each instrumental section. Ingenious rhythms, spicy dissonances, and memorable melodies by Menotti are enhanced with Lang's sense of instrumental color. *Sebastian Ballet* was first performed in 1944 by Ballet International in Paris. The waltz heard in the piece is Sebastian's first solo dance in the ballet.

JAN MEYEROWITZ
(Born in Breslau, Germany, 1913)

At the age of fourteen Meyerowitz went to Berlin where he studied with Zemlinsky at the College of Music. Compelled to leave Germany in 1933, he went to Rome where he studied composition at the Academy of St. Cecelia with Respighi and Casella. The outbreak of World War II occurred when he was in Belgium, and from there he went to southern France, where he lived underground much of the time. He immigrated in 1946 to the United States, where his musical reputation has grown steadily. A former member of the faculty at the Berkshire Music Center in Tanglewood and at Brooklyn College, Meyerowitz now lectures at New York City College. He has twice been the recipient of a Guggenheim Fellowship, in 1956 and 1958. His compositions, which have been performed frequently by major musical organizations throughout the world, include orchestral and choral works, operas, chamber music, songs, and compositions for organ and piano. (Jonathan Elkus, Lehigh University)

Three Comments on War (Ms., 1964. Gr = 4. T = 10:40.)

Three Comments on War was commissioned by the Southern Division of the College Band Directors National Association. The melody that serves as "Chorale" of the first movement, an anonymous secular French ballad of antiquity, is the folksong "Jean Renaud" that tells the story of a mortally wounded king who comes home to die. His mother makes desperate efforts to hide the tragic event from his queen who has just given birth to a son. The efforts are unsuccessful and the queen, in order to remain forever with Renaud, asks the earth to split open and to "swallow" her. The song is the cantus firmus of the beginning and the end of the Chorale Prelude. The middle portion is a plaintive cantabile crescendo evolved from the voices that support the cantus firmus in the opening section.

The second movement, Battle Music, has a program idea that is traditional enough. Examples of battle music are found in Renaissance and Baroque music. Their tone is heroic and somewhat humorous and the same appeal can be found in their late echo, Beethoven's *Wellington's Victory*. Modern war has certainly not eliminated the heroic aspect of battle, but its catastrophic grimness is quite unrelieved. The present Battle Music wants to be a reflection of this. It is written in sonata form with the minor but very noticeable irregularity that the two principal themes are "conjured up" by preparatory passages, and not stated directly. The first theme represents the battle events, the second is an anticipation of one of the songs of mourning of the finale.

The third movement, Epitaph, is a memorial piece for a soldier. The principal songlike theme, appearing in three sections of the piece, forms a five-point rondo with two other songlike episodes. A short quotation of "Jean Renaud" leads into a violent, ominous final fanfare. (Jan Meyerowitz, New York City)

DARIUS MILHAUD

(Born in Aix-en-Provence, France, 1892 — Died in Oakland, California, 1974)

Darius Milhaud was a student at the Paris Conservatory, where he won awards in violin, counterpoint, and fugue. His studies were interrupted by World War I and he did not return to Paris until 1919 when he became associated with the group of young French composers known as "Les Six." This group felt that French music had become a slave to impressionism and could be freed only through simplicity. They exerted a profound influence on modern French music, and Milhaud's artistic stature continued to grow until he became recognized as the major composer of France.

Milhaud was a distinguished composer, pianist, and lecturer. His style of composition shows the influence of American jazz and South American rhythm. He used polytonal and polyharmonic devices extensively. In 1940 when the Germans overran his native country, Milhaud came to the United States. He served as composer-in-residence at Mills College in Oakland, California, until his death.

Suite Française (Pub = LD, 1945. Gr = 4. T = 16:00. Rec = CR-9009, Un. of IL, Begian; MG-75093, Eastman, Fennell)

In 1945, the publishing firm of Leeds Music commissioned Milhaud to write an extended work for band as part of a proposed series of new works by contemporary composers. The result was *Suite Française*. The composer provided the following notes about the work:

> The five parts of this suite are named after French provinces, the very ones in which the American and Allied armies fought together with the French underground for the liberation of my country—Normandy, Brittany, Île-de-France (of which Paris is the center), Alsace-Lorraine, and Provence.
>
> I used some folk tunes of the provinces. I wanted the young Americans to hear the popular melodies of those parts of France where their fathers and brothers fought.

Suite Française was given its first performance by the Goldman Band in 1945. It was so successful that Milhaud was requested to rescore it for orchestra, in which medium it was first played by the New York Philharmonic.

REX MITCHELL
(Born in Pittsburgh, Pennsylvania, 1929)

An associate professor at Clarion State College in Pennsylvania, Rex Mitchell holds degrees from Muskingum College, Kent State University, and Pennsylvania State University, the latter being a doctorate in music education. He teaches instrumental music, arranging and orchestration. Among his compositions for concert band are *Caprice for Band, Concert Miniature, Panorama, The Silver Cornets* and *Song for the Young.*

Introduction and Fantasia (Pub = EM, 1970. Gr = 4. T = 9:00. Rec = CR-MID-70-14, North Hills H.S., Pittsburgh, PA, Mercer)

A slow and reflective introduction features a marimba solo and warm sonorities from the brasses. This is followed by a sudden percussion section feature setting the pace for a strongly accented, dynamic, fast moving theme. The higher registers of the flute and clarinet sections are prominent and the horn and trumpet sections are featured in syncopated figures. A legato section then features solos by the alto saxophone, horn, and oboe. The opening theme reappears briefly and is followed by the fast-paced second theme which brings the composition to a close.

DONALD I. MOORE
(Born in Farnhamville, Iowa, 1910)

Moore attended schools in Iowa, Minnesota, Colorado, and Michigan, receiving degrees from Carleton College and the University of Northern Colorado. He directed school bands in Iowa, Colorado, New York, and Texas. In 1948 he moved to Texas as director of the Baylor University Band and remained in that position for over twenty years. He has composed numerous works for band. Best known are *CBDNA March, Marcho Poco, Ides of March, March Forth, Dawn of Peace,* and *Rise and Shine.* He has also served in positions of leadership in several professional band organizations.

March Forth (Pub = SP, 1955. Gr = 3. T = 3:00)

A rousing concert march featuring the horn section at the trio, *March Forth* has been played by the U.S. Navy Band on tour and has been used as a warm-up contest march by bands all over the nation.

Marcho Poco (Pub = MM, 1948. Gr = 3. T = 3:00)

A composition well liked by bandsman and audiences, *Marcho Poco* has been listed by *The Instrumentalist* as one of the 100 most popular marches.

JOHN MORRISSEY
(Born in New York City, 1906)

John Morrissey earned his baccalaureate and master's degrees at Columbia University in New York City. He taught at Teacher's College, Columbia University and served as an officer in the music branch of Special Services, U.S. Army during

World War II. From 1938 to 1943 and again from 1946 until his retirement in 1968 he served as band director and head of the music department at Tulane University. His numerous works for band in the popular music style include *Caribbean Fantasy, French Quarter Suite, Viva Mexico, Music for a Ceremony, Concertino for Winds and Percussion,* and *Elegy for Band.*

Music for a Ceremony (Pub = CF, 1963. Gr = 3. T = 4:30. Rec = CF-BSS, Sym. Winds, Cacavas)

Composed to commemorate the inauguration of the President of Tulane University in New Orleans, Louisiana, this music combines the elements of a brilliant fanfare with a characteristic festive processional. The trio has a flowing, majestic-like melodic line.

Viva Mexico(Pub = EM, 1961. Gr = 3. T = 17:30)

Viva Mexico is a symphonic suite written as a result of Morrissey's travels and research in Mexico. The opening movement, Processional, alludes to the outskirts of Mexico City where the ancient pyramids of the Sun and the Moon stand, and where the Indian priests prepared their sacrifices to the gods. The music describes their processional as they mounted the steps of the Pyramid of the Sun at Teotihuacan. In the Fiesta of the Charros, brilliantly arrayed horsemen (charros) pass in review before applauding throngs, then perform amazing feats of daring as they compete in their annual Jaripeo (rodeo). The Bells of San Miguel section describes the haunting sound of church bells permeating the air from the smallest village to the largest city. Nowhere do they dominate the scene more poignantly than in the picturesque city of San Miguel de Allende where the beautiful cathedral rises imposingly at the edge of the Central Plaza. The Puebla de Los Angeles movement refers to the city of the same name, considered by many to be the most characteristically Spanish city in Mexico. With its colorful tiles and colonial architecture, Puebla still reflects the spirit of another era. Parade, the finale, describes the vitality, the sparkle, and the gaity of a parade in Mexico's great metropolis. In this final salute the composer pays tribute to a land replete with musical inspiration. (Myron R. Falck, Gustavus Adolphus College)

WOLFGANG A. MOZART

(Born in Salzburg, 1756 — Died in Vienna, 1791)

At the age of three, Wolfgang Mozart showed a remarkable love of music. He would listen to his sister Marianne's lessons and later would improvise similar tunes and chords. His father, Leopold, soon began directing his studies and later toured with Wolfgang and Marianne throughout Europe and England while the children were still very young. They were well received and widely acclaimed during these tours which continued for several years. The first of his serious compositions was completed and performed during that period.

At the age of twelve, young Mozart composed an opera, *La Finta Semplice,* at the order of the emperor of Austria, and it was performed at Salzburg. More writing and travels in Italy followed, with Mozart being honored at the Vatican and in several other Italian cities.

During his adult life when he wrote some of the world's greatest masterpieces, Mozart was almost always in debt and frequently in ill health. It is thought that he wrote his *Requiem* as a result of what he believed to be a forewarning of his own death. He left a fabulous legacy of opera, concerto, symphony, choral, and ensemble music to the world.

Alleluia (Arr = Barnes. Pub = LU, 1956. Gr = 3. T = 5:00.)

Mozart composed the motet *Exultate, Jubilate* in Milan, Italy, in his 17th year (1773). The review of the first performance lamented it as not being sacred music and compared it to one of his symphonies. In the use of melodies in the closing section Mozart, knowingly and indifferently, used four bars of Haydn's "Kaiser Hymn." The motet was originally written for soprano and small orchestra and still is in the repertoire of many singers. The *Alleluia* which is the third movement of the motet of one of gaity and jubilation, equivalent to a final symphonic movement. (Warrick L. Carter, University of Maryland, Eastern Shore)

Fantasia in F (Arr = Schaefer. Pub = SH, 1962. Gr = 3. T = 8:00. Rec = CR-ABA-72-4, Un. of TX, Moody)

Transcriptions for band are not unusual. The resetting of this Mozart fantasia is unique though, in that it was originally written for a mechanical clock. The three sections (in an ABA pattern) show examples of smoothly flowing lines gently intertwined and, in contrast, the contrapuntal opposition of short, crisp figures—all giving credence to the contention that Mozart could write for any medium. (Thomas J. Anderson, DeKalb College)

The Marriage of Figaro Overture (Arr = Slocum. Pub = MM, 1958. Gr = 4. T = 4:00. Rec = CR-MID-74-7, Northeast Intermediate, Midland, MI, Mead)

Mozart's famous opera, *The Marriage of Figaro,* composed in 1786, was the first of his greatest series of operas. The combination of Da Ponte's witty text and Mozart's sparkling music was irresistable, and the opera was an immediate success. The adventures of the resourceful barber (who appears again in Rossini's *Barber of Seville)* are illustrated by some of the most delightful music Mozart ever wrote. The overture, which is in one tempo throughout, is a pure gem of spontaneous melody and skillful design. (Paul B. Noble, Shenandoah Conservatory)

Romanza and Rondo from Concerto No. 3—French Horn Solo (Arr = Bardeen. Pub = KN, 1962 & 1964. Gr = 3/4. T = 7:45. Rec = CR-69-11, Clovis, NM, H.S., Howell)

Mozart composed several concertos for his friend Ignaz Leitgeb who was an excellent horn player but a cheesemonger by occupation. Having an unusual sense of humor, Mozart enjoyed playing practical jokes on his friend, and the manuscript for this concerto (K. 495) was written with a variety of ink colors and with extraneous comments directed to his horn-playing friend. It is apparent that the composer intended that his music should be enjoyed by both performer and audience. These two movements from the concerto are appropriate for either a program for serious listening or for a more informal concert. The solo part, while not exceptionally demanding on the performer, does require a very serious effort on his part, and several brief passages do call for virtuoso-like technique.

FLORIAN MUELLER

(Born in Bay City, Michigan, 1909)

Professor Emeritus of Music, the University of Michigan, Florian Mueller received the Master of Music degree from the American Conservatory of Music in

Chicago. He studied oboe with Alfred Barthel and theory and composition with Olaf Andersen. Mueller served as principal oboist with the Chicago Symphony Orchestra from 1927 to 1954. In 1960 he won the Ostwald Award of the American Bandmasters Association for his composition, *Concert Overture in G.* His compositions include works for orchestra, band, chamber music and pedagogical studies. Mueller now resides in St. Petersburg, Florida where he teaches and composes.

Concert Overture in G (Pub = BO, 1961. Gr = 4. T = 6:45.　　Rec = CR-MID-73-7, Lasalle-Peru, IL, H.S., Pontius)

The *Overture* is in sonata allegro form, the second theme of which is based on a melody known today as "Tallis' Canon," a psalm tune by English composer Thomas Tallis (1505-1585). The tune is presented in the form of theme and contrapuntal variations. This motif is heard throughout much of the work.

MODEST MUSSORGSKY

(Born in Karevo, Russia, 1839 — Died in St. Petersberg, 1881)

Modest Petrovitch Mussorgsky (also Moussorgsky) was tutored by his mother on the piano, and before he was nine he played the important works of Liszt and a concerto by Field. His original ambition, however, was military, and he eventually joined the Preobrajensky Regiment. His attitude toward music was that of an amateur until 1857, when he met Dargomijsky. Through him Mussorgsky was brought into contact with the members of the New Russian School.

His talent developed rapidly and his dramatic tendency was recognized by such men as Balakirev, Cui, Rimsky-Korsakov, Borodin, and Stassov. Military duties became irksome, so he resigned from the army and devoted himself to composition. Poverty forced him to take a clerical position in St. Petersberg (now Leningrad), an uncongenial occupation which proved to be a hindrance to his aspirations. Because of his high-strung sensitive nature and irregular mode of life, his health was impaired. Finally, he went to live with his brother Dimitri in Minkino, and it was there that he recovered sufficiently to do some of his best work. (Carl Fischer, Inc.)

Coronation Scene from Boris Godunov (Arr = Leidzen. Pub = CF, 1936. Gr = 5. T = 9:00. Rec = CR-CBD-69-4, Un. of So. MS, Drake)

Mussorgsky wrote two versions of *Boris Godunov* between 1868 and 1872, and the opera was rescored and revised by Rimsky-Korsakov after Mussorgsky's death. The drama is an intense and tragic story of a man tormented by his own mind. Boris has contrived the murder of the rightful heir to the throne and has proclaimed himself Tsar. The *Coronation Scene*, one of the most brilliant and colorful scenes in the opera, takes place in the square fronting the Kremlin in Moscow. A great throng of people has gathered to hail Boris as their new Tsar.

Boris appears in the middle of the *Coronation Scene,* and the ringing bells and shouting crowds fall silent. He is filled with a sense of doom, both for himself and his kingdom. He invokes God's blessing and asks the people to kneel in homage to the departed rulers of Russia. Once more they take up their cry of "Glory!" and the great bells of the cathedrals boom out as Boris proceeds to the royal apartments in the Kremlin. (Jack Snavely, University of Wisconsin at Milwaukee)

Pictures at an Exhibition (Arr = Hindsley, ms.; Leidzen. Pub = CF, 1938-42. Gr = 5 T = 28:00. Rec = IL-47, Un. of IL, Hindsley)

Written as a tribute to his close friend, the architect Victor Hartmann, Mussorgsky's suite for piano describes ten of the drawings which most impressed him from the some four hundred displayed in a memorial exhibition. The "pictures" are introduced and often interspersed with thematically recurring "promenades." The sequence of the suite is as follows:

Promenade
   The composer wandering about in the gallery.
(1) The Gnome
   A misshapen comical figure supposedly fashioned as a Christmas tree ornament.
   Promenade
(2) The Old Castle
   A troubadour sings before a medieval castle.
   Promenade
(3) Tuileries
   Children quarreling in the famous park in Paris.
(4) Bydlo
   A two-wheeled ox-drawn cart lumbering across the fields.
   Promenade
(5) Ballet of the Unhatched Chicks
   Dancers costumed as chicks emerging from their shells.
(6) Samuel Goldberg and Schmuyle
   A dialogue between a rich Jew and a poor one.
(7) The Market Place at Limoges
   Women haggling over prices in the market.
(8) The Catacombs
   Artist and friend studying a pile of skulls in the Paris Catacombs.
(9) Baba-Yaga's Hut
   A clock in the shape of the legendary Russian witch, Baba-Yaga.
(10) The Great Gate of Kiev
   The artist's plan for constructing a gate in Kiev through which will pass the pageant of Russian history.

(See March, 1981, *School Musician* for an analysis by Roger Farnsworth, Ed.)

VACLAV NELHYBEL

(Born in Polanka, Czechoslovakia, 1919)

Vaclav Nelhybel studied composition and conducting at the Prague Conservatory of Music and musicology at the Universities of Prague and Fribourg. He was already affiliated with Radio Prague as composer and conductor while still a student in Prague. By 1948 he had become active in Swiss National Radio as a composer-conductor. Since 1957 he has lived in New York, become a U.S. citizen, and is now active in America as composer, conductor, and lecturer. Since 1964 he has conducted his music and lectured at the invitation of universities in more than thirty states.

The most striking general characteristic of Nelhybel's music is its linear-modal orientation. Consequently, his cadences do not adhere to the modulatory usages of functional-harmony procedures so commonly followed in conventional music of an essential vertical or chordal nature. His concern with the autonomy of melodic line leads to the second, and equally important characteristic—that of movement and pulsation, or rhythm and meter. Separate lines often span many measures, interplacing one another in elaborate complementary rhythms and coinciding with punctuational emphasis at periodic intervals of the metric structure. The interplay between these dual aspects of motion and time, and their coordinated organization, results in a vigorous drive quite typical of Nelhybel's music. Add to these elements the tension generated by accumulations of dissonance, the increasing of textural densities, exploding dynamics, and the massing of multi-hued sonic colors, and you have the kind of whirl-wind propulsion of a well-integrated "sound and fury." (Chris Izzo, Western Illinois University)

Adagio and Allegro (Pub = EV, 1966. Gr = 4. T = 7:00. Rec = CO-1411, Un. of MD, Ostling)

Adagio and Allegro is dedicated to Frederick C. Ebbs and the University of Iowa Symphonic Band. The composition is in one movement with two contrasting themes. Ostinato technique is employed throughout the composition with fugal treatment of the patterns sustaining rhythmic interest. The Adagio opens with flutes and bells performing a soft and sustained ostinato in direct contrast to the agitated rhythm of the brass ostinatos in the Allegro. The work closes with brasses performing their motif in marcato chorale style against reiterated modal scales for the woodwinds and melodic percussion.

Andante and Toccato (Pub – FC, 1966. Gr – 4. T – 8:00.)

The Andante is written for the woodwinds in a solo and sectional style. It is expressive in character with the brass quality remaining for punctuation and excitement in the Toccata. (Jack Snavely, University of Wisconsin at Milwaukee)

Appassionato (Pub = FC, 1967. Gr = 3. T = 6:30. Rec = CR-MID-68-10, Vander-Cook Col. of Mus., Zajec)

Concerning *Appassionato,* Nelhybel wrote:

> The following short poem was given to me without signature by a young person from the audience after a performance of *Appassionato* —
>
> > A song—shy and tender—
> > Dreamy and nostalgic.
> > A song of sorrow and farewell,
> > Of hope and of despair;
> > A passionate outcry.
> > A song of agony and resignation.
> > A song of you and me.
>
> I cherish it deeply.

On the score, the composer added that *"Appassionato* is a composition with a strong emphasis on the woodwinds, the brass being reserved only for climactic moments. The complete absence of percussion allows the essential lyric mood of the composition to prevail."

Chorale for Symphonic Band (Pub = FC, 1965. Gr = 4. T = 6:00. Rec = CO-1260, Un. of KY, Miller)

The *Chorale* is based on a medieval Bohemian chant whose words are a desperate plea to St. Wenceslaus, the first king of Bohemia, not to forsake his people nor let them perish. This highly emotional chant, born out of fear of the plague, has been sung in Bohemia for centuries during times of war and danger. At the beginning of the *Chorale* a threatening atmosphere is evoked from which voices of despair emerge with the ancient chant emotionally pleading for help. However, the character of the composition gradually changes until the work closes with an ecstatic hymn of hope. Composer Nelhybel states, "In this composition I combined the modern concept of symphonic sound with the voice-leading techniques of the Middle Ages and the early Renaissance, in order to communicate the ancient theme to a contemporary audience. (Harold H. Hillyer, University of Texas at El Paso)

Estampie (Pub = FR, 1966. Gr = 4. T = 4:30. Rec = CR-MID-72-6, Harding Jr. H.S., Cedar Rapids, IA, Northrup)

Without being an overly difficult work, *Estampie* offers a vital and attractive artistic package revealing the keen imagination of the composer.

The "estampie" is a medieval dance pattern, in which a soloist alternated with the group singing and dancing in a kind of "round." Nelhybel employs this idea by alternating expressive woodwind passages with the marcato antiphonal sound of the brass choir. His unique ability to take advantage of the percussion, which has contributed to the distinct character of his writing, is again revealed in this composition. (Frank Bencriscutto, University of Minnesota)

Festivo (Pub = FC, 1968. Gr = 3. T = 6:00. Rec = CR-MID-76-6, East Ascension Jr. Hi., Gonzales, LA, Nelhybel; CO-S1501, OH St. Un., McGinnis)

Nelhybel states, "*Festivo* is an overture-type composition in which the woodwinds and the brasses are constantly confronting each other like two antagonists in a dramatic scene." The resulting percussive concept of wind performance which is prevalent in twentieth-century music provides a striking impact for the performer and listener.

Prelude and Fugue (Pub = FR, 1966. Gr = 4. T = 4:50. Rec = CO-1441, Un. of MD, Ostling)

The *Prelude and Fugue* is not a composition in two sections, but rather a composition in one movement with two contrasting themes. The slow opening is an intense search to formulate the main theme in a strong statement, first in the woodwinds, then in full brass, and finally in low brass and percussion. In the Allegro the theme emerges in full aggressive splendor, presented by brass and percussion. Immediately following the *Fugue* is the Vivace, literally a "running-away" from the theme. The fugal texture of the perpetuum mobile in the woodwinds generates a strong pull away from the marcato of the brassy main theme. The composition concludes with a struggle for supremacy between the driving eighth-note runs in the woodwinds and the imperative marcato of the brass. The work is dedicated to the University of New Mexico Concert Band. (Donald McRae and William E. Rhoads, University of New Mexico)

Suite Concertante (Pub = FC, 1967.   Gr = 4.   T = 11:00.   Rec = CR-MID-68-11, Brownsville, TX, H.S., Murphy)

The composition's title is a graphic explanation of its content. The term "suite" is apropos in that the work contains five separate movements—Bravado, Religioso, Rustico, Romantico, and Maestoso. "Concertante" denotes the typical and unique stylings in which Nelhybel writes; that is, the balancing of the various sections of the wind ensemble against the "ripieno," or large group. (Clayton Tiede, Mankato State College)

Symphonic Movement (Pub = FC, 1966. Gr = 5. T = 8:00. Rec = CR-CBDNA-73-4, Un. of IL, Kisinger)

Although he has written several large-scale works for band, the composer has described *Symphonic Movement* as "my first composition for band completely written on a symphonic level." The entire work is based on a single eight-note scale which is first stated in wide rhythmic spacing and later grouped in a closer melodic sequence. The remaining four tones of the twelve-tone scale are employed only twice; first, as counterpoint to the first entrance of the principal theme in the allegro section, and then as counterpoint to the last entrance of the theme in full brass. *Symphonic Movement* was dedicated to John Paynter and the Northwestern Band.

Symphonic Requim (Pub = FC, 1965. Gr = 5. T = 40:00.)

The opening movement of this four-part work is entitled Preambulum and is based upon the first four notes of the traditional *Dies Irae* chant, F-E-F-D. The second movement, Motet, uses only the double-reed and saxophone choirs and is based upon the *Dies Irae* theme in a changed order. The third movement, Passacaglia, is more aggressive and utilizes the brass and percussion instruments playing variants of the same theme. The final movement, Cantata, is a monologue for bass-baritone, the band providing a two-dimensional background with off-stage brass. This combination of closeness and distance, presence and absence, reflects the spirit of a contemplation on the matter of life and death. A translation of the Latin text of the Cantata—written by Venatius Fortunatus in the sixth century A.D.—is given as follows:

Time is gliding and flying by, we are deceived by the fleeing hours.
Though not alike, we all go toward the same end;
   no one returns once he has reached the final threshold.
What power have man's arms.
Beauty cannot last.
What, I ask you, what is the value of music?
   and what is the value of poetry?
In the final hour, even the songs of the Muses are useless,
   and it is senseless to prolong the melody.
Thus, while the moments are falling, the present is fleeing,
   the dice are snatched away from us and the game is over.
What remains in the end is the blessed flower of good deeds,
   sweet is the smell from the grave of the just.

Trittico (Pub = FC, 1965. Gr = 5. T = 10:30. Rec = BP-104, Un. of Houston, Matthews; UM-25456, Un. of MN, Bencriscutto)

Trittico was composed for William D. Revelli who conducted the University of Michigan Band in the first performance of the work in the spring of 1964. *Trittico* is defined as a triptych or painting on three panels such as is common on altars—the two side panels closing over the central panel. The title is most descriptive, as indicated in the following remarks found on the composer's score:

> The first and third movements are, in several ways, related to one another: their character is brilliantly forward-moving and energetic; the main theme of the first movement reappears in the culmination point of the third movement, and the instrumentation of the movements is identical (standard), with the individual instruments themselves being used quite similarly.
>
> The second movement is a strongly contrasting dramatic scene with turbulent recitatives and expressive woodwind solos, punctuated by low brass and percussion. The emphasis is on woodwinds and low brass: cornets and trumpets enter only at the very end with an extremely intense phrase to conclude the movement. The dramatic character is underlined by the strong use of percussion which is extended by a second timpani player, piano, and celesta.

Two Symphonic Movements (Pub = FC, 1972. Gr = 5. T = 14:00)

This work, composed in 1970 and dedicated to Michael Polovitz and the North Dakota Band, demonstrates the vigorous drive which is quite characteristic of Nelhybel's music. Nelhybel's personal magnetism and technical proficiency are evident in his compositions; the *Two Symphonic Movements* encompass the entire range of human emotions—the common denominator through which his artistic expression carries its universal appeal. All thematic material in these two contrasting movements is derived from four notes stated at the very beginning of the first movement, which is basically slow in tempo and of a free improvisational character. The second movement, in fast tempo, is a symphonic development of new thematic features of the four-note motif upon which the work is constructed. (Gale Sperry, University of South Florida)

RON NELSON

(Born in Joliet, Illinois, 1929)

Ron Nelson, a member of the faculty at Brown University, has many compositions to his credit. He began composing at the age of six and later earned degrees in composition from the Eastman School of Music. On a Fulbright Fellowship he studied at the École Normale de Musique in Paris with Arthur Honegger and Tony Aubin. His compositions include opera, film, band, and choral music.

Rocky Point Holiday (Pub = BH, 1969. Gr = 4. T = 5:30. Rec = CN-18, Cornell Un., Stith)

Ron Nelson's *Rocky Point Holiday* was commissioned by and composed for the University of Minnesota Concert Band. The composition is an exciting virtuoso work representative of a great number of American compositions which unite elements of jazz and classical construction into a new indigenous American style. Rocky Point is a wind-blown seaside resort on the coast of Rhode Island.

SAMMY NESTICO

(Born in Pittsburgh, Pennsylvania, 1924)

At the age of seventeen Sammy Nestico became staff trombonist for a radio station in Pittsburgh. Later he graduated from Duquesne University and accepted a teaching position in Wilmerding, Pennsylvania. Subsequently he joined the United States Air Force as director of the "Airmen of Note" and became known as an outstanding composer and arranger for service musical organizations. Nestico has over 400 compositions published and is known as one of the few composers who can write equally well for school musicians and professionals. Since retiring from the service, he has lived on the West Coast where he continues to write. (Kendor Music, Inc.)

Portrait of a Trumpet—Solo (Pub = KN, 1965. Gr = 4. T = 5:00)

Sammy Nestico provides this pleasant "mood" piece that exploits the colors of the full band with trumpet solo. The solo part requires solid musicianship including experience in playing jazz. The mood and style are largely legato with emphasis on musical blend, balance, and nuance.

A Tribute to Stephen Foster (Pub = KN, 1968. Gr = 5. T = 7:50. Rec = CR-MID-79-12, Hardaway H.S., Columbus, GA, Gregory)

Solos for horn, cornet, and bassoon are heard in this fine symphonic scoring of melodies by Stephen Foster. The score was originally created for the United States Marine Band, and its performance requires expertise and solid musicianship, traits that also account for its exceptional interest as a composition.

The music of Stephen Foster is filled with the nostalgia associated with mid-nineteenth century American history. His songs contain mixed emotions of humor and sadness that were symbolic of his life. The treasure of over 125 songs he left us have spanned the years. Many are still sung throughout our country and are known throughout the world.

The composer provides this personal note: "Stephen Foster has always been a personal favorite of mine, and it is with deep respect that I present the arrangement of his music. . . . "An old friend, with a new face."

Vaquero March (Pub = KN, 1967. Gr = 3. T = 2:15)

A concert march that is rhythmically, harmonically, and structurally fresh and colorful, *Vaquero* is dedicated to North Texas State University. The flavor strongly suggests the mood and excitement of vaqueros (Spanish cowboys).

JAMES NIBLOCK

(Born in Scappoose, Oregon, 1917)

James Niblock is professor of music at Michigan State University in East Lansing. A student of Paul Hindemith and Roy Harris in the field of composition, Niblock completed music degrees at Washington State College, Colorado College, and the University of Iowa. His output includes works for orchestra, choir, solo instruments, and piano; a concerto for violin and orchestra, film scores, works for organ, and various chamber works. His honors include an NEA grant for research in Mexican music.

Niblock is a versatile musician. In addition to his teaching responsibilities, he is an excellent violinist, he has written a book of music for high school choirs, and he still has found time to compose sixty major works. He and Mrs. Niblock are the parents of a daughter and a son.

La Folia Variations (Pub = MM, 1968. Gr = 3. T = 6:00. Rec = CR-MID-68-5, Muskegon, MI, H.S., Krive)

According to *The Oxford Companion to Music,* the story of the Folia is one of the most curious in the history of music. Originally the name of a wild Portuguese dance, one particular tune associated with the dance became universally familiar due to the treatment given it by Corelli in his *Twelfth Violin Sonata.* The whole melody is nothing but a little motif repeated nine times at various levels and yet for nearly two centuries this melody was used in various ways by many prominent composers. *La Folia Variations* states the famous Folia theme in baroque chorale style, presents three traditional variations beginning simply and increasing slightly in complexity, states two modern variations, and closes in traditional style. The general tone of the work is subdued and is not characteristic of the Portuguese dance origins. (Acton Ostling, Jr., University of Maryland)

Soliloquy and Dance (Pub = SO, 1957. Gr = 4. T = 8:00. Rec = MU-H80P-5838, Un. of MI, Revelli)

Niblock was a member of the music faculty at Michigan State University when he composed *Soliloquy and Dance.* The work became one of the compositions to represent the North Central Division membership of the College Band Directors National Association at its 1956 Chicago convention. In this composition, Niblock not only showed his talent for composition, but demonstrated keen insight into the sonorities of the symphonic band as well. The tranquility and loneliness of one's reflections upon himself and his own thoughts are beautifully portrayed in the opening section, and the dance reflects a sense of satisfaction, stately and exhilarating, but not wildly exciting. (Hubert H. Henderson, University of Maryland)

ROGER NIXON

(Born in Tulare, California, 1921)

Roger Nixon, a professor of music at San Francisco State University, received most of his professional training at the University of California at Berkeley, where his principal teacher was Roger Sessions. He also worked with Arthur Bliss, Ernest Bloch, Charles Cushing, and Frederick Jacobi, and in the summer of 1948 studied privately with Arnold Schoenberg. He was the recipient of the first Phelan Award in music composition. Among his numerous works are a viola concerto, an orchestral suite, much chamber music, choral music, songs, and music for symphonic band. (Carl Fischer, Inc.)

Elegy and Fanfare-March (Pub = CF, 1968. Gr = 4. T = 9:00. Rec = CR-MID-68-8, Northshore Concert, Wilmette, IL, Paynter)

The *Elegy* is a reflective, relatively quiet adagio movement, which is sharply contrasting in mood to the spirited *Fanfare-March.* The music was composed in 1956-57 and the first performances were by the University of California Band, James Berdahl conducting. In 1961, the *Elegy and Fanfare-March* was in the repertoire of the University of Michigan Symphony Band during its tour of the Soviet Union and satellite countries. Regarding the piece and its reception on this tour, William D. Revelli, conductor, wrote the following letter to the composer:

> Your *Elegy and Fanfare-March* is being played almost nightly for our Soviet audiences, and everywhere it is achieving great receptivity. The Russian people are great band fans and have evinced tremendous enthusiasm for your work. In fact, it is perhaps the most popular contemporary piece we are playing on this tour. I expect to perform it on our tour of the satellite countries, and am confident it will achieve the same enthusiastic response that we are enjoying throughout the Soviet Union tour. It is indeed a most effective and well-conceived band work. I hope that you will continue to provide us with additional repertoire from your talented pen. . . .

It has been found that American audiences respond with enthusiasm too, as the work has been programmed by college and high school bands across the country. (Carl Fischer, Inc.)

Fiesta del Pacifico (Pub = BH, 1966. Gr = 5. T = 8:00. Rec = DL-710157, Eastman, Geiger; GC-Revelli Years, Un. of MI, Revelli)

Fiesta del Pacifico is one of several festivals, held annually in various communities in California, which celebrate the "Old Spanish Days" of the state. This particular festival is held in San Diego for twelve days each summer and features a play on the history of the area with a cast of over 1,000, a parade, a rodeo, and street dances.

Reflections (Pub = TP, 1970. Gr = 5. T = 7:00. Rec = CR-CBDNA-75-6, Southern Oregon Col., McKee; GC-ATH-5062, Baylor Un., Floyd)

The composer states that "this music is reflective in both mood and shape, and its general character resembles that of a chorale prelude. It is monothematic, a germinal phrase played by the solo flute at the outset functioning as a basis for further melodic movement and motival development. The work is dedicated to the San Francisco State University Symphonic Band, Edwin C. Kruth, Director."

JACQUES OFFENBACH
(Born in Cologne, Germany, 1819 — Died in Paris, 1880)

Jacques Offenbach, Rhenish-Jewish composer and conductor, resided in France from early youth. Offenbach's father was cantor of the Hebrew synagogue at Cologne. In 1833 the boy entered the Paris Conservatory studying cello for one year with Vaslin; during this time he also played in the orchestra of the Opéra Comique. In 1849 he became conductor at the Théâtre Français, and in 1853 he began to compose stage pieces. In 1855 Offenbach opened his own theater, the Bouffes Parisiens, where many of his popular works were performed. From 1872 to 1876 he managed the Théâtre de la Gaîté, and in 1877 he made a tour of America. He was the most famous composer of light opera of his day, producing no less than ninety works in twenty-five years. Offenbach's most famous composition, *The Tales of Hoffman,* achieved great success, particularly in the United States, where it was first produced in 1907. (Carl Fischer, Inc.)

The Drum-Major's Daughter Overture (Arr = Odom. Pub = KJ, 1974. Gr = 4.
T = 6:40. Rec = CR-MID-74-13, Coronado H.S., Lubbock, TX, Anthony)

The last production by Offenbach, "La Fille du tambour-major," (1879) is no longer performed, but its overture remains in the symphonic repertory. The liveliness of the overture portrays the excitement and romance to be found in the operettas by Offenbach, master of this mid-nineteenth century medium which captivated the sophisticated audiences of Paris and, later, audiences in centers of culture throughout Europe and America.

Orpheus in the Underworld Overture (Arr = Lake-Kent. Pub = CF, 1917-46. Gr = 5.
T = 9:00. Rec = CR-MID-70-12, West Suburban Com., Dvorak)

The music of this overture is well known throughout the world. The plot of the opera, not so well known, concerns the mythological musician Orpheus and his wife, Eurydice. Their domestic life leaves much to be desired, and Orpheus seeks happiness with Chloe, the beautiful shepherdess. His wife is in love with the shepherd, Aristeus, who is Pluto in disguise.

On one occasion Eurydice is gathering flowers in the meadow, and by some mischance Orpheus mistakes her for Chloe; his perfidy is discovered, and Eurydice flies to Hades with Aristeus. Orpheus is delighted to have disposed of her so easily, but Popular Opinion demands that he make some effort to recover his spouse. Therefore Orpheus accuses Pluto before Jupiter, and all the gods of Olympus decide to accompany Orpheus to investigate the charges.

Eurydice is hidden in a secret chamber and is guarded by a stupid lout called John Styx. Jupiter, disguised as a fly, enters the chamber and buys Eurydice's love with the promise of freedom. Pluto is compelled to return her to Orpheus, who is to receive her only if he can reach the river without turning to look at his wife. But Jupiter is plotting to keep Eurydice himself and he causes a blinding flash of lightning, which forces Orpheus to turn his head and look back. Thus Jupiter retains Eurydice in subjection as a Bacchante and Orpheus returns happily to Chloe. (Carl Fischer, Inc.)

HIROSHI OHGURI

(Born in Osaka, Japan, 1918)

Like many composers in other countries Ohguri has combined the profession of composition with teaching. At the present time he is a professor of music at one of the leading schools in Japan, the Kyoto Girls College. His interest in composing for band has increased along with the growth of this medium in the schools. In 1958 only about ten per cent of the high schools in Japan had bands; by 1978 over ninety per cent of both junior and senior high schools had a band program. Although a large majority of the works played by Japanese bands are by European, American, and Russian composers (89% at the 1978 national band contest), an increasing number are by Japanese composers. Of the seven Japanese compositions played at the 1978 contest, one was by Hiroshi Ohguri. (Information from Paul Yoder, Troy State University)

Rhapsody for Band (Pub = ON.   Gr = 4.   T = 6:30.   Rec = CB-CBS-SONY-20AG-399, Izumo Jr. H.S., Katayose)

Although this work has the traditionally rather free rhapsodic form, varying from lento to allegro molto tempos, the effect of the music is still Japanese in character.

The rhapsody was composed in 1966 and was commissioned by the All Japan Band Association as required music for the high school division of the 1971 All Japan Band Contest. (Toshio Akiyama, Omiya, Saitama, Japan)

CARL ORFF

(Born in Munich, 1895

Carl Orff studied at the Munich Academy and privately with Heinrich Kaminski. In 1925 he helped to found the Gunter Schule which aims at the education of the lay public in creative musicianship. The principles developed by Orff have been adopted by elementary school educators in the United States and throughout the world.

Orff began his career as a composer in 1925 with realizations of Monteverdi's early seventeenth-century works. He sought to renew the musical theater in an ideology of his own. In 1935-36 his first stage work, *Carmina Burana,* was produced and was an outstanding success.

Carmina Burana (Arr = Krance. Pub = AMP, 1967. Gr = 5. T = 23:30. Rec = Excerpts-CR-ABA-73-3, U.S. Army Field, Enlx)

The original score of Carl Orff's *Carmina Burana* (1936), subtitled "Profane songs for singers and vocal chorus with instruments and magical pictures," calls for vocal soli, three choirs, and large orchestra. The band arrangement, however, is entirely instrumental in concept, the vocal music having been fully incorporated into the band itself.

Orff derived the inspiration and texts for his score from a thirteenth-century anthology of songs and poems written in medieval Latin, German, and French by the "goliards," the vagrant scholars, vagabond poets, and wandering monks of seven hundred years ago. Containing approximately two hundred songs and poems—both sacred and secular—the manuscript ranged in style and content from earthly simplicity to sophisticated symbolism, from religious contemplation to unabashed worldliness. The texts are frank avowals of earthly pleasure: eating, dancing, drinking, gambling, lovemaking; the beauty of life and glorious springtime!

Orff exhilarates us with throbbing rhythms and battering-ram tunes, and moves us with chaste tenderness and heartfelt simplicity. From the original twenty-five sections, John Krance has arranged thirteen.

(1) O Fortune, variable as the moon
(2) I lament fortune's blow
(3) Behold the spring
(4) Dance—on the lawn
.(5) The noble forest
(6) Were the world all mine
(7) The God of Love flies everywhere
(8) I am the Abbot
(9) When we were in the tavern
(10) I am suspended between love and chastity
(11) Sweetest boy
(12) Hail to thee, most beautiful
(13) Fortune, Empress of the world

(Thomas Giles, Mankato State College)

GLENN OSSER

(Born in Munising, Michigan, 1914)

Glenn Osser graduated from the public schools of Munising and received a Bachelor of Music degree from the University of Michigan. His career in New York started with his arranging for many of the well-known dance orchestras, including Bunny Berigan, Bob Crosby, and Red Nichols. He soon came to the attention of the radio conductors and started devoting his time to this field for such conductors as Al Goodman and Al Roth. The World War II years were spent in the Maritime Service, and after completing his enlistment, he was engaged by Paul Whiteman as an arranger. He was a staff conductor and arranger for the American Broadcasting Company from 1947 to 1968, and has been the music director for the Miss America Pageant since 1955. Currently, he also writes and produces music for television and recordings with vocalists.

Beguine Again (Pub = MC, 1967. Gr = 3. Rec = IL-48, Un. of IL, Hindsley)

Swirling woodwind chromatic figurations and soaring brass lines abound in this musical setting, a sequel to the composer's *Beguine for Band.*

Beguine for Band (Pub = EM, 1954. Gr = 3. Rec = DL-8157, American Sym. Band of the Air, Revelli)

In one of his earliest and most popular works, Osser has successfully organized the characteristic beguine rhythm for concert band. The beguine originated as a popular dance of the West Indies.

Bolero for Band (Pub = LD, 1962. Gr = 3. Rec = IL-31, Un. of IL, Hindsley)

A Spanish dance in three-quarter meter, the bolero produces a hypnotic effect with its ever-present, steady, and repetitious pulsation of duple and triple meter combinations of percussive and tonal sounds.

ERIC OSTERLING

(Born in West Hartford, Connecticut, 1926)

Eric Osterling graduated in music education from Ithaca College in 1948. Since that time he has been director of music education in the public schools of Portland, Connecticut, where he has developed an outstanding concert band. He was named "Man of the Year" by the Junior Chamber of Commerce and received the Distinguished Service Award in 1961. The recipient of several other honors and commissions, Osterling has received an annual award for his "outstanding contributions to band literature" from the American Society of Composers, Authors, and Publishers. (Carl Fischer, Inc.)

Bandology (Pub = CF, 1964. Gr = 3. T = 4:40. Rec = CF-BSS, Sym. Winds, Cacavas)

With its rich, full harmonies and interesting fanfare rhythms, *Bandology* is a light program piece designed to please audiences of all ages.

Mustang March (Pub = CA, 1966. Gr = 3. T = 2:30)

Mustang, a theatrical-type concert march, has the singing melody, full scoring, and strong beat which are the hallmarks of every successful Osterling opus. (Chappell and Co., Inc.)

Nutmeggers March (Pub = BO, 1954. Gr = 3. T = 2:50. Rec = OS-6706, Second All American Bandmasters)

Nutmeggers March was the first of several popular marches by Osterling to be published and to catch the fancy of the bandsmen and their audiences. All have a unique, lively, and cheerful sound.

The title for this march came from one of the two nicknames of Osterling's home state, Connecticut. The early Connecticut traders were said to have sold wooden nutmegs for real ones.

Symphonic Chorale (Pub = CA, 1969. Gr = 3. T = 3:30. Rec = CR-MID-69-9, Ouachita H.S., Monroe, LA, Swor)

Parellel triads sounding with a diatonic melody provide pleasant listening in this composition for school musicians. Rather than the traditional chorale sound, one hears flowing tone color with a variety of dynamic changes.

Thundercrest March (Pub = CF, 1964. Gr = 3. T = 2:50. Rec = CF-BSS, Sym. Winds, Cacavas)

Osterling has composed several concert marches which have proved popular with both bands and audiences throughout the country. *Thundercrest* with its stirring rhythm, rich harmonies, and distinctive melody, seems to catch the fancy of all audiences, young and old. (Carl Fischer, Inc.)

Totem Pole March (Pub = BO, 1962. Gr = 3. T = 2:50)

Pyramid effects are used to evoke a musical imagery of tribal totems piled one on top of the other, building an imposing structure. *Totem Pole* is one of many dynamic concert pieces by Osterling, a composer of concert marches with a special flare.

ROBERT PEARSON

(Born in Ossining, New York, 1924)

Robert Pearson received his early musical training in the state of New York. He earned his B.S. degree at Ithaca College and did graduate work at Hofstra University. Following college he was a member of and arranger for the Charlie Spivak, Eddy Duchin, and Russ Carlyle dance orchestras. Later he began directing school bands and orchestras.

Minuteman March (Pub = TE, 1964. Gr = 3. T = 3:20)

Minuteman is a stirring march which shows clearly the influence of Pearson's dance-band background in its harmony. While retaining the same general form as that used by Sousa and the other "march masters," this march achieves a delightful, modern sound.

The Minuteman—the pushbutton, land-based, solid-fueled mainstay of the United States nuclear arsenal—was the source of inspiration for Pearson's march for symphonic band. This exciting concert march recasts the sound in an unusual use of instrumentation—a sparkling addition to the general concert program.

KRZYSZTOF PENDERECKI
(Born in Debica, Poland, 1933)

Graduated from the Superior School of Music, Cracow, Poland in 1958, Penderecki has become recognized as a leader among international avant-garde composers and the most significant of today's Polish composers. In 1961 his *Threnody to the Victims of Hiroshima* brought him into the international spotlight. He maintains a residence in Poland but has also resided in Germany and served as composer-in-residence with the Buffalo, New York, Philharmonic Orchestra during the years 1968-1969.

Penderecki's music is new, strange, and foreign to the ear of the traditional audience, but to avant-gardists his works are in line with what they believe is to be the music of the near future and is already with us today. He provides his audiences with information—sound material in various shapes—totally different from the sounds and shapes of traditional concert fare. His music provides the ear with something that it has not heard before, but it is something to which the ear can respond and coordinate. Concepts such as keys and traditional melodic and harmonic structures are considered archaic, and freedom from preconceived rhythmic patterns on the part of the performer and conductor seems to be a goal sought after in his music.

Pittsburgh Ouverture (Pub = PET, 1967. Gr = 6. T = 12:00 Rec = Point Park College Recording Series No. KP101, American Wind Symphony Orch., Boudreau)

Commissioned by Robert Boudreau, conductor of the American Wind Symphony Orchestra, *Pittsburgh Ouverture* was first performed by that organization in 1968 at its permanent home of Oakmount Riverside Park in Pittsburgh. The music is scored for an ensemble of twenty-two woodwind instruments to be played by seventeen performers, fifteen brass instruments, and eighteen percussion instruments to be played by six performers. Some of the instruments called for are not normally found in wind ensembles in the United States. These include the bass flute in C, *oboe d'amore,* bass oboe, chimes with extended range, and a variety of other percussion instruments not found among standard manufactured equipment.

Numerous effects called for in the score are notated with special symbols not found in traditional music. There are no meter signatures nor are there any metronome marks. There are measure lines, sometimes quite widely spaced. Since a major ingredient of the composition is improvisation, the notation is designed to facilitate it. "Pitch content . . . is apparently derived from a twelve-tone set and is controlled by various serial procedures including permutations of the set. . . . However, Penderecki does not limit his pitch sources to the chromatic scale." Some microtones are called for and special notation symbols are utilized for these and other special sounds intended by the composer. (From "An Analysis of Penderecki's *Pittsburgh Ouverture"* by Thomas Tyra in the *Journal of Band Research,* Fall, 1973, and Spring, 1974)

FRANK PERKINS
(Born in Salem, Massachusetts, 1908)

After receiving a doctorate in economics from Brown University, Frank Perkins began a serious study of music, taking private lessons in piano, organ, trombone, saxophone, and percussion. Tibor Serly was one of his principal teachers. Perkins arranged for Fred Waring and then moved to Warner Brothers as a composer and conductor for motion pictures.

Fandango (Arr = Werle. Pub = BE, 1954. Gr = 4. T = 4:00. Rec = AC-6539, West TX St. Un.; EV-2084, Royal Horse Guards, Thirtle)

Originally published in 1952 as a piano solo, *Fandango* lends itself well to the band medium. The fandango is a Spanish dance in 3/4 time originally danced by a couple to the accompaniment of guitar and castanets. It first appeared in Spain in the early eighteenth century.

Perkins' *Fandango* has much of the descriptive feeling of the Spanish dance. Fire, spirit, and excitement pervade the beginning and ending. A midsection offers quiet contrast to the excitement of the remainder of the work.

VINCENT PERSICHETTI

(Born in Philadelphia, Pennsylvania, 1915)

Vincent Persichetti studied composition with Paul Nurdoff and Roy Harris and conducting with Fritz Reiner. He is a graduate of Combs College, Philadelphia Conservatory, and the Curtis Institute. Persichetti was head of the department of composition at the Philadelphia Conservatory from 1941 to 1947, and in 1947 joined the staff of the Juilliard School of Music in New York, where he is presently the head of the composition department. His works, in virtually every form and for all media, are played throughout the world; more than ninety of his compositions are published and many are recorded. Persichetti is a virtuoso keyboard performer and an energetic scholar. The influence of his musical mind is widely felt, thanks to his expert teaching and his book of the harmonic practices of this century.

Bagatelles (Pub = EV, 1962. Gr = 4. T = 5:00. Rec = CR-ATH-5055, Un. of KS, Foster)

Since the resounding success of his first published work for band, *Divertimento,* Vincent Persichetti has written prolifically for the concert band, including the use of this medium for his *Symphony No. 6.* A group of short pieces exemplified by the *Bagatelles,* however, seems to remain his favorite form of band writing. The four contrasting sections are titled Vivace, Allegretto, Andante sostenuto, and Allegro con spirito. *Bagatelles* was commissioned by Dartmouth College.

Chorale Prelude: So Pure the Star (Pub = EV, 1963. Gr = 4. T = 5:00. Rec = CR-ATH-5055, UN. of KS, Foster)

An original chorale melody is here given a contemporary treatment harmonically while retaining many of the characteristics of chorale preludes of the Baroque period. Sharply contrasting in style with most of Persichetti's band works, this beautifully constructed prelude was commissioned by the Duke University Band.

Chorale Prelude: Turn Not Thy Face (Pub = EV, 1963. Gr = 4. T = 4:30. Rec = CR-ATH-5055, Un. of KS, Foster)

At sixteen Vincent Persichetti was appointed organist of the prestigious Arch Street Presbyterian Church in Philadelphia. His understanding of the organ and chorus thus dates back to his earliest days, and it is not surprising that some of his most performed works are for church use. In *Turn Not Thy Face* he has revived an organ form popular in Bach's day, the chorale prelude, basing his flowing work on a chorale tune of his own which appears in his *Hymns and Responses for the Church Year.* The piece was commissioned by the Ithaca High School Band in memory of John Fitzgerald Kennedy. (Richard Franko Goldman, the Goldman Band)

VINCENT PERSICHETTI

Divertimento for Band (Pub = EV, 1951. Gr = 5. T = 11:00. Rec = MG-75086, Eastman, Fennell)

Divertimento consists of six short movements (Prologue, Song, Dance, Burlesque, Soliloquy, and March) which demonstrate rhythmic and contrapuntal savoir-faire blended neatly with tongue-in-cheek humor and lyrical nostalgia. The work was Persichetti's first for band and is still one of his most popular compositions. It was commissioned by the Goldman Band and premiered by that organization on June 16, 1950.

Masquerade (Pub = EV, 1966. Gr = 5. T = 12:00. Rec = DL-710163, Eastman, Hunsberger)

Persichetti's band works demonstrate the remarkable contrapuntal conciseness of his music which is basically tonal but with an independence of movement which often creates polytonal combinations. *Masquerade*, a theme with ten variations, was commissioned by the Baldwin-Wallace College Conservatory of Music, and the première was given at the conservatory with Persichetti as guest conductor. As in so much of the composer's music, the work incorporates complicated percussion parts which transcend their reinforcing functions to occupy an equal position with the winds in the basic fabric of the composition.

O Cool is the Valley (Pub = EV, 1972. Gr = 4. T = 6:00. Rec = CR-ATH-5055, Un. of KS, Foster)

Commissioned by the Ohio Music Education Association, *O Cool is the Valley* was given its premier performance by the Bowling Green State University Band in 1972. The work, subtitled *Poem for Band* after a poem by James Joyce, is essentially a three part composition. The first section is a slowly moving portion in simple meter. A section in compound meter follows; slow but with somewhat more motion. The final section is again in simple meter and slowly moving as in the first section.

Pageant (Pub = CF, 1955. Gr = 4. T = 7:00. Rec = NE-211, Northwestern Un., Paynter)

Pageant was completed for band in 1953 on a commission from Edwin Franko Goldman for the American Bandmasters Association. It was first performed under the composer's direction by the University of Miami Band. The work opens in a slow tempo with a motive in the horn that is used througout both sections of the composition. This solemn chordal section is succeeded by a vivacious parade, introduced first by the snare drum. In the final portion of the piece, the two principal subjects are developed simultaneously to an inspired climax.

Psalm for Band (Pub = EV, 1959. Gr = 4. T = 8:00. Rec = MS-IV, Morehead St. Un., Hawkins; CT-1247, OH St. Un., Persichetti)

Psalm for Band was commissioned by the Alpha Chapter of Pi Kappa Omicron National Band Fraternity at the University of Louisville. It was first performed in 1952 by the University of Louisville Concert Band with the composer conducting. He included the following note on the score:

> *Psalm for Band* is a piece constructed from a single germinating harmonic idea. There are three distinct sections—a sustained chordal mood, a forward-moving chorale, followed by a Paean culmination of the materials. Extensive use is made of separate choirs of instruments supported by thematic rhythms in the tenor and bass drums.

(John Wakefield, University of Maryland)

Symphony for Band (Pub = EV, 1958. Gr = 4. T = 16:00. Rec = CR-NEC-103, New England Conservatory, Battisti; IL-66, Un. of IL, Begian)

Vincent Persichetti's *Symphony No. 6 for Band*, commissioned by Washington University of St. Louis, could have easily been called *Symphony for Winds,* following as it did, the composer's *Symphony No. 5 for Strings.* Persichetti, however did not wish to avoid the word "band," which he felt no longer had the connotation of a poor quality of music. Some of his thoughts about band music were stated in an article in *The Journal of Band Research* (I, Autumn, 1964, p. 17): "Band music is virtually the only kind of music in America today (outside the pop field) which can be introduced, accepted, put to immediate wide use, and become a staple of the literature in a short time." The *Symphony for Band,* in fact, became a standard part of the literature for band almost immediately after its première at the national convention of the Music Educators National Conference in St. Louis, in March, 1956.

The four movements have forms with traditional implications. The opening horn call and a following scale-wise passage of the slow introduction section become the two principal themes, in reverse order, in the subsequent Allegro, which includes the standard exposition, development, and recapitulation of sonata form although the traditional key relationships are not completely retained. The slow second movement is based on "Round Me Falls the Night" from the composer's *Hymns and Responses for the Church Year.* The third movement, in trio form, serves as the traditional dance movement, and is followed by a finale in free rondo form, which draws thematic material from the preceding movements. (Max R. Tromblee, Phillips University)

WALTER PISTON

(Born in Rockland, Maine, 1894 — Died in Belmont, Massachusetts, 1976)

Walter Piston studied painting and drawing at the Massachusetts Normal Art School, graduating in 1916. Music was then a sideline. After serving in the U.S. Navy during World War I and playing saxophone in a service band, he entered Harvard University as a freshman at the age of twenty-six. Pursuing a general course of education, he studied theory and composition there and after graduation continued his music study in Paris with Nadia Boulanger. On his return to the United States he was appointed to the music faculty at Harvard.

Piston's numerous compositions include works for orchestra, chamber music, and solo instruments. He received many honors and awards, and his books on music theory are standard works in many American schools and colleges.

Tunbridge Fair (Pub = BH, 1951. Gr = 5. T = 5:00. Rec = MG-50079, Eastman, Fennell)

Commissioned by the League of Composers in 1950, *Tunbridge Fair,* subtitled "Intermezzo for Symphonic Band," is contrapuntal in texture throughout, utilizing informal early jazz-like rhythms and sonorities in a more formal structural setting. Two subjects are heard. The first is heavily accented and bouncy. The second is more flowing, yet syncopated, and is sounded with a hocket-like alternation of voicing. The work is bright and loud, yet quietly underscored with subtle humor. Its performance demands fine players in all choirs, for it must be played at a rapid pace with chromatic and octave doublings in practically all instrumental lines. It is full of brilliant upper passages with abrupt resolutions. The form is ABABA, with coda.

JAMES D. PLOYHAR
(Born in Valley City, North Dakota, 1926)

Ployhar's academic credits include a B.S. from Valley City State College, North Dakota, and an M.A. from Northern Colorado University. In addition, he has pursued graduate study in composition with Morris Hutchins Ruger at California State University at Long Beach and studied with Knud Hovaldt of the Danish Royal Philharmonic Orchestra. His successful career of twenty years as a public school music educator and writer of pedagogical materials for young musicians makes him in demand to give clinics and workshops at the college and university level. These frequent appearances as clinician and conductor have been enthusiastically welcomed throughout the United States and Canada.

Considered to be one of the most prolific writers for young school bandsmen, Ployhar's credits have appeared in well over 350 music publications, his compositions and scores have aired on network television, and his music is performed internationally in Europe and Japan. He is the author of the *Contemporary Band Course* published by Belwin-Mills Publishing Corporation of New York. The Ployhars have five children—all active in music.

Devonshire Overture (Pub = BE, 1976. Gr = 3. T = 5:00)

This work for school musicians is in a ternary form and begins with a soaring melodic line heard over the underlying rhythmic pulse of percussion and low brass. A slower middle section gives way to the often recurring melodic theme heard at the beginning of the composition. This work has been extremely popular as a concert and contest piece with both intermediate and more advanced bands throughout the United States and Canada. (James D. Ployhar)

Hammerfest March (Pub = BD, 1973. Gr = 3. T = 4:00)

This concert march is based on a Norwegian hymn tune. The original title is not known, and Hammerfest is actually a city in Norway. The melody is introduced by the clarinets and saxophones over a low brass accompaniment. The principal melody is then joined by a countermelody played by the flutes. Finally the melody is played in a grandiose style by the cornets with the countermelody being heard in the upper woodwinds. The march has been performed often as both a concert and contest selection. (James D. Ployhar)

The Original Thirteen March (Pub = BE, 1975. Gr = 2. T = 3:00)

Featuring the hymn-tune "Chester" by William Billings, this concert march is designed for performance by young school musicians. A countermelody is introduced in the flutes, piccolo and clarinets. The "Chester" melody then enters in the low brass and is finally heard with the entire brass section. The countermelody continues throughout. The work was written primarily for the United States Bicentennial celebration, but it continues to enjoy popularity beyond the festive year of 1976. (James D. Ployhar)

Variations on a Sioux Melody (Pub = BE, 1978. Gr = 4. T = 6:00)

The Dakota Indians once roamed freely over the Great Plains of North America. They were a nation made up of nomadic tribes sharing a common language. To the Indians, "Dakota" meant "allies." These allies were known to white men generally as the "Sioux," the word having been derived from "Nadouessioux," the French translation of a name given the Dakotas by some other tribe. *Variations on a Sioux Melody* was written especially for the International Music Camp Tour Band and performed at the John F. Kennedy Center for the Performing Arts in Washington, D.C. in 1978. (James D. Ployhar)

COLE PORTER
(Born in Peru, Indiana, 1892 — Died in Santa Monica, California, 1964)

The name Cole Porter immediately brings to mind a quarter-century's output of popular song classics, from "Begin the Beguine" to "True Love." Porter was born in Peru, Indiana, the only child of a prosperous druggist. He began his career as a composer while an undergraduate at Yale University, writing the famous football songs, "Yale Bulldog Song" and "Bingo Eli Yale." Porter was at once witty and sophisticated, enjoying the "high society" life of the well-to-do. In his prime, however he was thrown from a horse while riding and never fully recovered from the injuries sustained. Despite continued physical suffering, Porter went on to become one of the top Broadway composers, creating memorable scores for such shows as *Mexican Hayride, Can-Can,* and *Silk Stockings;* and the films *Born to Dance, Rosalie,* and *High Society.* The high point of Porter's achievement was *Kiss Me, Kate* which opened in 1948. His songs are satiric, sharp, nostalgic, sensual, and certainly the loveliest and most lyrical of his music written for the theater. *Kiss Me, Kate* is still performed in many countries, including England, Italy, Austria, and even Japan, and remains a favorite for revivals in this country. (Acton Ostling, Jr., Iowa State University)

Cole Porter—A Symphonic Portrait for Band (Arr = Robinson. Pub = CA, 1969. Gr = 4. T = 7:00. Rec = CR-MID-69-6, Waukegan, IL Grade Sch., Stiner)

Wayne Robinson has arranged this selection of perennial Porter favorites. "Another Opening, Another Show," "I Love Paris," "I've Got You Under My Skin," and "Wunderbar," are the four great Cole Porter songs included in this selection.

SERGEI PROKOFIEV
(Born in Sontsova, Russia, 1891 — Died in Moscow, 1953)

Sergei Prokofiev studied at the St. Petersburg Conservatory with such teachers as Rimsky-Korsakov, Liadov, and Tcherepnin. Subsequently he left his native country in the early twenties, spent considerable time in Paris, and returned to Russia in the early forties. Prokofiev was one of Russia's outstanding composers of the twentieth century. He himself listed the following as the four elements of his style: (1) classicism (neoclassicism); (2) innovation which at first was represented in an individual harmonic style, later as an expression of strong emotions; (3) the motoric element; and (4) lyricism. He regarded another element, the grotesque, as an outgrowth of the others. Much of his music, however, is flavored by a certain puckishness or humorous quality. He achieved popularity with the public and at the same time retained the admiration of musicians.

The catalogue of Prokofiev's works includes symphonies, band works, concertos, piano sonatas (as well as a number of separate piano pieces), and chamber music compositions.

Athletic Festival March (Arr = Goldman. Pub = MC, 1943. Gr = 4. T = 4:00. Rec = AN-S-40108, U.S.S.R. Defense Ministry, Sergeyer)

The *Athletic Festival March, Opus 79* was written directly for band. Its first performances in America were given by the Goldman Band. The work was written for a Russian athletic festival known as the Spartakiad. The music is full of lively humor and differs from the usual march in form.

March, Opus 99 (Pub = MC, 1946. Gr = 5. T = 5:00. Rec = MG-GI-SRI-75099, Eastman, Fennell)

It is entirely fitting that a composer of Prokofiev's stature and prolific output should also turn his attention to the band idiom. *March, Opus 99* is not the first of his works in this field; listeners may well remember the *Athletic Festival March* by the same composer.

March, Opus 99 was written in 1943, and received its premier performance on a broadcast conducted by Major Petrov, the leading bandmaster of the Soviet Union. This work was premiered in this country under the baton of Serge Koussevitzsky, conducting the Combat Infantry Band, on May 31st, 1945. (Richard Franko Goldman, the Goldman Band)

HENRY PURCELL
(Born in London, 1659 — Died in London, 1695)

Purcell was one of the greatest and most original of England's composers. When he was eighteen years old, he was appointed to the Chapel Royal as a composer, and five years later he became organist of the Chapel. His official duties led him to the composition of a large amount of church music. He also wrote much theater music, short opera masterpieces for school performances, popular ditties, and a large quantity of instrumental music for harpsichord and string instruments. A prominent feature of Purcell's music is a vigorous and steadily moving bass line, an idiom heard throughout the remainder of the Baroque era.

Battle Symphony (Arr = Schaefer. Pub = EM, 1976. Gr = 3. T = 7:50)

William A. Schaefer has compiled five short excerpts of music by Henry Purcell into a suite for band making this late seventeenth century music available for performance by school musicians and their audiences. The pieces were selected from three different works by Purcell—"The Married Beau," "Bonduca," and "King Arthur"—and assembled under Schaefer's title *Battle Symphony*. The five movements are Overture, To Arms!, The Battle, Song of Triumph, and Finale: The Order of the Garter. The selection brings the music of this important composer and the music of his era to the student in an enjoyable medium, and it makes interesting light program material for a band concert.

HENRI RABAUD
(Born in Paris, 1872 — Died in Paris, 1949)

Henri Rabaud had a notable career as conductor, teacher, and composer. After conducting at both the Paris Opera and the Conservatory, he succeeded Karl Muck as conductor of the Boston Symphony Orchestra in 1918. Two years later he returned to France to become the director of the Paris Conservatory. His major compositions include seven orchestral works, six operas, and four works for chorus, soloists, and orchestra. (Southern Music Co.)

Solo de Concours—Clarinet Solo (Arr = Gee. Pub = SO, 1960. Gr = 4. T = 6:00. Rec = SD-IV, Augustana Col., Lillehaug)

This famous solo was used for the clarinet competition at the Paris Conservatory in the years 1901, 1908, and 1937. For these competitions among students for honors in performance, French composers are invited to write solo compositions showing the virtuoso capabilities of the various instruments. This work in three sections is first rhapsodic, second lyrical, and finally quick-moving. Harry Gee provided the band accompaniment taken from the composer's piano score.

SERGEI RACHMANINOFF

(Born in Novgorod, Russia, 1873 — Died in Beverly Hills, California, 1943)

Sergei Rachmaninoff, distinguished composer, pianist, and conductor, was educated at the Moscow Conservatory. He disliked the drudgery of prolonged study, but with his natural gift for composition, did manage to win a gold medal for his opera *Aleko* while he was at the conservatory. In 1917 he escaped from the anarchistic revolution in Russia and a year later reached America where he resided until his death. He was a maligned yet widely-imitated composer. Critics found it difficult to forgive him for writing music in the twentieth century which they felt should have been written by Tchaikovsky during the nineteenth century. But there were composers who found the musical style of this aristocratic Russian the perfect way to intensify emotional impact.

Italian Polka (Arr = Leidzen. Pub = TE, 1941. Rec = VA-2124, Un. of MI, Revelli)

This engaging little work was originally written for two pianos. While in Italy, Rachmaninoff heard the tune played on an old-fashioned street organ, drawn through the streets by a donkey. Liking the tune, he immediately wrote it down. Later in Russia, it was arranged for the Imperial Marine Guard Band, and was performed with great success. The present arrangement was made for the Goldman Band by Erik Leidzen under the supervision of Rachmaninoff himself. (Richard Franko Goldman, the Goldman Band)

Vocalise, Opus 34 (Arr = Moehlmann; Snavely. Pub = WB, 1969; KN, 1970. Gr = 3. T = 7:30. Rec = CR-MID-70-8, Northshore, Wilmette, IL, Paynter)

This lovely work was originally scored for vocal solo with piano. It has gained acceptance and popularity in an orchestral transcription and is performed now with symphonic band. The vocal line, alloted to the first and second violins in the orchestra, is played by the first and second clarinets. (Jack Snavely, University of Wisconsin at Milwaukee)

ALFRED REED

(Born in Manhattan, New York, 1921)

Alfred Reed grew up in a musical home in Manhattan; he was well acquainted with most of the standard symphonic and operatic repertoire while still in elementary school. Beginning formal music training at the age of ten, he studied trumpet and was playing professionally while still in high school. He worked on theory and harmony with John Sacco and later, as a scholarship student, with Paul Yartin. Reed became deeply interested in band music while a member of the 529th Army Air Force Band during World War II producing nearly 100 compositions and arrangements for band before leaving military service. After the war he studied with Vittorio Giannini at the Juilliard School of Music and in 1948 began composing and arranging radio, film, and television music for NBC, and later, ABC.

Reed's academic degrees were earned at Baylor University, while he was conductor of the university orchestra, and he has an honorary doctorate from the International Conservatory of Music at Lima, Peru. He was the executive editor of Hansen Publications from 1955 to 1966 and since that time, has been a professor of music at the University of Miami—where he also heads the unique music merchandising degree program. With over 200 published works for band, wind ensemble, orchestra, chorus, and various smaller chamber music groups, Reed is one of the nation's most prolific and frequently performed composers. He is married to the former Marjorie Deley and the Reeds have two sons, Michael and Richard.

Armenian Dances (Pub = Part, I,SF, 1974; Part II. BA, 1978. Gr = 5. T = 10:30. Rec = Parts I & II, IL-78, UN. of IL, Begian)

The *Armenian Dances, Parts I and II,* constitute a four-movement suite for band based on authentic Armenian folk songs from the collected works of Gomidas Vartabed (1869-1935), the founder of Armenian classical music. Part I (first movement) is an extended symphonic rhapsody built upon five different songs, freely treated and developed in terms of the modern, integrated band or wind ensemble. Part II (second, third, and fourth movements) is built on three other Armenian folk songs.

Although the composer has kept his treatment of the melodies within the general limits imposed by its vocal, folk-song nature, he has not hesitated to expand the melodic, harmonic, and rhythmic possibilities in keeping with the demands of a symphonic-instrumental performance. Reed hopes that the overall effect of the music will remain true to the spirit of Gomidas Vartabed and that this rhapsody will help to promote interest in the work of the brilliant Armenian composer-musicologist. *Armenian Dances* was dedicated to Harry Begian and premiered by the University of Illinois Symphonic Band. (Alfred Reed, University of Miami)

A Festival Prelude (Pub = EM, 1962. Gr = 3. T = 4:45. Rec = CR-ATH-5057, MI St. Un., Bloomquist)

A Festival Prelude was written in commemoration of the twenty-fifth anniversary of the Enid, Oklahoma, Tri-State Music Festival and was first performed by the Phillips University Band with Reed conducting. The music is built up entirely from one main theme and two fanfare-like figures that occur throughout the score. The scoring of this work embraces the modern concept of the integrated symphonic band with the brasses separated into three distinct color groups and the woodwind writing centered around the clarinet choir. (Piedmont Music Company, Inc.)

Greensleeves (Pub = HN, 1961. Gr = 2. T = 7:30.)

Next to "Summer is icumen in," it is highly probable that the melody known to-day as "Greensleeves" is the oldest secular piece of music of which we have any documentary evidence. The song has been traced back to the early fourteenth century, thus making it over 600 years old to date.

It was already what we might call a "standard" in Shakespeare's time, and was used by him on several occasions in his plays, most notably in *The Merry Wives of Windsor*. Its melody was also taken as the basis of the beloved Christmas carol "What Child is This" and proved as adaptable for this purpose as in connection with its original lyrics as a song of unrequited love. Certainly a song with such vitality, capable of appearing in many forms during the centuries and showing no signs of a loss in popularity as the years and changing tastes go by, deserves to be called a "classic."

The present version was made in 1961 in response to a request for a concert setting of the melody for winds similar to Vaughan Williams' version for strings, harp, and flute. Following the success of this band setting, Reed was invited to transcribe the piece for orchestra in the summer of 1979.

A Jubilant Overture (Pub = BA, 1970. Gr = 3. T = 6:00. Rec = CR-MID-70-8, Northshore Concert, Wilmette, IL, Paynter)

Written in the spring of 1969, *A Jubilant Overture* has no program or descriptive basis of any kind, except, possibly, the natural ebullience of young spirits during the loveliest season of the year, in spring.

The music is cast in the traditional three-part overture form, beginning with the rousing Allegro con brio statement of three related themes in quick succession (from which the entire work is constructed). A broad, singing middle section (also derived from one of the opening themes) follows, and the music then returns to its original tempo and mood, plunging on to a brilliant coda in which the tonalities of D Major and B-flat Major are juxtaposed and combined, before ending in the key of B-flat Major. (Alfred Reed, University of Miami)

Othello (Pub = EM, 1977. Gr = 4. T = 18:45. Rec = IL-92, Un. of IL-II, Harris)

The works of William Shakespeare, soon to observe their 400th anniversary, un-doubtedly have inspired more musical compositions than those of any other writer in the English language. Incidental music for the plays on stage, in film, and on televi-sion, as well as concert works for a variety of media, appear every year. Reed's first version of *Othello* was as incidental music for a production by the University of Miami's Ring Theatre and was scored for sixteen brasses and three percussion. The present score utilizes some portions of this music in a completely re-composed setting and is the fourth in the series of commissions extended by Ithaca College in memory of Walter Beeler.

This concert suite is subtitled *A Symphonic Portrait for Concert Band/Wind Ensemble in Five Scenes (after Shakespeare)* with each movement characterizing musically the mood generated by a scene from the play.

The first movement, Prelude (Venice), establishes at once the tense, military at-mosphere that pervades so much of the play, and reveals itself in Othello's statement to the Duke of Venice in Act I, Scene III: "The tyrant custom hath made the flinty and steel couch of war my thrice-driven bed. . . ." The second movement, Aubade (Cyprus), is a morning song, or serenade, played by itinerant musicians under Othello and Desdemona's window (Act III, Scene I), titled appropriately, "Good morning, General." The third, Othello and Desdemona, portrays the deep feeling between them, passionate yet tender, and is prefaced by a quotation from Othello's famous speech to the Venetian Senate in Act I, telling of his wooing her: "She loved me for the dangers I had passed, and I loved her that she did pity them." The fourth movement, Entrance of the Court, is an amalgam of Shakespeare's Act IV, Scene I, and Boito's handling of essentially the same action in his libretto for Verdi's opera. Following the terrible scene in which Othello, driven half mad with rage and jealousy, first upbraids, then strikes Desdemona in full view of the court come to hail him as a hero, Iago mocks, "Behold the Lion of Venice!" The fifth movement, The Death of Desdemona, Epilogue, is a summation of the music and final resolution of the tensions heretofore generated, just as Act V, Scene II, sums up the play and resolves all the wrenching apart of human nature that has preceded it. The music here carries as its quotation of Othello's famous last lines, spoken to the dead body of Desdemona, "I kissed thee ere I killed thee. No way but this. . . ." (Piedmont Music Company)

Russian Christmas Music (Pub = SF, 1968. Gr = 5. T = 13:40. Rec = CR-CRE-9002, Un. of IL, Begian)

An ancient Russian Christmas carol ("Carol of the Little Russian Children"), together with a good deal of original material and some motivic elements derived from the liturgical music of the Eastern Orthodox Church, form the basis for this musical impression of old Russia during the jubilant Christmas season. Although cast in the form of a single, continuous movement, four distinct sections may be easily recognized. The composer originally sub-titled these sections Children's Carol, Antiphonal Chant, Village Song, and the closing Cathedral Chorus. All of the resources of the modern, integrated symphonic band are drawn upon to create an almost overwhelming sound picture of tone color, power, and sonority. (Alfred Reed, University of Miami)

Slavonic Folk Suite (Pub = HN, 1953. Gr = 2. T = 9:00.)

The ancient liturgical music of the Eastern Orthodox (Slavic and Russian) Church contains many beautiful and stirring melodies which, despite their antique origin and deep religious feeling, have never really received the attention and recognition they undoubtedly deserve. Inasmuch as the Eastern Church does not admit instrumental music as part of its services, most of the performances of this liturgical music have been vocal in conception as well as execution. The present version is a free adaptation of some of this material for the resources of modern symphonic band. This suite is drawn from the composer's larger symphonic work titled *Russian Christmas Music*. (Alfred Reed, University of Miami)

A Symphonic Prelude on Black Is the Color of My True Love's Hair (Pub = EM, 1963. Gr = 3. T = 4:20. Rec = CR-ABA-77-4, Riverview, FL, H.S., Melichar)

Although a great many of the early and traditional folk melodies of America are, not surprisingly, from English, Scotch, Irish, and Welsh folk songs, it is interesting to note that the words and melody of "Black is the Color of My True Love's Hair" are nowhere to be found in any of the folk song collections from the British Isles. It seems to be an authentic American product—one of the few from the period—and has been traced back to about 1740 in the Tennessee area of the Appalachian Mountains. In ten short bars of music and lyrics an unknown writer of that period captured an entire world of local color and feeling which has captivated listeners ever since.

A Symphonic Prelude takes the original melody as the basis for an elaborate chorale prelude, set for the concert winds as a work in its own right; not merely as an arrangement of the tune itself. The prelude was commissioned by the Hartford City High School Band and was premiered at the ASBDA convention in Elkhart, Indiana, in 1963, with the composer conducting. (Alfred Reed, University of Miami)

H. OWEN REED

(Born in Odessa, Missouri, 1910)

H. Owen Reed received his graduate degrees from Louisiana State University and the Eastman School of Music. He is the author of two textbooks and co-author of three. His teachers were Bohuslav Martinu, Howard Hanson, Roy Harris, and Helen Gunderson. Reed was professor of music and head of composition at Michigan State University until he retired in 1976. His best-known composition is *La Fiesta Mexicana,* a suite for band which he recently transcribed for orchestra. The orchestral version had its premiere with the Detroit Symphony. In 1975 Reed won the Neil A. Kjos Memorial Award with his unorthodox band score, *For the Unfortunate.* (Robert A. Jordahl, McNeese State University)

For the Unfortunate (Pub = KJ, 1975. Gr = 5. T = 13:00. Rec = MA-1158, MI St. Un., Bloomquist)

H. Owen Reed was commissioned to write *For the Unfortunate* by the McKeesport, Pennsylvania, Area High School Band in memory of Joseph P. Krysik who died with his wife and one-year-old son in a tragic airplane crash. The composer states in the score:

> The thought of writing such an emotionally-charged work was awe inspiring, but the challenge was irresistible so I accepted. The resulting composition, *For the Unfortunate,* has some programmatic connotations: It is a tragic work. It not only represents the tragedy of the Krysik family and his friends but tragedies which befall all mortals. Still, the imposition of "The Battle Hymn of the Republic," which occurs near the end (and in which the audience may participate), offers a ray of hope for the troubled. But I would urge the listener generally to follow the aesthetic theory of the absolute expressionist rather than that of the referentialist in listening to the music.

The score and parts to the music utilize both traditional and newer experimental notation. There are both metered and non-metered sections. An approximation of durations for rests and notes is indicated, but much margin for variation of durations of the elements of performance by the conductor and instrumentalists is called for. The composer describes the non-traditional symbols and their meaning in the score. A complex harmonic and melodic vocabulary results from the interpretation of these symbols. Much dissonance, in the traditional sense of the word, tone clusters, indiscriminately-pitched tones and quarter tones are heard. Instructions with the score state that the choral portion of the composition may be performed by a choir that moves on and off the stage during the presentation, or a pre-recorded choral performance may be used.

La Fiesta Mexicana (Pub = MM, 1954.   Gr = 5.   T = 21:00.   Rec = DL-710157, Eastman, Hunsberger)

This work is subtitled *A Mexican Folk Song Symphony for Concert Band,* and it was written after Reed had spent a year in Mexico studying folk music and composing on a Guggenheim Fellowship.   The entire work depicts a religious festival dedicated to the Blessed Virgin Mary and it faithfully represents all of the contrasts and contradictions of these festivals.   It is both serious and comical, festive and solemn, devout and pagan, boisterous and tender.   The first movement is a prelude and Aztec dance opening with the traditional pealing of the church bells and the noise of fireworks announcing the beginning of the fiesta.   The main part of the movement represents a midday parade (announced by the trumpets) featuring a group of brilliantly plumed and masked Aztec dancers who dance with increasing frenzy to a dramatic climax.   The second movement, titled Mass, is of a serious, liturgical nature.   The principal theme is chant-like and it is set amid coloristic sections representing the tolling of church bells.   The last movement, titled Carnival, is given over to unceasing entertainment and celebration.   At the beginning of the movement we hear the itinerant circus, then the market, the bull fight, the town band, and finally the "cantinas" with their band of "mariachis."   (Gene A. Braught, University of Oklahoma)

OTTORINO RESPIGHI

(Born in Bologna, Italy, 1879 — Died in Rome, 1936)

Ottorino Respighi studied violin at the Liceo Musicale of Bologna with Federico Sarti, and he studied composition with Luigi Torchi and Giuseppe Martucci.   He also studied privately in Russia with Rimsky-Korsakov.   Respighi performed in orchestras as a violist and violinist for many years and eventually turned to composing and teaching.   His compositions include opera, ballet, choral and orchestral works, chamber music, songs, and music for other media.   His symphonic works, particularly *The Fountains of Rome* and *The Pines of Rome,* made his name known internationally.

Huntingtower Ballad (Pub = RC, 1932.   Gr = 5.   T = 7:00)

During a visit to the United States in 1932, Respighi was commissioned by the Edwin Franko Goldman Band and the American Bandmasters Association to write this composition in memory of John Philip Sousa who had just died.   The premier performance was given in Washington at a memorial concert on April 17, 1932. Huntingtower is a castle in Scotland where Respighi spent some time.   The music is suggestive of Scotland and shows a fondness of the composer for Scotch melodies.

The Pines of Rome (Arr = Duker.   Pub = RC, 1966.   Gr = 5.   T = 19:20.   Rec = CR-CBDNA-73-8, Un. of IL, Begian)

The *Pines of Rome* was written in 1924 and was performed first in Rome in 1925. The composition is in four parts: The Pines of the Villa Borghese, The Pines near a Catacomb, The Pines of the Janiculum, and The Pines of the Appian Way.   It is based on the following program:

> Children are at play in the pine-groves of the Villa Borghese, dancing the Italian equivalent of "Ring around a-rosy"; mimicking marching soldiers and battles; twittering and shrieking like swallows at evening; and then disappearing. Suddenly the scene changes. We see shadows of

the pines which overhang the entrance to a catacomb. From the depths rises a chant which re-echoes solemnly, sonorously, like a hymn, and then is mysteriously silenced. There is a thrill in the air. The full moon reveals the profile of the pines of Gianocolo's Hill. A nightingale sings. Now it is misty dawn on the Appian Way. The tragic countryside is guarded by solitary pines. Indistinctly, incessantly, the rhythm of innumerable steps is heard. To the poet's phantasy appears a vision of past glories; trumpets blare, and the army of the consul advances brilliantly in the grandeur of a newly risen sun toward the Sacred Way, mounting in triumph the Capitoline Hill.

This setting for symphonic band was done by Guy Duker, Assistant Director of University of Illinois Bands since 1953. (Harry Begian, University of Illinois)

SILVESTRE REVUELTAS
(Born in Santiago, Mexico, 1899 — Died in Mexico City, 1940)

Silvestre Revueltas was educated at the Mexican National Conservatory and at the Chicago Musical College. He studied with Rocabruna, Tello, Sametini, Mayott, Borowski, and Sevcik. He conducted theater orchestras in the United States, concert orchestras in Mexico, and taught at the National Conservatory in Mexico City. In 1937 Revueltas went to Spain where he worked in the music section of the Loyalist government. His compositions include works for orchestra, ballet, string quartets, voice, and films.

A highly gifted composer, Revueltas had deep personal problems. Poverty and heavy drinking resulted in poor health and he died of pneumonia in his forty-first year.

Sensemaya (Arr = Bencriscutto. Pub = GS, 1980. Gr = 6. T = 7:00. Rec = AZ St. Un., Strange; CL-MS-6514, NY Phil., Bernstein)

The Mexican composer, Revueltas, has written an extremely complex and interesting composition primitive in flavor and using different meters such as 7/8, 5½/8, 7/16. *Sensemaya,* like many of this composer's works, contains compact melodic ideas which are woven into a vibrant texture of dissonant counterpoint and free polyrhythms. According to Leonard Bernstein it is "the work of a sophisticated composer with a very advanced technique handling an idea of savage primitiveness."

The Mayan word "sensemayá" refers to a popular ritualistic rhythm or song. This composition was inspired by the Cuban poet Guillén whose works often dealt with both African and Indian influences in Latin American cultures. In this instance the subject is a chant about the killing of a deadly snake.

JOSEPH J. RICHARDS
(Born in Cwmavon, Wales, 1878 — Died in Long Beach, California, 1956)

Joseph John Richards was brought to the United States as a child by his parents, and he grew up in Kansas. At the age of ten he studied horn and joined the town band. He later took up the cornet and soon joined the world of show business. By the age of nineteen he was the leader of a circus band. In subsequent years he played cornet and conducted the leading circus bands in America. During the off seasons he studied at Kansas State Teachers College and the American Conservatory in Chicago. Leaving the circus, Richards conducted concert bands in Florida and the Midwest. In the early 1920's he turned to teaching public school music in Pittsburg,

Kansas, and later taught in Illinois. While teaching in the schools, he continued to conduct professional and amateur bands as a side-line. In 1945 he became the director of the Long Beach, California, Municipal Band. He retired in 1950, making his home in Long Beach, but returning to Illinois periodically to conduct bands. During his career Richards wrote over 300 compositions for band, many of which were published by his friend C.L. Barnhouse. The Barnhouse Publishing Company still includes over forty of his works in its catalogue. Richards served as president of the American Bandmasters Association and was a member of ASCAP.

Emblem of Unity March (Pub = BA, 1941. Gr = 4. T = 3:45. Rec = CR-4171, Un. of KS, Foster)

The most popular of Richards' marches, *Emblem of Unity* was written while Richards was living in Sterling, Illinois, teaching in the public schools and directing community bands during the late 1930's. This march is Richards at his best. A classic and exciting composition, this music is heard as it is played by hundreds of school and professional bands each year all over the United States. Like the best marches, this march has unique features: the chord changes which precede the snare drum forzando in the introduction, the short lower brass breaks, and the final strain which sounds correct at either a constant, slower, or slow-to-fast tempo.

WALLINGFORD RIEGGER

(Born in Albany, Georgia, 1885 — Died in New York, 1961)

Riegger came from a musical family (his father was a violinist and his mother a pianist) and received an excellent musical education, but he did not begin to compose seriously until he was thirty-four. Even then he was forced to resort to making hundreds of choral arrangements, and editing, proofreading, and copying other composers' music in order to make a living. Recognition came very gradually and it was not until his *Third Symphony* was written in 1947 that Riegger's efforts in composition began to pay off financially.

As with most composers, Riegger's education and association with other composers had much to do with his style. He studied at Cornell for a year then entered the Institute of Musical Art (later known as Juilliard). After graduation he went to Berlin where he concentrated on cello but also studied composition with Max Bruch and Edgar Stillman Kelly. Later he taught at Drake University, at the Institute of Musical Art, and at the Conservatory in Ithaca. He became acquainted with Charles Ives, Henry Cowell, Edgar Varese, and Carl Ruggles and his composition style began to change from a solid German traditional basis to a more modern, experimental basis. He made use of the twelve-tone technique, but in a highly personal manner. Much of his music was atonal, but he reverted to tonality when it suited his musical ideas.

Riegger composed four symphonies, a concerto for piano and woodwinds, many other works for orchestra and band, a quantity of chamber and choral music, some piano pieces, and a number of works for modern dance groups. By the time he died, less than a month short of his seventy-sixth birthday, Riegger was considered by many musical authorities to be the dean of American composers.

Dance Rhythms for Band (Pub = AM, 1961. Gr = 4. T = 8:00)

Dance Rhythms is a minuet and trio structure with similar thematic material used in both large sections. The "trio" deviates from the tonic E-flat major to the lowered sub-mediant equivalent, B major. The transition to the reprise is by way of the initial motive and a short chordal trombone trio. The melodic and harmonic elements of *Dance Rhythms* are traditional; its interest comes from tone color and rhythmic variety.

NICHOLAS RIMSKY-KORSAKOV
(Born in Tikhvin, Russia, 1844 — Died in St. Petersburg, 1908)

Since his family belonged to the high aristocracy, it was considered necessary for young Rimsky-Korsakov to enter a profession suited to his station. At an early age, however, he displayed such a pronounced talent for musical composition that at the age of twelve, when enrolled at the Naval College of St. Petersburg for a six-year course, he was permitted to receive instruction in piano and cello in the intervals between his disciplinary studies. The turning point in his career came when he met Balakirev, the leader of the new Russian school of music, and was inspired by this master and his disciples, Cui, Mussorgsky, and Borodin, to study composition. A compulsory three-year cruise abroad in connection with his naval course did not dampen his ardor for music, for during the trip, under great difficulties, he composed a symphony which was performed under Balakirev's direction in St. Petersburg in December, 1865. This symphony and the compositions which followed—*Sadko* and *Pskovityanka*—directed the attention of the Russian musical world to this brilliant young composer. In 1871 he was appointed professor of composition and instrumentation at the conservatory. Two years later he retired from active duty in the navy and devoted his time to composition, to conducting the Free School and Russian Symphony concerts, and to his duties as inspector of naval bands.

Rimsky-Korsakov's music, for the most part, is joyous and gay. Unlike that of Tchaikovsky and Mussorgsky, it reveals the bright side of Russian life, being based almost entirely on national, historical, or legendary subjects. His art is said to be rooted in the Russian soil. (Carl Fischer, Inc.)

Concerto for Clarinet and Band (Arr = Fittelberg-Piket. Pub = OM, 1949. Gr = 4. Rec = ME-S-40108, U.S.S.R. Defense Ministry)

During 1876-77, Nicholas Rimsky-Korsakov, who was then inspector of the Tsar's naval bands, decided to write a series of solo pieces with band accompaniment which, he hoped, would improve the quality of the repertoire played by the Russian naval bands. The result of his work included the *Variations for Oboe,* the *Concerto for Trombone,* and a *Concertstück* for the clarinet. The clarinet work was never published during Korsakov's lifetime and remained in obscurity until 1936, when a piano reduction was made available. Although the work is entitled *Concerto,* it is in reality a single movement work which is divided into three sections, with the first and last containing the same material. (Thomas Tyra, Eastern Michigan University)

NICHOLAS RIMSKY-KORSAKOV

Concerto for Trombone and Band (Arr = Ivallin. Pub = BE, 1953. Gr = 3/5.
T = 8:00. Rec = CR-MID-77-14, Plymouth, MI, Centennial Park H.S., Griffith)

A musical discovery of major importance was made in 1951, when a forgotten work, Rimsky-Korsakov's *Concerto for Trombone and Military Band,* was found in Russia. The *Concerto for Trombone* opens with a nervously vivacious Allegro. The trombone enters with the band at once, making, with the repeated-note accompaniment, a rhythmic texture rather Schumannesque. Certainly this movement is charming and wholly un-Russian. The luscious cantilena of the slow movement (Andante) is so clearly Latin in profile that it could have come straight out of an Italian opera, perhaps one by Donizetti. The second movement moves without pause into the predominantly march-like finale and it is as Russian as can be. (Harold H. Hillyer, University of Texas at El Paso)

Procession of the Nobles from Mlada (Arr = Leidzen. Pub = CF, 1938. Gr = 4.
T = 4:20. Rec = CR-MID-77-7, Victoria H.S., TX, Junkin)

During the season of 1869-1870, the director of the Imperial Theater of St. Petersburg conceived the idea of staging an elaborate opera ballet based on a subject from the Slavic mythology. For this work, to be known as *Mlada,* he commissioned music from the Russian school of composition. The project was never realized, however, and most of the music which the composers had written found its way into other of their works. Not until twenty years later did Rimsky-Korsakov decide to use the subject for an opera ballet of his own. His *Mlada* was begun in 1889, and produced at the Marinsky Theater in 1892. (Richard Franko Goldman, the Goldman Band)

Scheherazade (Arr = Winterbottom; Hindsley, ms. Pub = BH, 1922. Gr = 5;6.
T = 42:00. IL-59, Un. of IL, Hindsley)

Rimsky-Korsakov preceded the score of this work by writing the story of how the Sultan Schahriar, persuaded of the falseness of women, swore to put to death each one of his wives after the first night. But the Sultana Scheherazade saved her life by interesting him in tales which she told him during one thousand and one nights. His curiosity piqued, the Sultan put off his wife's execution from day to day and at last gave up his bloody plan entirely.

Rimsky-Korsakov chose to start his musical "Thousand and One Nights" by telling the story of Sinbad the Sailor's seven voyages, each of which took him from luxury through tragedy and near-destruction, into many a fanciful land of absurd adventure, and back again to wealth and splendor. Here there is no attempt to retell in sound all the stories spun by this Oriental sailor-of-fortune; but rather, caught up in this impression-piece is the essence of the ships-at-sea, thundering waves, "Land ho!" and uninhibited adventure.

In the story of the Kalander Prince the plot concerns three beggars, each of whom is to tell a tale to save his life. Each claims to be the son of a king. Each has lost his left eye and claims he lost it at the close of some wondrous adventure. Rimsky-Korsakov has taken these alikenesses and, through the magical process of musical synthesis and poetic license, has made the three into just one Kalander Prince.

The movement devoted to the young Prince and the Princess is the idyll of the suite, an idyll both of the stories and the music. Here we are nearest to the touch of sentiment, apart from the mere drama of haps and mishaps. But there are all kinds of special events. The idyll begins straightaway, winds through a great variety of scenes and storms, sings out simply again and then its loneliness is enveloped and sealed in the last strains of the romance.

The final movement, Festival at Bagdad, begins with the motive of the sea, as does the first. The scene quickly changes, however, to the whirl and swirl of the festival.

Into the carnival atmosphere a reminder of the sea intrudes, other familiar figures flit by, including the evil jinn and the love idyll. Then in full festival array we seem to plunge back into the broad movement of the surging sea, straight on to the fateful event where the ship goes to pieces against a magnetic rock. There are no sighs or tears. Placidly the waves play softly about. Scheherazade herself reappears to conclude the tale quietly and tenderly. (Everett Kisinger, University of Illinois)

RICHARD RODGERS
(Born in Hammels Station, Long Island, NY, 1902 — Died in NY, 1979)

Richard Rodgers was educated in New York where he attended Columbia University. He has been awarded numerous honorary degrees and has served on the board of trustees of colleges, symphonies, and of the John F. Kennedy Center for the Performing Arts. In 1962, he became producer-director of the Music Theater of Lincoln Center in New York City. His Broadway theater scores, film scores, T.V. scores, and popular songs—all highly successful—number in the hundreds. Rodgers wrote twenty-eight stage musicals and eight films with lyricist Lorenz Hart; nine shows and a television musical with Oscar Hammerstein II; the musical *No Strings* alone; and teamed with Stephen Sondheim for the show *Do I Hear A Waltz?*. Rodgers has received several Pulitzer Prizes and many other awards.

The King and I, Selections (Arr = Bennett. Pub = WN, 1951. Gr = 4. T = 10:00. Rec = CR-MID-78-2, MI Youth Orch., Bialand)

Against the exotic background of the Imperial Palace in mid-nineteenth century Siam, *The King and I* unfolds an odd yet compelling story of an English school teacher and the "uncivilized" Siamese king. She is the West, he is the East, and the two meet in both electric conflict and warm understanding. Perhaps the most enchanting part of this unique musical drama is the deeply moving Rodgers and Hammerstein score. The songs are peculiarly appropriate to this unusual tale, and yet they possess that universal appeal which makes songs by Rodgers and Hammerstein everlasting favorites. For three uninterrupted years *The King and I* played to full houses on Broadway. (Lee A. Mendyk, Wayne State College)

Oklahoma, Selections (Arr = Leidzen. Pub = WN, 1944. Gr = 3. T = 6:30)

The musical show *Oklahoma* was the first on which Richard Rodgers collaborated with the lyricist Oscar Hammerstein II. They went on to become one of the greatest song-writing teams in musical history. Included in this selection are the songs "Oh, What a Beautiful Morning," "Many a New Day," "People Will Say We're in Love," and "The Surrey With the Fringe on Top."

The Sound of Music, Selections (Arr = Bennett. Pub = WN, 1959. Gr = 3. T = 10:30. Rec = SD-II, Augustana Col., Lillehaug)

The last of the Rodgers and Hammerstein collaborations is based on the true story of the unusual Trapp family. The result is a musical play of uncommon distinction and charm, a production framed with obvious taste and affection around a narrative that is at once warmly amusing and full of meaning. The songs in the present selection are "The Sound of Music," "How Can Love Survive," "My Favorite Things," "So Long, Farewell," "Do, Re, Mi," and "Climb Every Mountain."

Victory at Sea (Score = Bennett. Pub = WN, 1955. Gr = 4. T = 9:30. Rec = RCA-VCS-7064, NBC TV Production)

The cry of horns, trumpets, and trombones with which Rodgers begins his score for the television production, *Victory at Sea,* has in it all the vast restlessness and mystery of the sea itself. The *New Yorker* describes the music as "a seemingly endless creation, now martial, now tremendously moving." The symphonic sweep of Rodgers' score captures the moods and variations of the panoramic war at sea in all its terror and beauty and adds the elusive emotional dimension which neither camera nor words quite convey. Rodgers' music is greatly enhanced by the comprehensive arrangement of Robert Russell Bennett, who has long been a collaborator with Rodgers on Broadway.

BERNARD ROGERS

(Born in New York City, 1893 — Died in Rochester, New York, 1968)

Bernard Rogers attended Juilliard School of Music and studied privately with Bloch, Goetschius, Bridge, and Boulanger. He won many awards and honors, and he was commissioned to write several serious compositions. He served on the staff of the Eastman School of Music from 1929 to 1967. His works include music for orchestra, ballet, opera, and smaller ensembles, and he also wrote a book on orchestration.

Three Japanese Dances (Pub = TP, 1955. Gr = 5. T = 10:40. Rec = MG-75093, Eastman, Fennell; UM, Un. of MN, Bencriscutto)

Bernard Rogers composed his *Three Japanese Dances* for orchestra in 1933. It received its first performance by the Rochester Philharmonic Orchestra under the direction of Howard Hanson on May 3, 1934, at the Fourth Annual Festival of American Music of the Eastman School of Music. When Frederick Fennell, conductor of the Eastman Symphonic Wind Ensemble, suggested a band version in 1954, Rogers responded with considerable enthusiasm for the project. Among American composers, Rogers was unique for both his knowledge of instruments and his handling of them. In making this band transcription, he produced a vivid score for the modern band which reveals its capacity for nuance and delicate shading, for bold effect and rich sonority.

Since the "subject-matter" of the music is both unusual and unexpected, we provide the following notes by the composer himself which, while written for program notes of an orchestral performance, apply equally well to this new version.

. . . . There are no actual pictoral models. The three pieces are merely acts of fancy. In the first, a Dance with Pennons, the coloring is cool and gay, vernal and naive. Young girls weave to and fro casting ribbons of silk. The second is a Dance of Mourning. The dancer is clad in white (the color of mourning). An elaborate group of percussion instruments combine in a complex bell sonority against a primitive motive sounded by flute and bass flute. A distant mezzo voice, unaccompanied, adds a central episode, and the first material returns. The final panel is a Dance with Swords, suggested by the violent, distorted actor portraits of Sharaku. The music is fiercely rhythmic, propelled by thrusting rhythms and highly colored by percussion.

(Theodore Presser Co.)

GIOACCHINO ROSSINI

(Born in Pesaro, Italy, 1792 — Died in Paris, 1868)

Gioacchino Rossini studied for a short time in Bologna, abandoning that city to begin writing and producing opera in the larger European centers. After a cool reception in Vienna in 1823, he enjoyed a very successful season in London, and then took over management of the Italian Theater in Paris. The French government conferred on him the title of "premier compositeur du roi" accompanied by a handsome salary. He remained in Paris, pursuing a brilliantly successful career as composer and producer. At age thirty-seven, Rossini suddenly and mysteriously stopped composing opera. He spent the rest of his life teaching and doing some composing in Italy and France, finally settling again in Paris where he remained as the witty leader of the artistic world until his death at age seventy-two. (Educational Record Reference Library, Belwin-Mills)

The Barber of Seville Overture (Arr = Duthoit. Pub = BH, 1940. Gr = 5. T = 8:30. Rec = AN-535890, Philadelphia Orch., Karajan)

This overture was originally written not for *The Barber of Seville,* but for the earlier opera of Rossini's, *Aurelian in Palmyra* (1813), and did not make its way to the position it now occupies until three years later. None of its themes may be found in the opera, yet its light and bubbling gaiety, and the music's general resemblance to the ideal of Figaro are wholly expressive of what transpires in *The Barber of Seville,* both musically and dramatically. It is the most enduring, most popular, and perhaps, the master work of Gioacchino Rossini. (John Paynter, Northwestern University)

The Italian Girl in Algiers Overture (Arr = Cailliet. Pub = SF, 1952. Gr = 5. T = 8:15)

The Italian Girl in Algiers, an opera buffa, was the second of Rossini's works to achieve great success. It was produced in Venice in 1813. Like most of Rossini's operas it is no longer in the repertoire, but the sparkling melodies of the overture have made it a favorite on band and orchestra programs. (Richard Franko Goldman, the Goldman Band)

La Gazza Ladra Overture (Arr = Cailliet. Pub = SF, 1954. Gr = 5. T = 10:30. Rec = CR-MID-68-11, Brownsville, TX, H.S., Vezzetti)

The overture to "The Thieving Magpie" begins in a military manner with two rolls on the snare drum. The full band loudly presents the main melody, a vigorous march which is worked out briefly. Drum rolls, a brief crescendo, and five chords end this part of the overture. The allegro section contains two basic melodies: a glistening and delicate theme for the clarinets and a piquant subject shared by the entire woodwind section. As with other Rossini overtures, an exciting culmination is realized with the crescendo.

March for the Sultan Abdul Medjid (Ed = Townsend. Pub = TP, 1967. Gr = 4. T = 4:20. Rec = BP-111, Un. of MI)

This march is taken from a set of three written in honor of the Sultan Abdul Medjid, whom Giuseppe Donizetti served for twenty-five years in the capacity of bandmaster. He himself wrote one of the set for the Turkish potentate, and he commissioned the other two from the leading opera composer of the day, Rossini, and his own brother, Gaetano Donizetti. The scores for these works were discovered in the Turkish Institute in Istanbul by the American composer Douglas Townsend, who has edited them for performance by modern bands. (Richard Franko Goldman, the Goldman Band)

Scherzo for Band (Arr = Schaefer. Pub = EM, 1977. Gr = 5. T = 4:15.
Rec = CR-MID-78-13, Northshore Concert, Buehlman)

This original composition for band by Rossini was recently rediscovered, and it was rescored for contemporary band instrumentation by William A. Schaefer. The music, true to its title, moves rapidly in triple (3/8) meter, and must be performed sprightly and gently for the most part. There are opportunities for the brasses to demonstrate that they can perform boldly with vigor and almost immediately thereafter produce dainty staccato sounds. The woodwinds are required to show their technical dexterity throughout much of the work. The music is a welcome addition to the band repertory.

CAMILLE SAINT-SAËNS
(Born in Paris, 1835 — Died in Algiers, Algeria, 1921)

The possession of only mediocre talent is a hopeless problem for a would-be musician. Equally difficult in the opposite direction is extreme versatility. Camille Saint-Saëns, born of a rural but genteel family, was "burdened" with abilities enough for several persons. At the age of six he was playing Beethoven sonatas and was delighted with receiving the gift of a complete opera which he promptly learned. In adult life he became accomplished in astronomy, philosophy, mathematics, and other fields of advanced learning. He wrote musical and literary criticism and was the author of a book on mysticism. He traveled extensively and was familiar with most of the countries of Western Europe and the Mediterranean. He was known as a great wit and a gifted caricaturist. All this was in addition to playing organ in the famous Church of the Madeleine, Paris, teaching in the conservatory, and composing in almost all forms of music. (George Kreamer, Lake Charles, Louisiana)

Finale from Symphony No. 3 in C (Arr = Slocum. Pub = TN, 1974. Gr = 4.
T = 8:30. Rec = CR-MID-75-6, Northshore, Buehlman)

Camille Saint-Saëns' *Symphony No. 3 in C Major,* generally referred to as the "Organ Symphony," was his last major effort in the symphonic form. The work, bearing a dedication to Franz Liszt, was composed for the London Philharmonic Orchestra, and had its initial performance in the British capital under the direction of Saint-Saëns on May 19, 1886. The symphony was indeed modern for its day and was orchestrated with the sure hand of an expert. The organ, which gives the symphony its name, is frequently and effectively employed. This transcription of the finale for concert band by Earl Slocum also makes use of the organ. However, the work can be effectively performed without it by making use of cued notes for other instruments.

The Finale (Maestoso) begins with a sustained C major chord for organ followed by contrapuntal treatment of material vaguely reminiscent of the principal theme of the first movement. Then the initial theme, wholly transformed, is presented by the woodwinds and repeated by the organ with the full strength of the band. There follows a development (Allegro) built on a rhythm of three measures. An episode of a tranquil and pastoral character is twice repeated. A brilliant coda, in which the initial theme by a last transformation ends the work; the rhythm of three measures becomes naturally and logically a huge measure of three beats; each beat is represented by a whole note, and twelve quarters form the complete measure. After a fanfare by the trumpets and a solo passage for timpani, the movement finishes, as it began, with a chord in C major for organ and band. (TRN Music Publisher)

Marche Militaire Française (Arr = Hindsley, ms.; Lake. Pub = CF, 1913. Gr = 4. T = 4:10. Rec = CR-ABA-72-4, Un. of TX, Moody)

The subtitle of Saint-Saëns' *Algerian Suite* is "Picturesque Impressions of a Voyage to Algiers." Of its four movements, three are decidedly oriental in coloring. The fourth, the *Military March,* is by contrast quite French; it was intended to emphasize the contrast found at Algiers between the native and the French settlements. In a note on the score the composer emphasized the fact that he not only felt joyful at seeing French soldiers, but was conscious of the security he enjoyed under their protection. (Everett Kisinger, University of Illinois)

Pas Redoublé (Arr = Frackenpohl. Pub = SH, 1972. Gr = 4. T = 3:45. Rec = CR-ABA-73-3, U.S. Army Field, Neilson)

This "quick-step" concert march is reminiscent of Offenbach and perhaps is related to the nineteenth century galop. Originally written for four hand piano it was transcribed for band by Arthur Frackenpohl who is recognized as an American composer of merit. The music, as indicated by the title, moves at a fast and steady pace. There are three principal themes separated by interludes and then restated, the first being reiterated with a change of instrumentation and the second and third combined, leading to a coda.

TAKANOBU SAITOH
(Born in Tokyo, 1924)

Takanobu Saitoh was the conductor of the Japanese Central Air Force Band for many years before his retirement in 1976. Since that time he has been the director of the Tokyo Metropolitan Police Band. He is well known in Japan as a composer of band music as well as a highly experienced conductor.

Blue Impulse March (Pub = TA, 1973. Gr = 4. T = 3:28. Rec = TO-EMI-TA-6308-9; CR-ABA-80-8, Komazawa Un., Ueno)

"Blue Impulse" is the name given to Japan's F86 Saber acrobatic flying team. The music depicts the formation in a series of maneuvers which form beautiful pictures on the vast canvas of the sky. (Toshio Akiyama, Tokyo)

PETER SCHICKELE (P.D.Q. BACH)
(Born in Ames, Iowa, 1945)

Most audiences are unaware of the great diversity of Peter Schickele's musical pursuits. Not only is he the discoverer and purveyor of the long-neglected works of P.D.Q. Bach, but he is also a composer who, in the space of one year, wrote an orchestral work commissioned by the St. Louis Symphony, did the music for several

"Sesame Street" segments, contributed music and lyrics to the Broadway hit *Oh!* *Calcutta!,* appeared with the National Symphony, scored a TV commercial and an underground movie, sang and played in a rock group, and saw the release of a Vanguard album for which he arranged and conducted instrumental versions of songs by himself, Bob Dylan, and the Beatles.

As an undergraduate, Schickele was Swarthmore's only music major. By the time he graduated from the college in 1957 he had written and conducted four orchestral pieces, composed and performed a great deal of chamber and piano music, spent a summer studying intensively with Roy Harris in Pittsburgh, and become turned on by the music of Hindemith, Bartók, Stravinsky, Elvis Presley, Ray Charles, and the Everly Brothers—especially Stravinsky and the Everly Brothers. Schickele completed his schooling with an M.S. from Juilliard School of Music, where his principal composition teacher was Vincent Persichetti. Then came a Ford Foundation grant to write music for high schools in Los Angeles, after which he joined the Juilliard extension division for three years and also taught briefly at Swarthmore and at Aspen, Colorado. In 1959, he and a group of friends formed "Composers' Circle," a group that held workshop sessions and presented concerts of their own and other composers' music for over five years. (Keith Brion, Yale University)

Using his true name Schickele's compositions have ranged from *Three Folk Settings* for piano to cantatas titled *After Spring Sunset* and *The Birth of Christ.* As P.D.Q. Bach (1807-1742)? "who has justly been called 'history's most justly neglected composer,' and was the last and least of the great Johann Sebastian Bach's twenty-odd children, and he was certainly the oddest of the lot, . . ." a sampling of his titles includes *Pervertimento for Bagpipes, Bicycles, and Balloons; Iphegenia in Brooklyn;* and *Hansel and Gretel and Ted and Alice,* an opera-funnia for bargain counter tenor/harpsichord, beriberitone/calliope, and piano. In 1976 he published *The Definitive Biography of P.D.Q. Bach.* (Ed.)

Pavilion Piece (Pub = TP, 1971. Gr = 4. T = 3:00)

Composed while Schickele was on a Ford Foundation grant, writing music for selected high schools in Los Angeles, *Pavilion Piece,* as the title implies, was inspired by various bandstands in Aspen, Colorado, Central Park, and Schickele's former home town of Fargo, North Dakota. It was written "for those happy, balmy days when music really wafts in the mind. In form it's sort of like a song and a march—sweet and simple—music to eat potato salad by." (Keith Brion, Yale University)

Grand Serenade for an Awful Lot of Winds and Percussion (Pub = TP, 1976. Gr = 5. T = Who knows? Rec = You're kidding!)

The *Grand Serenade* was composed on commission from Prince Fred of Wein-am-Rhein, for some sort of outdoor occasion. P.D.Q. had originally wanted to write a really big work of thirty-five or forty minutes' duration, but he agreed to make it only a third as long when Prince Fred offered to triple his fee. Soon after it was played, a member of the Prince's household used the pages of the score to wrap six large sausages which were sent to Paris to be presented to Benjamin Franklin, from whom the Prince was anxious to obtain the specifications for building a glass harmonica, which Franklin had recently perfected. Eventually the manuscript made its way to an attic in Boston where the editor found it among the belongings of an eighteenth century Tory, in a box marked "Seditious Material." (Theodore Presser Co.)

FLORENT SCHMITT

(Born in Blâmont, France, 1870 — Died in Neuilly, France, 1958)

Schmitt began his first music lessons by studying piano with Hess and harmony with Sandre in the city of Nancy, not far from his home village of Blâmont in north-eastern France. When he was nineteen he went to the Paris Conservatory to study composition with Massenet and Fauré. He won the Prix de Rome in 1900 with the cantata, *Semiramis,* and composed several important works during the next four years in the Italian city. He settled permanently in Paris in 1906 where most of his early compositions were impressionistic in style, but his later writing evidenced a strong individuality including colorful and complex scoring. He visited the United States in 1932 to perform the solo part in his *Symphonie concertante* with the Boston Symphony, and he continued to compose a variety of instrumental and choral works until shortly before his death at the age of eighty-seven. Schmitt's music is characterized by vigor, eloquence, and passion.

Dionysiaques, Op. 62 (Pub = TP, Rental. Gr = 6. T = 10:00. Rec = CR-ABA-76-2, AZ St. Un., Strange; MI-MITCMS-003, M.I.T.)

Dionysiaques was composed in 1913 for the 100-member Garde Républicaine Band of Paris and first performed in 1925. The title, from Greek mythology, refers to the gods of drama and wine, similar to the Roman god Bacchus. Whether Schmitt considered the French band members as imbibers of too much wine is not known, however his sense of humor is a matter of record. Typical of his titles, for example, is his violin concerto, *Habeysée,* the phonetic representation of ABC, as pronounced in French.

ARNOLD SCHOENBERG

(Born in Vienna, 1874 — Died in Los Angeles, California, 1951)

Arnold Schoenberg came to the United States in 1933 and was on the faculties of the University of Southern California and the University of California in Los Angeles. Schoenberg's music reveals that his style of composition gradually changed through his years in Europe and the United States. His early works—before 1909—contain a wealth of counterpoint and remained tonal. Post-Wagnerian Romanticism describes his first period. The second style is evident in some of the piano works and the second *String Quartet,* in which he uses chords in fourths, little development, and atonality. The third style is seen in the *Five Piano Pieces, Opus 23* and the *Variations for Orchestra, Opus 31* (1927-28), in which he exploited the twelve-tone system, a method of composing of which Schoenberg is said to be the originator. In the fourth and last period of his career—the American phase—he refined the twelve-tone technique and even allowed tonal elements to co-exist with the twelve-tone style.

Theme and Variations, Opus 43a (Pub = GS, 1949. Gr = 6. T = 14:00. Rec = CR-1000, Cass Tech H.S., Detroit, Begian)

The *Theme and Variations* was written in 1943, eight years before the composer's death. Composed after Schoenberg had abandoned an exclusively atonal approach to composition, the G-minor tonality of the *Theme and Variations* is clearly defined.

Harmonically, these seven variations on a twenty-one bar theme which are played without break, are not daring or extravagant, but in them one may see a mastery of connection of thought and motivic division, an art of development, and a variety of character for which parallels can be found only among Schoenberg's own works.

The *Theme and Variations* was commissioned by Schoenberg's publisher, G. Schirmer. Excerpts from the composer's correspondence describe the conception of the piece:

> My dear friend, the late Carl Engel, then president of the G. Schirmer, Inc., had asked me frequently to write a piece for wind band. He complained that the great number of such bands had an important influence on the development of love for music in America, but unfortunately there are only a small number of good original compositions available, while for the most of their playing they are limited to arrangements. A considerable part of these arrangements reveals a poor or at least a low taste; and besides they are not even well orchestrated. . . . It is one of those works that one writes in order to enjoy one's own virtuosity and, in addition, to give a group of amateurs—in this case, wind bands—something better to play. I can assure you—and I think I can prove it—that as far as technique is concerned it is a masterpiece; and I know it is inspired. Not only because I cannot write even ten measures without inspiration, but I really wrote the piece with great pleasure.

It is interesting to note that while Schoenberg intended this work for the average amateur wind band, performance experience had shown the piece to be of such a level of difficulty that it had been performed only by unusually advanced ensembles. Schoenberg, therefore, transcribed the work for orchestra as *Opus 43b*, and it enjoys the unusual position of being one of the few works in the orchestral repertoire which was originally conceived for the wind band. (William E. Rhoads, University of New Mexico)

FRANZ SCHUBERT
(Born in Vienna, 1797 — Died in Vienna, 1828)

Son of a poor schoolmaster, Franz Schubert learned to play the violin and piano from his father and older brother and also studied with Michael Holzer, organist of the parish church at Lichtenthal. In 1808 Schubert was accepted as a choirboy in the court chapel which meant admission to the Imperial and Royal Seminary. He began composing at an early age, played the violin, sometimes conducted, and taught school.

Schubert was the classic example of a genius so devoted to his art that he never managed to live well or adjust to the world. He was one of the greatest creators of melody and perhaps the leading composer of lieder.

Living but to the age of thirty-one, he wrote an astonishing number of works including operas and other stage music, choral works with orchestra, choral works with piano and unaccompanied choral works, orchestral works, chamber music, solo instrumental works, and hundreds of songs.

Rosamunde Overture (Arr = Tobani; Hindsley, ms. Pub = CF, 1901. Gr = 5. T = 9:30. Rec = MG-2530422, Berlin Philharmonic Orch., Böhm)

Schubert wrote music for a number of singspiels—dramatic plays with set musical pieces—in the vain hope of achieving financial success. Little is known of this music, except for the overture to Helmine von Chezy's *Rosamunde,* a preposterous fairy tale.

Rosamunde was given for the first time with the overture Schubert had written for his opera *Alphonso and Estrella.* However the composer subsequently substituted still another overture, the one he had written for a singspiel called *The Magic Harp,* and it is this that we know as the *Rosamunde Overture.* It is the epitome of the fresh and innocent dawn of the Romantic period.

With the *Unfinished Symphony,* the *Rosamunde Overture* shares a measure of mystery: it lay unknown for many years after Schubert's death until it was rediscovered in 1867 by two famous English musicians, writer-historian George Grove and composer Arthur Sullivan. (Harold L. Hillyer, University of Texas at El Paso)

Symphony No. 8 in B Minor (Arr = Cailliet. Pub = CF, 1st movt., 1938; 2nd movt., 1942. Gr = 5. T = 1st movt., 11:50; 2nd movt., 9:00. Rec = RCA-LSC-2516, Chicago Symphony Orch., Reiner)

Schubert never completed his eighth symphony except for the first two of its proposed four movements. Known as the "Unfinished Symphony," it is considered a masterpiece of the orchestral literature even though incomplete. Schubert's creative genius for writing beautiful, flowing melodic lines with underlying harmonic figures is exemplified in these two movements.

GUNTHER SCHULLER

(Born in New York City, 1925)

Gunther Schuller's life has been literally steeped in music since his birth. As the son of a violinist with the New York Philharmonic Orchestra, he lived in an atmosphere of music from childhood. He joined the St. Thomas Choir School in New York at the age of eleven, began studying flute at twelve, then, at fourteen, he switched to French horn. He developed so rapidly that two years later he left both high school and the Manhattan School of Music (where he had been studying horn, theory, and counterpoint) to play professionally with the Ballet Theater Orchestra. He never returned to school and has no diploma of any kind—other than an impressive string of honorary doctorates. At seventeen he became first horn of the Cincinnati Symphony and at nineteen, he joined the Metropolitan Opera Orchestra, where he remained for the next fourteen years.

Schuller also composed a variety of works through these years, resigning from the Metropolitan Opera Orchestra in 1959 to devote more time to creative work. His *Symphony for Brass and Percussion* (1949) was premiered under the direction of Leon Barzin and was later performed and recorded by Dimitri Mitropoulos and the New York Philharmonic Orchestra. More recent examples of his compositions include *Concerto for Orchestra* for the Chicago Symphony; *The Visitation,* an opera for the Hamburg State Opera; *Tre Invenzioni,* a wind ensemble for the Fromm Music Foundation, *Violin Concerto* for Zvi Zeitlin and the Eastman School of Music, and a trumpet concerto for Gerard Schwarz and the Ford Foundation. In the late 1950's, Schuller coined the term "third-stream" in reference to music that synthesizes the popular and the traditional trends of musical expression. The term was consequently used to describe a fusion of jazz and "classical" music, and has more recently been used by Schuller to describe a global concept of music wherein there are no qualitative distinctions between categories of ethnic or cultural music. Schuller's writings, his compositions, and his performances as horn player and conductor in the field of jazz are widely known. In 1972 he presented the New England

Conservatory Ragtime Ensemble at a Festival of American Music premiering his reorchestrations of works by Scott Joplin. These renditions derived from the long-lost Red Back Book, a copy of which had been turned up by Joplin's editor, Vera Lawrence, and forwarded to Schuller. They were subsequently recorded by the same group, receiving a Grammy Award in 1973 as the best chamber music performance for that year, and have been credited with sparking the popular Ragtime revival that followed.

Schuller's works for band include *Combination March* (from the original version by Joplin), *Diptych* (brass quintet and band), *Meditation, Study in Textures for Concert Band,* and *Symphony for Brass and Percussion.* After ten years as president of the New England Conservatory, Schuller resigned that position in 1977 to devote full time to composing, writing, and conducting. (Information from Lou Chapin and James G. Roy, Jr. of BMI, and Schuller's personal vita)

Meditation (Pub = AM, 1965. Gr = 5. T = 6:00. Rec = Northern IL Un., Bird; Un-1, Un. of NE, Lentz; GC-Revelli Years, Un. of MI, Revelli)

Meditation for concert band is the composer's first work for band and its formal scheme can be described as ABCA with a Coda. Notable in the composition is the use of improvisation. At the beginning of the Coda, each of six flute and clarinet players is given four of the twelve notes with the following instruction: "Solo players improvise with the indicated pitches (always trilling), in any order, duration, or pattern." *Meditation* is contemporary music for band in the true sense of the term, i.e., not only written in our times, but representative of present-day compositional technique. (Donald L. Wolf, Northern Arizona State College)

Symphony for Brass and Percussion (Pub = SH, 1959. Gr = 5. T = 18:00. Rec = Argo, Jones Brass Ens.)

The composer has provided the following notes on his *Symphony for Brass and Percussion:*

> The purpose in writing this work was, of course, primarily to write a symphony. But secondarily it provided me with an opportunity to make use of my experiences of sitting day in, day out, in the midst of brass sections, and to show that the members of the brass family are not limited to the stereotypes of expression usually associated with them. Thus, there is more to the horn than its "heroic" or "noble" or "romantic" character, or to the trumpet than its usefulness in fanfares and calls. Indeed, these instruments are capable of the entire gamut of expression. Their full resources and the amazing technical advances in terms of performance made in the last thirty-odd years—especially in America—have been largely left unexplored by most contemporary composers.
>
> The concept of the *Symphony* is of four contrasting movements, each representing one aspect of brass characteristics. Unity is maintained by a line of increasing inner intensity (not loudness) that reaches its peak in the last movement. The introductory movement is followed by a scherzo with passages requiring great agility and technical dexterity. The third movement, scored almost entirely for six muted trumpets, brings about a further intensification of expression. The precipitous outburst at the beginning of the last movement introduces a kind of cadenza in which a solo trumpet dominates. A short timpani roll provides a bridge to the finale proper, which is a kind of perpetuum mobile. Running through the entire movement are sixteenth-note figures passing from one instru-

ment to another in an unbroken chain. Out of this chattering pattern emerges the climax of the movement, in which a chord consisting of all twelve notes of the chromatic scale is broken up in a sort of rhythmic atomization, each pitch being sounded on a different sixteenth of the measure. (Gunther Schuller, New England Conservatory)

WILLIAM SCHUMAN
(Born in New York City, 1910)

William Howard Schuman is one of America's leading composers. Completing study at the Malkin Conservatory in New York, at Teachers College of Columbia University, and at the Mozarteum Academy in Salzburg, Schuman became music instructor at Sarah Lawrence College, and later was appointed president of the Juilliard School of Music. Schuman began to acquire national prominence when in 1939 his *American Festival Overture* was performed by Koussevitsky and the Boston Symphony. A listing of his compositions includes an opera, six symphonies, concertos, choral works, band works, and chamber music. *Newsreel,* a delightful suite of descriptive music was Schuman's first venture into the band medium and was completed in 1941. In 1956 he composed a prelude *When Jesus Wept* and an overture *Chester* to be performed as a single composition. The music of Schuman is generally characterized by great emotional tension and rhythmic vivacity, with contrapuntal structures which reach great complexity.

Circus Overture (Arr = Owen. Pub = GS, 1972. Gr = 5. T = 7:00. Rec = CR-MID-74-9, Cambridge, OH, H.S., Treier)

In 1944 Schuman wrote *Circus Overture* for orchestra, but it was originally titled *Side Show.* The piece is energetic, rich in rhythmic ostinatos, and has long lively phrases. The listener will have no difficulty inventing pictures in his mind relating to a carnival or circus atmosphere.

Dedication Fanfare (Pub = TP, 1969. Gr = 4. T = 4:30. Rec = CR-MID-69-8, Northshore, Paynter)

Commissioned by the New Music Circle, St. Louis, Missouri, for the dedication of the Gateway Arch, this fanfare reflects the upward thrust and soaring lines of that striking welcome symbol. It proclaims the spiritual challenge and conquest represented by the arch. The constant rising surge of the music, the driving timpani part, the declamatory brasses, all propel the work to a mighty conclusion. (Norman J. Hunt, Sacramento State College)

George Washington Bridge (Pub = GS, 1951. Gr = 4. T = 7:00. Rec = CR-CBDNA-75-1, El Camino Jr. Col., Caldwell)

George Washington Bridge is subtitled "An Impression for Band" and the composer has included the following remarks with the score:

There are few days in the year when I do not see George Washington Bridge. I pass it on my way to work as I drive along the Henry Hudson Parkway on the New York shore. Ever since my student days when I watched the progress of its construction, this bridge has had for me an almost human personality, and this personality is astonishingly varied, assuming different moods depending on the time of day or night, the weather, the traffic and, of course, my own mood as I pass by. I have walked across it late at night when it was shrouded in fog, and during the brilliant sunshine hours of midday. I have driven over it countless times and passed under it on boats. Coming to New York City by air, sometimes I have been lucky enough to fly right over it. It is difficult to imagine a more gracious welcome or dramatic entry to the great metropolis.

(See April, 1981, *Music Educators Journal* for an analysis by Robert Garafalo, Ed.)

New England Triptych
  Be Glad Then, America (Pub = TP, 1975. Gr = 4. T = 7:00)
  When Jesus Wept (Pub = TP, 1959. Gr = 3. T = 5:00. Rec = CR-ABA-75-1, LA St. Un., Swor)
  Chester (Pub = TP, 1957. Gr = 4. T = 9:00. Rec = DL-8633, Goldman)

The music of William Billings, the early American composer, provides the basic material for this set. Billings is now seen as a major figure in American music. He wrote many simple sturdy tunes that were popular with the colonists, and he organized singing schools, composing music for them. Some of these singing school tunes were published in 1778 in a book called *The Singing Master's Assistant*.

Schuman wrote *New England Triptych (Three Pieces after William Billings)* for orchestra in 1956. In subsequent years he transcribed the music for band, greatly enlarging on some of it. The first movement, "Be Glad Then, America" is highlighted by timpani and a two part chordal counterpoint. Typical of Billings' music, it is noble and exciting. The second part of the triptych is a development of "When Jesus Wept," a round by Billings. Schuman's development of this sacred theme is superlatively sensitive music. The third and final portion is a brilliant climax for the set. The tune on which "Chester" is based was a famous American Revolutionary hymn and marching song of the same name. It was practically the unofficial national anthem during the war. Schuman developed and extended the orchestral version, making "Chester" into an overture for band, and it has become one of the great classics of band music in the United States. In the first section Schuman introduces the tune first in the woodwinds and then in the brasses. In the next section the melody is given a more contemporary setting with mid-twentieth century rhythmic and harmonic devices utilized to sustain interest. The closing section brings back the hymn-like treatment of the theme and the work is brought to a dramatic close.

DMITRI SHOSTAKOVICH
(Born in Leningrad, 1906 — Died in Moscow, 1975)

Dmitri Shostakovich studied at the Leningrad Conservatory from 1919 to 1925. At the age of nineteen, he composed his *First Symphony (Opus 10)* which subsequently became one of his most frequently performed works throughout the world. *Symphony No. 2* (1927) was less successful, and an opera, *The Nose* (1930), met with violent attacks from the Soviet press who called it a product of "bourgeois decadence" and it was soon withdrawn from the repertory. Shostakovich, despite efforts with a ballet, *The Golden Age* (1930), and *Symphony No. 3* (1931), failed to arouse the attention and praise of his first symphony. The opera *Lady Macbeth of Mtsensk* again found the attention of the Soviet press highly critical. Like many

Soviet composers, Shostakovich found himself constantly under pressure from restrictions imposed by the Soviet musical world with its concern for the moral and social rather than the purely aesthetic aspects of music—its wishes for works to be of immediate and practical value from the point of view of Soviet influence upon culture. The musical style of Shostakovich remains unbalanced with works containing crude parodies, programmatic devices, and conventional simplicity countered by works of originality, distinction, and significance. The composer's output includes three operas; three ballets; incidental music; scores for fifteen films; fifteen symphonies as well as other orchestral works; two jazz suites; a concerto for piano, trumpet, and strings; music for voice and orchestra; chamber music; songs; and music for piano. His *Symphony No. 5* (1937), to which he gave the subtitle "A Soviet Artist's Reply to Just Criticism," met with high approval in the Soviet Union and is probably his most well-known work. (Acton Ostling, University of Maryland)

Festive Overture, Opus 96 (Tr = Hunsberger. Pub = MC, 1965. Gr = 4. T = 6:00. Rec = CR-MID-70-5, Fort Hunt H.S., Wickes)

Shostakovich's *Festive Overture* was completed in 1954, in the period between his *Symphony No. 10* and the *Violin Concerto*. Arranged for the Russian Military Band by the composer in 1958, it has been scored for the American band by Donald Hunsberger. The *Festive Overture* demonstrates one of Shostakovich's distinctive talents—the ability to write a long sustained melodic line combined with a pulsating rhythmic drive. In addition to the flowing melodic passages, examples of staccato rhythmic sections set off the flowing line and the variant fanfares. It is truly a "festive" overture. (Miles H. Johnson, St. Olaf College)

Symphony No. 5, Finale (Tr = Righter; Schaefer. Pub = BH, 1947; SH, 1970. Gr = 5. T = 8:30. Rec = CR-MID-72-14, Cicero H.S., Codner)

Of the fifteen symphonies of Dmitri Shostakovich, the *Fifth* is the most performed. First played in 1937, this work re-established Shostakovich in the good graces of the Soviet government, after much criticism of his previous work, and won him a firm place among the world's first-rank composers. Because of the somewhat heroic nature of the music, the *Finale* seems especially well adapted to performance by the concert band. In free form, much of the movement is based on material derived from the first few notes of the opening theme. Contrast is offered by a very angular melody played by the solo cornets and a closely related but more sustained theme in the solo French horn. The ending provides one of the most thrilling climaxes in the band repertoire, stating the main theme in augmented form over a continually more insistent rhythmic pattern. (Hubert P. Henderson, University of Maryland)

FRANK SKINNER

(Born in Meredosia, Illinois, 1897 — Died in Hollywood, California, 1968)

Frank Skinner was educated at the Chicago Musical College and also studied music privately. Working as a pianist on river boats, in vaudeville, and in Broadway show orchestras, he learned the trade and soon began arranging music for publishers in New York. Later Skinner moved to Hollywood and composed outstanding film music including two works, *Tap Roots* and *Shawl Dance,* which he scored for concert band.

Tap Roots (Pub = SK, 1950, Out of print. Gr = 4. T = 9:10)

The concert version of the *Tap Roots* motion picture music is condensed from the original score into a descriptive tone poem. The opening theme describes the South before the Civil War followed by a musical picture of a cotton plantation with Negroes at work in the fields. Dusk falls and the Negroes sing with spiritual feeling around their cabins. In the master's mansion we hear a sentimental theme and then there is an abrupt announcement that war has been declared. The music then portrays the recruiting of men, soldiers on the march, the advance of the cavalry, and the battle. The war ends with defeat, surrender, desolation, and heartbreak. At the very lowest ebb the spiritual theme reappears, foretelling the reconstruction of the South, and the work ends with a confident grandioso.

CLAUDE T. SMITH

(Born in Monroe City, Missouri, 1932)

Claude T. Smith attended Central Methodist College and the University of Kansas. He was in the 371st Army Band during the Korean War and later taught instrumental school music in Nebraska and Missouri. He has more recently taught composition and conducted the orchestra at Southwest Missouri State University, served as education consultant for Wingert-Jones Music Company, and become staff composer for Jenson Publishing Company. Smith's instrumental and choral works have been performed by leading musical organizations in the United States and several other countries. Active as a clinician and guest conductor, he has been the recipient of numerous awards and honors including election to the presidency of the Missouri Music Educators Association. Smith is married and has one daughter.

Acclamation (Pub = WJ, 1969. Gr = 3. T = 12:00. Rec = CR-MID-69-11, Clovis, NM, H.S., Thompson)

Like most of Smith's band compositions, *Acclamation* is characterized by great rhythmic vitality. He employs frequent meter changes from 3/4 to 6/8 to 1/4 to 7/8 and back to 3/4. *Acclamation* has become a favorite concert selection on the programs of many all-state and all-district bands. The work was commissioned by the Getzen Company in honor of Nels Vogel of Moorhead, Minnesota.

Emperata Overture (Pub = WJ, 1964. Gr = 4. T = 9:00. Rec = PW-Accent Smith, Un. of KS, Bloomquist)

Emperata Overture opens with a fanfare-like statement by the brass section accompanied by percussion in the background. The main theme is then stated by the clarinets with a rhythmic brass background in 4/4 meter, but occasionally a 7/8 measure separates phrases. The middle section presents a lyrical statement of a new theme by a flute soloist followed by reiterations of the theme in various sections of the band as well as by the full band. The ending is highlighted by a change of key and a restatement of themes, making a very exciting finish. (Bardie Roberts, Jennings, Louisiana, High School)

Incidental Suite (Pub = WJ, 1966. Gr = 4. T = 10:00. Rec = PW-Accent Smith, Un. of KS, Bloomquist)

The *Incidental Suite* is written in three movements. The Tarantella provides a fast 6/8 dance characterized by the constant use of hemiola—a syncopated rhythm of three notes in two counts. In contrast, the Nocturne croons a slow, lazy melody accompanied by lush and sometimes dissonant harmonies. The Rondo opens in a rather martial style with the percussion section stating rhythmically that which becomes the main theme of this finale. Throughout the movement, short interludes of dialogue between the percussion section and other sections occur. For example in the last few bars, as the piece seems to have come to an end, the percussion section breaks back in with the final word. (Michael Jameson, Eastern Michigan University)

Sonus Ventorum (Pub = WJ, 1970. Gr = 3. T = 6:00. Rec = CR-MID-70-13, Richmond, MO, H.S., Smith)

Sonus Ventorum (Sound of the Winds) opens with a brief but powerful largo followed by a driving allegro section built on two main thematic ideas. The sound of the winds is enhanced by the percussion section throughout the work. The rhythmic figures which characterize Smith's music provide excitement and heightened interest for both the performer and listener.

HALE SMITH

(Born in Cleveland, Ohio, 1925)

Hale Smith enrolled in the Cleveland Institute of Music in 1946—after completing his World War II military service—and obtained both B.M. and M.M. degrees in composition. His principal composition teacher was Marcel Dick and he studied advanced theory with Ward Lewis. He has composed and arranged for various media including band, chamber ensemble, piano, voice, and orchestra. Two of his best known orchestra works are *Faces of Jazz* (1968) and *Rituals and Incantation* (1974). Most of Smith's compositions are highly concentrated and sensitive, showing a high degree of craftsmanship. His teaching experience includes two years at C.W. Post College (1968-70); since 1970 he has been an associate professor in the music department at the University of Connecticut.

Expansions (Pub = EM, 1967. Gr = 4. T = 6:30. Rec = CR-MID-68-7, Fenton H.S., Bensenville, IL, Smith; BP-107, Southern IL Un., Fjerstad)

Expansions was commissioned by and dedicated to the Southern Illinois University Symphonic Band. The title was in part suggested by the spreading two clusters of the beginning. It also refers to the fact that rhythms, intervals, dynamics, and instrumentation are all subjected to various procedures of augmentation and diminution. The entire piece is developed from the material presented in the first ten measures. The title seems also appropriate since the piece was conceived, not as an exercise in technique, but as a musical statement capable of involving the listener's emotions and imagination. (Educational Record Reference Library, Belwin-Mills)

Somersault (Pub = FR, 1964. Gr = 4. T = 4:00. Rec = BP-102, Baldwin Wallace, Snapp)

The title, *Somersault,* refers to the turning backward and upside down of the row forms that are so important to this piece. The flowing opening melody is an arrangement of all twelve tones of the chromatic scale which make up the twelve-tone series (or row) from which the harmonic and melodic material of this piece is derived. Sharp contrasts occur between richly harmonized passages dominated by the opening melody, and lean-textured, angular lines which seem to be suspended between blocks of heavily accented chords. The angular lines—really the opening melody in reverse—are crowded one on top of the other in a climactic pyramid at the end. (Harold Jackson, Southwest Baptist College)

KENNETH SNOECK
(Born in Detroit, Michigan, 1946)

Kenneth Snoeck graduated from Roseville High School in Detroit, Michigan, then enrolled at Central Michigan University where he received both B.S. and M.M. degrees. In addition to composition he is interested in the percussion instruments and has instructed both marching band and percussion at his alma mater. Examples of Snoeck's compositions and arrangements for marching band include *Quejada, Karnival,* and *Circus Spectacular.* Snoeck's most ambitious published work for concert band is *Scaramouch.*

Scaramouch—Symphony No. 3 for Winds and Percussion (Pub = SH, 1973. Gr = 5. T = 12:00. Rec = CR-CBDNA-73-3, Northwestern Un., Paynter)

"Scaramouch" is a stock character in the Italian commedia dell'arte who exists to parody the Spanish don; he has been variously described as a rascal, a scamp, and a cowardly buffoon. American composer Kenneth Snoeck remembers the character from an old Italian movie and the name Scaramouch as that given to a pet turtle by one of his friends. This symphony was completed in 1971 and premiered by the Central Michigan University Band. Two years later the work was voted by the members of the College Band Directors National Conference as "the best original manuscript submitted to CBDNA during the 1971-73 biennium."

Scaramouch uses a contemporary harmonic and melodic vocabulary, but remains traditional in its requirements for tonal individuality of the instruments. Much of the work's melodic importance is shared by the percussion section—the parts requiring six performers on varied assemblages of instruments and equipment. The most unusual scoring is in the second movement, Metal, which calls for four soprano flutes, alto flute, brass bells, automobile brake drums, metal plumbing pipes, multiple cymbals and multiple triangles. The full ensemble is used only in the first movement, titled With Restrained Energy, and the last movement, Vigorously. The third movement is called Wood and Membranophones (percussion instruments with skin heads). (Acton Ostling, Jr., University of Louisville)

JOHN PHILIP SOUSA
(Born in Washington, D.C., 1854 — Died in Reading, Pennsylvania, 1932)

The name of John Philip Sousa is almost synonymous with band music in America. Child of a Portuguese father (who was born in Sevilla, Spain) and Bavarian mother, he showed musical aptitude at an early age. At ten he was studying violin and harmony, soon learning to play wind instruments as well. He played with the Marine Band at thirteen, and later was appointed leader of the same band, a position he held for a dozen years before setting out to organize his own band. The Sousa Band became famous throughout America and Europe, playing concerts in both the United States and Canada and appearing at the Paris Exposition in 1900. After making four extensive European tours, the band was engaged for a world tour in 1910-11.

Along with ability to conduct, Sousa developed a distinct flair for writing marches. He seemed instinctively to know how to compose for band instruments, and his style, full of bouncing rhythms, brilliant instrumentation, and catchy tunes, earned for him the name of The March King. In his book, *John Philip Sousa—A Descriptive Catalogue of His Works,* Paul Bierley* writes that "If Sousa had a formula for composing successful marches, it was inspired simplicity. He was a master of counterpoint, but he used it prudently. . .his countermelodies and obligatos do not appear as mere embellishments or detract from melodic and rhythmic elements."

His output was extraordinary—several hundred pieces, including some comic operas as well as orchestral works. In addition, he wrote an autobiography entitled *Marching Along,* three novels, and an excellent method book for teaching instruments. A man of tremendous energy, he continued his extensive tours almost to the time of his death. His passing ended an era of military and marching band music which had become a positive force in American music at the turn of the century.

The Black Horse Troop March (Pub = SF, 1925; Fennell Ed., 1974. Gr = 4. T = 3:05. Rec = MG-GI-SRI-75064, Eastman, Fennell; BL-SABC-7-R, Detroit Concert, Smith; CA-SYB-2168, U.S. Army, Loboda)

Sousa loved horses, in spite of the fact that a fall from a high-spirited steed named Patrician Charley in 1921 limited the use of his left arm for the rest of his life. Only three years after the fall Sousa wrote *The Black Horse Troop* and dedicated it to the mounted troops of a Cleveland National Guard unit. Years before, in 1881, he had marched with his U.S. Marine Band and the same mounted troop unit in the funeral cortege of President Garfield. When Sousa and his band premiered *The Black Horse Troop* in Cleveland in 1925, the troopers rode their beautiful black horses right up on the stage with the band.

El Capitan March (Pub = JC, 1896; Helmecke Ed = TP, 1955. Gr = 3. T = 2:15. Rec = RC-LSP-2688, U.S. Navy; BL-SABC-1-R, Detroit Concert, Smith; MG-GI-SRI-75004, Eastman, Fennell)

Sousa was the composer of fifteen operettas, of which the best known is *El Capitan.* The march appears in the second act as a male chorus. Produced in 1896, the opera concerns a Peruvian viceroy of the sixteenth century who disguises himself as a notorious bandit to thicken the plot. In 1899 Sousa increased his band to over a hundred musicians for Admiral Dewey's victory parade and this march was used to salute the returning Spanish-American war veterans.

Corcoran Cadets March (Pub = CF, 1890. Gr = 3. T = 3:00. Rec = CA-SYB-2168, U.S. Army, Loboda; BL-SABC-4-R, Detroit Concert, Smith; MG-40007, Eastman, Fennell)

Sousa wrote this march for "the officers and men of the Corcoran Cadets," a Washington, D.C. drill team which averaged sixteen years in age and was the first company of cadets to be drafted into the National Guard. The team was named after William C. Corcoran who had once considered financing Sousa's musical education in Europe; Sousa's decision not to go might have disappointed Corcoran and could have been a factor in selecting the title for this march. The march was composed in 1890 and presumably was played by the "Corcoran's" band as well as other bands in the Washington, D.C. area at the time.

*Much of the information in this section is the result of Paul Bierley's research on the life and music of Sousa, and his kindness in sharing that knowledge. Although his *A Descriptive Catalogue of His Works* is out of print, a revised edition is planned. *John Philip Sousa: American Phenomenon* is still available. (Ed.)

The Fairest of the Fair March (Pub = JC, 1908; Helmecke Ed = TP, 1951; Fennell = TP, 1978. Gr = 3. T = 3:30. Rec = IL-40, Un. of IL, Hindsley; RC-CAL-125-Goldman; RC-LSP-2686, U.S. Air Force, Gabriel)

One of Sousa's favorite sayings was "A horse, a dog, a gun, a girl, and music on the side. That is my idea of heaven." Of the four first-named subjects, the fairer sex was by far the winner when all the titles of Sousa's compositions are examined. In this instance the subject was a pretty girl who worked at the annual Boston Food Fair. Even though the March King never met the girl, her memory inspired the title, *The Fairest of the Fair,* when he was preparing a new march for the food fair in 1908.

The Free Lance March (Pub = JC, 1906; Goldman Ed = TP, 1959. Gr = 3. T = 4:10. Rec = CA-SYB-2168, U.S. Army, Loboda; GC-Revelli Years, Un. of MI, Revelli)

Although Sousa is remembered primarily for his marches, he wrote considerable music of other types, including several operettas. One of these, titled *The Free Lance,* concerned a goatherd who left his goats, hired himself out as a (free lance) mercenary leader of two rival armies, maneuvered his troops so that neither side could win, and declared himself emperor of both countries. Whether Sousa needed another new march for his band in 1906 (he wrote no other marches that year) or whether he realized the limited future of his operetta, is not known, but he did piece several of the operetta tunes together in composing *The Free Lance March.* Sousa (along with Victor Herbert) devoted much time and energy in 1906 campaigning for composers' royalties on recorded music—a campaign which led to the passing of copyright laws still in effect. These laws protect the composer (another type of "free lance" artist) against infringement on the use of his product.

The Gallant Seventh March (Pub = SF, 1922; Fennell Ed = SF, 1971. Gr = 3. T = 3:00. Rec = MG-GI-SRI-75047, Eastman, Fennell; BL-SABC-6-7, Detroit Concert, Smith)

This march was written for the 7th Regiment, 107th Infantry, of the New York National Guard and the conductor of its band, Major Francis Sutherland. Sutherland had been a cornetist in Sousa's Band and left that organization to enlist in the army when the U.S. entered World War I. He remained in the 7th Regiment after the war and his band members joined with the members of the Sousa Band when *The Gallant Seventh March* was premiered at the New York Hippodrome in November of 1922. Written during the last decade of his composing career, this march is considered one of Sousa's best.

George Washington Bicentennial March (Pub = SF, 1930-66. Gr = 4. T = 3:40. Rec = CR-CBDNA-71-7, U.S. Air Force, Gabriel; BL-SABC-1-R, Detroit Concert, Smith)

To commemorate the two hundredth anniversary of the birth of George Washington, a Bicentennial Commission in Washington, D.C., was formed. A gala celebration was held, the climax being an impressive ceremony at the Capitol Plaza on February 22, 1932. The commission had asked Sousa to take part in the final ceremony, and he composed this march for the occasion. In this affair, one of two final appearances before his death, Sousa conducted the combined bands of the U.S. Army, Navy, and Marine Corps in the new march. Although written at the very end of his career, this brilliant and inventive march is one of Sousa's finest accomplishments. (Keith Brion, Yale University)

Hands Across the Sea March (Pub = JC, 1899; Helmecke Ed = JC, 1951. Gr = 3. T = 2:40. Rec = MG-GI-SRI-75099, Eastman, Fennell; CR-ABA-73-6, Inter-service, Harpham)

Several different ideas have been given concerning the title of this march. One suggests the title as a good-will gesture in preparation for the Sousa Band's first tour to Europe; another credits the incident where British Captain Chichester went to the aid of American Admiral Dewey during the Spanish-American War; the most likely, according to Paul Bierley, was the inspiration from reading a quote in an old play, "A sudden thought strikes me,—let us swear an eternal friendship." That line, combined with the conflicting emotions of America's part in the war, immediately suggested the title of *Hands Across the Sea.*

The Invincible Eagle March (Pub = JC, 1901; Helmecke Ed = JC, 1951. Gr = 3. T = 3:10. Rec = CA-SYB-2168, U.S. Army, Loboda; BL-SABC-2-R, Detroit Concert, Smith)

This march was dedicated to the Pan-American Exposition in Buffalo, New York, in 1901. If Sousa needed any additional motivation for this composition, it was provided by the fact that he knew Francesco Fanciulli was also writing a march for the same exposition. Fanciulli had followed Sousa as leader of the Marine Band in 1892 and was arrested and court-martialed in 1897 because he refused to obey a superior's order to play a Sousa march. After his discharge from the Marines, Fanciulli also formed a band, and the rivalry continued for some time. Although Fanciulli was a capable composer, his march for the exposition, *The Electric Century,* was never as popular as Sousa's *The Invincible Eagle March.*

King Cotton March (Pub = JC, 1895; Helmecke Ed = TP, 1951. Gr = 3. T = 2:40. Rec = RC-LSP-2688, U.S. Navy; MG-GI-SRI-75004, Eastman, Fennell; VA-VSD-2125, Un. of MI, Revelli)

During the long existence of his professional band (1892-1931), Sousa was credited with preventing many fairs and expositions from losing money. In this instance the Cotton States Exposition officials wanted to cancel the Sousa Band's three-week contract, but Sousa insisted that the contract be honored and his popularity, as usual, drew enormous audiences. The *King Cotton March,* written for the exposition, was a great hit during the concerts as it still is today.

The Liberty Bell March (Pub = JC, 1893; Helmecke Ed = TP, 1951. Gr = 3. T = 3:20. Rec = RC-LSP-2686, U.S. Air Force, Gabriel; BL-SABC-1-R, Detroit Concert, Smith; MG-GI-SRI-75047, Eastman, Fennell)

After learning many hard lessons through experience in the managing of band concerts and the publishing of his music, Sousa entered into a contract with John Church Company to publish his music on a royalty basis. Whereas formerly he had sold his music outright for nominal amounts only to see the publisher make handsome profits, he now could realize some profit for himself. *The Liberty Bell* was the first of his marches to be published under the new arrangement, and it became, and still is, one of the most popular of Sousa's marches. *The Liberty Bell* netted him over $40,000 in less than seven years. The title resulted from (1) Sousa and his manager seeing a huge painting of the Liberty Bell during a show in Chicago, (2) a letter from Sousa's wife the next morning telling how their son had marched in a Philadelphia parade honoring the Liberty Bell, and (3) Sousa's unashamed patriotism which predisposed him toward any title with a nationalistic ring.

Looking Upward Suite (Pub = JC, 1905. Gr = 3. T = 15:45. Rec = CR-MID-70-12, West Suburban Community, Dvorak)

Although John Philip Sousa is commonly known as "The March King," few people realize that he also wrote many operas, suites, light operas, vocal solos, and numerous other types of compositions. In this original suite for band, he depicts his conception of certain heavenly bodies. The movements are titled: By the Light of the Polar Star, Beneath the Southern Cross, and Mars and Venus. His predisposition to march rhythms is apparent in much of this music. Sousa wrote this suite in 1902, borrowing two of the melodies he had used for an operetta of 1899, *Chris and the Wonderful Lamp.*

Manhattan Beach March (Pub = JC, 1894; Helmecke Ed = TP, 1951. Gr = 3. T = 2:25. Rec = CR-ABA-73-2, U.S. Navy, Meyers; MG-GI-SRI-75064, Eastman, Fennell; VA-VSD-2125, Un. of MI, Revelli)

During Sousa's lifetime, Manhattan Beach was a highly fashionable New York summer resort. In 1893 he and his band began a long string of engagements there. With nineteen former members of Gilmore's Band, a dozen or so very capable players from Europe, and some of the most outstanding artists from other bands in his group, Sousa knew the musical and entertaining potential of his band. However his first business manager, David Blakely, was skeptical, and it was at the first Manhattan Beach concert series that he invited the most prominent critics and musicians in New York to hear the band and offer their criticism. Their comments were so flattering that Blakely was convinced Sousa was correct in his judgement. Sousa composed *Manhattan Beach March* during that first summer and several other important works during subsequent summers at the resort.

National Fencibles March (Pub = JC, 1888. Gr = 3. T = 3:15. Rec = PH-9500-151, Eastman, Fennell; CR-4040, Burke-Phillips All Star, Cailliet; BL-SABC-4-R, Detroit Concert, Smith)

Sousa's interest in marching units and drill teams was demonstrated many times by the titles of his marches. The National Fencibles was a popular drill team in Washington which had won the national competition and was recognized by Sousa with this march written in 1888. The trio of the march has words concluding with, "Onward we march with the Fencibles' swing," which are sometimes used as the title. Another subtitle is *The March Past of the National Fencibles.*

Nobles of the Mystic Shrine March (Pub = SF, 1923. Gr = 3. T = 3:00. Rec = CR-CBDNA-73-1, Un. of IL, Kisinger; BL-SABC-4-R, Detroit Concert, Smith; MG-GI-SRI-75047, Eastman, Fennell)

As might be expected of a person in his position, Sousa belonged to a large number of organizations; almost forty in all. When he became a member of the Ancient Arabic Order of Nobles of the Mystic Shrine in 1922, he was promptly named the first honorary director of the Almas Temple Shrine Band in Washington. In 1923 the Almas Temple hosted the national convention and Sousa conducted a band of 6,200 Shriners in Griffith Stadium; the largest band he ever conducted. In subsequent tours with his band, many of Sousa's appearances were arranged by the Shriners, and occasionally the host band joined in the playing of "their" march, *Nobles of the Mystic Shrine.*

The Pride of the Wolverines March (Pub = SF, 1926; Fennell Ed = SF, 1973. Gr = 3. T = 3:20. Rec = MG-GI-SRI-75064, Eastman, Fennell; VA-VSD-2125, Un. of MI, Revelli; BL-SABC-5-R, Detroit Concert, Smith)

When the Sousa Band was in Detroit for a concert in 1925, Mayor John W. Smith requested of the March King that he write a march for that city. The result the following year was *The Pride of the Wolverines,* dedicated to the mayor and the people of Detroit. For several decades this vigorous work was the official march of Detroit, but it has since been replaced by a composition written by Leonard B. Smith, *Hail Detroit.* Inasmuch as Michigan is the Wolverine State, Sousa's march might be appropriate for the entire state.

Semper Fidelis March (Pub = CR & JC, 1888. Gr = 3. T = 3:30. Rec = RC-LSP-2687, U.S. Marine; BL-SABC-3-R, Detroit Concert, Smith; PH-S-9500-151, Eastman, Hunsberger)

This march takes its title from the U.S. Marine Corps motto meaning "Always Faithful." It has been the Marine Corps' official march for many years, was regarded by Sousa as his most musical march, and has long been one of his most popular works, yet, it was purchased by the publisher Harry Coleman for thirty-five dollars! Part of the trio of *Semper Fidelis* was taken from Sousa's first published book (1886) titled *Trumpet and Drum.*

The Stars and Stripes Forever March (Pub = JC, 1897, Helmecke Ed = TP, 1951. Gr = 4. T = 3:20. Rec = CA-SYB-2168-U.S. Army, Loboda; CR-ABA-77-6, U.S. Marine, Foss; CR-ABA-73-5, U.S. Air Force, Mahan)

Of the genesis of this march, which is considered to be his greatest, Sousa tells us in his autobiography, *Marching Along:*

> Aboard the Teutonic, as it steamed out of the harbor on my return from Europe in 1896, came one of the most vivid incidents of my career. As I paced the deck, absorbed in thought, suddenly I began to sense the rhythmic beat of a band playing within my brain. It kept on ceaselessly, playing, playing, playing. Throughout the whole tense voyage, that imaginary band continued to unfold the same themes, echoing and reechoing the most distinct melody. I did not transfer a note of that music to paper while I was on the steamer, but when we reached shore, I set down the measures that my brain-band had been playing for me, and not a note of it has ever changed. The composition is known the world over as "The Stars and Stripes Forever" and is probably my most popular march.

(By permission of John Philip Sousa, Inc., New York City)

The Thunderer March (Pub = JC, 1889. Gr = 3. T = 2:40. Rec = MG-GI-SRI-75004, Eastman, Fennell; CRE-9005, Ithaca Col. Alumni, Beeler; VA-VSD-2125, Un. of MI, Revelli)

Three years after Sousa was "knighted" in the Knights Templar of Washington, D.C., he dedicated this march to that organization. *The Thunderer* was Mrs. Sousa's favorite march and was chosen by Sousa as one of five to be featured by his

Great Lakes Naval Training Station Band on their tour in behalf of the American Red Cross during World War I. The principal theme of the march trio is a bugle call taken from Sousa's *Trumpet and Drum* book which he had written in 1886. To this theme were added more and more countermelodies building to an exciting finale.

The Washington Post March (Pub = JC & CF, 1889. Gr = 3. T = 2:25. Rec = RC-CAL-125, Goldman; RC-LSP-2688, U.S. Navy; MG-GI-SRI-75004, Eastman, Fennell)

Composed in 1889, this march was written for the newspaper of the same name to help promote an essay contest sponsored by the paper. The 6/8 march happened to be appropriate for a new dance called the two-step and soon became the most popular hit tune in both America and Europe. Of the 136 marches which Sousa wrote, *The Washington Post* and the *Stars and Stripes Forever March* have been the most widely known.

ALBERT STOUTAMIRE
(See Vita in the Appendix)

The Minstrel Boy (Arr = Stoutamire. Pub = CO, 1976. Gr = 2. T = 3:15. Rec = CR-MID-76-12, Spring Woods H.S., Houston, TX, Wren)

The melody is an old Irish air which was very popular in the United States during the early nineteenth century. The arrangement begins as a subdued sentimental song with haunting "horn fifths" in the background played alternately by horns and trombones (and cued for other instruments). The arrangement builds in texture and volume, concluding with a stirring martial sound. Although written for advanced junior high school and senior high bands, the music makes attractive light program material for college and professional bands.

When Johnny Comes Marching Home (Arr = Stoutamire. Pub = BA, 1978. Gr = 2. T = 2:05)

The music was first published in 1863 by Patrick S. Gilmore, famed bandleader of the Union Army and organizer-conductor of "Peace Jubilees" following the American Civil War. Gilmore used the pseudonym of Louis Lambert, and after the song became popular, he claimed only to have written the words, identifying the melody as a traditional Negro melody. Some historians believe that the melody was an Irish tune that Gilmore heard sung by soldiers during the war. Regardless of its origin, with the new title and lyrics by Gilmore, "When Johnny Comes Marching Home" became very popular in the North during the war. The Confederacy thereupon adopted the melody with a comic verse titled "For Bales."

Following the Civil War, the melody became popular again, this time as the tune of "Abe Lincoln Went to Washington," a tribute to the President after his assassination. Still later, "When Johnny Comes Marching Home" became the song most frequently associated with the Spanish-American War. The song was revised and became popular once more during World War I.

Today the stirring melody continues to appeal to young and old alike. Stoutamire's adaptation is for young school musicians and is arranged to be well within the capabilities of advanced first year players but still of interest when performed by much more advanced musicians. In addition, it is especially effective as a pedagogical vehicle for teaching 6/8 meter in march tempo.

JOHANN STRAUSS

(Born in Vienna, 1825 — Died in Vienna, 1899)

Johann Strauss was not permitted by his father, Johann the elder, to study music, and after receiving a basic general education, he became a bank clerk. His mother, however, had him take music lessons in secret, and after the parents separated, Johann took up the study of violin and theory in earnest. At the age of nineteen, he formed an orchestra and presented concerts which soon began to rival those of his more famous father. Johann the younger became known as the "Waltz King" as a result of his numerous and popular waltz compositions. The best known of these include *Artist's Life; Tales from the Vienna Woods; Wine, Women, and Song;* and *The Blue Danube.* In his later years he wrote operettas, one of the best known being *Die Fledermaus.*

Overture to Die Fledermaus (Arr = Cailliet. Pub = BH, 1946. Gr = 4. T = 8:30. Rec = CR-MID-75-6, Northshore, Wilmette, IL, Paynter; GC, Revelli Years, Un. of MI, Revelli)

The famous waltz composer, Johann Strauss, Jr., wrote a number of operettas, the most famous and popular of which is *Die Fledermaus.* A standard item in the repertory of opera houses throughout the world, it was written in 1874, and received its first performance in Vienna. The overture contains many of the principal airs of the opera. (Richard Franko Goldman, the Goldman Band)

RICHARD STRAUSS

(Born in Munich, 1864 — Died in Garmisch-Partenkirchen, Germany, 1949)

A master of orchestration, Strauss expressed in his tone poems the whole gamut of human emotions. His art songs also achieved fame and success, among which "Allerseelen" became a great favorite and has been transcribed for both orchestra and band.

Strauss' father, Franz, was an eminent horn player in the orchestra of the Bavarian Court so music seemed a natural way of life in the Strauss home. By the time he was four, Richard was taking harp lessons and when he was eleven, he began the serious study of composition and orchestration. In 1886 he became court musical director at Munich followed by similar positions at Weimar, Munich, and at Berlin with the Royal Opera.

Strauss realized that sensationalism and commercialism were often closely related and the results were much in evidence in his operas *Salome, Der Rosenkavalier,* and *Elektra.* A highly successful conductor as well as composer, Strauss was also skillful in his business matters. He became one of Europe's wealthiest composers before he died at the age of eighty-five.

Allerseelen, Opus 10, No. 8 (Arr = Davis. Pub = LU, 1955. Gr = 3. T = 4:00)

The art songs of Richard Strauss achieved fame and success the same as his well-known tone poems. Among these art songs, *Allerseelen* (All Souls' Day) became a great favorite. Several times it has been transcribed for orchestra. In this transcription for the symphonic band the melody surges throughout, much in the style of Wagner. (James D. Pritchard, University of South Carolina)

A Hero's Life, Synthesis (Arr = Hindsley, ms. Gr = 6. T = 22:45. Rec = IL-40, Un. of IL, Hindsley)

A general and free ideal of great and manly heroism describing the inward battle of life which aspires toward the elevation of the soul is portrayed in Strauss' *A Hero's Life*. The opening sections depict the nobility of the Hero and the petty jealousies, hatreds, and suspicions of his enemies. This is followed by one of the great love expressions in music which is devoted to the Hero's helpmate.

The Hero plunges into battle, the victory is won, and later he is equally victorious in peaceful ventures. He has triumphed, but his achievements are belittled by his adversaries. His reward is envy and contempt, and at first he rebels. But finally he reaches the peace of fulfillment and contentment, a tranquility which nothing can disturb, and in this mood the Hero takes leave of the world.

Serenade, Opus 7 (Pub = BH, 1881. Gr = 4. T = 8:00. Rec = MG-90173, Eastman, Fennell)

The serenade was composed in 1881-82 when Strauss was seventeen years old. The composition brought Strauss to the attention of the great conductor Hans von Bülow who hired the young composer to be his assistant conductor with the Meiningen Orchestra, launching his well known conducting career. The music is cast in one large movement embracing a short sonata form. Although one of his first works, reminiscent of the andantes of Mozart, all of the typical Straussian qualities are present—the long arching melodic lines, rich harmonic textures and instrumental virtuosity. The delightful nature of the melodies and Strauss's knowledgeable use of the instruments make *Serenade, Opus 7* a gem in the wind instrument literature. It was scored for pairs of flutes, oboes, clarinets, and bassoons plus four horns and a contrabassoon.

Sonatina in F (Pub = BH. Gr = 5. T = 36:00. Rec = Bristol Collectors' Classics., The Boston Wind Ensemble, Simon. Bristol Laboratories, Inc., Not For Sale)

This chamber work for winds was composed more than sixty years after *Serenade, Opus 7*. During the summer of 1943 when he was recuperating from illness, Strauss began this work and gave it the humorous subtitle "Out of an invalid's workshop." He wrote for sixteen instruments—the thirteen used in *Serenade, Opus 7* plus a third clarinet, a basset horn, and a bass clarinet.

The first movement, Allegro moderato, begins on a solemn Wagnerian note but the mood is soon superseded by passages of elfin grace and Straussian wit. A contrasting middle section provides opportunities for the instruments to alternately intone expressive solo passages. A long drawn-out restatement ends in a melancholic coda.

The second movement, Romanza, is similar to the first movement in structure but with a graceful dance-like section presented in the middle section. The last movement, Molto allegro, displays a scherzo-like character.

Suite in B-Flat, Op. 4 (Ed = Whitwell. Pub = WIN. Gr = 4)

Hans von Bülow admired the *Serenade, Opus 7* and suggested to Strauss that he write another similar work. The result was this composition for the same thirteen wind instruments as the *Serenade* but an extended work in four movements: Allegretto, Romanze, Gavotte, and Introduction and Fugue. It was composed in 1884, two or three years after the *Serenade*. The music is more Brahmsian in character than Strauss's later works, but is delicate, charming and totally romantic writing for wind instruments.

Till Eulenspielgel's Merry Pranks (Tr = Hindsley, Ms.   Gr = 6.   T = 15:15.
Rec = IL-53, Un. of IL, Hindsley)

This symphonic rondo has been described as the most genial humoresque ever written in sound. Although the composer has declined to furnish a descriptive narrative, leaving it "to my hearers to crack the nut which the rogue had prepared for them," Wilhelm Klatte has written a lengthy analysis of the work, which may be summarized as follows:

> The whimsical Till rides his horse through a crowd of market women sitting chattering in their stalls; puts on the vestments of a priest and assumes an unctious mien, but feeling uncomfortable in the disguise, tears it off. He becomes a "Don Juan" and waylays pretty women; one bewitches him, but Till's advances are treated with derision. The rogue's anger is scarcely over when a troop of worthy Philistines appears, and these good people receive his gibes. Gaily he goes on his way playing waggish pranks, but Nemesis is upon him. Till is dragged by the jailer before the criminal tribunal. To each of the court's interrogations Till replies calmly, and lies. He is condemned to death and fear seizes him. The rogue is then strung up and his soul takes flight. The epilog, picking up the theme of the introduction, continues the people's murmuring and moralizing over the Till legend.

Aside from its musical evaluation and significance, *Till* has become somewhat of a virtuoso showpiece for orchestra, and it is even more of a challenge for the instrumentation of the concert band. (Mark Hindsley, University of Illinois)

Waltzes from Der Rosenkavalier (Arr = Cailliet. Pub = BH. Gr = 5. T = 15:00.
Rec = CR-ABA-77-1, FL A & M Un., Cailliet)

The "Knight of the Rose" has the honorary function of carrying the symbolic silver flower to the fiancee, and around this custom is woven a most complicated plot. *Der Rosenkavalier* is the fifth and finest of Strauss's notable contributions to the lyric theater. Some critics state that Strauss never wrote a more nearly perfect work. The waltzes from this opera, a sophisticated drawing room comedy in an eighteenth century Viennese setting, are most delightful.

IGOR STRAVINSKY

(Born in Oranienbaum, Russia, 1882 — Died in New York City, 1971)

Igor Stravinsky studied composition with Rimsky-Korsakov, but his early works did not show the influence of his teacher or the others of the so-called "Russian Five." They were more Brahmsian in style. Stravinsky was recognized as a successful composer with his ballets, *Petrushka* and *The Firebird,* but in 1913 the first performance of *The Rite of Spring* in Paris brought violent protests from the audience. Stravinsky came to the United States in 1925 where he appeared often as conductor of his own compositions. During an early period of his writing much of his work was based on Russian themes. Following World War I he began to acquire a new style of composing, and an important composition of this period was the suite of *Three Pieces for Clarinet Solo*. The contrast between these pieces of monodic style and the multitudinous *The Rite of Spring* was thought by some critics to indicate a change taking place in this composer's style. A religious aspect is evident in works of a later period. Probably no composer has had a greater impact on contemporary music.

IGOR STRAVINSKY

Berceuse and Finale from the Firebird Suite (Arr = Goldman. Pub = EM, 1947. Gr = 5. T = 6:00. Rec = CL-MS-7011, Columbia Sym. Orch., Stravinsky)

The *Firebird* marked the beginning of the now legendary collaboration between Igor Stravinsky and Serge Diaghilev, the impressario of the famous Ballet Russe. Stravinsky was a totally unknown pianist and composer in 1910, but *The Firebird,* followed by *Petrushka* and *The Rite of Spring,* catapulted him to the forefront of contemporary composers, a position never relinquished. Richard Franko Goldman has arranged two sections of the score for band, the Berceuse (Lullaby), and the Finale, which is itself based on an old Russian folk tune first "discovered" by Rimsky-Korsakov.

The story concerns the Firebird, a beautiful ballerina with orange wings, and Ivan, a young prince who hunts for the Firebird, finally capturing her. She gives him a golden feather as ransom and disappears. Later Ivan is captured by the demon, Kastchei, but he waves the golden feather and the beautiful Firebird comes to his rescue. He is taken to a metal box containing an egg which is the soul of Kastchei the Terrible. He smashes the egg, and the princess and nobles are forever freed of the spell of Kastchei and his followers.

Circus Polka (Pub = EAM, 1942. Gr = 5. T = 3:30. Rec = IL-32, Un. of IL, Hindsley)

This is one of the works written soon after Stravinsky's arrival in the United States. Composed in 1942 for the Ringling Brothers Circus at the request of the choreographer, George Balanchine, the polka was to accompany a ballet of elephants and was so first performed in an anonymous instrumentation for circus band.

The piece is brief, light, and charming, but at the same time, full of the kind of harmonic language (simple chord progressions with "one note too many" added) which gives it a piquancy identifying it unmistakably with its composer. During the simple polka tune in the woodwinds, horns, and cornets, the trombones and tubas occasionally interject a few notes. At the beginning, and every so often thereafter, an inexplicable rhythmic dislocation occurs, from which, somehow, the regular 2/4 meter flow emerges. The piece culminates with an extended quotation from Schubert's *Marche Militaire*—"an absolutely natural thing," according to Stravinsky. The difficulty of the writing and the need to make the piece sound lyrical and effortless combine to maintain the flavor of this unique mixture of the graceful and the grotesque; the dancing of elephants. While Stravinsky never saw the actual ballet, he once met Bessie, the young elephant for whom the polka was written, and he shook her foot. (Stephen Parkany, Yale University)

Concerto for Piano and Winds (Pub = BH, 1924. Gr = 5. T = 19:00. Rec = PH-839761, Bishop w. BBC Sym. Orch., Davis; CR-CBD-69-3, Peabody, Romersa)

This concerto was composed during the winter of 1923-24 when Stravinsky was living in France and touring as a concert pianist. The première was in Paris in 1924 with Koussevitzky conducting and Stravinsky as soloist. The work remained the exclusive performance right of Stravinsky who performed it around forty times in the next five years.

The scoring for the concerto is unconventional, employing a large band of woodwinds and brass made deliberately bottom-heavy by the addition of both timpani and double basses. Unfortunately, this concept was not clear to everyone at the time of the first performance. Stravinsky wrote some months later:

I remember that I was reproached on the subject of the constitution of the orchestra, which was said to be "incomplete" because of the absence of strings (except for the double basses). The unfortunate critic did not know at the time that there is such a thing as *un orchestre d'harmonie*. It is this *orchestre d'harmonie* (concert band) which I have chosen for my piano concerto, and not the symphonic orchestra, as an instrumental body more appropriate to the tone of the piano. Strings and piano, a sound scraped and a sound struck, do not sound well together; piano and winds, sounds struck and blown, do.

(Keith Brion, Yale University)

Symphonies of Wind Instruments (Pub = BH, 1926-52. Gr = 5. T = 12:00. Rec = LO-6225, Orch. Suisse, Ansermet; MG-SRI-75057, Eastman, Fennell)

The *Symphonies* was written in 1920 in memory of Claude Debussy and was premiered in London under the baton of Serge Koussevitzky. The initial performance was a disappointment to Stravinsky; he revised the work in 1947 and a subsequent performance conducted by Ansermet in 1948 proved to be much more acceptable to the composer. The composition is a series of highly contrasting, closely juxtaposed sections culminating in a chorale which is referred to throughout the work. Scored for twenty-three winds—the wind section of an orchestra. Stravinsky has described the *Symphonies of Wind Instruments* as an "austere ritual" which unfolds "in short litanies between different groups of homogenous instruments."

(See Fall, 1979, *Journal of Band Research* for an analysis by Richard Bowles, Ed.)

ARTHUR SULLIVAN
(Born in London, 1842 — Died in London, 1900)

Arthur Sullivan, unbridled genius of the musical theater, was the son of a military band clarinetist who was the first professor of clarinet when the Royal Military School of Music (Kneller Hall) opened in England at Sandhurst in 1857. Sullivan, with his collaborator William Gilbert, wrote numerous popular musical comedies, mostly subtle satires on British political themes. Included in these operettas, which captured the admiration of all English-speaking people, were *The Gondoliers, H.M.S. Pinafore, The Mikado,* and *Pirates of Penzance.*

Suite from the Ballet Pineapple Poll (Arr = MacKerras; Duthoit. Pub = CA, 1952. Gr = 4. T − 9:50. Rec = CR-CBDNA-71-3, Northwestern St. Un., LA, Smith; CR-MENC-80-33, Un. of WI-Stevens Point, Greene)

The ballet *Pineapple Poll* is a spoof of the Gilbert and Sullivan operettas. The plot is based upon "The Bumboat Woman's Story" of Gilbert's *Bab Ballads,* which was later developed by Gilbert into *H.M.S. Pinafore.* The story evolves around Pineapple Poll and her colleagues who are all madly in love with the captain of the good ship H.M.S. Hot Cross Bun. In order to gain admittance to the ship they disguise themselves in sailors' clothes, a fact which is kept secret from the audience until near the end of the ballet.

According to Charles MacKerras, the British conductor who composed this ballet, "The score is a patchwork quilt of tunes from most of the Gilbert and Sullivan operas. Every bar of *Pineapple Poll,* even the short bridge passages, is taken from some opera or other." *Pineapple Poll* was first performed in March, 1959, by the Sadler Wells Theater Ballet. (Robert E. Restemeyer, Southeast Missouri State College)

FRANZ VON SUPPÉ

(Born near Spalato, Dalmatia, 1819 — Died in Vienna, 1895)

Suppé's musical ability was recognized after he composed a Mass for the Franciscan church at Zara when he was only fifteen. He later became a musical director at Vienna and wrote more than sixty comic operas. He is best remembered, however, for his overtures *Light Cavalry; Morning, Noon, and Night in Vienna;* and *Poet and Peasant.*

Morning, Noon, and Night in Vienna (Arr = Tobani. Pub = CF, 1896. Gr = 4. T = 8:00. Rec = LO-6779, Vienna Philharmonic Orch., Solti)

Suppé composed much of his music during Emperor Franz Joseph's reign—a time of prosperity and *joie de vivre*—or so it seemed. Music was heard in Vienna, as it still is, "morning, noon, and night." Suppé's works were first performed in America as concert "curtain raisers" by the symphony orchestras. However, overtures like *Morning, Noon, and Night* were so suitable for bands that they soon became the park-band favorites and are still performed by many professional and school bands.

Poet and Peasant Overture (Arr = Myrelles-Safranek. Pub = CF, 1911. Gr = 4. T = 10:30. Rec = CL-MS-7085, NY Philharmonic Orch., Bernstein)

Two overtures associated with the old-time park band concert of the days when those events were at their peak in popularity are Rossini's *William Tell* and Suppé's *Poet and Peasant.* Although Suppe is noted as the composer of a great number of comic operas, this particular work did not belong to an opera until several years after its 1845 composition date. The themes from this overture are among the most often quoted material for comic effects for stage productions and animated cartoons probably because they represent, in sound, an era of nostalgia and are familiar to audiences of all age groups. It is for this reason, if no other, that the composition deserves to be heard in its original context as a serious but highly entertaining selection.

CARLOS SURINACH

(Born in Barcelona, Spain, 1915)

During the years 1936 to 1939 Surinach studied with Morera in Barcelona and from 1939 to 1943 he studied with Max Trapp in Berlin. Subsequently, he returned to Spain where he became the conductor of the Grand Teatro del Liceo in Barcelona. He also served as guest conductor in Lisbon and Paris.

In 1951 Surinach moved to New York City where he resides on the top floor of a one-hundred year old red brick house sandwiched between two high-rise apartment buildings. He became a U.S. citizen in 1952. In 1972 he received the highest Spanish honor possible for an artist: Knight Commander of the Order of Isabella I of Castile. He has composed seventeen ballets and numerous works for orchestra, band, choir, chamber groups, and other media.

Ritmo Jondo—Flamenco (Pub = AMP, 1967.   Gr = 4.   T = 8:00.   Rec = CR-MID-68-11, Brownsville, TX, H.S., Vezzetti; GC-Revelli Years, Un. of MI, Revelli)

Three flamenco rhythms form the basis of *Ritmo Jondo*, a composition in three movements, first performed in New York in 1952. The original version was written for clarinet, trumpet, xylophone, tamburo, timpani, and three hand clappers. A year later the composer produced an extended version for chamber orchestra, and subsequently transcribed the band edition.

The composer describes the three movements as follows:

> *Bulerias:* a gay, fast, flamenco dance, improvisatory in character with shifting rhythms. Originally the name appears to have been derived from "burlerias" (practical jokes), a reference which is evident in the style peculiar to this dance form. The "bulerias" constitutes the most characteristic example of the dances "por fiestas," or party dances, and its vehement and exciting rhythm, full of pitfalls in interpretation, has served as the basis for the majority of these dances.
>
> *Saeta:* a slow ritual song of Seville, sung in the streets as a prayer during the Good Friday procession. Instruments are prohibited during this season; however, muffled drums are allowed. The "saeta" form is linked with the purest and most remote sources of flamenco art originated by the Sephardim and the Berbers. A great deal of inner power is required to manifest the gripping ritual of this music.
>
> *Garrotin:* among the innumberable inventions of the festive dances, the "garrotin" is very prominent. The dances "por fiestas" offer an arena within the flamenco style in which all innovations and improvisations imaginable are admissible. The "garrotin" is an orgiastic and uncontrolled dance, happily contagious and charged with emotion and exuberance; though, at the same time, restrained by a certain stoicism and by the violence of its own racial origins.

JOHN TATGENHORST

(Born in East Liverpool, Ohio, 1938)

A graduate of Ohio State University, John Tatgenhorst resides in Columbus, Ohio, where he works as a composer and arranger. He has twenty original compositions and thirty-two arrangements published for band. His specialty is writing easy to moderately difficult pedagogical and light entertaining pieces for band, and he also composes music for films and television commercials.

Tanglewood—An Overture for Band (Pub = BA. Gr = 2. T = 4:12. Rec = CR-MID-72-12, Bay View H.S., Milwaukee, WI, Hepner)

An overture for both young and more advanced school bands, this work has appealing melodic lines and traditional harmony. There are three contrasting sections. The first is in a slow but moving 4/4 meter. The second is in *alla breve* meter at a stately march tempo, and the final section returns to the initial majestic tempo.

PETER I. TCHAIKOVSKY

(Born in Votinsk, Russia, 1840 — Died in St. Petersburg, 1893)

Peter Ilyich Tchaikovsky is primarily remembered as the great Russian composer of romantic and melodius symphony, ballet, and opera. However, he was also known as a theorist, teacher, and critic. Through much of his lifetime he was pensioned by his admirer, Mme. von Meck, and it is one of the oddities of music history that the composer and his benefactress never met. Intensely nervous, sensitive, and emotional, Tchaikovsky expressed himself through his music in a very personal way—he towers as one of the giants of his period. (Carl Fischer, Inc.)

Finale from Symphony No. 4 (Arr = Safranek. Pub = CF, 1912. Gr = 5. T = 11:30. Rec = CR-ABA-76-5, U.S. Armed Forces Bicentennial, Hunt)

The *Fourth Symphony,* by its magnificent power and brilliance, its flashes and humor, and its marvelous coloring, has won its way to a point in the favor of concert audiences which places it on an equal footing with its successors, and there are many who prefer it to the *Fifth*—and the *Sixth (Pathetique).*

The first performance of this composition took place on February 22nd, 1878, at Moscow, under the direction of Nicholas Rubinstein. The work made, at its production, only a mild success. When it was played for the first time in Petrograd, December 7, 1878, it met with brilliant success, and this triumph brought great happiness to Tchaikovsky. The first performance of the symphony in America took place February 1st, 1890, at a concert of the Symphony Society, conducted by Walter Damrosch, in the Metropolitan Opera House, New York. (Richard Franko Goldman, the Goldman Band)

Marche Slave (Arr = Laurendeau. Pub = CF, 1906. Gr = 4. T = 8:50. Rec = CR-NBA-78-7, U.S. Navy, Muffley)

The *Slavonic*—or *Russo-Serbian*—*March* dates from 1876, the year of the war between Turkey and Serbia, which was the occasion of a great outbreak of Pan-Slavonic enthusiasm. Nicholas Rubinstein organized a concert for the benefit of the wounded, for which Tchaikovsky, who was in full sympathy with the feeling of the hour, wrote this march. It had an immense success, and being a stirring expression of the emotions then dominant in Russia, it was regarded as in some measure prophetic of the triumphant Slavonic cause. (Richard Franko Goldman, the Goldman Band)

Nutcracker Suite (Arr = Lake. Pub = CF, 1924. Gr = 4. T = 17:15. Rec = CL-MS-6193, NY Philharmonic Orch., Bernstein)

The dainty and bewitching *Nutcracker Suite* was written for the Russian Imperial Opera, and first performed in 1892. It is based on the Hoffman fairy tale of the little girl, who, having indulged herself with Christmas goodies, dreams on Christmas night that she again sees the tree lighted in all its splendor, while all the toys and dolls are holding a revel, led by "Nut-Cracker, the Prince of Fairyland." The ballet met with such success that Tchaikovsky decided to use the most popular numbers and arrange a suite. The movements are called March, Arab Dance, Trepak, and Waltz of the Flowers. (Richard Franko Goldman, the Goldman Band)

Overture 1812 (Arr = Brown. Pub = BH, 1938. Gr = 5. T = 15:00. Rec = CR-MID-68-13, Sapulpa, OK, H.S., Brite)

Written in 1880, this overture is intended to be descriptive of the invasion of Russia in 1812, by the French under Napolean I, and their final defeat. After his victory of Borodino, the army of Napolean marched into Moscow and took possession of the Kremlin. Thereupon the patriotic Russians set fire to their city, forcing the French to retreat. The theme of the introduction is drawn from a Russian hymn, "God, Preserve Thy People," and this is soon succeeded by the vividly picturesque "battle music." The fight begins, and the French at first have matters all their own way. High above the tumult are heard fragments of the "Marseillaise," but soon a theme of obvious Russian extraction appears, a folk song from the government of Novgorod, the two motives alternating as the fight gives advantage, first on one side and then on the other. As time goes on the Russian theme becomes more and more predominant, and the "Marseillaise" dies gradually away. Napolean is beaten, and his army is in retreat. The victorious Russians give themselves up to rejoicing, the famous bells of Moscow peal forth gloriously in honor of Russian victory, and the fine rhythmic melody of the national hymn is heard triumphantly thundered out. (Richard Franko Goldman, the Goldman Band)

CARL TEIKE

(Born in Altdamm, Germany, 1864 — Died in Landsberg, Germany, 1922)

The son of a blacksmith and the fourth of fourteen children, Teike is known throughout the world today as the composer of some of the best march music of his era. Among his best-known marches are *The Conqueror (Graf Zeppelin* or *Count Zeppelin), Steadfast and True (In Treue Fest),* and *Old Comrades (Alte Kameraden),* the latter being the most popular in America.

Teike began his musical studies at the age of fourteen with Paul Bottcher, conductor of the Wollin Municipal Band. At the age of nineteen he entered the army as a musician in Ulm, but after several years he resigned to become a policeman. In the meantime he had supplemented his pay by playing in local theater orchestras and had taken private music lessons, earning recognition as a march composer.

In 1895, Teike and his family moved to Potsdam where he served with the Royal Police until 1908. After recovering from a serious illness, he took a position in the post office in Landsberg. After his death, a monument was erected to his memory by the people of Landsberg. (Information from Robert Hoe, Jr., Poughkeepsie, NY)

Old Comrades March (Arr = Laurendeau; Hautvast. Pub = CF, 1908. Molenaar, 1973. Gr = 3. T = 4:00. Rec = CR-MID-70-13, Richmond, MO, H.S., Seward; LO-99459, Dutch Navy)

At the turn of the century when one went to the park to hear a band play—and that was where band music was heard for the most part—one would most certainly hear stately, stirring strains such as those found in this march. *Old Comrades* characterizes the band style of that period very well. It is the epitome of Germanic military music.

The composer, Teike, had begun his musical career as an army musician and had earned recognition as a composer of marches. But when a new bandmaster disliked his new, yet unnamed, march and suggested that he destroy it, Teike decided to resign from the army. That march is now known around the world as *Old Comrades* or *Alte Kameraden,* and Teike is remembered as its composer.

GEORG P. TELEMANN

(Born in Magdeburg, Germany, 1681 — Died in Hamburg, 1767)

Georg Philipp Telemann received no formal education in music but diligently studied the scores of the great masters, Lully and Campra in particular. He studied languages and science at the University of Leipzig, served as church organist, founded a musical society among the students, and wrote operas for the Leipzig Theater in his late teens and early twenties. Later he served as music director at Eisenach, Frankfurt, Hamburg, and Bayreuth. Telemann's immense production included forty operas, forty-four Passions, twelve complete cycles of cantatas and motets, a large number of oratorios, and many orchestral works including over 600 French-style overtures.

Suite in A Minor—Flute Solo or Soli (Arr = Reed. Pub = SO, 1965. Gr = 5. T = 12:00. Rec = SD-III, Augustana Col., Lillehaug)

The *Suite in A Minor* is rather typical of the suites written during the Baroque period. Most were collections of popular dance forms such as minuets, allemandes, courantes, sarabandes, and gigues; often highly stylized and refined. The dances were usually written in the same (or closely related) key and often performed by different instrumental combinations of the period.

Alfred Reed's arrangement for band follows closely the original score written for flute and strings. It is in authentic eighteenth century style with alternating passages between the solo instruments and the ensemble, giving each the chance to come to the fore.

JAIME TEXIDOR

(Born in England, ca. 1900 — Died in England, ca. 1950)

Jaime Texidor was a pseudonym used by a British composer, Reginald Ridewood, not a Spanish composer of paso-dobles as previously believed by musicologists. Ridewood was recognized as a gifted composer and conductor by the officers and students at Kneller Hall where he graduated as a bandmaster in 1936. He composed the widely known *Amparito Roca* for military band, as well as *Bonds of Freedom* and *Carrascosa,* arranged by Winder for brass band, while he was a British military band master. His career was cut short by death due to cancer. (Information from Major Donald Keeling, Barrie, Canada)

Amparito Roca (Arr = Winter. Pub = BH, 1935. Gr = 3. T = 3:30. Rec = CA-DT-10022, Banda Municipal de Madrid)

This work reflects all the zest and flare of the Spanish national pastime—the bullfight. The march is arranged according to the traditional formula: an introduction is followed by three rather brief strains (each repeated, with slight variations introduced) and a trio heard three times (with variations) having the usual interlude before the last statement of the trio.

RONALD THIELMAN

(Born in Chicago, Illinois, 1936)

An associate professor of music at New Mexico State University, Ronald Thielman, in addition to his teaching duties, composes and serves as a clinician and adjudicator for bands throughout much of the United States. His academic preparation includes degrees from the University of Central Arkansas (B.M.E.) and North Texas State University (M.M.E.). His honors include several commissions from high schools and colleges and an honorary doctorate from the National Conservatory of Music in Mexico City.

Chelsea Suite (Pub = LU, 1965. Gr = 3. T = 9:30)

This composition was written and dedicated to the Marianna, Arkansas, High School Band while Thielman was serving as band director at that school. The work revolves around the opening statement in the trumpets which utilizes the interval of a fourth. The three movements of the suite suggest three contrasting moods: Intrada is in the style of a prolonged fanfare; Canzone is slow and song-like in character; and Allegro features the brasses and percussion, concluding the work in a lively spirit of festivity.

VIRGIL THOMSON
(Born in Kansas City, Missouri, 1896)

Virgil Thomson received his pre-college education in public schools, spent some time in the U.S. Army during World War I, and then attended Harvard University where he developed and refined his musical talents. At Harvard he met a number of persons who helped guide his musical career. He graduated from there in 1922 and went to Paris to continue his studies, Nadia Boulanger being one of his teachers. Returning to the United States, he began serving as an organist-choirmaster and began writing as a music critic. He continued to study piano, organ, and composition privately in the United States and in Paris. In 1940 Thomson became chief music critic for the *New York Herald Tribune*. His musical output with an innate "American" quality and an "un-mannered" musical idiom has made him a controversial figure in the musical scene of the United States. Among Thomson's works are two operas, *Four Saints in Three Acts* and *The Mother of Us All,* and a suite for orchestra from his music for a documentary film, *Louisiana Story.*

A Solemn Music (Pub = GS, 1949. Gr = 4. T = 5:00. Rec = UN-4-Un. of NE, Lentz)

A Solemn Music by Virgil Thomson was composed in 1949 on a commission of the Goldman Band League of Composers. Since then it has become a frequently performed work in the contemporary band literature. Known originally for his brilliant music criticism in the *New York Herald Tribune* and for outstanding film scores, Thomson turned to the purely symphonic field after the end of World War II with such compositions as *The Seine at Night* and *A Solemn Music.* In this piece, Thomson has developed a highly personal kind of atonal music based on free adaptation of the twelve-tone row technique perfected by Arnold Schoenberg. Writing in the idiom of a chorale-dirge, Thomson has created a profoundly expressive and dramatic score. (John Wakefield, University of Maryland)

EISEI TSUJII
(Born in Osaka, Japan, 1933)

Eisei Tsujii has been familiar with the music of bands since childhood as his father, Ichitaro Tsujii, has arranged and composed music for the government-sponsored professional Osaka Municipal Band, which he conducted, for many years. Eisei Tsujii received his B.A. degree in composition from the University of Osaka School of Arts in 1957. He is now an assistant professor at Sohai Girls College and Doshisha Girls College. (Toshio Akiyama, Omiya, Saitama, Japan)

Image Sonore II—Parfum d'iris (Pub = ON, 1972. Gr = 6. T = 8:00)

Image Sonore II was commissioned by the Ongaku No Tomo Sha (meaning "musical friend") Publishing Company of Tokyo for its thirtieth anniversary in 1972. It was premiered in Osaka during that year. The music is very contemporary in nature and it reveals both the imagination and scoring skill of its composer.

Tsujii's instructions for the performance of this work remind one of some of John Cage's aleatory pieces. For example the conductor is told that there are seven fragments in the piece; the odd-numbered parts are each to be performed independently without any other overlapping part; No. 1 should be placed preferably at the beginning, while No. 7 should be at the end. After several other "chance" possibilities are given, the conductor is advised that one option is to play the parts in the order of the numbers, i.e., No. 1 through No. 7.

MONTE TUBB

(Born in Jonesboro, Arkansas, 1933)

Monte Tubb received his Bachelor of Arts degree in music from the University of Arkansas in 1956. After majoring in composition at Indiana University, he was awarded a two-year Ford Foundation Grant as composer-in-residence for the Fulton County Schools in Atlanta, Georgia. In 1966 he became an assistant professor of music at the University of Oregon. (John Wakefield, University of Maryland)

Concert Piece for Band (Pub = TP, 1969. Gr = 5. T = 4:30. Rec = CR-CBD-69-4, Un. of S. MS, Drake)

Concert Piece is a fresh and imaginative work that musically suggests, in a tongue-in-cheek manner, a protest against "The Establishment." The protesting is accomplished by employing various instrumental groups that try to speak out against "The Establishment" represented by the band. One group of a bottle, side drum, and fife, improvises on a four-note motive. Another group, including an inexperienced violin player and a guitar, attempts to play the old gospel hymn "Bringing in the Sheaves." The third protester is represented by a pianist playing a polka as fast as possible. Another kind of protest is visibly demonstrated at one point by a clarinet player who stands up and conducts the clarinet section. Though the "protesting music" may seem initially alien to the "establishment music," the musical forces eventually blend into a congruent relationship with each other. (John Wakefield, University of Maryland)

TERIG TUCCI

(Born in Buenos Aires, Argentina, 1897)

Tucci was a scholarship student at the Instituto Musical Cesi in Buenos Aires. Later he organized and directed the Orquestra de Camera "Almafuerte" in Argentina. In 1923 he came to the United States and became a musical director and arranger for radio in New York City.

La Bamba de Vera Cruz (Arr = Hunsberger. Pub = SF, 1960. Gr = 4. T = 3:00)

La Bamba is a regional dance of the state of Veracruz which is located near the Gulf of Mexico. It is danced by a girl and boy with a flirtatious mood and feeling. The girl wears a red shawl that is converted into a ribbon which lies on the floor as they (the boy and girl) dance. The boy wears all white with a red scarf around his neck. The girl wears a light, white cotton skirt and blouse and flowers in her hair to accent color. The girl also wears a black hand-embroidered apron. (Harold L. Hillyer, University of Texas at El Paso)

Lola Flores (Arr = Krance. Pub = MA, 1966. Gr = 3. T = 4:00. Rec = CRE-9009- Un. of IL, Begian)

In Spanish-speaking countries, the popularity of the paso doble (double-step) as a dance is inherent and perennial. The special spirit and melodic appeal of Terig Tucci's music has captured the imagination of international audiences. One of Tucci's most famous paso doble compositions is *Lola Flores*. Here can be found all the color and excitement of the bull-ring. One can instantly visualize the eager anticipation of the crowd and the pride and pageantry of the matadors majestically entering the ring. (John Krance)

FISHER TULL

(Born in Waco, Texas, 1934)

Fisher Tull is chairman of the department of music at Sam Houston State University at Huntsville, Texas. He holds the degree of Doctor of Philosophy in composition from North Texas State University where he was a student of Samuel Adler. He has won numerous prizes in composition, among them the Ostwald Prize sponsored by the American Bandmasters Association for his *Toccata* in 1970, the Arthur Fraser Memorial Award (Huntsville, Alabama, Symphony) for *Three Episodes for Orchestra,* and the Walter Beeler Award for 1980. Tull has written a variety of compositions for band including *March for Tripod, Terpsichore, Antiphon, Studies in Motion, Cryptic Essay, Credo,* and *The Final Covenant* in addition to the three major works described below. He is a member of ASCAP and Pi Kappa Lambda. The Tulls have two children.

Reflections on Paris (Pub = BH, 1975. Gr = 5. T = 15:00. Rec = CR-ATH-5050, Sam Houston St. Un., Mills)

A one-movement programmatic work in six sections, the composition is based on the composer's impressions of a visit to Paris in 1972. Each section portrays a famous Parisian landmark, and each can be viewed as one strolls through the center of the city.

The first section, The Louvre, is depicted with a mood of mystical awe and profound grandeur. Leaving the Louvre one may stroll through The Jardins de Tuileries with its trees, flowers, people of all ages and many nations, and busy city traffic flowing around and through it. The walk eventually leads to The Place de la Concorde, a focal point of the city and of the history of modern France. Strains of *La Marseillaise* are now heard. The Avenue des Champs-Elysees, the beautiful and very busy street steeped in French tradition, continues in a straight line to The Tomb of the Unknown Solder in the center of The Arche de Triomphe. The music pays solemn honor to the many soldiers who gave their lives for France, and then swells to a triumphal surge through the portals which have welcomed French heroes from Napolean to DeGaulle.

the Unknown Soldier in the center of the Arche de Triomphe. The music pays solemn honor to the many soldiers who gave their lives for France, and then swells to a triumphal surge through the portals which have welcomed French heroes from Napolean to DeGaulle.

Sketches on a Tudor Psalm (Pub = BH, 1971. Gr = 5. T = 10:30. Rec = CR-ATH-5050, Sam Houston St. Un., Mills)

Sketches on a Tudor Psalm is based on a sixteenth-century setting of the *Second Psalm* by Thomas Tallis. The original version was in the Phrygian mode with the melody in the tenor voice. A modern adaptation is still used today in Anglican services. Its popularity is evidenced by its employment by Vaughan Williams as the basis for his *Fantasia for String Orchestra* in 1910.

The introduction sets the harmonic character by emphasizing the juxtaposition of major and minor triads. The theme is first presented by solo alto saxophone, continued by horns, and followed by a fully-harmonized version from the brass. The variation begins to unfold in an allegro section with a melody in the clarinets which was constructed from the retrograde of the theme. Subsequently, fragments of the theme are selected for rhythmic and melodic transformation. Finally, the opening harmonic sequence returns in highly punctuated rhythms to herald the recapitulation of the theme beginning in the low woodwinds and culminating in a fully scored setting of the climactic measures. A coda continues the development as the music builds to a triumphal close on a major chord. (Boosey & Hawkes, Inc.)

(See February, 1981, *Instrumentalist* for an analysis by the composer, Ed.)

Toccata (Pub = BH, 1970. Gr = 5. T = 10:30. Rec = CR-ATH-5050, Sam Houston St. Un., Mills)

The prize-winning composition of the American Bandmasters Association Ostwald Award in 1970, this work is based on three elements: a rhythmic motive stated first by percussion; a principal theme based on a twelve-tone series in brass; and a fughetta in the woodwinds based on a variant of the principal theme. As the music unfolds, these elements appear in combination, finally climaxed by a series of repeated chords which are a harmonic realization of the twelve-tone row. The music is economically scored with vigorous percussive emphasis—an excellent and exciting work. (Boosey & Hawkes, Inc.)

JOAQUIN TURINA

(Born in Seville, Spain, 1882 — Died in Madrid, 1949)

Joaquin Turina began his musical education in Spain and completed it in France where he studied composition with Vincent d'Indy and piano with Moritz Moszkowski. He developed a new and idiomatic Spanish style for his compositions. The first work in this style was the *Procession du Rocio* which was given its première in Madrid in 1913. (Donald McGinnis, Ohio State University)

Five Miniatures (Arr = Krance. Pub = AM, 1959. Gr = 5. T = 8:30. Rec = CR-CBDNA-71-3, Northwestern St. Un., Smith)

The miniatures are titled Dawn, The Sleeping Village, Promenade, The Approaching Soldiers, and Fiesta. This set typifies the music of Joaquin Turina, one of Spain's most representative nationalist composers. His style is that of the early impressionists, but colored with Spanish characteristics. These *Five Miniatures,* transcribed for band, are taken from Turina's set of *Eight Miniatures* for piano.

La Procession du Rocio (Tr = Reed. Pub = FC, 1962. Gr = 5. T = 7:30. Rec = CR-CBDNA-78-1, Coe Col., Slattery)

The published orchestral score carries the following descriptive note by the composer:

> Every year in Seville, during the month of June, there takes place in a section of the city known as Triana, a festival called the *Procession of the Dew* in which the best families participate. They make their entry in their coaches following an image of the Virgin Mary on a golden cart drawn by oxen and accompanied by music. The people dance the *soleare* and the *seguidilla.* A drunkard sets off firecrackers, adding to the confusion. At the sound of the flutes and drums which announce the procession, all dancing ceases. A religious theme is heard and breaks forth mingling with the pealing of the church bells and the strains of the Royal March. The procession passes and as it recedes, the festivities resume, but at length they fade away.

THOMAS TYRA

(Born in Chicago, 1933)

Thomas Tyra was educated in the public schools of Cicero, Illinois. He received both baccalaureate and masters degrees from Northwestern University and a Ph.D. from the University of Michigan. He has studied composition with Robert Delaney, George B. Wilson, and Leslie Bassett.

His teaching experience has included positions in the public schools of Des Moines, Iowa, and Cicero, Illinois; the United States Navy School of Music where he was staff arranger; Louisiana State University; Eastern Michigan University; and West Carolina State University. Bands under his direction have appeared in every major post-season football bowl game except the Rose Bowl, and he has served as adjudicator, clinician, and guest conductor in many parts of the country.

His compositions and arrangements have been performed nation-wide and he has written music for many media including winds, strings, and voices.

Tyra is a member of the American Society of Composers, Authors and Publishers; the College Band Directors National Association; Phi Mu Alpha; and he is presently national secretary-treasurer for Kappa Kappa Psi. (Barnhouse Music Co.)

Two Gaelic Folk Songs (Pub = BA, 1964. Gr = 3. T = 5:30)

Thomas Tyra's arrangement of two well-known songs, "Molly Malone" and "The Wearing of the Green," prove to be delightfully fresh material for band. With its unique harmonic treatment and its colorful display of the band's best sonorities, the score is a welcome addition to the light repertoire of the modern band. The slow first section stands in interesting contrast to the spirited second part with its lively rambling woodwinds.

DAVID VAN VACTOR
(Born in Plymouth, Indiana, 1906)

A graduate of Northwestern University in Evanston, Illinois, David Van Vactor became a flutist in the Chicago Symphony Orchestra and remained in that position from 1931 to 1943. During the next two years he served as flutist and assistant conductor with the Kansas City Philharmonic. In 1947 Van Vactor headed the department of fine arts at the University of Tennessee. He has toured Latin American countries as flutist and conductor and has served on the faculty at the Universidad de Chile. His musical compositions include works for orchestra, band, choir, and instrumental solos and ensembles.

Passacaglia, Chorale, and Scamper (Pub = SU, 1966. Gr = 4. T = 12:20. Rec = CR-MID-68-8, Northshore, Wilmette, IL, Paynter)

Commissioned by the University of Tennessee Concert Band in 1963, this work, as indicated by the title, has three contrasting parts. The Passacaglia begins with the *basso ostinato* stated in lower tessitura octaves by clarinets, low reeds, and low brasses. Sixteen variations on the theme follow without pause, each variation being different in character and difficulty. The Chorale is for brass alone and provides opportunities for many dynamic contrasts. The Scamper moves briskly and straightforwardly to an exciting conclusion.

RALPH VAUGHAN WILLIAMS
(Born in Gloucestershire, England, 1872 — Died in London, 1958)

Vaughan Williams spent two years between school and university in musical study at the Royal College of Music. After taking a degree at Cambridge, he returned to the Royal College in London for further study, then visited Germany where he heard the Wagnerian music dramas and stayed to study with Max Bruch. He returned to England to receive a doctorate in music at Cambridge.

With his friend, Gustav Holst, Vaughan Williams cut the ties that had bound English music to Germany and Italy. Instead of looking for good models on the Continent these two young Englishmen decided to seek them at home in England's own past. Vaughan Williams' music speaks of things English, but it also gives the English view of things universal.

Groves Dictionary of Music and Musicians states:

> Many of the traits discernible in Vaughan Williams' music, the vein of mysticism, the blunt speech, the air of the countryman still surrounding the town dweller, will be found in the personality of the man. In particular that mixture of radicalism and traditionalism which is found not infrequently in English public life is very strong in Vaughan Williams. His unchanged and unfailing zeal for the traditional songs and dances of England belongs to the obverse side of a mind which on its reverse is radical and protestant.

English Folk Song Suite (Pub = BH, 1924. Gr = 5. T = 9:30. Rec = MG-GI-SRI-75011, Eastman, Fennell)

Ralph Vaughan Williams, one of the most eminent of contemporary English composers, is known throughout the world for his splendid choral and orchestral works. Like many modern English composers, he found great inspiration in the study of folk music and in the work of early English masters such as Purcell. He made his own the modal harmonies and striking rhythms found in the traditional folk songs of Norfolk and Somerset, but formed an entirely individual style out of these elements. Vaughan Williams' interest in the wind band has nowhere found more satisfactory expression than in this suite. The score is remarkable for its originality.and masterful instrumentation. The musical subjects are all traditional, and reflect the composer's lifelong studies in the field of folk music. This suite, originally written for band, has also been transcribed for orchestra.

The movements are titled March—"Seventeen Come Sunday"; Intermezzo— "My Bonnie Boy"; and March—"Folk Songs from Somerset."

Scherzo Alla Marcia from Symphony No. 8 (Pub = OX, 1956. Gr = 4. T = 3:45. Rec = CR-MID-78-5, Wheeling, IL, Wind Sym., Williamson)

Symphony No. 8 was written in Manchester, England, between 1953 and 1956. It exemplifies Vaughan Williams' interest in wind and percussion instruments in that this entire movement was scored for winds, brass, and percussion instruments and excluded the string section.

Sea Songs (Pub = BH, 1924. Gr = 3. T = 4:45. Rec = BM-First Series)

Vaughan Williams, like his friends Gustav Holst and Dan Godfrey, knew the band idiom well as a result of conducting bands. *Sea Songs* is one of the simpler works by Vaughan Williams, and it was written for British military band in 1924. The composer loved the folk song heritage of his native land. He also knew the English sailing songs and he used three in *Sea Songs*—"Princess Royal," "Admiral Benbow," and "Portsmouth." The form is ABCA, the scoring is direct, and the music is most rewarding for player and audience alike.

Toccata Marziale (Pub = BH, 1924. Gr = 5. T = 4:30. Rec = MG GI SRI 75011, Eastman, Fennell)

English composer Ralph Vaughan Williams is most noted for his compositions for orchestra, the theater, and chamber groups, but his works for band, like the *Folk Song Suite* and *Toccata Marziale* (both published in 1924), demonstrate his unrivalled skill in scoring for this medium. Together with the two Holst suites for band, this music forms a set which has become a traditional cornerstone of concert band literature. Composed for the Commemoration of the British Empire Exhibition of 1924, the *Toccata Marziale* is a first-rate work by any measurement. The opening is somewhat akin to a fanfare, the movement in triads being especially effective. Its contrapuntal texture is determined by the juxtaposition of brass and reed tonal masses, and occasional lyric entrances soon give way to the primary brilliance of the basic theme. Another effective phrase is that first sung by the euphonium and then by the cornet, a broad flowing theme of wide range most effective against the constant movement of the basic theme which is never completely lost. Skillfully woven together into a unified whole, even though complex in rhythmic and harmonic content, the piece exploits the fundamental properties of the band's sonority, its virtuosity color, and places emphasis upon fine gradations between long and short, forte and piano. Of real contrast with the *Folk Song Suite, Toccata Marziale* has an immense non-contrived vigor perhaps unmatched in all band literature. (Acton Ostling, Jr., University of Maryland)

GIUSEPPE VERDI
(Born in Palma, Italy, 1813 — Died in Milan, 1901)

Showing unusual musical talent at a very early age, Verdi began his studies with the village organist. After being denied entrance to the Milan Conservatory in 1832 (they felt he showed insufficient talent), Verdi studied with several private teachers. In 1839 La Scala performed *Oberto,* the first of a long line of successful operas from this master's pen. His early operas are seldom performed today, being overshadowed by the brilliance of such later works as *Aïda, Rigoletto,* and *La Traviata.* After a sixteen-year period without producing any dramatic works, Verdi, now past the age of seventy, was to create his greatest masterpieces, namely *Otello* and *Falstaff.* These last works are vastly different and superior to his earlier productions, containing greater dramatic strength, greater artistic maturity, and, perhaps more important, a singular individuality—strikingly unique in a world otherwise overwhelmingly caught up in a tide of Wagnerism. (Carl Fischer, Inc.)

La Forza del Destino Overture (Arr = Lake-Kent. Pub = CF, 1946. Gr = 5. T = 7:45. Rec = CR-4035, Golden Crest, Beeler; CR-ABA-73-4, U.S. Marine, Moore)

La Forza del Destino originally began with a prelude leading without break into the first act of the opera. For the revision, Verdi lengthened and strengthened the prelude, making it into an overture coming to a full close before the curtain rises. Built from melodic, harmonic, and rhythmic matters dealt with in the opera itself, the overture quotes and combines several of the most striking melodies as well as the ominous, opening, three-chord motive and the rapid, repeated, ascending accompaniment-figure associated in the opera with tragic destiny.

Manzoni Requiem Excerpts (Arr = Mollenhauer. Pub = FC, 1961. Gr = 5. T = 16:10. Rec = CR-4035, Golden Crest, Beeler; GC-Revelli Years, Un. of MI, Revelli)

Shortly after Rossini's death in 1861, Giuseppi Verdi proposed that the leading Italian composers be invited to jointly compose a Requiem Mass in honor of their late colleague. Upon completion it was found that the separate parts, when viewed in the aggregate, lacked the necessary qualities of unity and cohesion. The individual parts were returned to their composer and the plan abandoned. Soon thereafter, when Verdi's music was returned to him, his close friend, Alessandro Manzoni, met a tragic end. Verdi wrote an entire Mass for his friend, using some of this music as a part of the Mass.

The *Manzoni Requiem,* written under the impulse of strong emotion, is as direct a composition as the world has known. By international appraisal, this musical work is regarded as a masterpiece. Emil Mollenhaur, the illustrious Boston musician, has scored the five excerpts for band. The Latin titles are Dies Irae, Tuba Mirum, Recordare, Ingemisco, and Rex Tremandae. Some of the greatest climaxes in all music are attained in this brilliant scoring. (William P. Foster, Florida A&M University)

Nabucco Overture (Tr = Cailliet. Pub = SF, 1959. Gr = 4. T = 8:00. Rec = MG-50156, London Sym. Orch., Dorati)

Nabucco, an opera in four acts by Giuseppe Verdi, was given its premier performance at La Scala in Milan on March 9, 1842. Its success proclaimed a new hero of the Italian opera, placing Verdi in the company of the masters—Rossini, Bellini, and Donizetti. Melodies in the overture depict Verdi's affinity for fleeting tunes that seem to leave an indelible impression on the listener. The crescendo employed here, which builds over lengthy spaces, became known as the "Rossini Crescendo" and was a popular device of opera composers of the period. (John Mitchum, DeKalb College)

Triumphal March from Aïda (Arr = Seredy; Caneva. Pub = CF, 1936; HL, 1969. Gr = 4. T = 10:00. Rec = SF-10600, London Philharmonic Orch., Linz)

Aïda, one of the most theatrically effective of all Verdi operas, was commissioned by the Khedive of Egypt for the inauguration of the new Cairo Opera House, and the commemoration of the opening of the Suez Canal. The première was delayed, however, owing to numerous difficulties and was never used for the inauguration. It was first performed on Christmas Eve in 1871 and received unanimous acclaim. It is an opera which might be called a spectacle with its constant excitement, dramatic action, and colorful pageantry. The most celebrated aria from the opera is, of course, "Celeste Aïda," although the *Triumphal March* presented here and the *Ballet Music,* both from the second act, are widely performed as concert pieces the world over. (Carl Fischer, Inc.)

HEITOR VILLA-LOBOS

(Born in Rio de Janeiro, Brazil, 1887 — Died in Rio de Janeiro, 1959)

Villa-Lobos is the foremost Brazilian composer to date. He was vitally interested in the folk music of Brazil and was instrumental in setting up the music education system of Brazil, emphasizing the native songs of his country. His interest in folk music resulted from the contacts made with the Brazilian people and their music during four years of travel as a concert cellist. Later he distinguished himself as a conductor, bringing many modern works to the attention of his audiences—and constantly composing. His output of over 2,000 works includes everything from chamber music to the larger forms. His lack of formal academic training, far from hampering his development, compelled him to create a technique that is most original. (Frank Bencriscutto, University of Minnesota)

Aria from Bachianas Brasileiras No. 5 (Arr = Krance. Pub = AM, 1971. Gr = 4. T = 6:15. Rec = CR-MID-72-3, Lawrence, KS, H.S., Williams)

The prolific output of Heitor Villa-Lobos includes the *Bachianas Brasileiras* suites, a group of pieces based on original melodies patterned after the folk songs and tribal chants of the Brazilian natives treated in a Bach-like way on Latin-American instruments. The *Aria* is arranged in an AABA form, with the first and last sections being performed by the soloist on a neutral syllable. The repeat of the first section by the wind instruments is followed by the "chant":

> Lo, at midnight clouds are slowly passing, rosy and lustrous,
>   O'er the spacious heav'n with loveliness laden,
> From the boundless deep the moon arises wondrous,
>   Glorifying the evening like a beauteous maiden.
> Now she adorns herself in half unconscious duty,
>   Eager, anxious that we recognize her beauty,
>   While sky and earth, yes, all nature with applause salute her,
> All the birds have ceased their sad and mournful complaining:

Now appears on the sea in a silver reflection
Moonlight softly waking the soul and constraining
Hearts to cruel tears and bitter dejection.

(Charles H. Luedtke, Dr. Martin Luther College)

ANTONIO VIVALDI
(Born in Venice, 1678 — Died in Venice, 1741)

Vivaldi received his early training from his father, a violinist, and he completed his musical studies with Giovanni Legrenzi, the director of music at St. Mark's Cathedral in Venice. His knowledge of instruments as shown in his orchestral compositions was considered one of the best of his day, and he was an excellent violinist.

From 1704 to 1740 the conservatory at the *Ospedale della Pieta* afforded Vivaldi a marvelous field for musical experiment, and like many teachers he may have learned much from his own pupils. This institution, one of the four famous Venetian music schools for girls, played an important part in the musical life of eighteenth-century Venice. During his stay at the conservatory, recurrent asthma attacks forced him to take long leaves of absence, but he also traveled to many European cities to perform or to produce his operas when his health permitted.

Vivaldi has been considered a composer for his own instrument, the violin; his original publications are indeed primarily for that instrument (with the exception of six concertos for flute), but his unpublished manuscripts comprise many instrumental works other than for strings and numerous important vocal works. Thirty-nine operas, for example, were produced between 1713 and 1739. Many of his works for clavier and organ were transcribed by J.S. Bach.

Concerto Grosso in D Minor (Arr = Antonini-Cacavas. Pub = CA, 1968. Gr = 4. T = 8:00)

The *Concerto Grosso in D Minor* is one of Vivaldi's best-known works. Published first in 1712 as a concerto for two violins, cello, and string orchestra, the work was transcribed for organ by J.S. Bach and considered one of his original compositions for several generations. Bach studied Vivaldi's music assiduously, transcribing three of his string concertos for organ and three for harpsichord. The *Concerto Grosso in D Minor* opens with an allegro-adagio-allegro, continues with a largo, and concludes with a busy allegro.

Concerto in B-Flat for Two Trumpets (Tr = Lang; Ham. Pub = FC, 1964; Mol, 1970. Gr = 3/4. T = 8:00. Rec = AR-38-352, La Follia Orch., de la Fuente)

The Baroque trumpet that Vivaldi knew was a "natural" valveless instrument and was difficult to play as the greatest number of notes were available only in the highest register. At this time, the trumpet was closely associated with the ruling nobility and this concerto illustrates a technical brilliance typical for the day. The fast-slow-fast structure of movements is typical of most of Vivaldi's works. (Roger L. Beck, Sioux Falls College)

RICHARD WAGNER
(Born in Leipzig, 1813 — Died in Venice, 1883)

Richard Wagner led a tempestuous life, characterized by poverty, political persecution, derision, and repeated failure. An ultra-precocious child, he learned much of value concerning the stage from his step-father, Ludwig Geyer, an actor of considerable talent. Inspired to become a musician, Wagner's phenomenal progress in the study of counterpoint and his intimate knowledge of the theater created in him a desire to compose operas with a dramatic story, with orchestral parts equal to the voice parts. His first attempts were notoriously unsuccessful. His marriage to Minna Planer, in 1836, was also a failure. His radical protests during the Revolution of 1848 led to another catastrophe, his exile to Switzerland. This exile was a blessing in disguise, for it was in Switzerland that he composed many of his best operas, including *Tristan and Isolde* and sketches for *Die Meistersinger.*

Franz Liszt, one of the first to recognize the composer's genius, helped him through many crises, both emotional and financial. Another unexpected benefactor appeared in the person of the monarch of Bavaria. The young King Ludwig placed a villa in Munich at his disposal, and the Wagnerian Festivals took place in that city under the King's patronage. Wagner's dream of recognition and tranquility was finally realized. His second marriage, to Liszt's daughter, Cosima von Bulow, a woman of artistic temperament and keen understanding, was supremely happy. He spent the last year of his life quietly and comfortably in Venice. (Carl Fischer, Inc.)

Elsa's Procession to the Cathedral from Lohengrin (Arr = Cailliet. Pub = RE, 1938. Gr = 5. T = 5:00. Rec = CR-MID-72-8, Stephens Co. H.S., Toccoa, GA, Sharretts; GC-Revelli Years, Un. of MI, Revelli)

"Elsa's Procession," with its medieval color and pageantry, prefaces her betrothal to Lohengrin, mystic knight of the Holy Grail, come to deliver the people of Antwerp from the Hungarian invaders. In the operatic presentation, a large double chorus (representing the people of Antwerp) adds its song of praise to that of the orchestra. It is in this music from the opera *Lohengrin*, first performed in 1848, that we find Wagner first striking out with those intense musical thoughts which were to culminate in *Tristan*, operas of "The Ring" and *Parsifal.* In this transcription, Lucien Cailliet has succeeded in building into the instrumental framework of the modern band a true representation of all that Wagner so eloquently describes with orchestra and chorus. (John Wakefield, University of Maryland)

Entry of the Gods into Valhalla from Das Rheingold (Arr = Godfrey. Pub = BH, 1955. Gr = 3. T = 6:00. Rec = CR-MID-72-14, Cicero, NY, H.S., Fennell)

Wagner composed four operas which together were called *The Ring of the Nibelungen. Das Rheingold* is the first of the four operas. Valhalla is a great castle built with the golden treasure stolen from the Rhine and is to be the home of the gods. After the completion of Valhalla, Donner, god of thunder, mounts a rock, gathers clouds about him, and strikes the rock with his hammer. With a flash of lightning and a clap of thunder the clouds vanish, and a beautiful rainbow bridge becomes visible—spanning the valley to Valhalla. The song of the Rhine daughters is heard as they lament the loss of the Rhine gold, but the motif of Valhalla ensues and rises to a majestic climax as Wotan, ruler of the gods, triumphantly leads the procession of the gods over the rainbow bridge into the castle.

Extended Finale from Tannhauser (Arr = Mayer.   Pub = SO, 1968.   Gr = 4.
T = 13:00.   Rec = CR-4035, Golden Crest, Beeler)

The extended "Finale" is intended to be the grand climax to the opera, but it is presented in abbreviated form in productions of the music drama because the complete form is considered too tiring for audiences. The extended form presented in this arrangement for band includes an introduction, the Absolution Motif, the solemn Men's Chorus scored here for trombones, the lyric Women's Chorus scored for trumpets, and the Pilgrim's Chorus scored for full band.

The Flying Dutchman Overture (Arr = Laurendeau.   Pub = CF, 1961.   Gr = 6.
T = 13:00.   Rec = CR-CBD-69-2, N. TX St. Un., McAdow)

The Flying Dutchman concerns a man condemned to sail the seas on a ghost ship. Every seven years he is cast on shore and given the opportunity to find a wife who will be faithful to him until death. Daland, a sea captain, upon promise of treasure, accepts him as fiancé for his daughter Senta. She consents and vows eternal fidelity. In spite of the opposition of her suitor, Erik, and the Dutchman's admission of his curse, she frees him from it by throwing herself into the sea. (Lucius Wyatt, Tuskegee Institute)

Good Friday Music from Parsifal (Arr = Slocum. Pub = MI, 1962. Gr = 6. T = 8:45.
Rec = MG-50276-SR-90276, Eastman, Fennell)

The opera *Parsifal*, composed in 1882, was the last of Wagner's great musical drama works. He called it a "religious stage-consecrating festival drama." The *Good Friday Music* occurs toward the end of Act III as Parsifal is recognized as a new knight of the Holy Grail and prepares to enter the Grail Castle. The musical style is solemn and dignified to depict the conflict of good and evil in the account of the hero, Parsifal, and his defense of the Holy Grail. The score of the *Good Friday Music* has been described by historians as among "the most exalted and magnificent pages in all of Wagner's compositions."

Huldigungsmarsch (Arr = Winterbottom; Schaefer.   Pub = BH, 1904; SH, 1971.
Gr = 4.   T = 5:00.   Rec = CR-CBD-69-2, N. TX St. Un., McAdow)

Wagner wrote this march to do honor to the new King Ludwig, II, who acceded to the Bavarian throne early in 1864. Wagner composed four works for band: *Trauermarsch* in 1844, *Huldigungsmarsch* in 1864, *Kaisermarsch* in 1871, and the *Centennialmarsch* in 1876. *Huldigungsmarsch,* in true Wagnerian fashion, is more of an overture in scope than a conventional march. It is reminiscent of *Die Meistersinger,* being composed in the same period of Wagner's career. Some few years later the music was transcribed for orchestra by Joachim Raff, and through the years it has often been played in that form. The music remained in the repertoire of bands, however, and it was played by a military band at the laying of the cornerstone of the Wagner Theatre at Bayreuth in 1872.

Introduction to Act III from Lohengrin (Arr = Drumm.   Pub = CF, 1937.   Gr = 5.
T = 4:00.   Rec = CR-MID-73-7, LaSalle H.S., Peru, IL, Pontious)

Lohengrin was first produced at Weimar in 1850, under the direction of Franz Liszt. The legend of the Holy Grail was the inspiration for the story of the opera. Lohengrin, Keeper of the Holy Grail, appears as a knight in silver armor to defend

Elsa of Brabant, unjustly accused of having killed her brother Godfrey, heir to the duchy of Brabant. Victorious in combat with Telramund, Elsa's accuser, Lohengrin marries Elsa, after having extracted from her the promise that she will never inquire his name, nor descent. When she, unfortunately, breaks her promise, Lohengrin publicly reveals his identity as Keeper of the Holy Grail and announces that he is compelled to leave the earth since his identity is known. As he is about to leave in a boat drawn by a swan, Telramund's fervent supplication breaks the sorceress' spell and Godfrey appears in his original form. As Lohengrin glides away, Elsa falls, unconscious, in her brother's arms.

The present work is the instrumental introduction to the third act which is followed by the festal music for the wedding of Elsa and Lohengrin. This introduction is neither traditional nor conventional, but is a free development of two strongly contrasting themes, with an interlude on a third theme.

The second theme, a period consisting of a phrase of four measures, twice repeated, rising a third higher each time, is an exceedingly impressive one. It was of this period that Berlioz wrote:

> Nothing comparable to this can perhaps be found in all music for grandiose vigor, force and brilliancy; launched forth by the brass instruments in unison, this theme turns the strong beats (Db, F, Ab in Band) at the beginning of its three phrases, into as many cannon shots which make the listener's breast quake.

(Carl Fischer, Inc.)

Invocation of Alberich from Das Rheingold (Arr = Cailliet. Pub = SF, 1940. Gr = 4. T = 5:10. Rec = MF-U4LM-8537, Un. of Miami, Fennell)

This composition is from *Das Rheingold,* the first opera of Wagner's tetralogy, "The Ring of the Nibelungen." Alberich is a hairy and uncouth gnome who makes amorous advances to the Rhine maidens who are guarding the gold in the river. They resist his advances and so he angrily renounces love and snatches the gold away. When Alberich acquires the gold, he achieves the power to enslave all of the Nibelungen. He promptly puts his slaves to work making various items for his pleasure and profit. As the present work begins we hear the anvils of the slaves making a furious clamor. This subsides and we hear a series of leading motives representing other characters of the music drama such as Freia and the Giants. Other motives represent places such as Valhalla, material things such as the Ring, or abstract concepts such as the Spell of the Ring. Cailliet has taken the motives and thematic development out of Wagner's original setting and made his own miniature symphonic poem for band. (Gene A. Braught, University of Oklahoma)

Liebestod from Tristan and Isolde (Arr = Bainum. Pub = KJ, 1964. Gr = 4. T = 6:40. Rec = CR-MID-74-8, Fraser, MI, H.S., Okun; GC-Revelli Years, Un. of MI, Revelli)

Both the music of this transcription and the opera from which it is extracted are too well known to need description. In the band transcription the sophisticated listener will miss the voices of the celli and others strings, but remaining are the tonal sequences which sing of desire and the avowing of love. The "Love-Death" is concerned with the indomitable determination to follow into nothingness the thing that makes life—Life. In Wagner's own words, ". . . it does not express the passion love or longing of such-and-such an individual on such-and-such an occasion, but passion, love, and longing in itself."

RICHARD WAGNER

Prelude from Die Meistersinger (Arr = Tobani-Kent. Pub = CF, 1948. Gr = 5. T = 10:15. Rec = CR-CBDNA-73-2, Un. of IL, Begian)

Operatic overtures of the nineteenth century were quite obviously related to the operas of which they were a part, since they usually were a collection of themes drawn from the main body of the operas themselves and prepared in such a way as to get the audiences into the proper mood for the opera which followed.

In the *Meistersinger Overture* Wagner has supplied us with a superb introduction to his opera which conveys much of the sentimentality and joyousness of this masterpiece. Yet the overture, when used in the opera, does not stand alone as in this concert version but leads directly into the action of the first act. This blending of the overture into the opera was used in varying degrees by Wagner but has been a predominant pattern ever since the dramatic values of opera have gained equal, if not superior, status to the music. (Stanislaw Skrowaczewski, Minneapolis, Minnesota)

Rienzi Overture (Arr = Meyrelles. Pub = CF, 1892. Gr = 6. T = 10:30. Rec = U.S. Army Field; Kucinski)

During his residence in Riga—a period of alternating hope and disappointment—Wagner sketched the opera, *Rienzi,* deliberately building it on such a stupendous scale that it could only be offered to some royal theater. He had read Bulwer Lytton's *Rienzi, the Last of the Barons* and "was carried away by this picture of great political and historical event." Wagner wrote as follows in explanation of the beginning of the work: "Grand Opera, with its scenic and musical display, its sensationalism and massive effects, loomed large before my eyes; the aim of my artistic ambition was not merely to imitate it, but with reckless extravagance, to outdo it in every particular." He carried out his intentions so well that the premier performance at Dresden in 1842 lasted six hours.

The overture is based upon thematic material from the opera, beginning with the long-drawn trumpet call, followed by Rienzi's prayer. This is followed by the allegro chorus of the first act finale and the battle hymn. The second act finale is then introduced, followed by the development section, which is based chiefly on the battle hymn. A brief recapitulation of the first part occurs and a brilliant coda brings the overture to its conclusion. With a wealth of colorful music, the overture has always remained popular—principally because of one noble melody, Rienzi's prayer for the people. (Everett Kisinger, University of Illinois)

Trauersinfonie (Rev = Leidzen. Pub = AM, 1949. Gr = 4. T = 6:00. Rec = DL-8633, Goldman)

Eighteen years after the death in London of Carl Maria von Weber, a patriotic movement in Germany resulted in the transference of his remains to his native land. In December of that year (1884) an impressive ceremony took place in Dresden, in which Wagner took a leading part. Besides reading the solemn oration, Wagner composed the march for the torch-light procession. This work, scored by Wagner for large band, was based on two themes from Weber's opera *Euryanthe,* and thus represented a musical homage to the earlier composer. The score remained unpublished until 1926, and the work has remained among the least known of all Wagner's compositions. (Richard Franko Goldman, the Goldman Band)

HAROLD WALTERS

(Born in Gurdon, Arkansas, 1918)

Harold Walters graduated from Little Rock High School, received his additional musical training at the Cincinnati Conservatory of Music, American University, and the Washington College of Music, and is now known the world over for his works for band. After serving in the United States Navy Band as chief arranger for almost six years, he conducted and wrote professionally for the next few years in Washington, D.C., and New York City for theater, newsreels, and various orchestras, for example the Sigmund Romberg Orchestra. For more than twenty years Walters has been associated with the Rubank Music Publishing Company as editor, composer, and arranger. He has written and published over 600 compositions and arrangements for band. (Rubank, Inc.)

Instant Concert (Pub = RU, 1970. Gr = 3. T = 3:10. Rec = CR-MID-70-10, Vander-Cook Col., Brittain)

Harold Walters has used melodies found on band concert programs the world over and condensed them into an *Instant* performance of three minutes and ten seconds. Most of the melodies are presented consecutively; however, there are places where two melodies are used contrapuntally. Listeners are often challenged to count the melodies recognized during the first performance and confirm their estimate as each "melody section" of the band stands during the repeat.

WILLIAM WALTON

(Born in Oldham, England, 1902)

Despite early acquaintance with eminent teachers, it may be said that Walton was virtually self-taught, for, showing exceptional promise as he did, his teachers were willing to let him go his own way, giving him guidance only when really necessary. Thomas Strong, dean of Christ Church, exerted his influence in enabling Walton to receive a baccalaureate degree in music at the exceptionally early age of sixteen. From that time on he was entirely self-taught.

Walton composed *Façade* in 1922 and *Crown Imperial* in 1937. He reworked *Façade* as *Suite No. 1* in 1926, and as *Suite No. 2* in 1938. Other works include a symphony, concertos, various other orchestral works, choral works, chamber music, a violin and piano sonata, and numerous songs. Among his many honors as a leading twentieth-century English composer was the reception of an honorary doctoral degree in music from the University of Oxford in 1942. He was knighted in 1951 and received the Order of Merit in 1968.

Crown Imperial March (Arr = Duthoit. Pub = BH, 1937. Gr = 4. T = 9:45. Rec = MG-SRI-75028, Eastman, Fennell; CR-ABA-73-4, U.S. Marine, Dunn)

This work, commissioned for the coronation of King George VI, was first performed at the coronation ceremony in 1937. The enormous vitality of the music finds ample breadth of sound in this brilliant coronation march. The first section has a quiet but rhythmic opening which gradually builds to a brilliant climax. This gives way to a broad and stately melody which is typically English in its majestic sonority. (Boosey & Hawkes, Inc.)

Façade (Arr = O'Brien. Pub = OX, 1969. Gr = 3. T = 25:00. Rec = CR-4040, The Burke-Phillips All-Star, Cailliet)

In 1922, William Walton composed a "melodrama" for seven instruments and reciting voice. The text was a series of sixteen abstract poems by Edith Sitwell. At the first performance, the text was recited, sing-song style, by Miss Sitwell from behind a curtain on which was painted a huge face with a megaphone mouth. From this music Walton later extracted two orchestral suites. The music is, as David Ewen has noted, filled with "parody, burlesque, mock seriousness, tongue-in-cheek sentimentality, and calculated cliches." The five movements included in this suite are Fanfare and Scotch Rhapsody, Popular Song, Jodelling Song, Old Sir Faulk, and Polka. This arrangement for band is by Robert O'Brien. (Thomas Tyra, Eastern Michigan University)

ROBERT WARD

(Born in Cleveland, Ohio, 1917)

Robert Ward studied composition at the Eastman School of Music, the Juilliard School of Music, and the Berkshire Music Center at Tanglewood where he was a student of Aaron Copland. He has served on the faculties of Columbia University and the Juilliard School of Music, and was music director of the Third Street Music School Settlement in New York. Later, he became managing editor of Galaxy Music Corporation and Highgate Press.

From 1967 to 1974 he was president and chancellor of the North Carolina School of the Arts. At present he serves on the boards of the National Opera Institute and the American Symphony Orchestra League in addition to his full-time schedule of composing and conducting. Ward has been awarded the Pulitzer Prize in Music, three Guggenheim Fellowships, and numerous commissions to compose. His published works include compositions for orchestra, band, choir, and various other media. He is married, has five adult children, and two grandchildren.

Jubilation Overture (Arr = Leist. Pub = GA, 1958. Gr = 4. T = 7:00)

The overture, *Jubilation,* was written in 1944-45, while Ward was bandmaster of the 7th Infantry Band which took part in the campaigns of Leyte and Okinawa. The overture does not reflect the grim atmosphere of war, but rather the hope and optimism that the conflict would soon be over. The work was first performed in 1946 by the National Orchestral Association conducted by Leon Barzin. The band transcription was made by Robert L. Leist at the request of the composer. (Richard Franko Goldman, the Goldman Band)

SAMUEL A. WARD

(Born in Newark, New Jersey, 1847 — Died in Newark, 1903)

An American composer of the latter part of the nineteenth century, Ward's only lasting composition is "Materna," a hymn tune published in 1892 in the *Episcopal Hymnal.* The melody was composed ca. 1882 as a setting for a hymn (set of words) written a century or more prior to that time, the text of which begins "O Mother Dear, Jerusalem." Ward's music survives today because of a marriage of his melody to the poetry of Katherine Lee Bates, a professor of English at Wellesley College in

New England, who was inspired to write the words in 1893 after her first visit to Pike's Peak. Traces of this inspiration are shown in such phrases as "spacious skies" and "purple mountain majesties."

America the Beautiful (Arr = Dragon. Pub = SF, 1963. Gr = 4. T = 4:30. Rec = SD-IV, Augustana Col., Lillehaug)

The poem "America the Beautiful" by Katherine Lee Bates was published in a magazine in 1894. The words were set to numerous tunes, but the melody that suited best was Samuel A. Ward's "Materna," which is still identified by that title in today's hymnbooks although the title of the hymn (the music and the words) is "America the Beautiful." So closely are these words and music associated by Americans today, that they usually assume that the two were conceived together. (Ed.)

Carmen Dragon, the arranger of this work, is a conductor, composer, arranger, music educator, and a radio and television personality—a complete musician. As music director-conductor of the Glendale, California, Symphony Orchestra, he has brought new excitement and personality to the Los Angeles concert scene. He has composed and conducted scores to thirty motion pictures and has released fifty-seven best-selling record albums. Personable, gregarious, at home in all areas of public performance, at ease before audiences young and old, Dragon is among the nation's most respected and beloved musicians. (Music Educators National Conference Convention Program, 1964)

DAVID WARD-STEINMAN
(Born in Alexandria, Louisiana, 1936)

David Ward-Steinman, winner of more than thirty awards, fellowships, grants, and honors, filled an appointment by the Ford Foundation Contemporary Music Project in 1970-72, as composer-in-residence for the Tampa Bay area at the University of South Florida. Following this commitment he returned to San Diego State University where, since 1961, he has been professor of music and was a recipient of the Outstanding Professor Award of the California State Universities and Colleges, given annually by the trustees to two of the 9,000 professors in the state system.

Among Ward-Steinman's distinguished teachers in the study of composition were John Boda, Nadia Boulanger, Wallingford Riegger, Darius Milhaud, and Milton Babbitt. He received his B.S. degree *cum laude* from Florida State University, and his M.M. and D.M.A. degrees from the University of Illinois.

His compositions cover all areas of music, including electronic and aleatory, and reflect his imaginative exploration of musical form. (Edward B. Marks Music Corp.)

Jazz Tangents (Pub = SF, 1969. Gr = 4. T = 12:00. Rec = CR-CBD-69-3, Peabody, Romersa)

Commissioned by the University of North Dakota Wind Ensemble, *Jazz Tangents* uses the rhythmic feel and harmonic vocabulary of modern jazz as a vehicle for an extended band work. It uses the jazz medium, combined with the more rigid aspects of formal construction. The central section of the final movement is a series of improvised jazz solos based on a twelve-bar blues chord progression. The movement titles reflect the idiom: With Tension—Fast and Swinging, Slow and Free, and Fast and Swinging. (Thomas Tyra, Eastern Michigan University)

ROBERT WASHBURN
(Born in Bouckville, New York, 1928)

Robert Washburn received his B.S. and M.S. degrees from the State University College of New York in Potsdam, where he is now professor of music. After four years in the United States Air Force he completed a Ph.D. in composition at the Eastman School of Music. He studied with Bernard Rogers and Alan Hovhaness at Eastman and later with Darius Milhaud at Aspen, and Nadia Boulanger in Paris.

In 1959-60 Washburn was composer-in-residence in Elkhart, Indiana, under a Ford Foundation Young Composers Grant. Additional honors include a full-year grant from the Danforth Foundation, a resident fellowship at the MacDowell Colony, a State University Research Foundation Summer Grant, a scholarship to attend the Bennington Composers Conference, and a recent invitation to participate in the Juilliard Repertory Project. He has received annual awards from ASCAP since 1961. Washburn's works have been performed by numerous leading ensembles here and abroad. (Oxford University Press)

Burlesk for Band (Pub = BH, 1961. Gr = 3. T = 2:30)

Burlesk for Band contains elements of humor and satire, such as unexpected changes of key, dissonances, "wrong notes" and suggestions of familiar tunes. The general mood of the work is light-hearted. After a more reflective and tranquil middle section, the humorous spirit returns. (Boosey & Hawkes, Inc.)

March—Opus '76 (Pub = BH, 1976. Gr = 4. T = 4:00. Rec = CR-ATH-5052, Crane, Maiello)

A commission of the New York State School Music Association to commemorate the Bicentennial and to honor Dean Harrington for his thirty-two years of service to the organization, *March—Opus '76* is a spirited concert march. It is in a contemporary idiom with an eighth-note series based on 1-7-7-6—1-9-7-6 of the major scale. (Boosey & Hawkes, Inc.)

Symphony for Band (Pub = OX, 1967. Gr = 4. T = 15:00. Rec = CR-CBDNA-71-6, Sam Houston St. Un., Mills)

Symphony for Band is in a traditional three-movement pattern. The first movement presents fragments of several themes in the slow introduction which later become fully presented, expanded, and combined in various contrapuntal manipulations. The second movement is in a large ABA design with a number of solo passages for the winds. The final movement employs asymmetric rhythmic groupings to some extent and again uses several contrapuntal devices to combine the various melodic and harmonic aspects of the movement. (Robert Washburn, The State University College at Potsdam)

CARL M. VON WEBER
(Born in Eutin, Germany, 1786 — Died in London, 1826)

Weber's childhood was concerned with a constant struggle between his music practice and a congenital hip-joint disease which prevented him from normal boyhood activities. He studied piano and violin with Michael Haydn in Salzburg and Abt Volger in Vienna. His ambitious father exposed the boy's talents in concerts all over Europe until the death of his mother finally stopped the exhausting tours and young Weber entered the choir-boys school in Salzburg.

Founder of the German romantic opera, Weber also takes high rank as a composer of concertos. When Mozart introduced the clarinet into the higher levels of music it rapidly became a favorite solo instrument. Weber was a great friend and admirer of Heinrich Baerman, the leading clarinetist of his day, and for Baerman, Weber wrote, among other works for clarinet, *Concertino for Clarinet* and the *Second Grand Concerto in E-Flat*.

Concertino, Op. 26—Clarinet Solo (Arr = Brown; Reed. Pub = BH, 1905; KN, 1962. Gr = 4/5. T = 8:10. Rec = CR-NBA-78-11, Kiel Mun., Thiessen)

Concertino, Op. 26 by Weber is one of the great works of the clarinetists' repertoire. Its first performance was on April 5, 1811, and the concert was such a success that the composer was commissioned to write two more selections for the clarinet. These fine works brought even greater fame to Weber, already a highly respected composer, and established the clarinet as a leading instrument for the expression of Romantic music. This concertino to this day remains the most popular solo in the clarinetists' repertoire.

The work opens with a slow introduction and proceeds to a leisurely theme followed by several contrasting variations.

Overture Euryanthe (Arr = Safranek. Pub = CF, 1915. Gr = 6. T = 9:30. Rec = AN-36175, Philadelphia Orch., Klemperer)

Although Weber wrote in various forms, his most inspired creative effort was directed toward opera. The overtures to his three greatest operas, *Der Freischutz, Euryanthe,* and *Oberon* have become favorites of the concert-going public and are mainstays of the standard orchestral repertoire.

The plot of Euryanthe is based on a variant of the "maligned wife" theme. Shakespeare used virtually the same story in "Cymbeline." *Euryanthe* was written in August 1823, and was last heard at the Metropolitan in 1914 with Toscanini conducting, but the overture has remained as a durable symphonic masterwork.

Second Concerto for Clarinet (Arr = Brown. Pub = BH, 1949. Gr = 4/5. T = 23:30. Rec = IL-38, Un. of IL, Hindsley)

The second and third movements are the more frequently performed portions of this concerto. The second movement Romanza is chiefly a test of sustained, expressive playing, although the middle section contains both animation and recitative. The concluding Polacca is a sparkling rondo with Polish dance rhythms. It is carefully constructed and a well-varied concerto for clarinet and band.

JAROMIR WEINBERGER

(Born in Prague, Czechoslovakia, 1896 — Died in St. Petersburg, Florida, 1967)

Weinberger studied with Hofmeister at the Prague Conservatory and with Reger in Leipzig. He taught for a semester at the conservatory in Ithaca, New York, in 1922, then returned to Europe to teach and compose. He lived in Prague most of the time until 1939 when he settled in St. Petersburg, Florida. He was best known for the work which brought him fame, the highly successful opera, *Schwanda, the Bagpiper.* Weinberger has, however, composed in many other forms, and his style represents a combination of modern idioms and traditional forms. His other works which have been transcribed or written for band include: *Czech Rhapsody, Homage to the Pioneers, Mississippi Rhapsody,* and *Prelude to the Festival.*

Polka and Fugue from Schwanda (Arr = Bainum. Pub = AMP, 1961. Gr = 5. T = 8:00. Rec = CR-CBDNA-73-1, Un. of IL, Kisinger)

The opera, *Schwanda the Bagpiper,* premiered in Prague in 1927 and became internationally famous. The *Polka and Fugue,* taken from the opera for use as a concert piece, has become even more successful.

Based on a Czech folk tale, the story involves Schwanda, the master bagpiper, and Babinsky, a robber who leads Schwanda on a series of adventures. The polka is taken from a scene in which Schwanda plays for Queen Iceheart who is waiting for someone who can melt her heart. His irresistable playing does the trick, and the queen and Schwanda decide to get married—sealing their vow with a kiss. However, Schwanda is already married so the marriage to the queen is called off. In response to his wife's questions of his fidelity, he cries, "If I have given the queen a single kiss, may the Devil take me"—and the Devil does. He is rescued from hell, however, by Babinsky, who plays cards with the Devil and wins everything he owns. He returns it all in exchange for Schwanda who plays the fugue on his bagpipe before he leaves, so that the servants of hell may hear the playing of a master bagpiper.

LAWRENCE WEINER
(Born in Cleveland, Ohio, 1932)

Though Weiner was born in Ohio, he acquired all his formal musical training at the University of Texas where he received the B.M. and M.M. degrees, majoring in composition. He was a member of the Fourth U.S. Army Band, Ft. Sam Houston, Texas, and performed the duties of composer, arranger, conductor, and piano soloist with the band. Weiner is presently a music educator in the San Antonio area. (Ludwig Music Publishing Co.)

Atropos (Pub = LU, 1966. Gr = 3. T = 4:00)

Atropos was one of the three Greek mythological goddesses of Fate; the first spun the thread of life, the second cast the lots, and Atropos, the third, cut the thread of life when she determined that it was long enough.

This composition, a scherzo for band, is an exciting work which portrays in sound the drama of Atropos' act. It captures the spirit and mood of the event—its agitation and restlessness and sense of inevitability. Though it is composed essentially of two basic motives or ideas, this work treats these in a variety of ways, employing among other things the use of sudden contrast with dynamics, texture, harmonies, and rhythm.

Atropos was first performed at a benefit concert for the John Philip Sousa Memorial at the National Cultural Center in Washington, D.C. (Ludwig Music Publishing Co.)

FLOYD WERLE
(Born in Billings, Montana, 1929)

Floyd Werle attended the University of Michigan and later entered the U.S. Air Force. Serving as chief arranger of the United States Air Force Band in Washington, D.C., he made many contributions to band literature through publications for that media. Both transcriptions and original compositions for band are among his writings.

Sinfonia Sacra—Symphony No. 1 (Ms., 1970. Gr = 5. T = 15:00. Rec = CR-CBDNA-71-7, U.S. Air Force, Gabriel)

Werle believes that contemporary composers and conductors of band works have tried to imitate the "artistic atmosphere and questionable programming practices" of the European-oriented symphony orchestra with disastrous results as shown by diminishing audiences and a failure to instill any interest in repertoire, band or otherwise. The following comments regarding *Sinfonia Sacra* were selected from a paper prepared by Werle for the 1971 meeting of the College Band Directors National Association:

> I am posing the same question to the 1970 symphonic band with *Sinfonia Sacra* that George Gershwin posed to the 1925 symphony orchestra with the *Piano Concerto in F*. The status of *Sinfonia Sacra* as a great work of art is, to my mind, secondary in importance to its being fun for the musicians to play and for an audience to hear. I frankly have written it because I am fed up to the teeth with two ascending perfect fourths followed by a descending minor third attempting to pass itself off as great art.
>
> *Sinfonia Sacra* is an extended work of full symphonic proportions. The title of this work is by no means facetious or ironic. The entire thematic material is derived from well known hymn tunes of various denominations; the title of each movement is also the name of the hymn tune which constitutes the principal or first tune. Of course other such tunes are used throughout besides those listed, but only one of these appears in anything resembling its original form—the "De Profundis" chant of William Croft is used for the passacaglia in the fourth movement.
>
> Each movement of the work can be classified as a "chorale fantasia" or "chorale prelude." There may be those who cannot conceive that these movements could be utilized as preludes, offertories, and voluntaries in a service of divine worship. These may be shocked to learn that they have already been utilized, and successfully, as such. Any opinions to the contrary, this is a piece having its origins in church and applied in its ministry. Maybe *Sinfonia Sacra* is not the right answer (to the repertoire problem), but it is my hope that it will either point in that direction or make somebody mad enough to go out and put forth some effort to find the right one.

PAUL WHEAR
(Born in Auburn, Indiana, 1925)

Paul Whear studied at Marquette, DePauw, Boston, and Western Reserve Universities, earning a doctoral degree from the latter university. He taught music at Mount Union College in Alliance, Ohio, and later moved to Doane College in Crete, Nebraska, where he directed the band and served as chairman of the music department. He is presently resident composer on the faculty of Marshall University and chairman of the theory-composition division of that institution. In addition, he serves on the theory-composition faculty of the National Music Camp at Interlochen, Michigan, and is conductor of the Huntington Chamber Orchestra and the Ohio University orchestras.

Whear has received thirteen annual ASCAP Serious Music Awards, two awards from the National Endowment for the Arts, a Japan Bandmasters Association Citation, and numerous other honors as a composer. He has written two operas, two symphonies for orchestra, three oratorios, three string quartets, and numerous other compositions for various media.

Antietam (Pub = LU, 1966. Gr = 4. T = 10:00. Rec = LU-1659, Capital Un.)

Antietam, in the fall of 1862, was the hardest-fought battle of the American Civil War. Though it was not a decisive victory for either side, it had a very important bearing on the outcome of the war. At this little creek in Maryland, the invasion of the North by the Confederate Army under General Lee was stopped. This battle also provided Lincoln with the opportunity for which he had been waiting, to issue the Emancipation Proclamation.

The composition, *Antietam,* was the prize winner of the first Kent State University composition competition. (Ludwig Music Publishing Co.)

Jedermann (Pub = LU, 1962. Gr = 3. T = 5:30)

A composition of medium difficulty for junior high school bands, this composition contains rhythmic interest and lyric melody in simple ABA form. The title was inspired by the production of the morality play *Everyman* presented in Salzburg, Austria, each year. (Paul Whear, Marshall University)

Wycliffe Variations (Pub = LU, 1969. Gr = 4. T = 9:30. Rec = CR-MID-69-8, Northshore Band, Wilmette, IL, Paynter)

Commissioned by the Wickliffe, Ohio, Community Association for the Wickliffe High School Band, Charles Frank, conductor, this set of variations is based on the well-known hymn tune "Stuttgart" from the *Psalmodia Sacra, Gotha,* 1715. The introduction uses the first four tones of the theme, first stated in baritones and tubas immediately following the short introduction. Five variations follow, the last of which forms the finale and restates the theme, slightly altered, in canonic form amidst fanfares. (Ludwig Music Publishing Co.)

KENNETH G. WHITCOMB

(Born in Battle Creek, Michigan, 1926)

Kenneth Whitcomb (George Kenny) is a composer who is interested in a wide variety of styles as a performer and as an arranger, as well as a composer of original works. Whitcomb grew up in the Midwest where he studied saxophone with Santy Runyon in Chicago, then moved to California where he studied film scoring with Eddy Manson in Los Angeles and received an Associate in Arts at Fullerton College. Since that time he has done free lance arranging for bands, orchestras, choruses, and various small ensembles, and has performed with various groups as a saxophone and woodwind specialist. At the present time he is an arranger and featured performer with the Disneyland Band in Anaheim, California.

Whitcomb's principal band works include an elementary band method written in collaboration with Barbara Buehlman, *Sessions in Sound;* a concert march, *Jet Stream;* a descriptive piece for young bands, *Stonehenge;* and an overture, *St. Elmo's Fire.* Works for other media range from *Gettysburg* for orchestra to *Space Dust* for stage band.

Coat of Arms March (Pub = SB, 1957. Gr = 4. T = 4:00)

This is one of the few marches that seems to work well at a slow tempo for commencement, a moderate tempo for a halftime routine, or a faster tempo for a concert. With interesting parts for all performers, different sections of the band may be featured ad lib. Whitcomb's (in this instance, Kenny) experience as a performer helps to make this march practical for the performers and enjoyable for the listeners.

DONALD H. WHITE

(Born in Narberth, Pennsylvania, 1921)

Donald H. White received the B.S. degree in music education from Temple University and the M.M. and the Ph.D. degrees from the Eastman School of Music. He also studied composition at the Philadelphia Conservatory of Music. His studies in composition have been under the direction of Howard Hanson, Bernard Rogers, Vincent Persichetti, and Herbert Elwell. White has written works in a variety of media—orchestra, symphonic band, chamber ensembles, choral works, and solo instruments. He is currently professor of music and chairman of the department of theory and composition at DePauw University.

Ambrosian Hymn Variants (Pub = LU, 1974. Gr = 3. T = 6:00. Rec = CR-MID-74-9, Cambridge, OH, H.S., Treier)

The composition opens with the theme, an ancient Ambrosian hymn used in the great church of Milan. The theme is followed by a set of four variations, the first of which is set in a lively 2/4 meter and makes use of contrapuntal imitation. Variation 2 is somber and establishes a religious mood commencing with sustained brass tones followed by woodwind and finally full band sounds. Variation 3 is in a fast 6/8 with duple rhythms interspersed into the melodic and chordal lines. The final variation follows variation 3 without pause and is announced by the trombones in unison punctuated by full band passages. The entire band then takes over the theme to build to the brilliant ending.

Dichotomy (Pub = TE, 1966. Gr = 4. T = 7:20. Rec = CO-S-1258, OH St. Un., McGinnis)

Premiered by the Grimsley High School Band in Greensboro, North Carolina, in April, 1965, with the composer conducting, *Dichotomy* was selected as the work to represent the North Central Division of the College Band Directors National Association at the 1967 national conference in Ann Arbor, Michigan. The following remarks concerning the composition are included with the score:

> In effect, the work is more than a single dichotomy, for this principle exists in the work with respect to tempi, dynamic contrast, and in scoring for opposing groups of instruments. It is set in traditional slow-fast-slow formal design with a quiet opening and conclusion.

Miniature Set for Band (Pub = TE, 1964. Gr = 4. T = 11:30. Rec = IL-37, Un. of IL, Hindsley)

Miniature Set was composed late in 1957 and first performed by the DePauw University Concert Band in March, 1958. Later that year the work was voted "the most outstanding contribution to the band's literature for 1958" by the College Band Directors National Association.

The collection has five brief movements titled Prelude, Monologue, Interlude, Dialogue, and Postlude. Each exploits a minute idea; a sonority, a melodic fragment, a rhythm, etc. The second movement features a contemplative solo by the flute, while the fourth movement engages solo trumpet and French horn in dialogue. These solo movements are set apart and enclosed by miniatures calling on the resources of the symphonic band. (Harold L. Hillyer, University of Texas at El Paso)

(See Spring, 1978, *Journal of Band Research* for an analysis by the composer, Ed.)

Patterns for Band (Pub = EV, 1969. Gr = 6)

Patterns is an attempt to exploit the coloristic palette of the modern band, in both transparent and thick textures. The composer's thorough knowledge of band-instrument color is evident in this attractive, contemporary work.

MAURICE WHITNEY
(Born in Glens Falls, New York, 1909)

Maurice Whitney earned degrees from Ithaca College and New York University. He attended Teachers College, Columbia University, the Westminister Choir School, and the New England Conservatory. A performer, a conductor, and an arranger of music for dance and theater orchestras, he has served as choir director and organist in churches, taught in school systems and colleges, and served in positions of leadership for music education. His works include theory and band texts and scores for small instrumental ensembles, band, and choir.

Whitney's professional honors include a citation from Ithaca College for outstanding work in music education, New York State Teacher of the Year award, and an honorary doctorate from Elmira College. He is retired and lives in Sun City Center, Florida.

Introduction and Samba—Saxophone Solo (Pub = BO, 1951. Gr = 4. T = 5:00.
Rec = IL-83, Gregory W. Un. of IL, Begian)

Introduction and Samba is dedicated to saxophone virtuoso Sigurd Rascher. The
range and delicacy of the instrument is exploited to excellent advantage.

CHARLES E. WILEY

(Born in Abilene, Texas, 1925)

Charles "Pete" Wiley came from a band oriented family; his father and uncle
were both famous college band directors in the states of Texas and Kansas, respectively. Charles Wiley started clarinet lessons at age nine but soon changed to oboe,
which he has continued to play, and teach, during his music career. His college
career was interrupted by military service time as a navigator in the navy during
World War II. He returned to college (Texas Tech) after the war and received a
degree in mathematics. After changing to a music curriculum at the Universities of
Kansas and Texas, he earned his masters degree at the latter university in 1950 and
later a doctorate at the University of Colorado.

Wiley went to Lamar University (then Lamar Technical College) in 1952 and
found a band of twenty students. At present the instrumental program includes 350
students in the marching band, 100 in the concert band, and ninety in the symphonic
band. Under Wiley's guidance, the Lamar University Bands have performed for
numerous national conferences and nationally-televised football games. In 1972, the
Board of Regents awarded Wiley a $2,000 cash prize and the lifetime title of Regent's
Professor for his distinguished teaching. In 1974, with the assistance of his wife,
Wiley founded the TRN Publishing Company—the name, "That's Really Nice,"
typifies his droll sense of humor. His compositions and his arrangements bear the
imprint of a talented musician with practical experience.

Antonito (Pub = TN, 1973. Gr = 4. T = 3:45. Rec = CR-MID-77-10, VanderCook
Col., Zajec; TN Promotion Record, Lamar Un., Wiley)

This pasodoble (two-step) has the expected Spanish-American flavor from the
strong introduction straight through to the finale. The "march" begins in the key of
F minor but modulates to the major key of A-flat during a triumphal sounding transition. The low woodwinds and brasses are challenged throughout to play their parts
with precision. The attractive countermelodies, the surprising phrase lengths, and
contrasting dynamics also help to maintain interest in this excellent pasodoble for
band.

Old Scottish Melody (Pub = TN, 1977. Gr = 3. T = 2:30. Rec = CR-MID-77-7, Victoria, TX, H.S., Junkin)

The melody for this arrangement is the old Scottish tune, "Auld Lang Syne,"
scored for band in the style of Percy Grainger's *Irish Tune from County Derry*. In-
tellectual music is for the head; rhythmic music is for the feet; this expressive
arrangement by Wiley is for the heart.

CLIFTON WILLIAMS
(Born in Traskwood, Arkansas, 1923 — Died in Miami, 1976)

Clifton Williams' early musical experience was in school bands and orchestras of Malvern and Little Rock, Arkansas. His formal education in music composition included studies at Louisiana State University with Helen Gunderson and at the Eastman School of Music with Bernard Rogers and Howard Hanson. A member of the faculty at the University of Texas in Austin for seventeen years, he became chairman of the department of theory-composition at the University of Miami School of Music in 1966.

Most widely acclaimed as a composer of serious music for the concert wind band, he composed in many forms and his prizes, awards, and honors were numerous. Of particular import is the continuing impact of his work upon the standard of literature for school, college, and military concert bands. His compositions in this medium have become basic repertory for American, Canadian, European, and Japanese bands.

In addition to his many other honors, those most recently listed include election to membership in the American Bandmasters Association, appointment to the Ostwald Memorial Band Music Competition Committee, appointment as Governor of Province 13, Phi Mu Alpha Sinfonia National Professional Music Fraternity, and the honorary degree of Doctor of Music conferred by the National Conservatory of Music at Lima, Peru.

The musical idiom of Williams' music is conservative, and yet contemporary in concept. His use of modern instrumentation was skillful and delights those who perform it as well as the listener. His early and untimely death brought an end to one of the most creative talents of the past two decades. (Logan O. Turrentine, Hialeah, Florida, High School)

Air Force Band of the West March (Pub = SO, 1965. Gr = 4. T = 3:30)

A concert march, the *Air Force Band of the West* was written for and dedicated to Lt. Col. Samuel Kurtz, U.S.A.F. Retired, to coincide with his retirement from the United States Air Force on October 31, 1964. Kurtz served as a military band leader for over twenty-one years and is nationally known for his work with the Air Force Band of the West at Lackland (San Antonio), Texas. He initiated the band name during his first tour of duty at Lackland Air Force Base. (Harold L. Hillyer, University of Texas at El Paso)

Caccia and Chorale (Pub = BA, 1976. Gr = 3. T = 6:45. Rec = CR-MID-76-10, VanderCook Col., Zajec)

Clifton Williams provided the following program note on this work:

> While it remains open to question whether music can convey any message other than a purely musical one, composers often tend to attempt philosophical, pictorial, or other aspects within a musical framework. Such is the case with *Caccia and Chorale,* two title words borrowed from Italian because of their allegorical significance. The first, Caccia, means hunt or chase, and is intended to reflect the preoccupation of most people in the world with a constant pursuit of materialism. The Chorale is, by contrast, an urgent and insistent plea for greater humanity, a return to religious or ethical concepts.

Knowing the seriousness of his illness when he began this work and feeling that he might not survive an impending operation, Williams intended to write only the *Caccia*. However the surgery seemed to be successful and the Chorale movement was thus composed as a personal prayer of thanksgiving along with a sincere plea for ethical regeneration by all mankind. (Joseph M. Tate, Barbe High School, Lake Charles, Louisiana).

Concertino for Percussion and Band (Pub = SB, 1960.   Gr = 4.   T = 8:00. Rec = IL-27, Un. of IL, Hindsley)

William F. Ludwig, Sr., president of the Ludwig Manufacturing Company, commissioned this work as part of an endless campaign to raise the standards of percussion performance and to better the appreciation for the art of drumming. The composition is demanding of high performance from the percussion section as can well be heard in the cadenza in the middle of the piece. Each member of the percussion section must be capable of performing on several different instruments. Instruments called for are: timpani, snare drum, tenor drum, bass drum, tom-toms, small cymbals, crash cymbals, suspended cymbals, triangle, bells, chimes, and gong. (Donald A. Stanley, Mansfield State College)

Dedicatory Overture (Pub = EM, 1964.   Gr = 4.   T = 8:00.   Rec = CO-955, Un. of MD, Ostling)

Dedicatory Overture was commissioned by Epsilon Upsilon Chapter of Phi Mu Alpha Sinfonia National Honorary Music Fraternity at Evansville College (Indiana), for use in services dedicating a new music building. A concert overture in form, *Dedicatory Overture* employs the composer's own setting of the Evansville College Alma Mater hymn contrasted with much original material. (Blase S. Scarnati, Slippery Rock State College)

Dramatic Essay—Trumpet Solo (Pub – SU, 1958.   Gr – 3/4.   T – 4:40.   Rec – CR-MID-77-12, DiMartino w. Clark H.S., Winchester, KY, Campbell)

Commissioned by the educational services department of the Conn Corporation, *Dramatic Essay* was written especially for Don Jacoby, who, at that time, was representing the Conn Corporation as a clinician and trumpet soloist. The work is indeed a dramatic dialogue between the soloist and the band.

Fanfare and Allegro (Pub = SU, 1956.   Gr = 5.   T = 5:45.   Rec = MG-75094, Eastman, Fennell)

Fanfare and Allegro was the first composition to win the Ostwald Award for original band literature. The award was presented at the American Bandmasters Association convention in 1956. It is written in an exciting contemporary style with brilliant scoring. The work opens with a declamatory fanfare section which leads directly to the allegro movement. It features ostinato figures, brilliant brass, and percussion. Although rhythmically complex, the music is impressive and straightforward, and its resonance and sonority are ideally suited to the medium of the modern band.

Festival (Pub = SU, 1962. Gr = 5. T = 5:35. Rec = CT-1502, OH St. Un., McGinnis)

Festival was composed in 1961 for band and orchestra simultaneously. A "tour de force" in instrumentation, the objective of this show-piece was to generate a festive mood—one of gaiety and excitement. This is a tightly knit composition, with both the fast and slow sections based on the same thematic material.

Laredo (Pub = SO, 1964. Gr = 3. T = 3:50. Rec = IL-XCSV-126554, Un. of IL)

At the suggestion of Elmo Lopez, supervisor of instrumental music in the Laredo (Texas) public schools, this Spanish two-step was composed as a gesture to the international friendship existing between the sister cities of Laredo, Texas, and Nuevo Laredo, Mexico. The cities responded by naming May 4, 1963, "Clifton Williams Day," with a parade and other honors along with two international concerts which featured the "Laredo Paso Doble." The Texas Senate and House of Representatives cited Williams for furthering international goodwill through music.

Unable to resist the musical temptation, Williams used the syllables la-re-do as the work's principal motive. (Harold L. Hillyer, University of Texas at El Paso)

Pastorale (Pub = SB, 1957. Gr = 4. T = 4:05)

Written for the University of Texas Band, this work offers a challenge to the listener as well as the player. The score frequently shifts tonalities and there are many fresh adventures in sounds and many opportunities for expressive soloistic style. The one movement work is written in a quasi choral style and is a refreshing contrast to the driving, dynamic works which are more typical of Williams.

The Ramparts (Pub = EM, 1967. Gr = 5. T = 6:00; 7:00 w. chorus. Rec = CR-MID-70-13, Richmond, MO, H.S., Seward)

The Ramparts was written for the United States Air Force Academy at the request of Major Herman Vincent who was director of bands at the time. Its first performance was at the academy during "June Week" (preceding graduation) in 1965. The title refers to the Rampart Range of the Rocky Mountains near Colorado Springs, where the academy is located. Immediately after the première, the Cadet Chorale adopted the hymn in *The Ramparts* and it is still used as an unofficial alma mater. The text of the hymn, titled "What Great Thing," is as follows:

> From the Ramparts we will go into the sky,
> Far away from comrades here to whatever fate may bring:
> Fame or glory, even death.
> But no matter what may come,
> Life is better, purpose more, honor bright
> Because 'twas here we first beheld
> What greater thing could be.

The work's opening theme is the "Adjutant's Call" which is sounded by trumpets to begin each formal parade at the academy. This theme is developed and reaches a climax before the hymn (which is optional). The chorale melody is then developed by the instruments of the band to bring the piece to a brilliant, exciting ending. The quiet, echoing chord in the woodwinds at the end—like an airplane disappearing over the Ramparts—was intended by the composer as a reminder that we should all search for the "greater things."

Both Williams and his wife, Maxine, considered this composition to be his most serious and best work. Mrs. Williams wore a charm bracelet composed of a charm for each work deemed "a major contribution to the art." The charm for *The Ramparts* was the largest of the set. (Herman Vincent, McNeese State University)

The Sinfonians March (Pub = EM, 1960. Gr = 4. T = 5:20. Rec = CN-9, Cornell Un., Stith)

A symphonic march, *The Sinfonians* was commissioned by Phi Mu Alpha Sinfonia Fraternity of America. "Hail Sinfonia! Come, brothers, hail!" Thus begins the principal song of the fraternity with words by Charles Lutton set to music of Arthur Sullivan. It is after an extended fanfare introduction in the march that the theme underlying these opening words is stated by the horns. The song is then completed, embellished, and added to in the distinctive style of the composer.

Strategic Air Command March (Pub = SO, 1965. Gr = 3. T = 3:45)

Written at the request of the U.S. Strategic Air Command staff through Capt. Herman Vincent, commander of SAC Bands, this march was premiered at the SAC Band's annual concert in Omaha, Nebraska, July 14, 1963, and was conducted by the composer. Near the end of the march the audience may detect "sonic booms," a trademark of the Strategic Air Command in its mission of eternal vigilance in the security of the country. (Harold L. Hillyer, University of Texas at El Paso)

Symphonic Dance No. 2, The Maskers (Pub = SF, 1968. Gr = 4. T = 6:20)

This work is one of several compositions by Williams which show him to be a master of writing music for band in a light flowing style. *The Maskers* and *Fiesta (Symphonic Dance No. 3)* were both premiered by the University of Miami Band in 1967.

Symphonic Dance No. 3, Fiesta (Pub = SF, 1967. Gr = 4. T = 6:20. Rec = CR-MID-68-13, Sapulpa, OK, H.S., Brite)

Fiesta depicts the pageantry of Latin America celebrations—street bands, bull fights, bright costumes. It is one of a group of five originally commissioned for the twenty-fifth anniversary of the San Antonio Symphony Orchestra. It was first performed by that orchestra in January, 1965. The composer then scored the work for band, and it was first performed in March, 1967, by the University of Miami Band, under the composer's direction. (Robert E. Restemyer, Southeast Missouri State University)

Symphonic Suite (Pub = SB, 1965. Gr = 4. T = 7:10. Rec = BP-102, OK City Un., Neilson; CR-ABA-79-3, Hardaway H.S., Gregory)

The music consists of five movements related through the use of the principal theme. In each movement a new theme is also introduced and in the last movement several themes are developed simultaneously. The suite begins with an Intrada which suggests a solemn processional in fanfare style. The following movement, Chorale, is based on a melody in the first cornet which has more than a hint of the "blues" in it. The March is marked allegro vivo and is based on a short fanfare-like motive heard at the beginning. After many repetitions it works up to a fine climax for full band at the end. The Antique Dance features a modal melody in the flute with percussion accompaniment. The concluding Jubilee is the climactic movement of the suite. Marked allegro con brio, it is written in sonorous triadic harmony throughout. With a few contrasting sections, the movement is based primarily on a chordal-rhythmic motive. *Symphonic Suite* was the Ostwald Award-winning composition of the American Bandmasters Association in 1957. (Gene A. Braught, University of Oklahoma)

Variation Overture (Pub = LU, 1962. Gr = 3. T = 5:45)

It is a relatively recent phenomenon for a composer of major stature to write music for instrumental ensembles utilizing mature techniques of composition within a simple framework and well within the performance capabilities of young student musicians. Williams has done an admirable job of achieving such a goal in this composition. The basic thematic material consists of the first three notes of the major scale. The three tones are skillfully woven into the composition so that one never forgets them but never tires of hearing them. It is a delightful piece of music for young players and for young at heart audiences.

HAYDN WOOD

(Born in Slaithwaite, England, 1882 — Died in London, 1959)

When he was only two years old Haydn Wood went with his family to live on the Isle of Man, situated in the Irish Sea between England and Ireland. He later studied violin and composition at the Royal Academy of Music in London and at the Brussels Conservatory. His compositions include numerous works for chamber ensembles and string orchestra, yet he is unquestionably better remembered for his music for band, works which are of a light, folk-song nature.

Mannin Veen (Pub = BH, 1937. Gr = 5. T = 10:00. Rec = CR-CBDNA-73-5, Western Div. Community Col. Honor, McGinnis)

The title of this tone poem means "Dear Isle of Man," and the composition is based on four Manx folk tunes. The first, "The Good Old Way," is an old and typical air written mostly in the Dorian mode. The second tune, which introduces the lively section of the work, is a reel—"The Manx Fiddler." The third tune, "Sweet Water in the Common," relates to the old practice of summoning a jury of twenty-four men, comprised of three men from each of the parishes in the district where the dispute took place, to decide questions connected with watercourses, boundaries, etc. The fourth and last tune is a fine old hymn, "The Harvest of the Sea," sung by the fishermen as a song of thanksgiving after their safe return from the fishing grounds.

NAOZUMI YAMAMOTO

(Born in Tokyo, 1932)

Naozumi Yamamoto was born in 1932, two years after the school band program began in Japan. He was a child living in Tokyo during the first few years of the band contests. Although the contests were dropped during World War II, Yamamoto was much impressed by the American military bands which were stationed in Japan after the war, and he joined with other talented composers in writing works for band after the contests were resumed in 1956. At the present time he is engaged in a wide variety of music activities in addition to composing.

This Glorious White World March (Pub = TA, 1972. Gr = 4. T = 3:30. Rec = RC-RCA-Victor-SJV-1239)

This march was composed in 1972 at the request of the organizing committee for the eleventh Olympic winter games held in Sapporo, a city in northern Japan. Although originally intended as music to inspire marching units, the composition is equally appropriate as music for concert audiences.

PAUL YODER

(Born in Tacoma, Washington, 1908)

Paul Yoder graduated from the University of North Dakota and received his Master of Music degree in 1941 from Northwestern University in Evanston, Illinois. He was awarded an honorary Doctor of Music degree by the University of North Dakota on the occasion of the seventy-fifth anniversary of that institution.

The composer and arranger of music for school bands since 1933 and past president of the American Bandmasters Association, Yoder continues to be a distinguished leader in the field of music education. He has contributed arrangements of some of the most widely performed works in the literature of band music. As a clinician and traveller to many other countries, Yoder may truly be considered an "international ambassador of good will."

Pachinko (Pub = VO, 1966. Gr = 3. T = 2:30)

Pachinko is a musical composition of a Japanese pin-ball game which is very popular in that country. Many of these machines are assembled in a large room, and when up to 200 players are operating these devices, the sound effects are astounding.

The percussion section depicts most of these sounds, but the woodwind passages are intended to portray the speed and excitement of the game. The melody carried by the flutes and alto saxophones is written in one of the Japanese scales which approximates our harmonic minor scale without the 4th or 7th degrees. (Paul Yoder, Fort Lauderdale, Florida)

Tin Pan Gallery (Pub = HN, 1968. Gr = 3. T = 4:00. Rec = CR-MID-68-9, Coral Gables, FL, H.S., Yoder)

This concert novelty includes various songs associated with food and cooking. It was written as a musical companion to the cook book titled *Tin Pan Galley* by the composer's wife, Roselyn Yoder. This cook book contains recipes contributed by the wives of band directors. Hence the title which is, of course, a "take-off" on the famous tin-pan alley of New York and the more recent tin-pan valley of Nashville. Yoder believes that, all in all, the possible variations on the original title have been just about exhausted. (Paul Yoder, Fort Lauderdale, Florida)

LUIGI ZANINELLI

(Born in Raritan, New Jersey, 1932)

Following high school graduation, Luigi Zaninelli was awarded a scholarship in composition with Gian-Carlo Menotti at the Curtis Institute of Music. He won the Steinway Composition Award in 1954. While a student he received a Curtis scholarship for study in Italy with Rosario Scalero. Upon his return to the United States,

Zaninelli resumed his studies with Menotti and following graduation pursued advanced study in composition with Vittorio Giannini and Bohuslav Martinu.

In 1964 he returned to Italy to compose music for films, and during that period he became musical director for Metropolitan Opera soprano Anna Moffo. The publication of two arrangements for band, *Americana* and *Trinity,* in 1975 and 1978 respectively, concurred with his position as composer-in-residence and associate professor of music at the University of Southern Mississippi, Hattiesburg, Mississippi. (Shawnee Press, Inc.)

Americana (Pub = SH, 1975. Gr = 4. T = 8:00. Rec = SH-8, Ithaca Col., Gobrecht)

Three familiar American folk songs, "Shenandoah," "Skip to My Lou," and "Sweet Betsy from Pike," comprise the material used in this setting for band with optional choral parts. The instrumentation is for full symphonic band with complete contemporary instrumentation and with various percussion instruments including xylophone, bells, chimes, and vibraphone. The arrangement is dedicated to the University of Southern Mississippi Band, Joe Barry Mullins, conductor.

Trinity (Pub = SH, 1978. Gr = 3. T = 5:15)

Trinity is comprised of three familiar hymn tunes widely sung throughout Christendom. "Angels from the Realms of Glory" is one of the best known hymns based on the stories in Matthew and Luke. The rugged melody of "How Firm a Foundation," a favorite of U.S. presidents, is believed to be a folk tune, although some musicologists attribute it to the writer of the text—R. Keene. The text has been called "a sermon in verse."

"We Plow the Fields and Scatter" is from Germany, and was first published in 1872. The popular, somewhat boisterous melody is sometimes called "a peasant's song." (Shawnee Press, Inc.)

JOHN ZDECHLIK
(Born in Minneapolis, Minnesota, 1937)

As a high school jazz trumpeter and pianist, Zdechlik developed an interest in creative writing for jazz bands. In 1957 he began studies in music education at the University of Minnesota. Upon graduating, he taught two years at the secondary level and then returned to the University of Minnesota to study theory and composition. He served as associate band director at the university while earning his master's degree. He then taught full time at the same university but soon resumed his studies, this time working for a Ph.D. degree in composition and theory which was completed in 1970.

At the conclusion of his studies at the University of Minnesota, Zdechlik took a position at the Lakewood Community College in White Bear Lake, Minnesota, where he serves as band director and department chairman.

Chorale and Shaker Dance (Pub = KJ, 1972. Gr = 4. T = 9:00. Rec = CR-MID-72-14, Cicero, NY, H.S., Codner)

Commissioned by the Jefferson High School Band, Bloomington, Minnesota, Earl Benson, conductor, *Chorale and Shaker Dance* has become a standard in the band repertoire since its première at the national convention of the Music Educators National Conference in 1972. The work contains two basic ideas: the chorale, which is a simple, single phrased melody, and the Shaker song, "The Gift To Be Simple." These melodies are used in alternation, combination, and with extreme rhythmic variation throughout the composition.

Dance Variations (Pub = KJ, 1977. Gr = 4. T = 7:20. Rec = CR-MID-77-8, Clinton, TN, H.S., Barnes; PW-Zdechlik, Luther Col., Nyline)

The composition is comprised of a theme made up of a unique combination of intervals and is stated three times. Six variations on the theme follow. Variation I is allegro and in common time. The woodwinds and brass play the theme antiphonally. Variation II is a molto allegro tempo with alternating measures of 4/4 and 5/4 meter. The theme is developed by brass, woodwinds, and percussion. Variation III presents the theme by the trombones in a chant-like statement while polychords sound in the high woodwinds. Variation IV features the bassoons, oboes, and low reeds at a moderate tempo with a giocoso feeling. Variation V has a polychordal setting for woodwinds and trombones with fragments of the theme played by French horn and trumpet. Variation VI is in a moderate rhythmic setting which starts quietly and builds steadily to the end.

The work was commissioned by Gamma Pi Chapter of Kappa Kappa Psi, Purdue University Bands, Al G. Wright, Conductor.

APPENDICES

CONTRIBUTORS — INDIVIDUALS
(With former and most recent known position)

Toshio Akiyama	Toyko, Japan
Thomas J. Anderson	DeKalb College
Mary Arthur	Fond du Lac, Wisconsin
Thomas J. Ashbaugh	Graceland College
Grayson W. Babcock	Fort Atkinson (Wisconsin) High School
Harold Bachman	University of Florida—(Deceased)
George E. Baggett	Harding College
Carl Barnett	Will Rogers (Tulsa, Oklahoma) High School
Donald J. Bastarache	Westfield State College
A.E. Beck	U.S. Navy Band
Roger L. Beck	Sioux Falls College
Walter Beeler	Ithaca College—(Deceased)
Harry Begian	University of Illinois
Paul W. Behm	Mason City (Iowa) High School
Marvin C. Belford	Millikin University
Frank Bencriscutto	University of Minnesota
Paul Bierley	Columbus, Ohio
Jerry Bilik	Ann Arbor, Michigan— Los Angeles, California
Kenneth Bloomquist	Michigan State University
Earl W. Bohm	St. Louis Park, Missouri
A.G. Bortz	Lansing Michigan
Carmine M. Both	Slippery Rock State College
Lee Bowling	National Intercollegiate Bands Englewood, Colorado
Jack W. Bowman	Alma College—Cameron University
Edward A. Boynton	University of Maine at Fort Kent
J. Raymond Brandon	North Little Rock, Arkansas
Gene A. Braught	University of Oklahoma
Keith Brion	Yale University—New Haven, Connecticut
Keith Brown	Temple University
Merrill Brown	University of Toledo
Richard L. Brown	Lambuth College
Paul Bryan	Duke University
Henry E. Busche	MacMurray College
Milton Bush	University of New Orleans— Louisiana State University at New Orleans
Ernest C. Cadden, Jr.	Amory (Mississippi) High School
Raoul Camus	Queensborough Community College

Don Caneva	San Diego, California
Dean R. Canty	Pan American University
Daniel J. Carbone	Little (Colorado) Senior High School
James Carlson	University of Minnesota at Morris
Warrick L. Carter	University of Maryland at Eastern Shore
George Cavender	University of Michigan
Lou Chapin	Broadcast Music, Inc.
Claude Christnach	Luxembourg
James Clark	Berry College
John W. Coker	University of South Florida
Russell Coleman	Central Missouri State College
Thomas H. Cook	Central College
Milton Cooper	Delaware State College
Aaron Copland	Peekskill, New York
John Corley	Massachusetts Institute of Technology
Paul Creston	Central Washington State College— San Diego, California
Roger L. Dancz	University of Georgia
Oliver Daniel	Broadcast Music, Inc.
Patrick Deaville	Lake Charles (Louisiana) High School—- Jennings (Louisiana) High School
Stanley DeRusha	Michigan State University
Vincent R. DiNino	University of Texas
Edward J. Downing	Interlochen Natinal Music Camp
Janet W. Ebert	Urbana College
Orville M. Eidem	North Dakota State University
Jonathan Elkus	Lehigh University— Provincetown, Massachusetts
Wilber T. England	Indiana University
Myron R. Falck	Gustavus Adolphus College
Leonard Falcone	East Lansing, Michigan
Frederick Fennell	University of Miami
Linda S. Ferguson	Santa Ana, California— Lake Charles, Louisiana
Paul G. Fisher	Millersville State College
C. Dale Fjerstad	Southern Illinois University— University of the Pacific
Robert C. Fleming	University of Tennessee at Martin— Arizona State University
Robert E. Fleming	Youngstown State University
Richard L. Floyd	Baylor University
Kirby W. Fong	California Institute of Technology
Guy F. Foreman	LaPorte (Indiana) High School
Robert Foster	University of Kansas
William Foster	Florida A & M University

Bertram W. Francis	Mansfield State College
Kenton R. Frohrip	St. Cloud State College
Arnald D. Gabriel	United States Air Force Band
Loren D. Geiger	Lancaster, New York
Donald S. George	Wisconsin State University— University of Wisconsin at Eau Claire
Thom Ritter George	Quincy, Illinois
Thomas Giles	Mankato State College
John Gilfry	University of Southwestern Louisiana
Rick Gilpin	Jennings (Louisiana) High School
Samuel Goldfarb	Rockville (Connecticut) High School
Richard Franko Goldman	The Goldman Band
Robert W. Gordon	Sterling College
W.B. Green	Buena Vista College
Donald E. Greene	Wisconsin State University at Stevens Point
Isaac Greggs	Southern University
Gerald K. Grose	University of Wisconsin at Milwaukee
Charles M. Grove	Kosciusko (Mississippi) High School
Ron Grundberg	Highland Park, Illinois
Egil A. Gundersen	Skien, Norway
Dan Hanna	DePauw University
Herbert Hazelman	Grimsley (Greensboro, North Carolina) High School
Fred Heath	University of Maryland—University of Maine
Joseph Hebert, Jr.	Loyola University
Allan Hein	Washburn University
James G. Hejl	Mississippi State University
Hubert Henderson	University of Maryland
Walter Hendl	Eastman School of Music
M.Q. Hennessey	University of Notre Dame
William R. Higgins	Messiah College
Harold L. Hillyer	University of Texas at El Paso— Eastern Illinois University
Mark Hindsley	University of Illinois
Maurice Hinson	The American Music Teacher
Robert Hoe, Jr.	Poughkeepsie, New York
John M. Hoover	University of Louisville
Dennis Hopkins	Memorial (Houston, Texas) High School— McNeese State University
Alan Hovhaness	C.F. Peters Corporation
James E. Howe	Surrey, England
Calvin R. Huber	Wake Forest University
Donald R. Hunsberger	Eastman School of Music
Norman J. Hunt	Sacramento State College
Karel Husa	Cornell University

Paul D. Husby	The Minnesota Winds
John L. Iltis	University of Alberta
Kenley Inglefield	University of Toledo
Christopher Izzo	Western Illinois University
Harold J. Jackson	Southwest Baptist College—
	Northwest Missouri State University
Marion L. Jacobs	Grand Junction, Colorado
Robert Jager	Tennessee Tech University
Michael Jameson	Eastern Michigan University
Eldon Janzen	University of Arkansas
Arthur Jefferson	Detroit Public Schools
Lloyd S. Jensen	Modesto Junior College
Bryan Johnson	Oakland-Craig (Nebraska) Schools
Clyde E. Johnson	University of Minnesota at Morris
Dennis L. Johnson	Western Illinois University
Miles H. Johnson	St. Olaf College
William V. Johnson	California Polytechnic State University
Darrell Johnston	San Jose City College
L. Bruce Jones	Louisiana State University— (Deceased)
Sam L. Jones, Jr.	Millsaps College
Robert A. Jordahl	McNeese State University
James Jorgenson	University of Redlands
Masaru Kawasaki	Tokyo, Japan
Harvey W. Kellner	Otero Junior College
Dale E. Kennedy	Oklahoma City University
Everett Kisinger	University of Illinois
Otis Kitchen	Elizabethtown College
Kiyoshige Koyama	Kobe Yamate Girls Junior College
Joel L. Kramme	University of Missouri at Rolla
John Krance	New York
George Kreamer	Lake Charles, Louisiana
Bruce Lambert	Sam Houston (Lake Charles, Louisiana)
	High School
Caesar La Monaca	Miami, Florida
Ross A. Leeper	Eagle Grove (Iowa) Middle School
Bennett Lentczner	Radford College
Leland A. Lillehaug	Augustana College
Clifford Lillya	University of Michigan
Stuart J. Ling	College of Wooster
Newell H. Long	Indiana University
Gordon E. Louts	Shippensburg State College
Charles H. Luedtke	Dr. Martin Luther College
Maurice McAdow	North Texas State University
Lanny McAlister	Gordon Military College
W. Francis McBeth	Ouachita University

Lamar K. McCarrell	Campbell College
Donald McGinnis	Ohio State University
Donald McRae	University of New Mexico
Chester Mais	Cornell University
Gregg E. Magnuson	University of Maine at Orono
Charles Martyn	West Virginia Tech
Lee A. Mendyk	Wayne State College
	Winona State University
Jan Meyerowitz	New York City
Duane J. Mikow	University of Alaska
John Dale Miller	Lenoir (North Carolina) High School
Vondis Miller	Winston Churchill High School—
	University of Lethbridge
Charles Minelli	Ohio University—Athens, Ohio
John Mitchum	DeKalb College
William J. Moody	University of Texas—
	University of South Carolina
David Nelson	University of Michigan
Melbern W. Nixon	Emporia State University
Paul B. Noble, Jr.	Shenandoah Conservatory of Music
Weston Noble	Luther College
Raymond Nutaitis	Wilkes College
Gary B. Nyberg	Nebraska Wesleyan University
David L. Oakley	University of Missouri at Rolla
Robert F. O'Brien	University of Notre Dame
Howard G. Oliver	Bethany Nazarene College
Acton Ostling, Jr.	Iowa State University—
	University of Louisville
Donald L. Panhorst	Edinboro State College
Steve Parkany	Yale University
John Paynter	Northwestern University
Bob Peckham	Athens, Georgia
Wayne Pegram	Tennessee Tech University
James A. Perkins	Chatfield, Minnesota, Music Lending
	Library
Roger A. Perley	Moline, Illinois
G. David Peters	University of Illinois
Jon R. Piersol	Bowling Green State University
Francis Pieters	Kortrijk, Belgium
Max Planck	University of Eastern Michigan
James D. Ployhar	c/o Belwin Mills Publishing Corp.
Michael Polovitz	University of North Dakota
John Powell	University of South Alabama
James D. Pritchard	University of Northern Iowa
Stanley E. Radcliffe	Cameron College
Gregg Randall	Las Cruces (New Mexico) High School

Malcolm Rayment	Queensborough Community College
Alfred Reed	University of Miami
Robert E. Restemyer	Southeast Missouri State University
H. Robert Reynolds	University of Wisconsin— University of Michigan
William E. Rhoads	University of New Mexico
Bardie Roberts	Jennings (Louisiana) High School— Baton Rouge, Louisiana
Edward Roberts	Tarkio College
James D. Robertson	Shepherd College— Eastern Oregon State College
W.C. Robinson, Jr.	Florida Memorial College
Arvin E. Rogers	Jacksonville University
C. Ward Rounds	Northwest Missouri State College
James G. Roy	Broadcast Music, Inc.
Clarence E. Sawhill	University of California at Los Angeles
Blase S. Scarnati	Slippery Rock State College
William Schaefer	University of Southern California
John C. Schector	Cumberland College
Gunther Schuller	New England Conservatory of Music
Julian Scaman	New York City
Edmund P. Sedivy	Montana State University
Bill D. Shellenbarger	Oral Roberts University
Kent Sills	Mississippi State University
James Sinclair	Yale University
Thomas F. Sirridge	Kappa Kappa Psi, Stillwater, Oklahoma
Stanislaw Skrowaczewski	Minneapolis, Minnesota
Thomas C. Slattery	Coe College
Gene C. Smith	Baylor University
Leonard B. Smith	The Detroit Concert Band
Pamlyn J. Smith	New York City
Jack Snavely	University of Wisconsin at Milwaukee
Gordon A. Solie	Portland State University
John Phillip Sousa III	New York City
R. John Specht	Queensborough Community College
Gale Sperry (Deceased)	University of South Florida
Randall Spicer	Washington State University
Donald A. Stanley	Mansfield State College
D.W. Stauffer	United States Navy
Ward Stauth	Corydon, Indiana
Marice W. Stith	Cornell University
J.C. Sweet	New Canaan, Connecticut
Lonn M. Sweet	Southern State College
William Swor	Louisiana State University— Indiana State University

CONTRIBUTORS — INDIVIDUALS

Tom Tapscott	Northwest (Clarksville, Tennessee) High School
Joseph M. Tate	Barbe (Lake Charles, Louisiana) High School—Ball (Galveston, Texas) High School
Edward Thompson	Lake Arthur (Louisiana) High School
James M. Thurmond	Lebanon Valley College
Clayton Tiede	Mankato State College
Max R. Tromblee	Phillips University
Logan O. Turrentine	Hialeah (Florida) High School
Thomas Tyra	University of Eastern Michigan— Western Carolina University
Stuart J. Uggen	North Park College
C.R. Varner	College of William and Mary
Susan Vaughan	Hibbing State Junior College
William T. Verran	Cairo, Georgia
Herman G. Vincent	United States Air Force Academy— Lake Charles, Louisiana
Rick Van Santvoord	Glen Cove, New York
Raymond Vun Kannon	Hofstra University
Ralph Wahl	University of South Carolina
John E. Wakefield	University of Maryland
David L. Walters	Jacksonville State University
Harold L. Walters	Miami, Florida
Robert Washburn	State University College at Potsdam
Robert Weatherly	Southeastern Louisiana University
Walter C. Welke (Deceased)	University of Washington
Paul Whear	Marshall University
Ray C. Wifler	University of Wisconsin at Fond du Lac
Don Wilcox	West Virginia University
James Wilcox	Southeastern Louisiana University
Charles A. Wiley	Lamar University
Russell L. Wiley	University of Kansas
Arthur L. Williams (Deceased)	Oberlin College
Robert E. Williams	University of Minnesota at Duluth
Cecil B. Wilson	Case Western Reserve University
George C. Wilson	National Music Camp, Interlochen
Robert H. Wojciak	University of Cincinnati— University of Southern California
Donald L. Wolf	Northern Arizona University
William H. Woodworth	William Paterson College
Lucius R. Wyatt	Tuskegee Institute
James A. Yarrington	Western State College

Paul Yoder	Ft. Lauderdale, Florida—
	Troy State University
James C. Young	Louisiana Tech University
Raymond G. Young	University of Southern Mississippi—
	Louisiana Tech University

CONTRIBUTORS — ORGANIZATIONS

ABA Research Center (McKeldin Library, University of Maryland)
Alfred Publishing Company
American Music Teacher
Barnhouse Music Company
Belwin-Mills Publishing Corporation
Boosey and Hawkes, Incorporated
Chappell and Company, Incorporated
College Band Directors National Association
Franko Colombo Publications
Carl Fischer, Incorporated
Sam Fox Publishing Company
Galaxy Music Corporation
The Instrumentalist
Journal of Band Research
Kendor Music, Incorporated
Leblanc Publications, Incorporated
Ludwig Music Publishing Company
Edward B. Marks Music Corporation
Mills Music, Incorporated
Molenaar's Musiekcentrale
Edwin H. Morris and Company
Music Educators National Conference
Oslo University Library
Oxford University Press
C.F. Peters Corporation
Phi Mu Alpha Sinfonia
Piedmont Music Company, Inc.
Podium Publishing Company
Theodore Presser Company
Rubank, Incorporated
G. Schirmer, Incorporated
Shawnee Press, Incorporated
Southern Music Company of San Antonio
Studio P/R
Teine and Corporation, Limited
TRN Music Publisher
Volkwein Bros., Incorporated
M. Witmark and Sons

APPENDIX II

KEY TO PUBLISHERS*

ACA   **American Composers Alliance,** 170 W. 74th St., New York, NY 10023

ACC   **Accura Music,** Box 887, Athens, OH 45701

AL   **Alfred Publishing Co.,** 15335 Morrison St., Sherman Oaks, CA 91403

AMP   **Associated Music Publishers, Inc.,** 866 Third Ave., New York, NY 10022

BA   **C.L. Barnhouse Co.,** 100 B. Avenue East, Oskaloosa, IA 52577

BD   **Byron-Douglas Publications,** (See **BE**)

BE   **Belwin-Mills Publishing Corp.,** 25 Deshon Drive, Melville, NY 11746

BH   **Boosey & Hawkes, Inc.,** 24 W. 57th St., New York, NY 10019

BL   **Bandland, Inc.,** 20962 Mack Ave., Grosse Pointe Woods, MI 48236

BO   **Bourne Co.,** 1212 Avenue of the Americas. New York, NY 10036

BR   **Broude Brothers Ltd.,** 56 W. 45th Street, New York, NY 10036

B3   **The Big Three Music Co.,** 729 7th Ave., New York, NY 10019

BVC   **Bregman-Vocco and Conn, Inc.,** (See **HN**)

CA   **Chappell and Co., Inc.,** (See **TP**)

CF   **Carl Fischer, Inc.,** 62 Cooper Square, New York, NY 10003

CH   **Charter Publications, Inc.,** Box 850, Valley Forge, PA 19482

CO   **M.M. Cole Publishing Co.,** 919 Michigan Ave., Suite 1602, Chicago, IL 60611

DUR   **Durand et Cie,** (See **TP**)

EAM   **European American Music,** 195 Allwood Road, Clifton, NJ 07012

EB   **Edwin H. Morris and Co., Inc.,** (See **HN**)

EFK   **Edwin F. Kalmus and Co., Inc.,** P.O. Box 1007, Opa-Locka, FL 33054

EM   **Edward B. Marks Music Corp.,** (See **BE**)

EMS   **Educational Music Service,** 905 Gaffield, Evanston, IL 60201

EV   **Elkan-Vogel Co., Inc.,** (See **TP**)

FC   **Franco Colombo, Inc.,** (See **BE**)

FE   **Forest R. Etling, Publisher,** 1790 Joseph Ct., Elgin, IL 60120

FI   **Fillmore Music House,** (See **CF**)

FR   **Frank Music Corp.,** 30 W. 54th St., New York, NY 10036

* Abbreviations conform with *Band Music Guide,* The Instrumentalist Company, courtesy James T. Rohner

FZ	H.T. Fitzsimons Co., Inc., 357 W. Erie St., Chicago, IL 60610
GA	Galaxy Music Corp., 2121 Broadway, New York, NY 10023
GE	Gershwin Publishing Corp., (See TP)
GL	G. Leblanc Corp., 7019 30th Ave., Kenosha, WI 53141
GS	G. Schirmer, Inc., 866 Third Ave., New York, NY 10022
HA	Harms, Inc., (See BE)
HI	Mark Hindsley, 1 Montclair Road, Urbana, IL 61801
HL	Hal Leonard Publishing Corp., 8112 W. Bluemound Rd., Milwaukee, WI 53213
HM	Hollis Music Co., (See TR)
HN	Hansen House Miami, 1870 West Ave., Miami, FL 33139
HT	Harold Brasch, 2707 S. June Street, Arlington, VA 22202
IP	Interlochen Press, P.O. Box 395, 8 Bunting Ln., Naperville, IL 60540
JB	Jerry H. Bilik, 50 Hollyhill Lane, Greenwich, CT
JC	John Church Co., (See TP)
JP	Jenson Publications, 2880 S. 171st St., New Berlin, WI 53151
JWP	J.W. Pepper and Son, Inc., Valley Forge, PA 19482
KJ	Neil A. Kjos Music Co., 4382 Jutland Drive, San Diego, CA 92117
KK	K.L. King Music House, (See BA)
KN	Kendor Music, Inc., Main & Grove Streets, Delevan, NY 14042
LD	Leeds Music Corp., (See BE)
LU	Ludwig Music Publishing Co., Inc., 557 E. 140th St., Cleveland, OH 44110
MA	Edward B. Marks (See BE)
MAL	Malcolm Music Limited, (See SH)
MC	MCA Music, (See BE)
ME	Mercury Music Corp., (See TP)
MG	Musicians Publications, P.O. Box 7160, West Trenton, NJ 08628
MIS	Michigan State University Bands, East Lansing, MI 48824
MJ	MJQ Music, Inc., (See SF)
MOL	Molenaar's Muziekcentrale n.v., B.P 19, 1520 AA Wormerveer, Holland
MM	Mills Music, Inc., (See BE)
MP	Music Publishers Holding Corp., (See WB)
OM	Omega Music Co., (See SF)

KEY TO PUBLISHERS

ON	**Ongaku-No-Tomo Sha Co., Ltd.,** 6-30 Kagurazaka, Shinjuku-ku, Tokyo 162, Japan
OX	**Oxford University Press, Inc.,** 200 Madison Ave., New York, NY 10016
PA	**Panella Music Co.,** 58 Warren St., Apt.2, Pittsburgh, PA 15205
PD	**Podium Music, Inc.,** 360 Port Washington Blvd., Port Washington, NY 11050
PE	**Piedmont Music Co., Inc.,** (See **BE**)
PET	**C.F. Peters Corp.,** 373 Park Avenue South, New York, NY 10016
PI	**Peer International Corp.,** 1740 Broadway, New York, NY 10019
PO	**Pro Art Publications,** (See **BE**)
PR	**Studio P/R, Inc.,** 224 S. Lebanon St., Lebanon, IN 46052
RC	**Ricordi & Co.,** (See **GS**)
RE	**Remick Music Corp.,** (See **WB**)
S&	**Schmitt Publications,** (See **BE**)
S&C	**Schott & Co., Ltd.,** (See **EAM**)
SB	**Summy-Birchard Co.,** Box CN27, Princeton, NJ 08540
SF	**Sam Fox Publishing Co.,** P.O. Box 850, Valley Forge, PA 19482
SH	**Shawnee Press, Inc.,** Delaware Water Gap, PA 18327
SN	**Southern Music Pub. Co., Inc.,** 1740 Broadway, New York, NY 10019
SO	**Southern Music Co.,** 1100 Broadway, P.O. Box 329, San Antonio, TX 78292
SP	**Shapiro, Bernstein & Co., Inc.,** 10 E. 53rd St., New York, NY 10022
TA	**Toha Music Publishers,** 6-32 Kagurazaka, Shinjuku-ku, Tokyo 162, Japan
TE	**Templeton Publishing Co.,** (See **SH**)
TN	**TRN Music,** Box 10077, Lamar Station, Beaumont, TX 77710
TP	**Theodore Presser Co.,** Presser Place, Bryn Mawr, PA 19010
TR	**TRO,** 10 Colombus Circle, New York, NY 10019
VO	**Volkwein Bros., Inc.,** 117 Sandusky St., Pittsburgh, PA 15212
WB	**Warner Brothers Publications, Inc.,** 75 Rockefeller Plaza, New York, NY 10019
WIM	**Wimbledon Music Inc.,** 1888 Century Park East, Century City, CA 90067
WIN	**W.I.N.D.S.,** Box 513, Northridge, CA 91328
WJ	**Wingert-Jones Music Inc.,** 2026 Broadway, Box 1878, Kansas City, MO 64141
WN	**Williamson Music, Inc., c/o Boston Music Co.,** 116 Boyleston St., Boston, MA 02116
WS	**Witmark & Sons,** (See **WB**)

APPENDIX III

KEY TO RECORD COMPANIES

AC   **Austin Custom Records**, P.O. Box 9057, Austin, TX 78756

AN   **Angel**, (See **CA**)

AR   **Arion Corporation**, 825 Boone Ave. N., Minneapolis, MN 55427

AT   **Arkansas Tech University**, Russellville, AR 72801

BH   **Boosey & Hawkes, Inc.**, P.O. Box 130, Lawson Blvd., Oceanside, NY 11572

BL   **Bandland, c/o Detroit Concert Band**, 20962 Mack Ave., Grosse Pointe Woods, MI 48236

BM   **Belwin-Mills Publishing Corp.**, 25 Deshon Drive, Melville, NY 11746

BP   (See **BM**)

BR   **Brewster**, 50 River St., Old Saybrook, CT 06475

CA   **Capitol Records**, 1750 N. Vine St., Hollywood, CA 90028

CB   **CBS Records**, 51 W. 52nd St., New York, NY 10019

CC   **Century Custom Recording Service**, P.O. Box 308, Saugus, CA 91350

CF   **Carl Fischer, Inc.**, 62 Cooper Square, New York, NY 10003

CL   **Columbia Broadcasting System**, 51 W. 52nd St., New York, NY 10019

CN   **Cornell University Band Office**, Lincoln Hall, Ithaca, NY 14850

CO   **Coronet Instructional Media**, 65 E. South Water St., Chicago, IL 60601

CR   **Crest Records, Inc.**, 220 Broadway, Huntington Station, NY 11746

CS   **Connoisseur Society, Inc.**, 390B West End Ave., New York, NY 10024

CT   **Coronet Recording Co.**, 4971 N. High St., Columbus, OH 43214

DE   **Desto Records**, 14 Warren St., New York, NY 10007

DG   **Deutsche Grammophone** (See **PO**)

DL   **The Decca Record Company, Ltd.**, 539 W. 25th St., New York, NY 10001

EV   **Everest Rec. Group**, 2020 Avenue of the Stars, Century City, CA 90067

EMI   **EMI Angel** (See **CA**)

FAMU   **FAMU Foundation**, Box 224, Florida A & M University, Tallahassee, FL 32307

FS   **Fidelity Sound Recording**, 23 Don Court, Redwood City, CA 94062

GC   **Golden Crest Records, Inc.**, 220 Broadway, Huntington Station, NY 11746

HI   **Mark Hindsley**, 1 Montclair Road, Urbana, IL 61801

IL   **University of Illinois**, Harding Band Building, 1103 S. Sixth St., Champaign, IL 61802

JC	Japan Columbia, (See CL)
LC	Luther College, Dept. of Music, Decorah, IA 52101
LO	London Records, Inc., 539 W. 25th St., New York, NY 10001
LOU	Louisville Recording Society, 211 Brown Building, 321 W. Broadway, Louisville, KY 40202
MAC	Mace Records, 947 US Hwy 1, Rahway, NJ 07065
MA	Mark Educational Recordings, Inc., 10815 Bodine Road, Clarence, NY 14031
ME	Melodiya/Angel, (See CA)
MF	University of Miami Bands, Coral Gables, FL 33124
MG	Mercury Record Productions, Inc.,110 W. 57th St., New York, NY 10019
MH	Musical Heritage Society, 14 Park Road, Tinton Falls, NJ 07724
MI	MIT Concert Band, Kresge Auditorium, Cambridge, MA 02139
MM	(See MA)
MO	Molenaar's Muziekcentrale N.V., P.B. 19, 1520 AA Wormerveer, Holland
MS	Morehead State University Store, Morehead, KY 40351
MU	University of Michigan Band, 350 E. Hoover St., Ann Arbor, MI 48109
NE	New World Music Corp., 75 Rockefeller Plaza, New York, NY 10021
NO	Nonesuch Records, 962 La Cienega, Los Angeles, CA 90069
NW	Northwestern University Bands, Evanston, IL 60201
OD	Odyssey (See CL)
OH	Ohio State University Bands, Columbus, OH 43210
OS	On the Spot Recording Company, 11369 S. Lothair, Chicago, IL 60600
PH	Phillips, Evelyn House, 62 Oxford St., London W.1., United Kingdom
PO	Polydor, Inc., 810 Seventh Ave., New York, NY 10019
PR	Studio P/R, Inc., 224 S. Lebanon St., Lebanon, IN 46052
PW	Werlein's for Music, 605 Canal St., New Orleans, LA 70130
QU	Quintessence, Pickwick International, Inc., 7500 Excelsior Blvd., Minneapolis, MN 55426
RC	RCA Records, 1133 Ave. of the Americas, New York, NY 10036
SC	Southern CA School Band & Orch. Assoc., 127 N. Madison, Pasadena, CA 91105
SD	Augustana College Band, Sioux Falls, SD 57102

SE Seraphim, (See CA)

SF Sam Fox Music Sales Corp., 1540 Broadway, New York, NY 10036

SH Shawnee Press, Inc., Delaware Water Gap, PA 18327

SO Southern Music Co., 1100 Broadway, P.O. Box 329, San Antonio, TX 78292

TA Toha Music Publishers, 6-32 Kagurazaka, Shinju-ku, Tokyo 162, Japan

TE Telarc Records, 23293 Commerce Park Road, Cleveland, OH 44122

TN TRN Music Publishers, P.O. Box 10077, Lamar Station, Beaumont, TX 77710

TO Toshiba, Makabe Bldg., 3-4-3 Akasaka, Minato-ku, Tokyo 153, Japan

TT Tennessee Tech University Bands, Cookesville, TN 38501

UM University of Minnesota Bands, 84 Church St. S.E., Minneapolis, MN 55455

UN University of Nebraska Bands, Room 123, Westbrook Music Building, Lincoln, NE 68508

VA Vanguard Recording Studio, 71 W. 23rd St., New York, NY 10010

APPENDIX IV

INDEX OF TITLES, with COMPOSERS, GRADE, PERFORMANCE TIME, and RECORD AVAILABILITY

TITLE	COMPOSER	PAGE	GRADE	TIME	RECORD
Academic Festival Overture	Brahms	37	5	9:15	Y
Acclamation	C. Smith	208	3	12:00	Y
Adagio and Allegro	Nelhybel	167	4	——	Y
Aegean Festival	Makris	154	5	10:00	Y
Air for Band	Erickson	67	3	3:15	Y
Air Force Band of the West March	Williams	252	4	3:30	N
Alla Barocco—Folk Rock	Giovannini	85	4	5:30	N
Allegro Tempestuoso from Symphony No. 5	Mennin	159	5	8:00	Y
Alleluia	Mozart	164	3	5:00	N
Allerseelen, Opus 10, No. 8	R. Strauss	217	3	4:00	N
Ambrosian Hymn Variants	White	249	3	6:00	Y
Americana	Zaninelli	258	4	8:00	Y
American Civil War Fantasy	Bilik	31	3	8:00	Y
American Folk Rhapsody No. 2	Grundman	98	3	5:00	Y
American Folk Rhapsody No. 3	Grundman	98	3	6:30	Y
American Folk Song Suite	Frackenpohl	75	3	7:45	Y
An American in Paris	Gershwin	80	4	5:45	Y
American Overture for Band	Jenkins	128	4	5:00	Y
American Patrol	Meacham	157	3	4:00	Y
American Salute	Gould	92	4	5:00	Y
American Weekend March	De Gastyne	57	4	4:15	Y
Americans We March	Fillmore	71	3	2:50	Y
America the Beautiful	Ward	243	4	4:30	Y

TITLE	COMPOSER	PAGE	GRADE	TIME	RECORD
Amparito Roca	Texidor	226	3	3:30	Y
Analogue	Leckrone	142	3	5:10	Y
Anatolia	Creston	53	5	8:00	Y
Andante and Toccata	Nelhybel	167	4	8:00	N
Andante et Allegro—Trombone-Euphonium Solo	Barat	15	3/4	4:10	Y
Antietam	Whear	248	4	10:00	Y
Antiphony for Winds	Kechley	132	4	5:00	Y
Antonito	Wiley	251	4	3:45	Y
Appassionato	Nelhybel	167	3	6:30	Y
Apotheosis of This Earth	Husa	119	6	25:00	Y
Aria from Bachianas Brasileiras No. 5	Villa-Lobos	235	4	6:15	Y
Ariane Overture	Boyer	36	4	10:00	N
Armenian Dances	Chobanian	48	4	13:20	Y
Armenian Dances	Khachaturian	133	4	6:00	Y
Armenian Dances	A. Reed	186	5	10:30	Y
Army of the Nile March	K. Alford	6	4	3:00	Y
Athletic Festival March	Prokofiev	184	4	4:00	Y
Atropos	Weiner	246	3	4:00	N
Avatara	Leckrone	142	3	——	N
Bagatelles	Persichetti	179	4	5:00	Y
Balladair	Erickson	67	3	3:00	Y
Ballad for Band	Gould	92	4	8:10	Y
Ballet for Young Americans	R. Hermann	111	4	13:00	Y
Ballet Music from Faust	Gounod	93	4	18:50	Y
La Bamba de Vera Cruz	Tucci	229	4	3:00	N
Bandology	Osterling	176	3	4:40	Y
The Barber of Seville Overture	Rossini	197	5	8:30	Y
Barnum and Bailey's Favorite March	King	134	4	2:30	Y

TITLE	COMPOSER	PAGE	GRADE	TIME	RECORD
The Battell Suite	W. Byrd	39	4	12:00	Y
Battle Symphony	Purcell	184	3	7:50	N
Beatrice and Benedict Overture	Berlioz	26	5	7:30	Y
Beguine Again	Osser	176	3	——	Y
Beguine for Band	Osser	176	3	——	Y
Berceuse and Finale from the Firebird Suite	Stravinsky	220	5	6:00	Y
The Big Cage Galop	King	134	3	1:30	Y
The Black Horse Troop March	Sousa	211	4	3:05	Y
Block M March	Bilik	31	3	3:00	Y
The Blue and the Gray	Grundman	99	3	9:00	Y
Blue Impulse March	Saitoh	199	4	3:28	Y
Blue Lake Overture	Chance	45	4	5:30	Y
Bolero for Band	Osser	176	3	——	Y
Bravura March	Duble	62	4	2:45	Y
Brighton Beach March	Latham	141	3	3:15	N
Broadway Curtain Time	Krance	138	4	9:00	Y
Bugler's Holiday—Trumpet Trio	Anderson	7	3	3:20	Y
Burlesk for Band	Washburn	244	3	2:30	N
Burnished Brass March	Cacavas	41	2	2:30	Y
Burst of Flame March	Bowles	36	3	3:30	N
Caccia and Chorale	Williams	252	3	6:45	Y
Cantique and Faranade	McBeth	151	3	7:00	Y
Canto	McBeth	151	2	4:30	Y
Canzona	Mennin	159	5	5:00	Y
El Capitan March	Sousa	211	3	2:15	Y
Carmina Burana	Orff	175	5	23:30	Y
Celebration Overture	Creston	53	4	7:30	Y

TITLE	COMPOSER	PAGE	GRADE	TIME	RECORD
Chant and Jubilo	McBeth	151	3	7:00	Y
Chapultepec for Band	Chavez	47	4	8:25	N
Chelsea Suite	Thielman	227	3	9:30	N
Chicago Tribune March	Chambers	44	4	3:30	Y
Children's March, Over the Hills and Far Away	Grainger	95	3	7:00	Y
Chimes of Liberty March	E.F. Goldman	88	3	3:00	Y
Chorale and Alleluia	Hanson	103	4	5:20	Y
Chorale and Capriccio	Giovannini	86	4	5:30	Y
Chorale and Shaker Dance	Zdechlik	258	4	9:00	Y
Chorale for Symphonic Band	Nelhybel	168	4	6:00	Y
Chorale Prelude: So Pure the Star	Persichetti	179	4	5:00	Y
Chorale Prelude: Turn Not Thy Face	Persichetti	179	4	4:30	Y
A Christmas Festival	Anderson	7	3	5:45	Y
The Circus Bee March	Fillmore	71	3	3:00	Y
Circus Overture	Schuman	205	5	7:00	Y
Circus Polka	Stravinsky	220	5	3:30	Y
Citadel March	Erickson	67	2	2:00	N
Clarinet Carousel—Duet	Bennett	21	3	——	N
Classic Overture in C	Gossec	91	4	5:00	Y
Coat of Arms March	Whitcomb	249	4	4:00	N
Colas Breugnon Overture	Kabalevsky	129	4	4:30	Y
Cole Porter—A Symphonic Portrait for Band	Porter	183	4	7:00	Y
Colonel Bogey March	K. Alford	6	4	3:17	Y
Colonial Song	Grainger	96	4	6:00	Y
Colossus of Columbia March	Alexander	4	4	2:40	Y
Come Sweet Death—Komm Susser Tod	Bach	10	3	3:50	Y
Commando March	Barber	16	4	3:00	Y

TITLE	COMPOSER	PAGE	GRADE	TIME	RECORD
Concert Fanfare	Bielawa	30	4	4:06	Y
Concertino for Alto Saxophone and Band	Bilik	31	4/5	12:00	Y
Concertino for Marimba and Band	Creston	54	4/5	15:00	Y
Concertino for Percussion and Band	Williams	253	4	8:00	Y
Concertino for Tuba and Band	Bencriscutto	20	5	10:00	Y
Concertino for Woodwind Quintet and Band	Long	149	4	7:30	Y
Concertino, Op. 26—Clarinet Solo	Weber	245	4/5	8:10	Y
Concertino, Op. 107—Flute Solo	Chaminade	45	4/5	8:00	Y
Concert Music for Band	Hindemith	113	5	——	Y
Concert for Alto Saxophone	Dahl	55	5/6	19:00	Y
Concerto for Alto Saxophone and Concert Band	Husa	120	5	20:00	Y
Concerto for Band	Jacob	123	4	12:30	Y
Concerto for Clarinet and Band	Rimsky-Korsakov	193	4	——	Y
Concerto for Horn	R. Hermann	111	4	8:50	N
Concerto for Piano and Winds	Stravinsky	220	5	19:00	Y
Concerto for Trombone and Band	Rimsky-Korsakov	194	3/5	8:00	Y
Concerto for Trumpet	Haydn	107	3/4	14:30	Y
Concerto for Trumpet	Hummel	119	4/5	——	Y
Concerto for 23 Winds	Hartley	105	6	16:00	Y
Concerto Grosso, Op.6—Two Flutes and Clarinet	Handel	102	4	12:45	Y
Concerto Grosso in D Minor	Vivaldi	236	4	8:00	N
Concerto in B-Flat for Two Trumpets	Vivaldi	236	3/4	8:00	Y
Concerto in G Minor, Op. 25 —Piano Solo	Mendelssohn	158	4	6:30	Y
Concert Overture in G	Mueller	165	4	6:45	Y
Concert Piece for Band	Tubb	228	5	4:30	Y
Concert Suite	Ashe	9	4	10:30	N
Corcoran Cadets March	Sousa	211	3	3:00	Y
Coriolanus Overture	Beethoven	19	4	8:00	N

TITLE	COMPOSER	PAGE	GRADE	TIME	RECORD
Coronation Scene from Boris Godunov	Mussorgsky	165	5	9:00	Y
Country Band March	Ives	121	5	4:00	Y
Court Festival	Latham	141	3	5:30	Y
Crown Imperial March	Walton	241	4	9:45	Y
Daikagura for Band	Koyama	136	—	6:00	Y
Dance and Intermezzo	Carter	43	3	——	Y
Dance Rhythms for Band	Riegger	193	4	8:00	Y
Dance Variations	Zdechlik	259	4	7:20	Y
Danza Final from Estancia	Ginastera	85	4	4:00	Y
Danzon from Fancy Free	Bernstein	28	4	2:45	Y
Dedication Fanfare	Schuman	205	4	4:30	Y
Dedicatory Overture	Williams	253	4	8:00	Y
Designs, Images, and Textures	Bassett	18	5	11:00	Y
Devonshire Overture	Ployhar	182	3	5:00	N
Diamond Variations	Jager	125	5	12:00	Y
Dichotomy	White	250	4	7:20	Y
Dionysiaques, Op. 62	Schmitt	201	6	10:00	Y
Divertimento for Band	Kaneda	130	5	7:30	Y
Divertimento for Band	Persichetti	180	5	11:00	Y
Double Concerto for Trumpet, Trombone, and Concert Band	Erickson	68	5	11:30	N
Down to the Sea in Ships	Bennett	22	5	12:30	N
Dramatic Essay—Trumpet Solo	Williams	253	3/4	4:40	Y
Drammatico	McBeth	152	4	7:40	Y
Dream Sequence	Krenek	139	5	15:00	Y
The Drum-Major's Daughter Overture	Offenbach	174	4	6:40	Y
Echigo Jishi	Koyama	137	5	6:00	Y
Egmont Overture	Beethoven	19	5	8:30	Y
Elegy and Fanfare-March	Nixon	172	4	9:00	Y

TITLE	COMPOSER	PAGE	GRADE	TIME	RECORD
Elegy for a Young American	Lo Presti	149	4	5:30	Y
Elegy for Symphonic Band	Kaneda	130	5	8:10	Y
An Ellington Portrait	Ellington	66	4	7:00	N
Elsa's Procession to the Cathedral from Lohengrin	Wagner	237	5	5:00	Y
Emblem of Unity March	Richards	192	4	3:45	Y
Emblems	Copland	49	5	10:45	Y
Emperata Overture	C. Smith	208	4	9:00	Y
Endearing Young Charms—Euphonium Solo	Mantia	156	5	4:30	Y
English Dances for Band	Arnold	8	4	8:00	Y
English Folk Song Suite	Vaughan Williams	232	5	9:30	Y
Enigma Variations	Elgar	66	5	15:30	Y
Entry of the Gladiators March	Fucik	78	4	2:35	Y
Entry of the Gods into Valhalla from Das Rheingold	Wagner	237	3	6:00	Y
Estampie	Nelhybel	168	4	4:30	Y
Expansions	H. Smith	209	4	6:30	Y
Extended Finale from Tannhauser	Wagner	238	4	13:00	Y
Facade	Walton	242	3	25:00	Y
The Fairest of the Fair March	Sousa	212	3	3:00	Y
Fandango	Perkins	179	4	4:00	Y
Fanfare and Allegro	Williams	253	5	5:45	Y
Fanfare for the Common Man	Copland	50	5	3:30	Y
Fanfare from La Peri	Dukas	62	5	1:00	Y
Fantasia for Band	Giannini	82	4	7:00	Y
Fantasia in F	Mozart	164	3	8:00	Y
Fantasia in G Major	Bach	10	4	6:30	Y
Fantasies on a Theme by Haydn	Dello Joio	59	5	14:00	Y
Fantasy for Band	Erickson	68	3	4:00	N
Fantasy for Symphonic Band	Kawasaki	132	5	7:09	N
Fantasy on American Sailing Songs	Grundman	99	3	5:30	N

TITLE	COMPOSER	PAGE	GRADE	TIME	RECORD
Festival	Williams	254	5	5:35	Y
A Festival Prelude	A. Reed	186	3	4:45	Y
Festive Overture	Shostakovich	207	4	6:00	Y
Festivo	Nelhybel	168	3	6:00	Y
Fetes	Debussy	56	5	7:00	Y
Fiddler on the Roof	Bock	34	4	6:30	Y
Fiesta del Pacifico	Nixon	173	5	8:00	Y
La Fiesta Mexicana	H.O. Reed	190	5	21:00	Y
Finale from Symphony No. 1	Kalinnikov	130	4	8:30	Y
Finale from Symphony No. 2	Ives	122	4	11:00	Y
Finale from Symphony No. 3 in C	Saint-Saens	198	4	8:30	Y
Finale from Symphony No. 4	Tchaikovsky	224	5	11:30	Y
Finale from Symphony No. 5 in E Minor	Dvorak	64	5	10:30	Y
Fingal's Cave Overture	Mendelssohn	158	4	10:00	Y
First Suite in E-Flat	Holst	114	4	10:00	Y
First Swedish Rhapsody	Leidzen	143	4	7:30	N
First Symphony for Band	Erickson	68	5	12:00	N
Five Miniatures	Turina	230	5	8:30	Y
Flag of Stars	Jacob	123	5	11:00	Y
Florentiner March	Fucik	78	4	4:50	Y
The Flying Dutchman Overture	Wagner	238	6	13:00	Y
La Folia Variations	Niblock	172	3	6:00	Y
The Footlifter March	Fillmore	72	3	3:00	Y
For the Unfortunate	H.O. Reed	189	5	13:00	Y
La Forza del Destino Overture	Verdi	234	5	7:45	Y
The Foundation March	R.F. Goldman	89	3	3:30	Y
Four Contrasts for Winds	Ford	74	3	7:30	Y
Four Freedoms Overture	Forsblad	74	3	3:00	Y
Four Pieces for Band	Bartok	17	2	3:05	N
Four Preludes for Band	R. Bennett	23	5	12:40	N

TITLE	COMPOSER	PAGE	GRADE	TIME	RECORD
Four Scottish Dances	Arnold	9	4	9:00	Y
The Free Lance March	Sousa	212	3	4:10	Y
From Every Horizon	Dello Joio	59	4	9:00	Y
From Shire and Sea	Davis	56	2	5:00	Y
From the North Country	Hattori	106	3	5:00	N
From Tropic to Tropic March	Alexander	4	4	2:40	Y
Fugue a la Gigue	Bach	11	5	4:00	Y
Gallant Men March	Cacavas	41	2	3:00	N
The Gallant Seventh March	Sousa	212	3	3:00	Y
La Gazza Ladra Overture	Rossini	197	5	10:30	Y
Geometrics No. 1, Op. 22	Mailman	154	4	6:00	Y
George Washington Bicentennial March	Sousa	212	4	3:40	Y
George Washington Bridge	Schuman	205	4	7:00	Y
Gigi	Loewe	147	3	8:00	N
Giles Farnaby Suite	Farnaby	70	4	19:00	Y
Good Friday Music from Parsifal	Wagner	238	6	8:45	Y
Grand Funeral and Triumphal Symphony, Op. 15	Berlioz	27	5	28:00	Y
Grand Serenade for an Awful Lot of Winds and Percussion	Schickele	200	5	——	N
Great Themes from Italian Movies	Cacavas	41	3	6:00	N
Greensleeves	A. Reed	187	2	7:30	N
Il Guarany Overture	Gomez	90	5	7:00	Y
Hammerfest March	Ployhar	182	3	4:00	N
Hammersmith—Prelude and Scherzo	Holst	114	4	12:45	Y
Handel in the Strand	Grainger	96	3	3:35	Y
Hands Across the Sea March	Sousa	213	3	2:40	Y
Here's the Band	Leckrone	142	4	5:00	Y
A Hero's Life, Synthesis	Strauss	218	6	22:45	Y
Highlights from Hello, Dolly!	Herman	110	3	8:00	N

TITLE	COMPOSER	PAGE	GRADE	TIME	RECORD
Highlights from Mame	Herman	110	4	9:00	N
Highlights from Oliver	Bart	16	3	4:30	Y
Highlights from Promises, Promises	Bacharach	13	4	6:00	Y
Hill Song No. 2	Grainger	96	5	4:30	Y
His Honor March	Fillmore	72	3	3:15	Y
Huldigungsmarsch	Wagner	238	4	5:00	Y
Huntingtower Ballad	Respighi	190	5	7:00	N
Hymn and Fuguing Tune No. 1	Cowell	52	—	5:00	Y
Hymn to Yerevan	Hovhaness	117	3	4:00	Y
If Thou Be Near	Bach	11	3	—	N
Image Sonore II—Parfum d'Iris	Tsujii	228	6	8:00	N
Incantation and Dance	Chance	46	4	7:30	Y
Incidental Suite	C. Smith	208	4	10:00	Y
Instant Concert	Walters	241	3	3:10	Y
In Storm and Sunshine March	Heed	109	4	2:30	Y
Intermezzo from Vanessa	Barber	16	5	4:00	N
Introduction and Capriccio—Piano Solo	Chance	46	4	7:00	N
Introduction and Fantasia	Mitchell	162	4	9:00	Y
Introduction and Samba—Saxophone Solo	Whitney	251	4	5:00	Y
Introduction to Act III from Lohengrin	Wagner	238	5	4:00	Y
Invercargill March	Lithgow	146	4	2:15	Y
The Invincible Eagle March	Sousa	213	3	3:10	Y
Invocation of Alberich from Das Rheingold	Wagner	239	4	5:10	Y
An Irish Rhapsody	Grundman	99	3	6:50	Y
Irish Tune from County Derry and Shepherd's Hey	Grainger	97	3 4	3:30 2:15	Y
Irving Berlin—A Symphonic Portrait	Berlin	26	3	6:05	Y
The Italian Girl in Algiers Overture	Rossini	197	5	8:15	N
Italian Polka	Rachmaninoff	185	—	——	Y

TITLE	COMPOSER	PAGE	GRADE	TIME	RECORD
Jalousie	Gade	79	4	6:30	Y
Japanese Folk Song, Itsuki no Komoriuta	Fujita	78	4	3:30	N
Japanese Folk Song, Warabe-Uta	Kaneda	131	3	7:30	Y
Japanese Songs for Band	Akiyama	3	2	5:45	Y
Jazz Tangents	Ward-Steinman	243	4	12:00	Y
Jazz Waltz	Maltby	155	4	5:00	N
Jedermann	Whear	248	3	5:30	N
Jericho Rhapsody	Gould	93	5	11:00	Y
Jesu, Joy of Man's Desiring	Bach	11	3	3:45	Y
Joi	Logan	148	3	5:00	N
Le Journal du Printemps, Suite No. 3	Fischer	73	4	——	N
Joyant Narrative	McBeth	152	4	7:28	Y
Jubilance	Giovannini	86	4	5:45	Y
A Jubilant Overture	A. Reed	187	3	6:00	Y
Jubilation Overture	R. Ward	242	4	7:00	N
Jubilee March	Goldman	88	3	3:00	Y
Kaddish	McBeth	152	4	7:00	Y
Kentucky March	Goldman	88	3	3:00	N
The King and I, Selections	Rodgers	195	4	10:00	Y
King Cotton March	Sousa	213	3	2:40	Y
The Klaxon March	Fillmore	72	3	3:15	Y
Kobiki-Uta	Koyama	137	5	10:00	Y
Laredo	Williams	254	3	3:50	Y
Latina	Bencriscutto	20	3	2:40	Y
The Leaves Are Falling	Benson	24	6	11:30	Y
Legend	Creston	54	5	7:00	Y
Les Preludes	Liszt	145	6	14:00	Y
The Liberty Bell March	Sousa	213	3	3:20	Y

TITLE	COMPOSER	PAGE	GRADE	TIME	RECORD
Liebestod from Tristan and Isolde	Wagner	239	4	6:40	Y
Lincoln Portrait	Copland	50	5	10:30	Y
Lincolnshire Posy	Grainger	97	5	15:00	Y
Little Concerto for Piano and Band	Cowell	52	—	12:00	N
Liturgical Music for Band	Mailman	154	4	10:00	Y
Lola Flores	Tucci	229	3	4:00	Y
London Suite	Coates	49	4	11:45	Y
Looking Upward Suite	Sousa	214	3	15:45	Y
Lyric Dance	Bencriscutto	20	4	4:05	Y
The Mad Major March	K. Alford	6	3	2:55	Y
Manhattan Beach March	Sousa	214	3	2:25	Y
Mannin Veen	Wood	256	5	10:00	Y
Man of La Mancha	Leigh	144	4	4:30	N
			3	1:45	N
Manzoni Requiem Excerpts	Verdi	234	5	16:10	Y
March and Procession of Bacchus	Delibes	58	4	5:00	Y
March Dramatic	Jager	126	4	2:30	Y
Marche Ecossaise	Debussy	57	5	6:15	Y
Marche Hongroise—Rakoczy	Berlioz	27	5	4:00	Y
Marche Militaire Francaise	Saint-Saens	199	4	4:10	Y
Marche Slave	Tchaikovsky	224	4	8:50	Y
March Forth	Moore	162	3	3:00	N
March for the Sultan Abdul Medjid	Donizetti	61	4	3:15	Y
March for the Sultan Abdul Medjid	Rossini	197	4	4:20	Y
March from Symphonic Metamorphosis on Themes by Carl Maria von Weber	Hindemith	113	4	7:30	Y
March of the Belgian Parachutists	Leemans	143	4	2:50	Y
Marcho Poco	Moore	162	3	3:00	N
March—Opus '76	Washburn	244	4	4:00	Y

TITLE	COMPOSER	PAGE	GRADE	TIME	RECORD
March, Opus 99	Prokofiev	184	5	5:00	Y
March With Trumpets	Bergsma	25	4	6:00	Y
The Marriage of Figaro Overture	Mozart	164	4	4:00	Y
Masque	McBeth	152	4	7:15	Y
Masquerade	Persichetti	180	5	12:00	Y
Meditation	Schuller	204	5	6:00	Y
Meditation from Thais—Flute Soli	Massenet	156	4	5:00	Y
Merry Mount Suite	Hanson	104	4	9:30	Y
Military March	Beethoven	19	3	5:30	Y
Military Symphony in F	Gossec	91	3	5:00	N
Miniature Set for Band	White	250	4	11:30	Y
The Minstrel Boy	Stoutamire	216	2	3:15	Y
Minuteman March	Pearson	177	3	3:20	Y
Mogura-Oi	Koyama	137	5	2:15	Y
Monterey Jack. March	Kinyon	135	3	2:15	N
Moorside March	Holst	115	4	4:00	Y
Morceau Symphonique—Trombone Solo	Guilmant	100	4/5	6:00	Y
Morning, Noon, and Night in Vienna	Suppe	222	4	8:00	Y
Mosaic	McBeth	152	5	8:00	Y
Musica Boema	Lukus	150	5	——	Y
Music for a Ceremony	Morrissey	163	3	4:30	Y
Music for a Festival	Jacob	124	5	26:00	Y
Music for Prague, 1968	Husa	120	5	18:30	Y
Music for Winds and Percussion	Del Borgo	58	5	6:45	Y
Mustang March	Osterling	176	3	2:30	N
My Fair Lady	Loewe	147	3	9:00	Y
Nabucco Overture	Verdi	234	4	8:00	Y

TITLE	COMPOSER	PAGE	GRADE	TIME	RECORD
National Emblem March	Bagley	14	3	2:50	Y
National Fencibles March	Sousa	214	3	3:15	Y
New Colonial March	Hall	101	3	2:45	Y
New England Triptych	Schuman				
Be Glad Then, America		206	4	7:00	N
When Jesus Wept		206	3	5:00	Y
Chester		206	4	9:00	Y
Night Soliloquy—Flute Solo	Kennan	133	4	4:00	Y
Nobles of the Mystic Shrine March	Sousa	214	3	3:00	Y
Nocturne	Hermann	112	3	4:40	Y
North Sea Overture	Hermann	112	4	8:00	N
Nutcracker Suite	Tchaikovsky	224	4	17:15	Y
Nutmeggers March	Osterling	177	3	2:50	Y
O, Cool Is the Valley	Persichetti	180	4	6:00	Y
Oklahoma, Selections	Rodgers	195	3	6:30	N
Old Comrades March	Tcike	225	3	4:00	Y
Old Scottish Melody	Wiley	251	3	2:30	Y
Olympia Hippodrome March	Alexander	4	4	3:00	Y
On the Mall March	Goldman	89	3	3:15	Y
An Original Suite	Jacob	124	4	9:15	Y
The Original Thirteen March	Ployhar	182	2	3:00	N
Orlando Palandrino Overture	Haydn	107	3	——	Y
Orpheus in the Underworld Overture	Offenbach	174	5	9:00	Y
Otemoyan	Koyama	137	5	2:00	Y
Othello	A. Reed	187	4	18:45	Y
An Outdoor Overture	Copland	50	5	9:30	Y
Overture 1812	Tchaikovsky	225	5	15:00	Y
Overture and Caccia	Menotti	160	5	7:30	Y
Overture Euryanthe	Weber	245	6	9:30	Y

TITLE	COMPOSER	PAGE	GRADE	TIME	RECORD
Overture for Band	Beyer	30	4	6:30	N
Overture for Band	Mendelssohn	158	4	7:00	Y
Overture for Winds	Carter	43	3	5:30	N
Overture in B-Flat	Giovannini	86	4	4:50	Y
Overture in C	Catel	44	4	5:30	Y
Overture to Candide	Bernstein	29	5	4:00	Y
Overture to Die Fledermaus	J. Strauss	217	4	8:30	Y
Pachinko	Yoder	257	3	2:30	N
Pageant	Persichetti	180	4	7:00	Y
Pageant Overture	Lo Presti	149	4	6:30	N
Pageantry Overture	Edmondson	65	3	5:12	Y
Paint Your Wagon	Loewe	147	3	10:00	Y
Panis Angelicus	Franck	76	3	3:00	N
Pas Redouble	Saint-Saens	199	4	3:45	Y
Passacaglia and Fugue in C Minor	Bach	11	5	20:00	Y
Passacaglia, Chorale, and Scamper	Van Vactor	232	4	12:20	Y
Passacaglia for Symphonic Band	Kaneda	131	4	6:04	Y
Passacaglia in G Minor	Bright	38	4	5:00	N
Pastorale	Williams	254	4	4:05	N
Patterns for Band	White	250	6	——	N
Pavilion Piece	Schickele	200	4	3:00	N
The Pearl Fishers Overture	Bizet	33	4	——	N
Pentland Hills March	Howe	118	3	2:20	Y
Phedre Overture	Massenet	156	4	9:30	Y
Pictures at an Exhibition	Mussorgsky	166	5	28:00	Y
The Pines of Rome	Respighi	190	5	19:20	Y
Pittsburgh Ouverture	Penderecki	178	6	12:00	Y
The Planets	Holst	115	3	9:30	Y

TITLE	COMPOSER	PAGE	GRADE	TIME	RECORD
Poet and Peasant Overture	Suppe	222	4	10:20	Y
Polka and Fugue from Schwanda	Weinberger	246	5	8:00	Y
Polyphonies for Percussion	Benson	24	4	5:50	Y
Porgy and Bess, Selections	Gershwin	81	4	12:00	Y
Portrait of a Trumpet—Solo	Nestico	171	4	5:00	N
The Power of Rome and the Christian Heart	Grainger	97	5	12:00	Y
Praeludium	Jarnefelt	127	4	2:40	Y
Praeludium and Allegro	Giannini	82	5	7:30	Y
Prelude and Allegro	Guilmant	100	3	4:40	Y
Prelude and Dance	Creston	54	5	7:00	Y
Prelude and Fugue	Nelhybel	168	4	4:50	Y
Prelude and Fugue in E Minor	Bach	12	5	4:45	N
Prelude and Fugue in F Minor	Bright	38	4	6:50	Y
Prelude and Fugue in G Minor	Bach	12	3	3:00	Y
Prelude (D Minor), Chorale and Fugue	Bach	12	5	8:30	Y
Prelude from Die Meistersinger	Wagner	240	5	10:15	Y
Preludium and Fugue	Frescobaldi	77	3	4:50	Y
The Pride of the Wolverines March	Sousa	215	3	3:20	Y
La Procession du Rocio	Turina	231	5	7:30	Y
Procession of the Nobles from Mlada	Rimsky-Korsakov	194	4	4:20	Y
Proclamations	George	79	4	7:00	Y
Proud Heritage March	Latham	141	3	4:00	Y
Psalm for Band	Persichetti	180	4	8:00	Y
Psyche and Eros	Franck	76	4	5:30	Y
Purple Carnival March	H. Alford	5	4	3:50	Y
Ragtime Dance	Joplin	129	4	4:30	N
Rakes of Mallow from Irish Suite	Anderson	7	3	——	Y
The Ramparts	Williams	254	5	6:00	Y

TITLE	COMPOSER	PAGE	GRADE	TIME	RECORD
Reflections	Nixon	173	5	7:00	Y
Reflections on Paris	Tull	229	5	15:00	Y
Renaissance Triptych	Kirck	136	3	6:00	Y
Rhapsodie Francaise	Lijnschooten	145	3	6:10	Y
Rhapsody for Band	Ohguri	174	4	6:30	Y
Rhapsody from the Low Countries	Lijnschooten	145	3	6:00	N
Rhapsody in Blue	Gershwin	81	4/5	22:00	Y
Rienzi Overture	Wagner	240	6	10:30	Y
The Ringmaster March	Burden	39	3	2:10	N
Ritmo Jondo—Flamenco	Surinach	223	4	8:00	Y
Ritual Fire Dance	Falla	69	5	4:15	Y
Rocky Point Holiday	Nelson	170	4	5:30	Y
Rolling Thunder March	Fillmore	72	4	2:30	Y
Roman Carnival Overture	Berlioz	27	4	8:50	Y
Romanza and Rondo from Concerto No. 3— French Horn Solo	Mozart	164	3/4	7:45	Y
Rosamunde Overture	Schubert	202	5	9:30	Y
Royal Fireworks Music	Handel	102	5	15:00 21:00	Y
Royal March	Kinyon	135	2	2:00	N
Russian Christmas March	A. Reed	188	5	13:40	Y
Russian Sailors' Dance from the Red Poppy	Gliere	87	5	3:00	Y
Ruy Blas Overture	Mendelssohn	158	4	12:00	Y
St. Anthony Divertimento	Haydn	108	3	11:00	Y
The Saints	Bowles	36	3	3:20	N
El Salon Mexico	Copland	51	5	11:00	Y
Scaramouch—Symphony No. 3 for Winds and Percussion	Snoeck	210	5	12:00	Y
Scarborough Fair	Kinyon	135	2	——	N
Scenes from the Louvre	Dello Joio	59	4	10:30	Y
Scheherazade	Rimsky-Korsakov	194	5/6	42:00	Y

TITLE	COMPOSER	PAGE	GRADE	TIME	RECORD
Scherzo Alla Marcia from Symphony No. 8	Vaughan Williams	233	4	3:45	Y
Scherzo for Band	Rossini	198	5	4:15	Y
Sea Songs	Vaughan Williams	233	3	4:45	Y
Sebastian Ballet—Excerpts	Menotti	160	5	7:45	Y
Second Concerto for Clarinet	Weber	245	4/5	23:30	Y
Second Prelude	Gershwin	81	4	4:00	N
Second Suite	Jager	126	4	10:00	N
Second Suite in F	Holst	116	4	14:00	Y
Second Symphony for Band	Erickson	68	4	17:00	N
Selections from West Side Story	Bernstein	29	4	8:30	Y
			5	4:30	
Semper Fidelis March	Sousa	215	3	3:30	Y
Sensemaya	Revueltas	191	—	——	Y
Sequoia	LaGassey	140	4	6:00	N
Serenade for Alto Saxophone and Band	Bencriscutto	21	3/4	4:30	Y
Serenade for Band	Latham	141	3	5:00	N
Serenade in D Minor, Op. 44	Dvorak	64	4	17:00	Y
Serenade, Opus 7	R. Strauss	218	4	8:00	Y
Serenade, Op. 22	Dvorak	64	3	6:15	Y
Serenata	Anderson	7	3	3:55	Y
Sholom Aleichem	Ades	2	3	5:15	Y
Shoonthree	Cowell	52	5	5:00	Y
A Short Ballet for Awkward Dancers	Hazelman	108	4	5:40	N
S.I.B.A. March	Hall	101	3	2:15	N
Sinfonia Nobilissima	Jager	126	3	8:00	Y
Sinfonia No. 4	Hartley	105	6	10:00	Y
The Sinfonians March	Williams	225	4	5:20	Y
Sinfonia Sacra—Symphony No. 1	Werle	247	5	15:00	Y
Sinfonietta	Dahl	55	5	17:00	Y

TITLE	COMPOSER	PAGE	GRADE	TIME	RECORD
Six Concert Fanfares	Bencriscutto	21	4	0:15	Y
Sketches on a Tudor Psalm	Tull	230	5	10:30	Y
Slavonic Folk Suite	A. Reed	188	2	9:00	N
Sleigh Ride	Anderson	8	3	——	Y
A Solemn Music	Thomson	227	4	5:00	Y
Soliloquy and Dance	Niblock	172	4	8:00	Y
The Solitary Dancer	Benson	24	5	5:50	Y
Solo de Concours—Clarinet Solo	Rabaud	185	4	6:00	Y
Somersault	H. Smith	209	4	4:00	Y
Sonata for Winds	Carter	43	3	——	N
Sonatina for Band	Giovannini	86	4	9:05	Y
Sonatina In F	R. Strauss	218	5	36:00	Y
Songs of Abelard	Dello Joio	60	5	16:00	Y
Sonus Ventorum	C. Smith	209	3	6:00	Y
The Sorcerer's Apprentice	Dukas	63	6	10:30	Y
The Sound of Music, Selections	Rodgers	195	3	10:30	Y
The Southerner March	Alexander	5	4	2:40	Y
Southwestern Sketches	Adler	3	5	13:00	Y
Spectrum	Bielawa	30	4	6:00	Y
Star Dust	Carmichael	42	4	4:30	N
Stars and Bars March	Jager	126	4	2:30	N
The Stars and Stripes Forever March	Sousa	215	4	3:20	Y
Strategic Air Command March	Williams	255	3	3:45	N
Stratford Suite	Cable	40	4	12:30	N
Suite Concertante	Nelhybel	169	4	11:00	Y
Suite for Band	Hovhaness	117	3	10:00	N
Suite Francaise	Milhaud	161	4	16:00	Y
Suite from the Ballet Pineapple Poll	Sullivan	221	4	9:50	Y

TITLE	COMPOSER	PAGE	GRADE	TIME	RECORD
Suite in A Minor—Flute Solo or Soli	Telemann	226	5	12:00	Y
Suite in B-Flat, Op. 4	R. Strauss	218	4	——	N
Suite in Minor Mode	Kabalevsky	129	2	4:00	Y
Suite Italienne	Bilik	32	3	7:00	N
Suite of Old American Dances	R. Bennett	23	4	15:25	Y
Summertime	Gershwin	82	3	——	N
Symphonic Chorale	Osterling	177	3	3:30	Y
Symphonic Concert March	Bonelli	34	4	6:30	Y
Symphonic Dance No. 2, The Maskers	Williams	255	4	6:20	N
Symphonic Dance No. 3, Fiesta	Williams	255	4	6:20	Y
Symphonic Jazz Suite—Soloists and Combo	Benciscutto	21	5	21:00	Y
Symphonic Moment for Band	Kaneda	131	5	9:27	Y
Symphonic Movement	Nelhybel	169	5	8:00	Y
Symphonic Overture	Carter	43	3	4:20	Y
A Symphonic Prelude on Black Is the Color of My True Love's Hair	A. Reed	188	3	4:20	Y
Symphonic Requiem	Nelhybel	169	5	40:00	N
Symphonic Songs for Band	R. Bennett	23	4	12:27	Y
Symphonic Suite	Williams	255	4	7:10	Y
Symphonie Fantastique	Berlioz	27			
2. A Ball		27	6	5:00	N
4. March to the Scaffold		27	6	5:00	Y
5. Dream of a Witches' Dance		27	5	8:30	Y
Symphonie for Band	Jadin	125	3	5:40	Y
Symphonies for Wind Instruments	Stravinsky	221	5	12:00	Y
Symphony for Band	Bilik	32	5	15:00	Y
Symphony for Band	Gould	93	5	20:00	Y
Symphony for Band	Persichetti	181	4	16:00	Y
Symphony for Band	Washburn	244	4	15:00	Y
Symphony for Brass and Percussion	Schuller	204	5	18:00	Y

TITLE	COMPOSER	PAGE	GRADE	TIME	RECORD
Symphony in B-Flat	Fauchet	70	5	30:15	Y
Symphony in B-Flat	Hindemith	113	6	16:50	Y
Symphony in D Minor-First Movement	Franck	76	5	8:00	N
Symphony No. 1 for Band	Jager	126	4	18:00	Y
Symphony No. 2—First Movement	Borodin	35	5	6:30	N
Symphony No. 3	Giannini	83	5	23:00	Y
Symphony No. 3, Finale (Excerpts)	Mahler	153	3	7:00	Y
Symphony No. 3—Ilya Murometz	Gliere	87	4	8:30	Y
			5	7:00	
Symphony No. 4	Hovhaness	117	4	18:00	Y
Symphony No. 5, Finale	Shostakovich	207	5	8:30	Y
Symphony No. 5½	Gillis	84	5	15:00	N
Symphony No. 8 in B Minor	Schubert	203	5	20:50	Y
Tanglewood—An Overture for Band	Tatgenhorst	223	2	4:12	Y
Tapor No. 1	Hovhaness	117	3	5:00	Y
Tap Roots	Skinner	208	4	9:10	N
Tenth Regiment March	Hall	101	3	3:15	Y
Theme and Variations, Opus 43a	Schoenberg	201	6	14:00	Y
Things to Come	Bliss	33	—	11:00	N
Third Suite	Jager	127	4	8:05	Y
This Glorious White World March	Yamamato	257	4	3:30	Y
Three Chorale Preludes	Latham	141	3	6:30	Y
Three Comments on War	Meyerowitz	160	4	10:40	Y
Three Dance Episodes	Khachaturian	133	5	13:00	Y
Three Japanese Dances	Rogers	196	5	10:40	Y
Thundercrest March	Osterling	177	3	2:50	Y
The Thunderer March	Sousa	215	3	2:40	Y
Till Eulenspiegel's Merry Pranks	R. Strauss	219	6	15:15	Y
Tin Pan Gallery	Yoder	257	3	4:00	Y

TITLE	COMPOSER	PAGE	GRADE	TIME	RECORD
To Be Fed By Ravens	McBeth	153	6	11:35	Y
Toccata	Frescobaldi	77	4	5:20	Y
Toccata	Tull	230	5	10:30	Y
Toccata and Fugue in D Minor	Bach	12	5	8:40	Y
Toccata for Band	Erickson	68	4	5:15	Y
Toccata for Winds, Op. 104	Jenkins	128	5	8:00	Y
Toccata Marziale	Vaughan Williams	233	5	4:30	Y
Totem Pole March	Osterling	177	3	2:50	N
Tournament Galop	Gottschalk	92	4	3:00	Y
Transitions	Badings	14	5	12:00	Y
Transylvania Fanfare March	Benson	24	5	3:10	Y
Trauersinfonie	Wagner	240	4	6:00	Y
A Tribute to Stephen Foster	Nestico	171	5	7:50	Y
Tribute to Youth	Ford	74	3	5:20	Y
Trinity	Zaninelli	258	3	5:15	N
Trittico	Nelhybel	170	5	10:30	Y
Triumphal March from Aida	Verdi	235	4	10:00	Y
Tulsa	Gillis	84	5	10:25	Y
Tunbridge Fair	Piston	181	5	5:00	Y
Two Gaelic Folk Songs	Tyra	231	3	5:30	N
Two Moods Overture	Grundman	99	3	3:00	N
Two Symphonic Movements	Nelhybel	170	5	14:00	N
Universal Judgment	De Nardis	60	4	9:00	Y
Valdres March	Hanssen	104	4	3:25	Y
The Vanished Army March	K. Alford	6	4	2:40	Y
Vaquero March	Nestico	171	3	3:25	N
Variants on a Medieval Tune	Dello Joio	60	5	11:40	Y
Variation Overture	Williams	256	3	5:45	Y

TITLE	COMPOSER	PAGE	GRADE	TIME	RECORD
Variations and Fugue	Giannini	83	5	14:30	Y
Variations for Tuba and Winds	Frackenpohl	75	4/5	5:30	Y
Variations on a Kitchen Sink	Gillis	84	3	4:00	N
Variations on a Korean Folk Song	Chance	46	4	6:30	Y
Variations on America	Ives	122	5	7:00	Y
Variations on a Shaker Melody	Copland	51	4	5:45	Y
Variations on a Sioux Melody	Ployhar	182	4	6:00	N
Variations on Jerusalem the Golden	Ives	122	4	4:00	N
Victory at Sea	Rodgers	196	4	9:30	Y
Viva Mexico	Morrissey	163	3	17:30	N
Vocalise, Opus 34	Rachmaninoff	185	3	7:30	Y
The Voice of the Guns March	K. Alford	6	4	2:30	Y
Waltzes from Der Rosenkavalier	R. Strauss	219	5	15:00	Y
Washington Grays March	Grafulla	94	4	3:50	Y
The Washington Post March	Sousa	216	3	2:25	Y
Water Music Suite	Handel	103	4	20:00	Y
When Johnny Comes Marching Home	Stoutamire	216	2	2:05	N
William Byrd Suite	Byrd	39	4	16:45	Y
Wycliffe Variations	Whear	248	4	9:30	Y
Ye Banks and Braes O' Bonnie Doon	Grainger	98	2	3:00	Y

APPENDIX V
VITA

Norman E. Smith was born in Cape Girardeau, Missouri, in 1921. He attended public schools in Missouri, Oklahoma, and Louisiana, and earned the B.A. degree in music at the University of Southwestern Louisiana in 1943. After service time as an AAF pilot, he taught band, orchestra, and music theory in high schools for nine years. Graduate education included the University of Nebraska, Louisiana State University (M.M.E. degree), University of Michigan, and Florida State University (Ph.D.).

Smith taught at McNeese State University from 1954 to 1978 where he was a professor of music education, teaching graduate classes in band literature, conducting, and brass methods; undergraduate classes in acoustics and music appreciation; and trumpet and French horn applied music. He was director of bands at McNeese for eighteen years and is still active in the College Band Directors National Association. He has guest conducted honor bands and served as an adjudicator in Texas, Louisiana, and Mississippi band and orchestra festivals. He plays trumpet with the Lake Charles Civic Symphony and violin with the university orchestra.

Smith's interest in music acoustics, trumpet pedagogy, and baroque brass instruments has motivated several research trips to Europe and to many other universities in the United States. He and his wife Aline, are the parents of Linda and Pamlyn, and the grandparents of Chris and Ted.

Albert Stoutamire was born in Broadway, Virginia, in 1921, and he attended public schools in Richmond, Virginia. His undergraduate college education, interrupted by three years service in the United States Army during World War II, was completed in 1947 at the Virginia Commonwealth University (B.S. degree). Graduate education degrees were earned at Teachers College, Columbia University (M.A.) and the Florida State University (Ed.D.).

Stoutamire's teaching experience includes directing bands and orchestras in the public schools of Richmond, Virginia, teaching at LaGrange College in Georgia, and since 1961, teaching at McNeese State University in Louisiana. His professional performing experiences include playing trombone in several symphonies and numerous theater, studio, and dance orchestras.

Among his publications are more than a dozen articles in leading music education journals, several book reviews, a music history book; and numerous musical arrangements and compositions for band, orchestra, choir, and instrumental solos and ensembles. These works for young musicians include ten sets of books. A method book for band has recently been released, and a technique book for band will be published soon.

Stoutamire's wife Anne, plays violin and viola, and their son Robert, plays tuba in a high school band.